A Future for the American Economy

A Future for the American Economy

The Social Market

SEVERYN T. BRUYN

STANFORD UNIVERSITY PRESS
STANFORD, CALIFORNIA

Stanford University Press
Stanford, California
© 1991 by the Board of Trustees of the
Leland Stanford Junior University

Printed in the United States of America

CIP data appear at the end of the book

Acknowledgments

MY ACKNOWLEDGMENTS go most gratefully to colleagues who read my manuscript with care and know the scientific arguments very well. My distinguished readers, the sociologist S. M. Miller, and the economist Burton Weisbrod, were strongly critical and simultaneously sympathetic to the interdisciplinary problem I posed, and thus vital to my formulating the argument with more clarity.

Editorial work goes beyond what most people think. Readers are not normally aware of the generous contributions that copy editors make in a production process. Few recognize that copy editors will have offered alternative ideas to the author that would avoid a reviewer's criticism, cleaned paragraphs that were lost in verbiage, redesigned sentences to make a point clear, repositioned paragraphs to make a chapter coherent, suggested a change in the title of a chapter to make it more apt, questioned scientific assertions that may not fit the data, and interrogated the author about the logic of an idea to the point that it is made more meaningful in the text. It required considerable stamina for my editors to make sense out of a manuscript that was filled with tortuous and twisted avenues of thought, but they did all the things I have mentioned above to our benefit.

I want to thank Betty Seaver for help on the initial draft. Then Barbara Brandt began working on the order of the argument and questioned the intricate turns in logic that made it difficult for readers to follow. And finally, my thanks to Barbara Mnookin, who skillfully and magnificently performed all of the tasks needed to bring the manuscript into publication.

Not the least, I want to thank my graduate students whose systematic questioning of my lectures became an editorial work in itself and spurred me to follow those ideas to their logical conclusion.

S.T.B.

164019

Contents

viii   *Contents*

A Future for the American Economy

Introduction

THE AMERICAN ECONOMY is filled with so many contradictions today that it foils the best prophecies and most sophisticated forecasts by economists. This book is about those contradictions and the directions the economy could take in the future. In particular, it is about the central contradiction: government control vs. market freedom. How this contradiction is resolved is important not only for the United States but ultimately for countries around the world.

My main thesis is that social factors—rather than purely economic factors—are at the root of this contradiction between market freedom and government control. I argue that the way markets are socially organized is critical to their profitability and their capacity for operating independent of government controls. In essence, the social organization of the private economy is the key to the free market system.

In other words, the economy can function more productively and humanely with less government regulation. I believe that the study of market organization is essential to understand how it can operate in the interest of the society. Furthermore, I believe that research can be combined with public policies to reduce state controls and create a market system that is more self-regulated.

The character of such a change can be far-reaching. At a philosophical level, this overall dynamic of development was proposed by Georg Wilhelm Friedrich Hegel, as conceived in the dialectical idea of *Aufhebung*. This concept turned scientific thought around from a static and descriptive outlook on the world—as with Linnaeus's classification of plants—to a view of the world as a dynamic process of change and transformation—as with Darwin's theory of evolution. *Aufhebung* was an abstract concept that referred to the unification of opposites, a complex process by which contradictions in history were transcended. It became part of an idealistic philosophy that assumed the whole world could be con-

ceived accurately in the realm of thought, a philosophy so powerful in its implications that it led Karl Marx to chart his course of the
study of the political economy from this perspective.

Marx first developed this new perspective in the *Economic and
Philosophic Manuscripts of 1844*. In this work, he dealt directly with
Hegel's abstract concept of "alienation," the separation of human
beings from nature and material life, now interpreted concretely as
embodied in the class structure of society. But a theory about the
transformation of opposites is not easily applied to the realm of
political economy, any more than it is easily applied to the world
of ideas. The transformation of the class structure in history was
much more complex than Marx could successfully interpret in the
gross terms of a dialectical process. We know today from the history of socialist states that the alienation of labor and the contradictions of capitalism could not be transcended either by violent revolution or by state decree.

The notion of *Aufhebung* and the grand solutions it implied for
resolving the dilemmas of human life therefore remain a mystery in
philosophy and social thought; the problem that stimulated Marx's
work is still with us. How does the transformation of opposites
really happen? How is it possible to achieve a unity of opposites
between doing and thinking, between being and having, between
means and end, between public and private life, between production and consumption, and between theory and practice? We are
still puzzled over the way these opposites are transcended, but I
believe that Marx gave us the clue in his compelling critique of the
political economy of capitalism.

Marx said that the concepts of capitalism are defined traditionally
in economic terms; but the truth is that these economic concepts
have a social root. Finding that social root is the first step toward
transcending the contradictions. This step requires that we see
how concrete individuals are able to express their humanity in the
life of the economy itself. Marx argued that a social reality should
become incorporated into the framework of economics. He argued
that individuals become part of the economy through certain forms
of human (i.e., social) interaction, not just through their objectification in economic categories such as commodity prices or wages.
It is by understanding the humanness in economic interchange
that we move toward the transcendence of opposites.

Put another way, Marx argued that the more people are able to create themselves as "social individuals," the less conflict results between themselves as individuals and their human character, between individuality and society, indeed—in Marx's philosophical terms—the less intense "the strife between existence and essence, freedom and necessity, the individual and the species."

This same contradiction between the individual and the community in the market economy has been central to the thinking of scholars like Martin Buber, who sought a connection between the "I" and the "Thou," and the sociologist Amitai Etzioni, who has posed the problematic of the market in the contradictions between "I" and "We."

Marx said that the problem under capitalism is that individuals do not have an opportunity to create themselves socially, that is, to act on behalf of their own humanity. In order for people to become social individuals, they must take an active part in determining all aspects of their own lives, from the most immediate concerns to the broadest general issues of the political economy, including its organization and culture. In short, people must become authors of their own fate through structures that allow them to express themselves as human beings.

The creation of such structures and processes is a powerful challenge. In this book, we will examine the human organization and culture of the market economy as the basis for evaluating its capacity to become more humane and self-regulating. I do this by making the social categories of economic life a little more visible.

Marx's critique of capitalism was so compelling that it turned nations around as well as philosophies. The rise and spread of socialism have been the major characteristic of political thought in the twentieth century. And though the conclusion of this century may be characterized by its very opposite—the fall of state socialism—the social basis of the economic order remains an essential question today. Therefore, I believe that studying the "sociality" of economic life will still be on the agenda for us in the next century.

Although the social factor in the market economy is important to study, as Marx claimed in his *Manuscripts of 1844*, my interpretation of it takes a totally different turn from that put forward in the Marxist ideologies of socialist countries. I believe that social research can clarify both how the market is a human phenomenon and how it can become more self-regulatory. Public policies and research must take account of the social factor both because it plays a key role in the economy and because its importance will increase in the future. Understanding the role of the social factor can help us to reduce state regulation of the economy.

One factor that inhibits this understanding is the paradigm of economics today, which is constructed to depict a market system devoid of social life; as a result, economic studies of the market as such are highly restricted and often inaccurate. This limited conception is also held by the general public, transmitted by the mass media's discussions of economic indicators, Laffer Curves, inflation rates, unemployment statistics, and the GNP. These economic categories keep people from seeing the patterns of human design and the cultural values that shape market life.

I believe that a new paradigm must be constructed, one that shows how social factors are closely intertwined with economic factors, and how the market actually rests on a social foundation.

As we shall see, a social paradigm of the economy has been emerging for over a century, through the evolution of interdisciplinary fields of research. This new paradigm could take various names in the future, but for our purposes, let us call the way economic exchange is organized in the context of society "the social market." A key principle in this paradigmatic view of the economy is "social self-governance." This concept refers to managing markets outside the aegis of the state, that is, by the organizing of corporations, associations, partnerships, and individuals who manage markets in social systems of exchange relatively independent of state controls.

This image of a socially self-governing system of economic exchange stands in contrast to other, more familiar images, including those of the unregulated free enterprise system that swings between depressions and prosperity; the regimented and totally state-dominated socialist or communist economy; the inefficient and cumbersome liberal welfare state; and the neocorporate state that has its extreme version in the fascist economy, controlled by powerful corporations embraced by the government.

Despite the popular belief that the market's invisible hand leads to the general good, government policies have always played a major role in determining whether the market will function in the public interest. The government today has become the visible hand, along with corporate giants that dominate various market sectors.

The crucial question in this book, therefore, is whether the market can function to regulate itself in the public interest apart from government, with fewer market concentrations, oligopolies, and government interventions.

My assumption is that a market *can* govern itself better than it does today, but that its success in doing so is dependent on the recognition of complex social factors. This view is not a theory in the full sense, only a systematic concept of social exchange that assumes the market contains within itself a power for self-generation and self-regulation.

By offering various case studies and pointing to empirical research, I describe how self-regulatory mechanisms in the market come about through the integration of social and economic factors. I discuss how the sociolegal system can hinder or encourage the development of self-regulation, and suggest future public policies that may advance economic self-governance. Just as the market we know today was created by government policies, so new government policies can help to bring about a market shaped by greater self-regulation.

This book is not a critique of the market system in the conventional sense. I do not focus on the destructive and exploitive side of markets, as important as such studies are. Studying the dark side of capitalism is important and should continue because it illuminates the problems, but my focus is on the potential for social development that resides within the existing system as we move toward the end of the twentieth century.

The book speaks to public policy in many ways. For example, the whole edifice of the market economy today is constructed on business law based on the principles of competition and self-regulation. They are touted as the essential values of business, but I argue that such principles remain largely a fiction, and that bringing the idea of market self-regulation into reality requires altering business law in a way that recognizes that certain types of cooperation between currently antagonistic associations can be legitimate and work in the public interest.

The principle of self-regulation can be applied to many types of problems. Take the industries suffering from overseas competition in domestic markets, for example. I believe that a legal restructuring of trade associations could provide the research, capital, and management required to help these industries gain a competitive footing against foreign firms. This requires cooperation—not competition—in selected instances to strengthen the economy in a global market.

Still, implementing such public policies is a complex and knotty problem, and that is why greater attention to social research is needed to accompany the process. To move in this direction of self-regulation requires that the government and private sector work together experimentally with the help of a new field of socioeconomic studies. Economic studies are not sufficient by themselves. We are all familiar with economic indexes that measure economic growth and evaluate the status of the market. But these do not measure either the social organization of the market or its capacity for social development. Social indexes are needed to understand the subtleties of market organization, to measure the capacity for industrial self-regulation, and to supply information to policy makers who wish to increase the self-governing powers of the economy.

The idea of a social market has an analytical dimension and a normative dimension. That is, one can simply describe how markets work—by measuring their degree of self-regulation, for example. Or one can explore the question of how they might work to raise the degree of self-regulation. Throughout this book, I examine the social market from both angles.

It may seem anomalous to suggest that Adam Smith and Karl Marx both had a vision of an economy operating outside the control of the state. But though these founding fathers of capitalism and socialism had many differences, they both believed that the economy has origins in the life of society, and that the processes of society (not the state) should guide it. This common vision of the future, however, was never realized.

Adam Smith hated big corporations and believed that a self-regulated market could only operate with small firms in competition with each other; but within the next century, big corporations had emerged and big government developed to regulate them. Karl Marx hated the state and believed that while a revolutionary takeover by the workers would be necessary in some cases, the state should be dismantled and would soon wither away, leaving a type of economy that could regulate itself through society.

If we were to integrate the views of Smith and Marx into a single vision, the new market system to emerge would be characterized not by corporate or state monopoly, but by a system of decentralized and equitable exchange, grounded in both competition and co-operation, integrated by both individual and community values, founded on principles of both freedom and justice, and created by the processes of society operating within the economy, apart from the state. Thus, the essence of the modern democratic state—its capacity for self-governance—is transferred into the economy.

To increase the level of self-governance in the economy requires making many changes in the organization of the market. It means moving from a system based on the classic separation between labor and management to systems of social management; moving from a system of investment based on pure financial criteria to a system of social investment that integrates economic and social criteria; moving from a system of destructive competition between firms to a market system grounded in conflict resolution and co-operation. It means a private sector organized to promote competition not in self-interest alone, but also in the public interest, a system yielding greater dividends to society in health, safety, nutrition, and environmental protection.

I argue that the market economy is developing in such directions of participatory governance, from the workshop to the corporation to the industry and to the economy as a whole, in other words, from the "I" to greater degrees of the "We." Opportunities for individual employees to integrate their own self-interest on the job with the broader interests of fellow workers, for example, are increasingly evident today; this means creating a "We" relationship with fellow employees through work rules made in autonomous groups, quality circles, and worker councils. But in some firms this structural change has gone further: employees integrate their self-interests through high levels of participatory management and corporate ownership, with employee representation on boards of directors.

This pattern of individual representation can also be seen developing vertically through democratically constituted trade associations, where common rules are forged by competitive firms in the interest of a whole industry. The representation of the "concrete individual" continues to integrate with others (the I-We relation) through the democratic formation of trade associations under a still larger scope of common responsibility—such as that represented in the American Standards Association, which sets technical standards in the interest of the whole economy without state regulations. Firms in all trades come together to integrate the specific interests of American firms with the larger public interest.

Trade associations often function against the public interest today, but I argue that they could be the seeds for greater self-regulation and public responsibility. Peak federations like the American Standards Association, the Chamber of Commerce, the National Association of Manufacturers, and the Council of Institutional Investors are in an incipient stage of development. Public incentives and policies could encourage them to work more directly in the public interest. The breadth of their member representation gives them the capacity for accomplishing a larger human purpose hidden in the market system.

Proceeding in this direction of organizational self-development requires resolving contradictions, that is, making syntheses of old oppositions. This paradox of social development is perhaps best expressed in the seeming oxymoron the "private social market," that is, a private market that becomes publicly oriented. Furthermore, a public corporation need not signify a government corporation; "the public" is not synonymous with the state. A broadly based, democratic trade association could become a public corporation operating in the private sector, independent of the state. The market would still be private and competitive, but it would be socially structured by more cooperation so as to serve the public interest.

By moving in this direction and looking beyond the ideologies of capitalism and communism, we could establish a new competitive economy with manifest social foundations. To clarify how this could come about, I begin, in Part I, with a review of the historical and theoretical perspectives on socioeconomic research. I argue that new breeds of social economists and economic sociologists are needed to study this developmental process.

Part II presents examples of emerging trends as choices for policy research: in the labor market for the study of social management; in the capital market for the study of social investment; and in the whole private market for the study of the human dimensions of economic life.

Part III explores the capacity of the market to become more socially empowered, pointing out that corporations today are already cooperating—as well as competing—with each other, and that they generate self-regulatory norms that introduce the values of society selectively into the marketplace. Case studies from Europe, Japan, and the United States demonstrate various structures of cooperation. A theory of self-regulation by opposing associations then enables us to develop indexes to measure their accountability. This means examining how the larger culture—societal values and norms—is introduced into the market.

I believe that social indexes can measure workable *cooperation* in the same manner that economic indexes measure workable *competition*. When these two kinds of indexes are combined, they should provide a better measure of how well the market is performing in the public interest, and when refined operationally, can assist agencies such as the Antitrust Division of the U.S. Department of Justice and the Federal Trade Commission in making decisions about market effectiveness, including the extent to which trade associations can assume greater powers of self-governance. The rationale for government policies should also be based on balancing the principles of efficiency and equity regarding corporate development in an open market.

Part IV describes how organizational research and new public policies can promote a self-regulatory market, leading toward the elimination of the welfare state, and how changing definitions of key economic terms point toward a new social order of markets.

The Appendix reviews global issues, such as international debt, military tensions, the rise of multinational corporations, and their impact on the U.S. economy. It examines how problems may be resolved by research on mutual systems of international governance in the monetary system, codes of conduct for multinational enterprises, and institutions that can strengthen local communities operating in a global market.

Social development in the market economy is a highly subtle process—one requiring the kind of voluntary actions that government legislation could never produce on its own. This is why the individual action of people in every sector of the economy, the tedious empirical task of each researcher, the unpublicized work of each professional business consultant, and the vision of a social market put together by scholars in many different disciplines are all important to the successful process of change and development in the market economy.

The future cannot be detailed in the gross terms of dialectical theory or be planned by any sequence of legislation. The dimensions of this development process must be explored, reviewed, debated, studied, analyzed, and shaped by people working at all levels of the economy. Thus, this book's overriding message for future researchers and policy makers is that the most important source of social change originates in the imagination and self-direction of people in all stations of life, including every individual who is affected by the marketplace.

PART I

The Social Market

The worst error of all is to suppose that capitalism is simply an economic system, whereas in fact it lives off the social order.

> Fernand Braudel
> *Civilization and Capitalism*, vol. 3:
> *The Perspective of the World*

CHAPTER 1

A Social Orientation to the Market

THE MARKET ECONOMY we know in America today is neither static nor eternal. It has changed—and will continue to change— over time. In this book, I describe certain changes taking place in the system today that I believe could bring us to a dramatically different kind of order. Before we look at these developments, however, I would like to raise the crucial question of the analytical paradigm used for studying and interpreting our economic system.

In modern times, the task of interpreting the capitalist system and its uniquely characteristic institution, the market, has typically been assigned to the field of economics. If, as is commonly claimed, the purpose of business is to make profits, our economic system is best explained on the basis of economic principles. Accordingly, in both academia and the public policy arena, we turn to economists to help us make sense of the ever-shifting economic picture.

The interpretation presented in this book, however, is based on the assumption that our economic system is grounded primarily in a societal order, and that social and economic influences must be studied together in order to understand the changes taking place in the market. This approach may sound unorthodox, but an increasing number of economists are coming to acknowledge that the critical role of social institutions and organizations as autonomous forces must be recognized in order to understand and make predictions about market behavior, and that the "bottom line" for business today consists of social as well as economic factors.

From the perspective of this book, the changing relationship of the social sciences to the study of the market has been central to the evolution of capitalism itself. We will therefore begin our analysis of the key changes taking place today by exploring the changing views on the market economy over the years.

Conceptual Approaches to Studying the Market Economy

Let us begin by identifying trends of thought in economics, sociology, and history relating to the study of the market, locating them in the categories of classical economics, neoclassical economics, social economics, economic sociology, and social history.[1]

Classical Economics

The concept of the economy was originated by Aristotle to mean the wise and legitimate government of the household for the good of the family. For Aristotle and other early Greek philosophers, the economy was part of the polis; the various dimensions of the larger economy, such as trade and exchange, were simply part of the politics of the city-state. It was to be centuries before the concept was applied systematically to the societal domain. The mercantilist Antoine de Montchrétien's study *Traicte de L'Economie Politique* (1615) is thought to mark the first use of the term "political economy."[2] Because Montchrétien was mainly interested in issues of state finance, the term was employed not in connection with an analysis of industry or a critique of commerce, but simply to signify a survey of French industries motivated by a high degree of patriotism. Other mercantilists also described the management of trade and treasure in terms of national interests. The mercantilists introduced the concept of the economy to describe the state's trade and industry but did not yet define economy as we do, and none distinguished the economy as a separate entity within society.

In the eighteenth century, the French Physiocrats, following in the wake of the mercantilists, began to see the economy as an autonomous entity, separate from government and operating under a supply-demand-price mechanism. This leap seems to have been possible only with the breakdown of feudalism, the rise of international commerce, and the introduction of money as a major form of exchange. Furthermore, the concept of the economy gained greater prominence at the same time that the concept of the market as an institution did so. Attributes of the economy (such as trade and prices) had certainly been seen and reported before this time; but with the Physiocrats, the market as an activity independent of the state was becoming evident in the fluctuating system of prices. Old as the notion of prices was, they had never been conceived as constituting a natural system of their own. By custom, medieval cities had regularly controlled prices and money and kept them stable. Moreover, medieval thought had always associated prices with the concept of justice: attributes of the economy were considered a branch of moral philosophy. But over the following centuries, the penetration of foreign trade into local markets gradually transformed them into an arena in which prices were in flux.

Not only did the Physiocrats propose that both the market and the economy were autonomous systems; it is especially significant that they saw the market economy as an expression of Nature, operating under "natural law." François Quesnay was among the first to propose that the economy was based on both positive and natural law. In fact, some historians designate him as the first political economist, in the sense that he believed that the wealth of a nation required scientific study to determine the precise conditions that would ensure its optimum production and distribution.

According to the Physiocrats, the laws of nature (*droit naturel*) in the economy were to be discovered through scientific study; the laws of government were seen in acts of the legislature (*droit legitime*). Furthermore, the Physiocrats held natural law to be superior to the laws of government. Here we see a concept that would shape economic thought for the next two centuries. On high abstract grounds, the Physiocrats arrived at the principle of government nonintervention, which they described as the doctrine of laissez-faire.

As time passed, fluctuating prices for products were followed by fluctuating prices for land and labor. Prices became independent of guild control and local custom, shaped instead by the convergence of separate but competing interests in the new arena of the marketplace. The price system thus became a kind of collective reality sui generis. The price for labor could be seen in the changing order of wages, the price for land in the changing order of rent, and the price for money in the changing interest rates. This new reality came to be identified as the "economy," and within the philosophic framework of that day, it was a system based on natural law.

Although Adam Smith drew on the Physiocrats for the notion of a "hidden hand" that leads the mass of unregulated economic transactions to the best overall outcome for society, he did not follow them in many other important respects. A product of the less feudal and more monetarized economy of England, he saw no need to mystify agriculture as the key to the wealth of nations, as the Physiocrats did. He was able to include wages and rents in the group of prices operating in the market and was the first to link the production of wealth to a system of integrated markets. It was in this sense that Smith became the acclaimed founder of political economy. He recognized, however imprecisely, the interdependence of different kinds of prices resulting from competitive markets. Laissez-faire, the principle of nongovernmental intervention in the markets, would now become a fundamental of political economy.

The concept of the economy was thereafter to be closely identified with the concepts of the market and the private sector, though the early economists themselves never saw the economy as limited to the private sector. Both Quesnay and Smith tended to see the study of the economy operating broadly across history even as they identified it with an emerging autonomous market. Quesnay saw surplus as inherent in farming (apart from farming's position in the private sector), observable in the difference between the cost to create a product and the selling price. Smith saw the economy as rooted in the "truck, barter, and exchange" of primitive society as well as in the autonomous market.

Interestingly, because Adam Smith was not inclined to separate his study of the economy from the influence of society, many classical sociologists have recognized Smith's work as significant to the development of an integral perspective between the disciplines of economics and sociology. Auguste Comte considered Smith's analysis "illuminating," and Marx was also highly appreciative of his work. Albion Small thought of him as virtually a sociologist. Emile Durkheim's *Division of Labor in Society* was greatly influenced by Smith's work.

Economics emerged as a distinct field toward the end of the nineteenth century. Until then, all writing about production and trade had been within a framework of social thought, such as ethics, logic, or philosophy. Aristotle had made his observations about the economy in *Nicomachean Ethics* and *Politics*, believing that economic relations fell in the category of justice. Thomas Aquinas and medieval scholastics continued with the concept of justice as the basis for discussing issues of trade and commerce, and the mercantilists developed political economy as a subject to be examined within the framework of government. Only the Physiocrats began to separate the economy as an independent entity for scientific study. Now following Smith and his contemporaries, the discipline of economics could arise to focus on the market system, and to study the economy apart from politics and the state.

We are indebted to these classical theorists for analyzing the evolving self-regulatory power of the market. But since they were writing before political scientists and sociologists could interpret the larger meaning of this institutional separation between the market and the state, they could not be conscious of the complex institutional development that we discuss later. This development begins to become clear with a recognition of the social factor in the market.

Neoclassical (Traditional or Mainstream) Economics

Neoclassicism is the prevailing trend of thought in economic departments in the United States and is widely represented in public policy. It has various theoretical orientations and specialities, as well as a vast store of research and data with contrasting premises and conflicting arguments, but for our purposes this view is distinguished by its focus on the market's economic aspects with no intentional or systematic consideration of the social factor. Indeed, when a social factor becomes recognized as important in studies by mainstream economists, their work is often called "nontraditional." Throughout this book, therefore, I will refer to the neoclassical approach as "traditional economics" or "mainstream economics."

The field of economics took an especially big leap in the late nineteenth century with the work of W. S. Jevons, Karl Menger, and Alfred Marshall. The transition between political economy and economics can be seen most dramatically in the studies of the British economist Jevons, who wanted to create a field of study based on the model of physics. His major work is *The Theory of Political Economy* (1871), but the unfinished volume he left behind at his death was titled *Principles of Economics*.[3] Menger published his first and most influential work, *Principles of Economics*, in Vienna in 1871. It dealt with the general conditions that create economic activity, value, exchange, price, and money. What made it distinctive was its explanation of value derived from an analysis of the conditions determining the distribution of scarce goods among competing uses. In short, Menger created what has been called the means-ends structure that came to define the subject matter of modern economics.

In Cambridge, England, Marshall began his studies in the field of political economy as early as 1867; his main ideas appeared in *Principles of Economics* (1890). The book was an instant success, and he is widely considered the founder of the discipline of economics. For Marshall, values were expressed in the ratios of exchange between goods; the money system caused the values, which were transferred into prices that basically reflected supply and demand.

Alfred Marshall distinguished economics as a science that interpreted the economy in purely instrumental terms, arguing from a scientific view that the economy was to be understood as an autonomous system of exchange and studied as a natural phenomenon, rather than viewed as a set of moral principles based on an ethical concept of justice. This view has long remained a controversy in scientific studies of the economy. The fact is that a valuative order is present in every field of action, including the field of economics. Indeed, the values of economic theory developed in the context of nineteenth-century philosophies such as utilitarianism (how happiness could be created for the greatest number of people), individualism (how self-interest could be advanced), and naturalism (how the world could be viewed as composed of objects obeying the laws of Nature). Traces of all three philosophies, combined with Darwin's "competitive struggle for survival," can still be found in the theories of modern economics.

Economists abstracted the different concepts of the individual, utility, competition, and the natural from the beliefs of the times and integrated them selectively into a scientific framework. The underlying assumption of economics in this cultural context was in effect that individual self-interests should be allowed to rein in the pursuit of utilities (wants and preferences) under the natural conditions of a competitive market because it would ultimately lead to the greatest happiness for all. These are the very assertions about how the market operates that are studied and measured today in mainstream economics.[4]

The term "neoclassical" was first used by Thorstein Veblen in 1900 to characterize Marshall's work, a recognition of the new discipline's continuity with classical economics on the alleged basis of a common utilitarian approach and a common assumption of a hedonistic psychology.[5] The term gained a certain popularity in the 1920's and 1930's in the writings of such economists as Wesley Mitchell, J. A. Hobson, Maurice Dobb, and Eric Roll. But it came into its own after the Second World War, when other economists began to use it routinely and even extended its meaning to embrace marginalist theory in general.[6] It entered the general vocabulary after 1955, when Paul Samuelson identified his popular economics textbook as a "grand neoclassical synthesis."[7]

Although the neoclassical theory's ideas reflected the society's values, it saw economics as a science separated from society; the laws of economic behavior were independent of social relations and societal values. There are many strains of neoclassical thought, but the one emphasizing economic science assumed that the cross-cultural (universal) subject of economics involved (1) separate actors, (2) any situation where choice and scarcity were present, (3) exclusively rational actions with an emphasis on choice and the maximization of profits, (4) a tendency toward equilibrium, (5) with predictions extrapolated from reality. On these assumptions, people naturally seek the lowest price available to them in a range of choices, and the proper role of government is to help maintain this autonomous system and to intervene only to re-establish the basis for fair competition.[8]

Neoclassical economics derived from Menger's premise that the appropriate concern of economics is the allocation of insufficient means to provide the necessities of life. For most academic economists, however, the normative question of how to allocate the means is not an issue because it is not a scientific question. They assume, rather, that the pertinent issue is how the allocation happens; the formal ends are assumed to be given by the society. Although economists do engage in normative studies, the mainstream theory is still guided by the assumption that a natural law governs the economy that can be discovered through scientific study.

The field of economics today has a dozen definitions of its subject matter, but the usually accepted one rests in the means-end schema. From this perspective, economists argue that the discipline is applicable anywhere that the concept of economizing is appropriate. When asked to write on "the most important economic problem" facing the United States in 1958, the economist Frank Knight said, "The question has no definite answer. Most problems involve some use of means, hence demand 'economizing,' avoiding waste and futility. Accordingly, the economic problems form no distinct class, and any list would be largely arbitrary."[9]

Many economists say that within the means-end schema, the subject of economics lies in any arrangement in which items are marketable—capable of being purchased by money. In other words, the economy is located wherever there is an exchange of items translatable into monetary terms. Some economists state that it exists in any exchange that has the potential to be expressed in money.

The term "market," from the Latin *mercatus*, also has a distinctly economic meaning in the conventional vocabulary. As the *International Encyclopedia of Social Sciences* notes, economists take two approaches to the meaning of the word. In one, they consider the general conditions under which buyers and sellers exchange goods and services, studying such types of competition as monopoly and oligopoly. In the second, they identify specific groups of buyers, sellers, and commodities within a geographically identified exchange area, for example, the fluid-milk market for New York City or the cement market for the Upper Midwest.[10] In both approaches, the primary determinants of the market are assumed to be economic factors involving at least some monetary capability in a system of competition, and the economy is therefore defined as any method that provides for the marketability of exchange objects.

But as more and more prominent economists today are recognizing, traditional economics is in trouble because of its failure to acknowledge the social factor. Lester Thurow, for example, has said that the premise that human behavior can be modeled and explained by "rational utility (income) maximization" is increasingly suspect and without empirical foundation; the field of economics is in a crisis because the idea of "utility maximization" survives despite the lack of empirical support for it. Indeed, he sees the whole idea emptied of empirical content. For example, consumer preferences

are not being distorted by advertising, but are instead being formed endogenously in the market by a wide variety of *social* forces that include deliberate advertising. There is no such thing as "true" independent individual preferences. Human preferences are like an onion, because when the layers of social influence are peeled away, nothing is left. So the rock of stable preferences on which equilibrium price-auction markets are founded is in fact little more than quicksand.[11]

Further:

To reconstruct a theory of economic behavior, a more complex vision of the interaction between society and its citizens is paramount. Societies are not merely statistical aggregations of individuals engaged in voluntary exchange but something much more subtle and complicated. A group or a community cannot be understood if the unit of analysis is the individual taken by himself. A society is clearly something greater than the sum of its parts despite what the price-auction model would maintain. . . . In the final analysis, human preferences are not individually but socially determined, involving intense interaction between society and the individual.[12]

Social Economics

Like neoclassicism, social economics has many trends of thought, but it is distinguished from traditional economics by the fact that the social factor is recognized as an influence on the market, if not vital to the market's formation. The term itself has independent origins in the fields of economics and sociology among researchers working on the assumption that the market is based on more than an economic foundation.

One of the first economists to acknowledge the social factor as vital was Friedrich von Wieser, who in 1914, at the behest of the eminent sociologist Max Weber, then editing a series of social science publications, the *Grundriss der Sozialökonomik*, produced a treatise called *Social Economics*. As successor to Menger at the University of Vienna, von Wieser developed a variant of economic doctrine that drew heavily on his reading of Herbert Spencer's *First Principles*. By showing how a balance of forces between competitive drives and government regulation acted to modify the classical concepts of private property, von Wieser linked theory to policy, an interest that persists today among social economists. He wanted to show how the social economy was constituted through the process of exchange—the mechanism through which he believed single individuals expressed their economic interest. He also recognized the role of class structure in determining market behavior in selective ways. The stratifying of prices, for example, seemed to him to reflect the growth of different categories of goods related to the different classes of society.[13]

From these beginnings, social economics branched out into specialized fields, including welfare economics, evolutionary economics, and institutional economics. The last is the name for much heterodox thought in economics. Institutional economists have worked largely within the United States, representing a continuation of the German and English historical traditions that included

Max Weber and John Hobson. They reject both neoclassical and Marxian economics, and it is significant for our purposes that their work has swung so widely between the fields of sociology and economics. The sociological perspective originated with Thorstein Veblen, who focused on the progressive role of technology and the inhibitions of institutions, the economic perspective with John Commons, who, less interested in the power of technology, approached institutions more neutrally as market forces.

The core of institutional analysis lies in its opposition to mainstream economics. Institutional economists assert that the traditional analysis of levels of income and output cannot reveal the forces driving the market; what is at issue is the organization and control of the economic system, particularly the power structure. Where the mainstream economist sees the market from a purely economic orientation, these nontraditional economists argue that the market itself is a complex of institutions that interacts with society's other institutional complexes. In short, the economy is more than a competitive market mechanism; therefore accurate studies in economics need to include the institutions that shape the operation of the market. The focus of institutionalists is on the larger economy, which effectively allocates resources.

Institutional economists also accent a concept of value that transcends price. They are concerned both with the values represented in the habits and customs of social life and a society's latent constructive values—values that are not always recognized by the general public but are visible in an analysis of the power structure. One example is Veblen's emphasis on status emulation as a principal force in the formation of economic behavior, including the impact of what he called conspicuous consumption and invidious comparisons on the formation of consumer demands. But a broader concept of value is inherent in many studies, including Commons's analysis of the social evolution of business law; John Maurice Clark's study of the social control of business; Wesley Mitchell's study of the economy as a pecuniary phenomenon; and Selig Perlman's analysis of the labor union movement as a mode of social change. Thus from the beginning institutional economists tended to avoid methodological individualism and the mathematical modeling that seemed so much a part of traditional economics and removed its adherents from the social realities of the market.[14]

The most widely known contemporary economist in this field is John Kenneth Galbraith, who has explored the institutional nature of corporate power, the complex planning modes of the business system, and the social forces that influence the formation of opinion and policy in the public sector. Indeed, my view of the market extends the meaning of Galbraith's concept of "countervailing powers" toward what I call a concept of "social self-governance."

Welfare economics is rooted in a debate over Adam Smith's idea of an invisible hand transforming the self-interest of the many into the common good. In this debate, the field drew some inspiration from Vilfredo Pareto and his principle of optimality, which defines a set of optimal outcomes for the allocation of resources and the distribution of incomes.[15] But the work of Arthur Pigou laid perhaps the stronger base for contemporary studies in cost-benefit analysis. When Alfred Marshall retired from Cambridge in 1908, he left Anglo-Saxon economics in the hands of Pigou, who showed his own genius in the study of economic welfare. In *Economics of Welfare*, Pigou asserted that a study of welfare economics could improve the human condition. Welfare was a state of consciousness that could be measured in terms of greater or less, and economic welfare was subject to the measuring rod of money. But economic welfare was not an index of total welfare, which included additional aspects such as the quality of work, environment, human relationships, and status. Pigou's legacy may be seen most prominently today in the notion that the negative externalities of business, such as the impact of waste on the environment, can be measured in cost-benefit terms; such studies have become an important part of the assessment of corporate social responsibility.[16]

Social economics has continued as a subfield as well as a generic name. The Association for Social Economics is largely made up of economists concerned with the ethical and moral dimensions of economic science, and regularly publishes a journal called *Review of Social Economy*. A somewhat different orientation, socioeconomics, has only recently emerged. It began informally in 1989 during a conference held at the Harvard Business School sponsored by a new professional association, the Society for the Advancement of Socio-economics. The movement is too new to report on in detail. Suffice it to say that its intent is to bridge the gap between sociology and economics and provide an empirical basis for recommendations on public policy.[17]

Though each of these subfields has its own emphasis, most continue to accept the assumptions of the economic model. For example, social economists have developed theories about social relations of exchange and consumption in the fields of crime, education, and marital relations, but the individualist and economic view of the market has been kept as a basic orientation. While making important contributions to understanding the social market, these studies have maintained the economic model, never altering the premise that the market is based on the rational calculation of costs, benefits, and price mechanisms. Put another way, many studies in this genre do not go so far as to assume that the whole economy is based on a social foundation. For many social economists, the market is a phenomenon in which social relations simply play a conditioning or even a disruptive role, not a central, shaping role.[18]

The same picture can be drawn for research by sociologists and anthropologists who have studied markets in banking, contracts, and labor. This may seem a pejorative view of their work, but I believe the deeper social foundations of the market are being revealed in these studies even though the authors themselves may not yet realize the full implications of their research. Indeed, they can be thanked in good part for the growing recognition that the social factor plays more than a minor role in market behavior. So each piece of social research that is done in this tradition expands the professional, and oftentimes public, awareness of the depth of the social factor operating in the market economy.

In sum, although social economics acknowledges the social factor as an influence on the market, in my judgment it is as yet not a truly interdisciplinary field, in the sense that the frameworks of both economics and sociology are fully integrated and equally recognized for their importance in the study of the market. I believe that such an integration will take place only with (1) increasing scientific awareness of the social factor among economists and sociologists who study the market, allowing for an improved perception of a relationship between their research categories; and (2) sociolegal (objective) changes in corporate structure and business law. We will speak later about these changes, some of which are taking place today.[19]

Economic Sociology

Economic sociology has roots primarily in sociology. Although its theoretical orientations overlap with social economics, this field definitively assumes that the market is grounded in society, and thus that any system of exchange will generate different norms and organizations according to the nature and culture of the society. In this tradition, the market is clearly observed to have a social foundation.[20] Neil Smelser succinctly describes its aims this way:

Economic sociology is the application of the general frame of reference, variables, and explanatory models of sociology to that complex of activities concerned with the production, distribution, exchange, and consumption of scarce goods and services.

The first focus of economic sociology is on economic activities alone. The economic sociologist asks how these activities are structured into roles and collectivities, by what values they are legitimized, by what norms and sanctions are they regulated, and how these sociological variables interact.

The second focus of economic sociology is on the relations between sociological variables as they manifest themselves in the economic context and sociological variables as they manifest themselves in non-economic contexts. How, for instance, do familial roles articulate with the occupational role of a local community and the control of its political structure?[21]

Although the focus of market studies is from a sociological rather than an economic perspective, the field of economic sociology finds common ground conceptually with social economics around many topics, and the two share a list of early founders, including Marx and Weber. These two social analysts offer a basis for us to interpret the social market from both its subjective and its objective aspects.

The subjective approach can be illustrated in the work of Max Weber, who defined "social action" as that which "takes account of the behavior of others and is thereby oriented in its course." The Weberian methodological tradition leads the sociologist to examine the way the actors themselves interpret the world in everyday life, rather than the way an objective observer might interpret the world. The method tends to be inductive, in the sense that these subjective data then become the basis for sociological interpretation and analysis.[22]

Weber's definition is in some ways close to key definitions in economics.[23] It starts where people see the system as it manifestly exists. His definition of social action allows us to interpret the market as socially determined from within itself, rather than being externally influenced from the outside either by the government or by law. On the other hand, unlike mainstream economics, his conception of economy as based on "autocephalous" (autonomous) economic action within society allows us to investigate the customs of social (not government) regulation that also act on the market system.

By contrast, Karl Marx saw the market from the objective distance of a historical observer who takes a more critical overview. He interpreted the market as part of the changing order of society in the context of history, seen not as a competitive struggle for prices but as a class struggle for power. From Marx's perspective, the field of political economy (or economics), which interprets the market economy as a natural order of prices, fails to account for its historical context and social dynamics. Furthermore, Marx viewed the economy as socially grounded; it began historically when people sought subsistence together. Marx used the term "social concept" in two different ways. Sometimes it referred to "cooperative relations," one historical mode of production in his scheme, and sometimes he used it interchangeably with the concept of being human—to be "human" is to be "social." In both cases, however, the social concept was the conceptual foundation for Marx's critique of political economy.[24]

Marx asserted that the rise of the market economy changed the social relations between people into quantitative relations: exchange (market) relations were a fiction, even though they were measured by economists as if they had some reality. In his view, people living in a commercial (market) society lose any sense of the value to be found in their labor, and the exchange (market) values do not represent the value that labor originally created in the production of commodities. The exchange system reifies "things" (commodities) so that they seem to be the real values of society, and products and market prices become excessively valued and fictionalized.

These two complementary ways of analyzing social reality, Weber focusing on the subjective and Marx focusing on the objective, bear some similarity to two major concepts we will employ through the rest of this book: the "manifest" and "latent" dimensions of society and of the economy. As I use them, these two dimensions do not coincide perfectly with their analyses, but the differences in their work stimulated new thought in economic sociology; we shall note later how the sociologist Robert Merton came to refine these terms for middle-range research.

Like Marx and Weber, Karl Polanyi could be placed equally in the categories of social economics and social history, but I want to trace his thought here because his work focuses so directly on the sociological issues of the market. For our purposes, he is more than a social historian; he is a social analyst who offers a unique concept of the market as increasingly divorced from a purely economic orientation.

Polanyi's main argument is that in capitalism, the economy is "disembedded" from society. The modern market has a special culture for economizing in ways that distinguish it from markets in other periods of history. Thus economizing principles are not universal.[25] For Polanyi, there is a "formal" economy and a "substantive" economy. The first refers to the logical relationship between means and ends, as in "economizing" or "economical." It is from this definition that the principle of efficiency is applied to marshal scarce means to achieve formal goals. This formal economy, characterized by "economic man" and "rationality," can be seen in Paul Samuelson's famous definition of economics as simply the study of "how . . . we choose to use scarce productive resources with alternative uses." Substantive economy studies the elemental facts of survival, that is, the necessity of meeting human needs in the physical world. In this sense, the field of economics is concerned simply with the material means for living, and the subject matter of economics—that is, the economy—includes the society's history and institutions.[26] Substantivism has gone far to foster what might be called nontraditional economics, whose main strains we have discussed as institutional economics, welfare economics, and social economics. Polanyi himself is associated closely with this nonmainstream tradition.

Polanyi noted that the market has also been defined in two ways. In one meaning, it is the place where the necessaries of life can be bought and sold, or exchanged, in small quantities; this type of market goes back to antiquity and has existed in all societies. In the second meaning, it is an exchange system in which a supply-demand-price mechanism enables trade; this definition applies to the capitalist period, governed (on the classicists' view) by price mechanisms that respond to supply and demand apart from local custom or moral standards.

Polanyi himself proposed redefining the market as an *institution* composed of "market elements" that may or may not involve a supply-demand-price mechanism. These elements included site, available goods, a supply crowd, a demand crowd, custom or law, and equivalencies needed to make the exchange. He also proposed that the rate of exchange need not be influenced solely by the market mechanisms so familiar to economics, but may also be influenced by custom, administration (organization), and law. In effect, he asserted that the market economy may be determined by tradition and organizational dynamics as much as by economic principles.

Polanyi's historical analysis of the development of markets reveals three important things: (1) the market system as we think of it today did not exist in early societies; (2) historical studies show that the economy has always been embedded in society; and (3) nonmarket forms of exchange existed in early societies and continue to exist today in what Polanyi described as "reciprocal" and "redistributive" systems.[27] In drawing these distinctions, Polanyi's aim was to develop a theoretical framework to accommodate nonmarket economics, one that would prove applicable to any society, from ancient systems to the modern market economy. This contribution, as with the rest of Polanyi's distinguished work, was a major step in exploring how social factors must continue to be taken into account in studying the nature and development of economic systems.

Since Polanyi's time, economic sociology has become a field too replete with theories and research to cover fully here, but the publication of *Economy and Society* by the sociologists Talcott Parsons and Neil Smelser in 1956 must be mentioned. Understandably enough, this work, a theoretical attempt to examine the institutional roots of the economy, was not read by the public because of its extremely high level of abstraction. But it was also ignored by economists because it did not seem relevant to their field, and Marxists rejected it because it seemed too strongly in the tradition of Weber and economic theory.[28] It nevertheless represents a landmark work in theory that takes society as the basis for interpreting the market economy.

In my judgment, economic sociology needs to develop further as a field of study in universities, if for no other reason than to counterbalance the distortion of reality that stems from the heavy emphasis on economics both in public policy and in all professional studies of the marketplace, a tendency that the prominent economist Kenneth Boulding called "economic imperialism" in university studies.[29] Indeed, it is increasingly assumed in academic circles that an economic analysis can be applied to all dimensions of society even more effectively than social analysis. Consider, most outstandingly, Gary Becker's well-known studies of "human capital" and their elaboration in *The Economic Approach to Human Behavior*.[30]

Richard Swedberg suggests that a rapprochement is needed between sociology and economics around four approaches: economic imperialism, the structural-individualistic research program, the new political economy, and socioeconomics. The reader is encouraged to read his excellent review of the literature on the late developments in this field.[31]

Social History

Social historians concerned with the market economy have their own perspective, one that is in accord with a major premise of this book: that the market has a foundation in society. Although all the traditions mentioned above contribute to the social concept of the market, some notion of how the market has developed in history will give us a better understanding of the changes evolving in the American economy today.

When historians attempt to determine the point at which capitalism began as an epochal system, they necessarily incorporate factors of social organization into their explanations. In the process, they each tell us something about what to consider the social essence of capitalism. The French historian Henri Pirenne believed that profit making was the essence of capitalism, and so by his lights the capitalist system began in the twelfth century, when commercial traders started roaming the earth selling goods for profit. This interpretation puts capitalism's beginnings farther back than most other historians are willing to accept.[32]

The German historian Werner Sombart argued that the nature of every new epoch was found in the shape of its economy, which should be examined in terms of its culture—the new attitudes and values brought to the life of a people. Sombart saw the capitalist system evolving from feudalism through a new spirit characterized by the principles of "unlimited acquisition," "rationalism," and "competition," which to him meant that the first signs of capitalism emerged in the seventeenth century.[33] In contrast, Maurice Dobbs, a British Marxist who held that the system was defined by the way labor and capital were organized, and specifically by a mode of production in which the class of producers (the laborers) were subordinated to a class of people with money (capitalists), saw capitalism as emerging at the end of the eighteenth century. And for John Commons, the clue to the system's history lay in the type of institution controlling the profit-making system. He therefore believed that capitalism developed in stages: merchant capitalism in the 1600's, employer capitalism in the 1850's, and banker capitalism in the 1900's.[34]

Max Weber distinguished between industrial capitalism and political capitalism (involving historic opportunities by groups for profit through the exploitation of subordinate groups).[35] Political capitalism had existed throughout history in different forms. Industrial capitalism, known by the "method of enterprise," was typified by "capital accounting"—a process of determining its income-yielding power by the striking of a balance—and was historically located only in the modern period. But though the striking of a balance was first proposed in 1698 by a Dutch theorist, Simon Stevin, Weber noted, that by itself did not fully define industrial capitalism. This form of capitalism developed uniquely out of feudalism and was characterized by six features: the appropriation of all physical means of production (land, apparatus, machinery) by private enterprises; freedom of the market (i.e., the absence of outside trade limitations based on class privilege); a rational technology based on calculation; calculable law, free from arbitrary interruptions by royalty; free labor (i.e., the availability of persons "economically compelled to sell their labor" on the market without restriction); and the commercialization of economic life (i.e. the general use of paper instruments to represent share rights in enterprises and property ownership).[36]

This is not the whole story of the way capitalism has been interpreted by historians, but these accounts are sufficient to suggest that its development has many dimensions. Together, they suggest that the market economy originated slowly and developed new traits incrementally. The rise of merchants in the twelfth century was a seed-trait that helped to form the new system; another seed appeared later, in the system of accounting for the calculation of profit; another was the emergence of a labor (propertyless) class; and of course the spirit of competition and "unlimited acquisition" developed to characterize the culture. The key point is that not only do historians help us build a more complete picture of capitalism, but they all recognize socal factors as the means for analyzing its evolution. They recognize that a new social order of economy arises very slowly with many different traits emerging during different periods of history.

The Social Market

The concept of the social market is indebted to all the traditions mentioned above. It is strongly rooted in the perspective of economic sociology, but it is also a contextual interpretation in the tradition of socioeconomics; it draws as well from the historic foundations of neoclassical thought and becomes part of a larger history of social economy. Keeping in mind these disciplinary perspectives in the concept of the social market will aid us in recognizing the fundamental changes evolving in the U.S. economy today. But we need to add one final conceptual approach, that is, understanding the market as a system of exchange that is based on both social and economic foundations.

I assume that any market system is rooted ultimately in society. My focus here is on the contemporary period of capitalism, which is distinguished by its emphasis on a market with an economic orientation—that is, a market *perceived by its participants* as characterized by exchange based primarily on economic principles. Yet in reality, the market in contemporary capitalism is also embedded in a complex system of social exchange and social organization. Although still largely unrecognized, *society is the ultimate arbiter of market organization, and social factors infuse the market's very life and being, and are therefore fundamentally involved in determining its future course and direction.*

One very important point: the concept of "society" is quite different from the concept of "the state." Society refers to the interactions and organization, both formal and informal, of people, and to the norms and values, both conscious and unconscious, that shape people's lives together. The state refers to the formal, institutionalized government system that is only one aspect of society. The relationship of the state to society, and the impact of both on the economy, will be explored in detail in a later section.

Applying the concept of the social market to the contemporary economy, we have said that social factors have a crucial, if widely unrecognized, impact on the nature of business. Such social factors are therefore often seen either as hidden or as ideal dimensions of the market, although they exist analytically and can be researched empirically so that they can become documented as real in the public mind. They are objectively real, in the ways people act in the everyday life of the market, however unconsciously; and they are also becoming real as a widening social consciousness leads people to take them into account to guide their own conduct, for example, by altering corporate structure or business law. As we will see, though still "latent" in the market today, social factors of the last sort can be expected to develop as a more visible part of the future economy.

But exactly how do social and economic factors interplay to influence the market in everyday life? To answer that question, we need to examine the concept of exchange—the central concept of a market—from a sociological perspective.

Exchange Theory

Although criticized by Lester Thurow and other economists, the field of economics continues to maintain its traditional view of exchange theory. In the widely accepted *New Palgrave Dictionary of Economics*, Robert Wilson states:

> The accepted purview of economics is the allocation of scarce resources. Allocation comprises production and exchange, according to a division between processes that transform commodities and those that transfer control. For production or consumption, exchange is essential to efficient use of resources. . . . If two agents have differing marginal rates of substitution then there exists a trade benefiting both. . . .
> Most theories hypothesize that each agent acts purposefully to maximize (the expected utility of) gains from trade. Some behavior may be erratic . . . but experimental and empirical evidence substantially affirms the hypothesis of "rational" behavior, at least in the aggregate.[37]

Exchange theory began with the utilitarian philosophies of David Ricardo, Adam Smith, John Stuart Mill, and Jeremy Bentham between 1750 and 1850. This tradition assumed—given some exceptions and variations—that exchanges among people are based on (1) profit-oriented, rational decision making that is free of external restraint and (2) a search for full information surrounding what are primarily economic transactions. The classic studies of Herbert Spencer and Emile Durkheim that followed, as well as the more recent studies of Talcott Parsons and George C. Homans, have exposed the fictions underlying many of these assumptions. The classic conditions of profitability, economic rationality, freedom from restraint, and access to full information may exist in the marketplace, but then again, they may not. Indeed, exchanges can be characterized by the opposite: lack of a profit incentive, motives that are nonrational, decisions based on external constraints, and no clear information. The fact is, every kind of condition can come into play within an exchange system.

Unlike economic exchange, social exchange involves symbolic interaction, and it is thus connected to other types of institutional life, including religious institutions, schools, governments, and other associations. It includes the symbol of money as an artifact of exchange and has multiple meanings to people who are engaged in marketing. It can include a potential for competition but also a potential for cooperation in the exchange relationship.

The Concept of Social Exchange

The famous anthropologist Bronislaw Malinowski was perhaps the first noneconomist to challenge the popular picture of exchange in the utilitarian tradition. In his study of the Kula Ring, Malinowki described a circle of exchange relations among members of South Pacific Trobriand Islands communities. This system saw armlets traveling in one direction along the Kula Ring of islands exchanged for necklaces moving in the opposite direction. Observing that this arrangement was primarily a social exchange aimed at solidifying interpersonal relationships, Malinowski argued against the belief that all transactions are primarily economic (though it is worth noting, for our purposes, he also saw that economic factors existed latently within the Kula; they simply were not dominant).

Influenced by Malinowski's observations, a number of social scientists began to study the phenomenon of social exchange within economic exchange. Before we turn to them, however, one extremely important theoretical point must be emphasized here. The assertion that social exchange exists in the midst of economic exchange, or, put another way, that social factors play a crucial role in what is defined as economic exchange, is from my theoretical perspective simply an observation about reality. It does not imply that the existence of social factors in economic interactions is either desirable or undesirable. Nor does it imply that the impact of these social factors is either necessarily harmful or necessarily beneficial to the outcome of that exchange.

In his study of the Kula Ring, Malinowski emphasized the constructive and integrative aspects of the noneconomic exchange. He demonstrated that the dominant factors among the Trobriand Islanders were their impulses to share, display, and bestow, and that the most fundamental purpose of their exchange was to fulfill societal needs and maintain a positive sense of community. But this may not always be the case. As we shall see later, the social factor can play either a constructive or a destructive role in the market. I do not equate social factors with "good"; the social is simply one aspect of the overall system. Whether or not the social factors operating in the economy lead to desirable or undesirable outcomes depends on many other factors and criteria.

Other Social Theories of Exchange

Marcel Mauss took Malinowski's Kula example and reinterpreted it in its collective or structural dimension. Mauss asked why people who receive gifts feel compelled to reciprocate, concluding that all exchange is based on collective rules that become compelling for the individual. For Mauss, exchange relations create, reinforce, and serve group morality; and morality, further reinforced by exchange patterns, comes to regulate still other activities.[38]

Claude Lévi-Strauss insisted that exchange should be seen as an expression of society rather than as an expression of individuals in interaction. He lifted the focus from a micro to a macro perspective, arguing that "various forms of social structure rather than individual motives are the critical variables in the analysis of exchange relations," and that "[it] is the exchange that counts and not the things exchanged."[39] This prescient view anticipated the fact that social exchange can structure markets, a condition we see increasingly evident, for example, in the service economy.

Behaviorists like George Homans and B. F. Skinner developed exchange theories closest to those of economic exchange, asserting that the classic tradition of utilitarianism works through all exchange. For their own purposes, these theorists reinterpreted the concept of utility as "reward" and the classic concept of punishment as "cost"; this then allowed them to interpret economic behavior in terms of social-psychological relationships and human needs. Homans thus revised exchange theory from a focus on collective norms toward a series of scientific propositions about human interaction. In analyzing interactions among members of diverse groups, he observed key regularities that led him to frame the following propositions (among others): as the frequency of interaction between two or more people increases, the degree of their liking for one another increases, and vice versa; people whose liking for one another increases express these sentiments in increased activity, and vice versa; the more frequently people interact with one another, the more alike their activities and their sentiments tend to become; and the higher a person's rank in a group, the more his or her activities conform to its norms.[40] It is ironic to note that although Homans's theories were quite close to those of economic exchange, propositions such as those he discovered might well contradict economic principles of the marketplace.

While Homans tended to accent interpersonal exchange in his work, other theorists emphasized that exchange operates at both the micro and the macro level of organization, and an understanding of their interconnections is vital. One writer who has sought to create bridges between the collective orientations of Mauss and the individual orientations of Homans is Peter Blau, who sees exchange as the most elementary and basic process of social life, serving as the foundation of the economy operating in society. Blau proposes that people are attracted to social life by intrinsic and extrinsic rewards through an exchange process in which the economic factor is only one expression. To enter into exchange with others, people direct their behavior toward values or ends through social interaction, adapting the means to reach their ends in a process determined only in part by competition. This complex process gives rise to systems of stratification and power differentiation among various classes of people. An entire system of exchange is affected, then, by the distribution of power, not simply by the economics of the market.

Blau further states that complex systems are always based on simpler systems, and that the larger complex systems (e.g., conglomerate corporations) operate in systems of exchange that in turn affect the smallest units of human interaction. He thus leads us from the smallest units of interaction, considered so important to the social behaviorists, to the larger organizational structures of exchange in society. But for Blau it is not a one-way system of exchange from top to bottom, because exchange systems exist at different levels, each with its own dynamics. Starting with the smallest units, group norms emerge to regulate the exchange transactions, including "the fundamental and ubiquitous norm of reciprocity," which makes failure to discharge obligations subject to group sanctions. These social obligations are no less critical than economic obligations in the marketplace.[41]

The Social Factor in the Market Economy

Up to this point, our brief historical review of major conceptual approaches to studying the market economy has shown how the concept of the social factor has continually been broadened and deepened as an analytical keystone. Let us now look at some of the concrete implications of this approach. As should be clear by now, this requires that we look at the market from a sociological perspective as well as from an economic one.

From a sociological perspective, the market is embedded in a human order, and its behavior is understood in a societal context. It is composed of people in organizations that are rooted in processes of social exchange. People engaged in the market have collective attitudes, habits, informal networks, and associations that affect their behavior—not all of which fall within the field of economics or business management. In fact, an organization that engages in the market need not be a business, and the social processes need not be based primarily in competition. Further, the market may be based not only on scarcity, but also sometimes on abundance; not only on supply and demand, but also on social norms regarding the use of property, the conventions of stock payments, the rites of passage for money; not only on the profit motive or an interest in efficiency, but also on a set of customs and organizational rules. From this perspective, the cadences of work within a corporation and the measures of time, weight, and space are socially and culturally determined. They cannot be understood simply in terms of economizing in the use of scarce means.

The field of economics is not reduced by this perspective. On the contrary, it broadens the subject matter of economics and brings it down to the real. The discipline of economics is critical to understanding the transformations taking place today, but by itself it is not sufficient: plainly, too many noneconomic variables operate within the market and help determine its behavior. Two current examples will illustrate the point.

The contention of Malinowski and his followers that social exchange is often hidden in, and can actually shape, what is apparently economic exchange is obviously true in international finance today. The decision of a big nation or a world bank to lend capital to a small nation may be made in contravention of its economic principles because social factors make it essential to solidify a relationship. A large country's loan may encourage the smaller nation's support of the lender-nation's military base on its territory. Such a decision, however, may not be justified on purely economic grounds within the popular view of the market. Moreover, the fact that political factors dominate international finance is becoming well known, despite rhetoric to the contrary. Robert Ayers talks of the World Bank's providing capital to Chile against the logic of economic analysis, simply for political reasons.[42] Such social and political factors can have a powerful impact on supposedly economic transactions and decisions. Yet though public recognition of them is growing, they remain unnoticed and unmeasured in economic textbooks and are thus still part of the latent economy.

We also saw that some exchange theorists conceived of social exchange as a collective reality. A social reality that influences individuals and motivates them to other than self-initiated actions has always disturbed neoclassical economists, contradicting as it does the predominant belief in individualism—that each person determines his or her own behavior, independent of any collective behavior or custom. Despite this central assumption of economics, however, it is increasingly apparent to the public today that the New York Stock Exchange's behavior cannot be understood merely by examining individual behaviors alone. For our purposes, it is significant that recent studies of the organizational dynamics in the stock market are beginning to show how the market's behavior is socially determined. Indeed, the "Black Monday" crash (October 19, 1987) and the close call on October 16, 1989, have led analysts to call for an altering of the social norms, social technology, and organizations that regulate the stock market. There is much more to be done, but the major question is how to do it without more government controls.[43]

State and Society

In our now-completed discussion of theoretical orientations for analyzing the economic system, we have seen the key role of the social factor and briefly explored its meaning. The next chapter presents a model for understanding the current transformations of the market economy, including a more extensive consideration of the meaning and role of social factors in these transformations. Before we turn to these topics, however, let us investigate further two issues implied by our discussion of the social factor and the economy: the presently large role of state control over the economy and the role of society vis-à-vis the state.

No one would deny that both modern socialist and modern capitalist nations are characterized by significant state control over their economies. The ironic fact, however, is that their founders never embraced government control as an ideal. Adam Smith, as we have seen, championed laissez-faire and minimum state control over the economic order. Opposition to state control over the economy has always characterized capitalism and continues to do so today. The objections range from the carefully wrought theories of economic scholars to the demands of politicians, business leaders, and average citizens for a drastically reduced government role in business matters. Many political conservatives and business spokespeople, in particular, claim that the government's extensive involvement in the business sector is harmful to the development of the economy. Not only is it oppressive, but it also creates waste— through its expenditures on a juggernaut of regulatory agencies; its vast government bureaucracies, which impede the efficiency of business; and so on.

Both Lenin and Mao—the vanguard of twentieth-century Marxism—reinterpreted the Marxist tradition to include the assumption that the takeover of the economy by state institutions would result in a democratically designed socialist order. But many observers, both Marxist and non-Marxist, acknowledge today that the state has become idealized in this revolutionary process far beyond anything Marx envisioned. In fact, the point about much of nineteenth-century socialist thought was its anti-statist character. Karl Marx himself hated the state and foresaw the development of socialism as a system governed by society, not the state.[44]

This book is guided by the assumption that the state's currently large role in shaping our economy can recede, while the role of society can become more conscious and integral to its operation. This assumption is not new. It was stated quite emphatically during the nineteenth century by early critics of capitalism like Owen, Fourier, Engels, Bakunin, Proudhon, Saint-Simon, and Marx himself. (It is surely one of the great paradoxes of history that Marx is popularly equated with an economic system under total state control.) Marx and the other writers mentioned above saw in capitalism's economistic market the seeds for its own destruction. They believed that this flaw would become the basis for capitalism's transformation, and that the next economic system to evolve would rest on social foundations.

The concept of society is a root concept underlying any theoretical orientation to the market, because a society infuses the nature of every market order, and the nature of a particular society determines the particular nature of its markets. A concept of society was basic to Adam Smith's theory of free enterprise, just as it was basic to Karl Marx's theory of socialism.

In the Western world, the concept of society, as distinct from the state, came rather late in the Age of Reason, when philosophers were searching for secular foundations to support a critical analysis of political institutions. Intellectual historians locate the origin of the concept of society in the "social contract" described by Thomas Hobbes, who insisted there was a distinction between the organized state and the law of Nature. Later liberal thinkers of the Enlightenment wanted to justify a secular rational criticism of the state and drew sharper distinctions. In developing a critical doctrine, John Locke (and others) began to distinguish the law of Nature from the social contract that had formed the state. Locke claimed that there was a natural human order derived from the interdependence of people and their natural rights, an order that existed prior to and outside the political institutions and the state. The state was merely a utilitarian device for ensuring a more efficient human (social) order. In other words, Locke defined the state as a dependent sector of a larger social order.[45]

According to Locke, people contract to form a civil society; this contract, an "obligation mutually undertaken," has as its specific object the preserving of life, liberty and property. The notion of a social contract greatly influenced the writing of the U.S. Constitution and early American political theory. Although as a doctrine it faded away in later history, it fulfilled the purpose of directing attention to the importance of consent in any system of society. The sociological concept of solidarity fashionable in France at the beginning of the twentieth century also had a contractual basis.[46]

The work of Hobbes and Locke inspired other thinkers to make analytical distinctions between church and state, leading to the complementary concepts of civil society and religious society, which were defined as two aspects of the larger society.

Adam Smith asserted that the duty of the state was to furnish instructions about and protect the natural order of society. Since for maximum productivity competition in economic affairs had to be completely free, the sphere of government should be reduced, leaving natural forces to reconcile the requirements of the individual and the group.

By directing that industry in such a manner as its produce may be of greatest value, he [the individual] intends only his own gain, and he is in this, as in many other cases, led by an invisible hand to promote an end which was not part of his intention. Nor is it always the worse for the society that it was not part of it. By pursuing his own interest he frequently promotes that of the society more effectually than when he really intends to promote it.[47]

Hegel took a more positive view of the state. He held that its origins lay in the eternal and universal pure intelligence of the will, and that the laws of the state were a form of the universal will in which personality, property, and contract were realized. Civil society, by contrast, was guided by the principle that individuals pursued only their own interests. The state, therefore, became the fulfillment of the spirit, the highest of ethical communities.

Marx was appalled by this view, which he labeled a total misconception. Indeed, on reading Hegel, he changed the focus of his own analysis from politics to the nature of civil society. He argued that the state does not stand above society, but is part of society, which made it necessary for him to analyze social life as a first step.

In his essay "On the Jewish Question," Marx elaborated on the concept of political alienation. He substituted the idea of "species-life" (humanity) for Hegel's concept of "universality," and described the split between political life as a heavenly pursuit and the actual, earthly life of civil society. In Hegel's heavenly state of politics, people see themselves as communal beings with common ends, whereas in civil society they see themselves as private individuals. But by pursuing their own ends, Marx held, they reduced themselves to means and thereby became the plaything of alien powers. Thus Marx was very much concerned about alienation within civil society as alienation in relation to the state. Political emancipation gained through bills of human rights, he argued, was a great step forward, but it failed to address the social nature of people and to make humanity real. Full emancipation required democracy, where the sovereignty of people became a "tangible reality, a secular maxim." Thus he said in his *Essay*:

Only when the actual, individual man has taken back into himself the abstract citizen and in his everyday life, his individual work, and his individual relations has become a species-being, only when he has recognized and organized his own powers as *social* powers so that social force is no longer separated from him as *political* power, only then is human emancipation complete.[48]

In effect, as has often been asserted, Marx stood Hegel on his head. Not only did Marx see society as the primary authority and power in governing people's lives, but society (or community)— and not the state—was the evolving ruler of the economy:

And out of this very contradiction between the interest of the individual and that of the community the latter takes an independent form as the *State*, divorced from the real interests of the individual and community, and at the same time as an illusory communal life, always based, however, on the real ties existing in every family and tribal conglomeration.[49]

Marx concluded that the real struggles were to be found outside the state, and that the state would eventually diminish. Thus, he saw a dynamic relationship between what we might call the hidden versus the overt expressions of an evolving society. The state is the overt, manifest regulator of the economy—that is, people *think* the government plays the key role in determining their lives—but this is a delusion. Social analysis reveals that the "real" power lies elsewhere, hidden. This real power becomes evident (manifest) to people only through struggle and the social evolution of the economy.

To Marx, the creative dimensions of the economy were found in its social life, realized more in the process of cooperation than in competition. Indeed, Marx occasionally identified the term "social" with cooperation in his analysis of the productive economy:

The production of life, both of one's own in labour and of fresh life in procreation, now appears as a double relationship: on the one hand as a natural, on the other as a social relationship. By social we understand the cooperation of several individuals, no matter under what conditions, in what manner and to what end. It follows from this that a certain mode of production, or industrial stage, is always combined with a certain mode of co-operation, or social stage, and this mode of co-operation is itself a certain productive force. Further, that the multitude of productive forces accessible to men determines the nature of society, hence, that the "history of humanity" must always be studied and treated in relation to the history of industry and exchange.[50]

Put another way, Marx believed that the often oppressive state system was a false substitute for society. If one were to elaborate on this interpretation, one could say that the state draws the social life (or society) out of the economy and curbs its creative potential by regulating it from the outside. *The state substitutes outside laws for the natural, social (normative) life of the economy.*

The nineteenth-century French sociologist Emile Durkheim was more interested in studying socialism than in promoting it. His search for a common denominator in the theories of socialism he studied produced the following definition:

One calls socialist those theories which demand a more or less complete connection of all economic functions or of certain of them, though diffused, with the directing and knowing organs of society.

This definition calls for a few comments.

We have already observed that we were saying "connection" and not "subordination," and one cannot too strongly stress this difference, which is essential. Socialists do not demand that the economic life be put into the hands of the state, but into contact with it. On the contrary, they declare that it should react on the state at least as much as—if not more than—the latter acts on it. In their thinking, this rapport should have the effect, not of subordinating industrial and commercial interests to "political" interests, but rather of elevating the former to the rank of the latter. For once this constant communication is assured, these economic interests would affect the functioning of the government organ much more profoundly than today and contribute in much larger measure to its course. Very far from relegating economic interests to a second place, it would much rather be a question of calling upon them to play, in the whole of social life, a considerably more important role than is permitted today, when precisely because of their distance from the directing centers of society, they can activate the latter only feebly and intermittently. Even according to the most celebrated theoreticians of socialism, the state as we know it would disappear and no longer be the central point of economic life—rather than economic life being absorbed by the state. For this reason, in the definition, we have not used the term "state," but the expression—expanded and somewhat figurative—"the knowing and managing organs of society."[51]

Durkheim considered how society might develop so as to deal with such problems as suicide, which he believed were created by the anomie of the unregulated, free market economy. What was needed, he suggested, were new kinds of "intermediary groups" to regulate people's specialized occupational life. His own plan called for occupational communities, with representation in a national assembly outside the state. We will return to Durkheim's concept when we look at how trade associations create social norms and a sense of community within their trade areas.

The revisions in both the capitalist and the socialist states during the past century fall far short of the dream of those nineteenth-century socialist philosophers who envisioned that the new ideal society would go not only beyond capitalism, but also beyond the dominion of the state. It is generally conceded today that the process by which the new society may appear will be much more nuanced and difficult to achieve than these philosophers thought. But I believe that subtle changes rooted in social factors are already taking place in business institutions, and that though it is too early to name the economy at this stage, a system beyond contemporary capitalist or socialist models is visible on the horizon.[52] In the next chapter, we will explore how oppositional forces within the U.S. economy are bringing about the first stages of this transformation.

CHAPTER 2

A Theory of Oppositional Dynamics in the Market

THE FUTURE of the market economy has always been a subject of intense interest to both supporters and opponents of the system, and over the years a vast body of literature has grown up around the topic. Proponents have often focused on how the system is changing and do not concern themselves with the question that generally preoccupies opponents: when and how capitalism will end and be transformed into something else.

Whether or not one wishes to see the end of capitalism, we can all agree that the system has continued to change throughout its history and is still changing today. I believe we can find useful information from both proponents and opponents to help us analyze these changes and project the system's future direction.

For example, many Marxists define capitalism by the traditional division between labor and management, and the ownership of corporations by a capitalist class that exploits workers. This definition has implications for defining a postcapitalist system in the relatively near future, because in the United States today we can observe that workers are beginning to participate in higher management and are even becoming owners of the corporations for which they work through ESOPS (Employee Stock Ownership Plans). According to the classic definition of capitalism, such a trend toward worker management and ownership, if continued successfully into the future, would signal the end of capitalism.

I suggest that there is more to the story than this. Even if workers were eventually to own and manage all their own firms, in effect ending the traditional Marxist division between capital and labor, those firms would still compete in the marketplace, where—all things being equal—they would still be guided primarily by profit motives and corporate self-interest. They would still want to extract maximum returns from the consumer and would tend to exploit the environment in their corporate interest, and thus there would still be a need for government regulation to protect the public. Although a competing system of labor-based firms would make a significant change in the attitudes of the employees and the character of capitalism, it would not, therefore, have changed the system in some essential respects.[1]

I think that a deeper change in the nature of capitalism would be the development of cooperation to the point where it surpasses competition and becomes the main feature—the dynamic—of the economy. Such a development would require not only the cultivation of employee participation and ownership—what is described later as "social management"—but also the development of intercorporate systems of cooperation among businesses and an increased role for industry-wide associations designed to operate in the public interest. Such developments would lead much further to a different social order. But that alone would not be enough. A new social order different from capitalism would also require a new legal system and a new culture. I believe that the seeds of all these changes currently exist in the current economic system, and that though their presence is not yet visible to most people, they have the potential to move toward greater public expression.

In his brilliant work *The Coming of Post-Industrial Society*, Daniel Bell notes that a new social system does not always arise within the manifest characteristics of the old one but sometimes comes from outside them. European feudal society, for example, was structured around gentry, noblemen, soldiers, and priests whose wealth was based on land, but the mercantile and industrial society emerged from the bourgeois sector that began to appear in the thirteenth century, composed of artisans, merchants, and free professionals whose property lay in their skills or their willingness to take risks, whose everyday values were far removed from the fading chivalric style of feudal life, and who gathered in the free towns that arose outside the feudal landed structure. "So, too, the process today," Bell says:

The roots of post-industrial society lie in the inexorable influence of science on productive methods, particularly in the transformation of the electrical and chemical industries at the beginning of the twentieth century. But as Robert Heilbroner has observed: "Science, as we know it, began well before capitalism existed and did not experience its full growth until well after capitalism was solidly entrenched." And science, as a quasi-autonomous force, would extend beyond capitalism. By this token, one can say that the scientific estate—its ethos and its organization—is the monad that contains within itself the imago of the future society.[2]

Bell argues that capitalism's transition toward a new social order is much more subtle and nuanced than Marx could have imagined in the nineteenth century. It involves a major shift in the entire culture, including not only the change from an industrial to a service orientation but also major technological changes and new forms of professional and scientific estates that help shape the foundations of the new society.

In order to understand where capitalism is now heading, I suggest that we need to look at its transition from the standpoint of *the social dimensions of the market system becoming manifest*. Thus we will see a new system emerging from within the old, but also emerging outside its main characteristics.

An Analytical Framework

I believe the essence of capitalism is found in the nature of the market. I define capitalism as a social system of exchange that emphasizes an economic orientation and operates through a dynamic equilibrium of opposing forces. These opposing forces within the market economy are the basis for initiating change. They include the class structure in the traditional sense. However, "class" inequities also operate today in the form of monopolies within the multi-leveled corporate system of exchange from producer to consumer. The market's class structure, as expressed in the unequal power balance occurring at each point through the entire chain of supply-to-production-to-distribution-to-retail-to-consumption also needs to be examined. Understanding the oppositions at each of these competing intersections and the process by which they are resolved allows us both to anticipate and to take advantage of pathways toward the system's future.

I begin by describing these oppositions at a high level of abstraction, interpreting them as occurring first between the manifest and the latent dimensions of the economy; and then, at a second, related yet independent level of analysis, between the economic and social orientations of the market. These oppositions represent the overall categories within which a large-scale transition can be observed taking place in the day-to-day life of market operations.

From this perspective, we can anticipate the economy moving over the long range in the two major patterns of change now taking place: first, the economy is moving from a system characterized by the manifest traits of a business society toward a system characterized by the development of its latent traits; and second, at the same time it is moving from a system of exchange defined by an economic orientation toward a system defined by a social orientation. The concepts behind these two patterns of change are important to understand because they help explain other kinds of oppositional dynamics at other levels of operation in the market economy.

The Manifest and Latent Economies

The concepts of "manifest and latent functions," which were developed by the sociologist Robert Merton in the late 1940's to provide a basis for analyzing organizational behavior (what Merton called "middle-range analysis"), offer us a framework for studying the social transition of the market economy. Merton defined "functions" as the consequences of social structure that people intend and that are adaptive to the system under study; latent functions are adaptive consequences that are unintended and often unconscious.[3]

The "manifest economy" for the purposes of this book is defined both subjectively and objectively. *Subjectively*, it refers to the way people understand the market in the popular sense: an economic order determined by principles such as profits, productivity, and efficiency. At the same time the market is defined *objectively* and intentionally by law: business is designed legally to produce profits, productivity, and efficiency. In this sense, the manifest economy could be defined as "the profit sector."

The "latent economy," defined as that which is unseen or less visible, although not necessarily less important, includes the larger economic order interpreted in part by Karl Polanyi as the "substantive economy" where "people make a living," an order characterized broadly by social principles in the sense that it operates beyond the purposes of profit, productivity, and efficiency. In other words, the latent economy is not characterized primarily by "economizing principles," even though they operate to some degree within it.

This latent economy includes the whole voluntary nonprofit sector that participates in the market system: trade associations, trade unions, religious institutions, universities, fraternal orders, and so forth. Although these nonprofit organizations are technically part of "the economy," the mainstream economist and the public generally "see" the economy only as consisting of the profit sector.[4] It also includes much more of the societal order than just the nonprofit sector—the family household and the informal organization of the neighborhood—as well as certain unseen socially oriented parts of the profit sector that we shall come to shortly.

In this latent economy, economic principles are secondary. For example, the family is not designed primarily to act on economic principles because it has more important purposes, but it must still maintain an income and balance a budget to survive. The economic orientation of the family is thus a latent (yet important) part of its purpose. However, in special cases, latent "economizing principles" can manifest themselves in the family and even dominate its character and direction. A marriage can fall apart over money issues. But since money problems are complexly intertwined with social (interpersonal) issues, such problems can be the unintended consequences of a marriage that is not working according to its manifest purposes: that is to say, the economic problems in a marriage are often unforeseen because the family is defined in terms of noneconomic matters such as being in love and raising children.[5]

Other examples of the latent economy can be seen in the many informal helping systems that are crucial to the economic survival of families in lower-income working-class communities. In her study of blue-collar marriages, Mirra Komarovsky found that the emotional and economic support provided by the extended family played a crucially important part in the survival of young families. Komarovsky describes the economic arrangements among kin in the form of "reciprocal aid":

Thus, a widowed father shares his home with a married son who pays no rent but is responsible for household expenses; a widowed mother residing with her daughter works as a waitress, paying rent and her share of the grocery bill; a widow and her bachelor brother inherited the parental home and rented rooms to a married daughter who is the homemaker for the whole group and expenses are shared.[6]

Similarly, in her study of a community suffering from severe economic depression, Carol Stack found that extensive networks of kin and friends reinforced people's schemes for self-help and strategies for economic survival.[7]

In his *Critique of Political Economy*, Karl Marx first defined the economy as "the total ensemble of social relations entered into in the social production of existence"; only after this definition did he narrow his concern to a critique of the market economy specifically. Similarly, in *Origin of Private Property and the State*, Frederick Engels attempted to write a history of the family from an economic viewpoint, viewing the reproduction of "immediate life" as the key to history; by "reproduction" he meant not just physical reproduction, but also the "care and protection" supplied through social institutions. In attempting to explain the dynamics of economic life in the local neighborhood, Martin Lowenthal relies on Marx's larger definition, as well as on theories from anthropology and sociology, to explain the economic order of community life.[8] He is describing the latent economy.

Economic and Social Orientations in the Market System

The latent-vs.-manifest dynamics of change are master categories of change, but other terms explaining this transition operate in concert with them. The social-vs.-economic orientation, for example, corresponds to the latent-manifest traits, but also operates autonomously in the transitional process, as we shall see.

An early revelation of the fact that business operated on social principles came from social science research. In the classic 1920's study of the Hawthorne Plant of the Western Electric Company in Chicago, the working assumption was that physical and economic factors were the primary factors motivating workers, and so experiments were conducted to measure how changes in employee pay, lighting, rest periods, and the like affected productivity and work performance. The surprising results of this famous study changed the course of research and indeed caused professionals to challenge the ideology of the economic orientation for many decades thereafter.

In brief, the researchers found that even though they lowered the lighting, took away rest periods, and lowered the pay of the factory workers, morale and productivity increased. The social attention given the workers through the experiment turned out to provide a major incentive for them to work harder: dignity, recognition, status, and respect were more essential to work motivation than economic matters.

Since then, social experiments have proliferated to advance business's awareness of the power of the social factor. Even the most benighted managers are now at least conscious that social factors are vital to the work process; the profit sector cannot be defined solely from an economic orientation in modern management.

To think further about the hidden and often subtle relationships between social and economic factors, imagine a big retail store with all sorts of merchandise on display: furniture of all kinds, hardware, music supplies, clothes hanging on racks, and more. All these goods were designed, manufactured, packaged, and displayed according to a particular set of ideas, which means that for this display to become reality, a social exchange had to take place. In other words, there was an exchange of ideas, a symbolic interaction, behind the floor display. You and I might not ordinarily think of social interactions or "sets of ideas" as part of the market system, but they are all-pervasive; the latent, unseen dimension.

Take this case one step further into its professional implications. The store design was formed by someone with aesthetic principles and a logic of order independent of economic principles and yet intersecting with them. This marketing of artful design occurred at each stage of manufacture and distribution. We will see later how the "marketing of ideas" and consultation in "organizational development" are burgeoning fields in business; the increasing incorporation of artistic and psychological principles into business further challenges the idea that the profit sector is rooted solely in an economic orientation.

Once you begin to think about it seriously, you realize that the whole retail store—and every business anywhere—survives and thrives on patterns of social interaction. Since no business could exist without a social organization, in this sense business rests on a social foundation. If you follow this logic, you can see why an increased study of the types of social organization and governance systems in business should change the picture of what constitutes the bottom line. Increasingly we hear that "the bottom line is people," by which is meant their attitudes, customs, folkways, the way people organize, and so on. Business is a social enterprise as much as it is an economic enterprise.

Although the social factor has always shaped markets, and many people in the business world know this intuitively from their own experience, the shift toward a social orientation is nevertheless not simply a matter of consciousness. The manifest economy—the profit sector—must play by the rules and obey an economic orientation because of statutory and common law. The activities of business are legally mandated to be economically oriented, and in certain cases corporate policies *cannot* be socially designed. Fiduciaries who forsake "prudent" profitability out of social concern could be violating the law, for example. Social investment practice represents a major intersect, changing the dynamics between the social and economic orientations in the market economy.

The intersection of categories at the organizational level. We said that our master categories—the manifest-latent and the social-economic—are at once related to each other and autonomous. This means that they intersect independently in the explanation of critical change, crisscrossing at middle-range levels of analysis from case to case. Here are two concrete examples appropriate to functional analysis.

First, a nonprofit university's manifest goal is not to maximize profits because its broad social purpose to transmit and create knowledge transcends economic motives. At the same time, let us say that university officials in certain departments engage in transactions oriented primarily to profit making. Let us add that though top university officials are not conscious of the administrative shift to an economic orientation, it gradually becomes apparent to the larger community. Such a development can become not only dysfunctional because the university is not fulfilling its manifest goals of education; it is also illegal. Here we see a need for functional research to let us know how long these activities remain unrecognized by top officials and what constitutes the "unintended consequences."

Second, let us say that a profit corporation is making such large charitable gifts to this university that the action is questioned by its stockholders. The action may be defended by the corporation as good public relations and part of its long-range planning, and thus be accepted by its corporate board, but at some point, let us say, it becomes known that the gifts exceeded the legal limit. If the stockholders can prove the gift went over the percent permissible by law, they have a case for a transgression that should yield them some economic returns. The company's chief executive might have been motivated by high ideals, but he or she has now broken the law and must report to the stockholders about what happened.

These two cases illustrate how the master categories of the social and the economic orientations intersect at the corporate level. This intersect is one of the frontlines of change in the market economy. As corporate executives begin to take more account of social factors—for example, the corporate impact on consumers, on the environment, on energy resources—they are increasingly altering their view of profit making from "maximizing" toward what is called "profit optimization." In fact, because so many businesses have moved from the nineteenth-century concept of maximizing profit to a new approach accounting for "social factors," thanks largely to the growth of labor, consumer and government power, some scholars have begun using a new term—"satisficing"—to replace the concept of maximizing.[9]

Indeed, one could posit that in both the profit and the nonprofit sector, the "optimization" of profits is tending to become the guiding principle. The nonprofit sector today is increasing its interest in profit making, meaning optimizing, while the profit sector, which is taking account of more countervailing powers such as the government, consumer, and environmental groups, is constraining its profit-maximizing tendencies and thus also leaning to a concept of optimizing profits under the changing organization of the market.[10]

Although I would argue that the social factor has a slightly greater power over the long term, this shift in goals can go either way in the short run, since the social and economic factors are closely intertwined. At present, the profit sector is socializing and the nonprofit sector is economizing within their fundamentally opposing orientations but since the short-run trends may show the reverse, the process requires careful study to see where the emphasis in either sector will go in the next decade.

In the profit sector, the seeming shift from social to economic orientations in the short run can be illustrated with an example from the labor movement. Some labor analysts claim that in the early history of the market economy, unions were more strongly devoted to social goals, such as human dignity and respect, than to economic goals, such as wages and benefits, and that the shift toward an economic orientation—labeled "business unionism"—occurred in the historic transition of the 1930's, when collective bargaining was legalized. But while unions may have shifted toward an economic orientation, they cannot manifestly be profit making; furthermore, a careful analysis of their operations would reveal their fundamentally social character. Still further, it might be argued that in certain industries the style of labor leadership has a greater impact on market prices than the competitive behavior of the firms in the market. In other words, we can see from such examples how the shift in orientation from social to economic can take place within the legal limits of the market in a matter of decades, while the social factors are always latent and powerful, although generally unseen even in the case of labor unions.

It could be said that these oppositional dimensions—the latent-manifest and the social-economic—are like high-level magnetic fields waiting to be energized at their "meeting points," like negative and positive poles that create arcs of electricity when they come close to one another. But such analytical concepts are mere speculation without observing their actual meeting points. Accordingly, let us turn once again to an example of a real-world meeting point. Let us say a group of religious orders decide to alter their investments in a corporation because it is not acting according to their "social purposes." Here the intersect between the positive and negative poles can issue a powerful electrical impulse. I have witnessed the charged opposition that takes place when religious groups engaged in the practice of social investment confront business executives engaged in profit making. The charges and countercharges that fly between the participants become strongly moral—within each of their opposing orientations. This creative (and sometimes not so creative) opposition between the manifest-latent and social-economic dimensions of a corporation, and the ramifications of that opposition, go far to making changes in business law as well as in the role of government agencies.

This changing dynamic can also be seen with the fiduciary's court challenge over the legal meaning of "prudent man" when social investments are on the law's borderline, and it can also be observed in federal agencies like the Securities and Exchange Commission and the Federal Trade Commission when their staffs must reinterpret their rules to business executives who seek guidance on establishing codes of ethics in trade associations. Although these abstract oppositions are helpful in orienting theory, they must be concretized and resolved through continuous empirical research at organizational levels.[11]

The potential destructiveness of the social factor. The social factor is a neutral concept: its role in the workings of the economy is neither "good" nor "bad." Although every analysis implies what is harmful or beneficial about the nature of the social factor in the market, the term itself is value-free. I believe that the concept of sociality has value first because its public recognition is important in the affairs of the market; and second, because once we know how it operates, we will be able to see how this factor can lead us to a self-regulating economy. But the social factor itself is not a matter of ethical good or bad.

The harmful and destructive results that occur when the economic factor is dominant are well known; in fact, its dominance in capitalism has been cited for causing the rise of the socialist state. Nevertheless, the economic factor has an important role to play in the market, as we shall see below. Likewise, the social factor, if allowed to dominate, can lead to harmful results. For example, the state as an institution within society is broadly an expression of this social factor; but the state itself can function either for good or for evil. The market is also a social institution that can operate either functionally or dysfunctionally in the context of society. The social factor, therefore, broadly conceived here in conceptual opposition to the economic factor, should not be idealized. Just as the economic factor was interpreted as an "evil" by early socialists, so the social factor can be considered a potentially evil force.

The drive for power, the drive of people to dominate and exploit each other apart from a drive for economic revenue or any type of economic advantage is an example of how the social factor can be a destructive force in the market. Let us consider the power of a private gift of, say, a beautiful necklace, which the buyer at a retail store receives from a distributor wishing to influence a sale. The gift of the necklace may be reciprocated not by an armlet in this system of social exchange (as in Malinowski's Trobriand Islands), but by the buyer's quiet agreement to purchase items sold by the gift-giving distributor. The economic factor is still important in this hidden social contract because the firm must still make profits, but the personal gift, along with all that it implies, is powerful, and the social factor may have more power in this immediate exchange than the economic factor, even though that predominates in the thinking of the firm itself; the company must make money regardless of what buyers do to add to their own riches. Thus, there is a subtle mix of social and economic factors determining the source of supply in this buyers' market, a mix that can be revealed by social research. Social researchers are thus revealing the negative power of social factors hidden in the symbolic life of the market economy, as well as their positive power.

When social and economic factors are not working together, they are generally working against each other, and the result is destructive. More, they can be self-destructive, as for example when a corporation so monopolizes a market sector as to become regulated by the state. Such an outcome is self-destructive according to the firm's own manifest purposes, because it must pay taxes to have an outside authority regulate its behavior, not only losing money thereby but also having its own freedom to operate productively in the market curtailed. Similarly, a church's drive for power can offend enough people that they revolt against it, with the result that it loses its economic base and ultimately whatever power it originally had in the community.[12]

To offer a salient example of the destructive power of the social factor in recent political history, the revolutionary fervor in Cuba, based on manifest *social*(ist) ideals, has led at times to the near-destruction of the Cuban economy. One of the revolutionaries' earliest mistakes was to kill a large portion of the bulls in the countryside in order to provide meat for the peasants, who had so long been denied this food by the landlords. Unfortunately, this empathic act not only destroyed the basis for breeding new cattle, to the point that the cattle industry suffered for many years thereafter, but also meant the costly purchase of new bulls to rebuild the stock of cattle. Thus this social action in the marketplace, which totally ignored the economic factor, had disastrous effects on key phases of rural development, something the leaders had most idealized in their new socialist nation.

The Cuban revolutionary government also idealized the motives of workers, ignoring how important the economic factor can be to labor. Cuban leaders believed that all the workers would join together as a social unit in the factories to serve the higher goals of the society, regardless of issues relating to their comparative income. The economics of the labor market were thus downplayed as secondary to the collective ideal of working together to build a new society. When productivity did not meet goals, managers again turned to social (not economic) incentives, such as giving public recognition to model workers without raising their income. Since these rewards did not always produce results, they turned to social competition, offering model workers higher status positions in the Communist Party. When these approaches still failed to produce desired results, leaders finally turned to economic incentives. The economic factor, so despised ideologically because of its role in capitalism, soon began to reveal its significance in a depressed socialist production system like Cuba's. The Cuban experience is much more complex than this brief account suggests, because it includes positive social developments, but it is true that the economic factor—once so denigrated—has since become a larger consideration in state planning in the country.[13]

I mention such cases to illustrate how either the social or the economic factor can play positive or negative roles in the development of society. Just as the state-managed societies are finding the economic factor important in new ways, they stand both in contrast and in parallel with the market societies, which are increasingly finding the social factor important. The need for Cuban leaders to motivate workers with economic incentives differs markedly from—but also mirrors—the growing need of corporate managers in the United States to give social recognition to employees through participation in management and corporate ownership. Clearly, the social and economic factors are intricately interwoven into the market.[14]

My theory proposes that the social factor should tend to become more conscious and influential in the American economy over the long run; we can now understand why there is no guarantee that such an outcome will necessarily be beneficial. I believe that *both* social and economic factors must be a conscious part of planning in order to maximize desirable outcomes for the market, and I argue strongly for joint studies by both economists and social scientists to illuminate public policy and help us learn of the intricate mix of these different factors operating together. Indeed, socioeconomic studies may then become a basis for policies that stimulate self-regulation in the private economy.

A Sociological Perspective: Process, Organization, and Governance in the Market

Three sociological categories will help guide our analysis of the market as an exchange system: social process, social organization, and social governance. There is no need to define them rigorously here because we are not working at that level of theory, but a brief word about each will help the reader understand how these categories can be used in this analysis of the economy and its transformations.

Social process in our context means the way people exchange goods and services within and between their organizations. Early sociologists like Albion Small, Charles Cooley, and Robert Park saw the social process as central to their work. Indeed, Small traced the origins of sociology to Adam Smith's theory of sympathy developed in his *Theory of Moral Sentiments* and saw the fundamental processes as a coordination of the natural forces within society. Cooley considered the social process the very essence of society, which he saw as a cooperative network of communications between actors and subgroups, characterized by the reciprocal action of people in sympathetic communication. Park distinguished four social processes: competition, conflict, accommodation, and assimilation, with competition as a universal and continuous process that reflected the natural order.[15]

The differences between Cooley and Park, the one stressing the role of cooperation and the other stressing competition, are reflected in my theory of how the market operates in society. I see these two processes operating together, and focus on finding the proper balance between them so that they can function in the public interest.

Social organization in our context means the way people structure themselves in groups. It includes such categories as stratification, norms, roles, informal and formal relations, corporation, association, oligarchy, and democracy. This sociological concept stands in contrast with the economist's focus on the tasks of production and distribution that yield measurable amounts of total output in goods and services. The importance of this difference is discussed later, but since the thesis of this book is that the social organization of production and distribution makes a key difference in total output, this concept is critical for understanding the way market organizations operate.

Social governance in our context means the way people manage their lives together. It is a master concept that includes such subconcepts as command governance, mutual governance, and self-governance. Our focus with social governance and its various aspects is not on formal government, that is, state governance, but rather on the various self-generated systems of governance that shape the private market.

"Command governance," which is usually manifest in the private sector's corporate economy, is a system of authority based on obedience as people work in hierarchical relationships. In the business corporation, for example, authority is formally structured from top to bottom. Although corporations are the most visible representatives of command governance in business, they always exhibit a manifest-latent interlacing of the command system with some form of mutual governance. It should be noted that command governance exists in all forms of organizations, including democratic structures such as trade associations.

"Mutual governance" refers to systems in which there is some measure of reciprocal influence in the patterns of authority and decision making. It is a form of governance in all exchange systems, because reciprocal influence is always present, but in this study its presence is particularly noted in democratic organizations, where it is manifest and institutionalized; thus trade organizations, trade unions, and cooperatives are seen as mutually governed associations operating in the market. However, though members of such organizations have the right to influence others and participate in their own governance, the organizations also operate with hierarchical authority.

"Self-governance" refers to the capacity of people to manage their own affairs apart from outside controls. All social exchange shows some characteristics of it, since all human beings are self-governing to some degree; even slaves have some degree of governance over their physical movements and their thinking. It often exists latently in business in the sense that people in every position have some measure of self-governance over their work.

The concept of self-governance applies at every level of the economy, from the individual who is relatively self-governing in a workshop, to the work team, to the corporation, to the industry, and finally to the relatively self-governing economy as a whole. At each level, the degree of self-governance is interdependent with the self-governing structure above and below it.

The three types of social governance described here are really principles through which people manage their organizations and their systems of exchange. They exist in different forms and degrees in all types of social organization in the economy, and it will be our task to examine how they are latent or manifest in the changing market.

A final note. I use the term "social management" instead of social governance in discussing the internal organization of the corporation, but the terms are interchangeable for our purposes: the difference is a matter of the emphasis given to the concept of social governance as a form of administration. This emphasis is important in policy research designed to increase the degree of self-governance operating at all levels of the private sector.

The Concept of the Self

The possibility of social self-regulation of the economy outside the state depends in part on people's capacity to expand their own concept of the self. Although that concept can be traced back to ancient times, its significance for our purposes begins in the thinking of the man who so influenced Marx—Georg Wilhelm Friedrich Hegel. Hegel said that although people desire to appropriate things around them in ways that constitute their self-identity, each person comes to feel in the process that these things are not the true end of his or her desire; the true end of one's self is fulfilled only through *association* with other individuals. Thus self-consciousness attains its satisfaction only in another's self-consciousness. People become who they are, gain their very existence, their selfhood, by "being for another." This social relation, however, is not attained simply through harmonious cooperation; it is attained through a life-and-death struggle between essentially unequal individuals.

For Hegel, the struggle was expressed symbolically in history as the relation between "master" and "servant." People acquire a greater level of self-consciousness by fighting out the battle between all expressions of this symbolic relationship, which Hegel saw as the only way to acquire freedom and complete self-realization. The truth of the self is therefore ultimately found not in the "I" but in the "we," and people's developing social relationships are the foundation of self-consciousness.

Hegel interpreted "labor" as a process that transforms the relationship between master and servant. Laborers learn that the product of their labor is an expression of themselves, part and parcel of their being, and the master, seeing that the product bears the hallmark of the subjects, begins to see that he is not an independent "being for himself," but dependent on other beings. Once each individual recognizes that his or her own essence is to be found in the other, the opposition between subject and object begins to lessen in intensity.

Although we can see Hegel's idealism here, we also see a theory of social consciousness developing through the awareness of the existence and role of others in the world. For Hegel, this growing consciousness was the beginning of freedom, an achievement of self-sufficiency and independence from all "externals," in which all externality was appropriated by the subject—in this case, the self. Thus Hegel set forth the modern framework for a theory of self-governance as a social concept, a system ruled by oppositional forces and leading gradually toward total fulfillment.

In applying Hegel's concept to the political economy, Marx retained the master-servant metaphor but rejected Hegel's concept of the state as representative of the ultimate community: on the contrary, the self was alienated by its identity with the state. More significantly, Marx sought to rectify Hegel's idealism by grounding the "rational kernel" of his thought in the material foundations of society, applying the concept of alienation to the class structure of capitalist society. He identified the core of the struggle for self-identity in the division between the bourgeoisie and the proletariat, the resolution of which required their class struggle.[16]

Our concept of self-governance grows from the best of this original thought on selfhood by Hegel and Marx. The self is a social entity that develops its integrity through association with wider and wider levels of organization in the market economy, expanding and achieving an identity in its expressions in ever higher hierarchical and broader geographical levels of organization. In politics, one's self-identity is activated from the local community to the state, to the nation, by voting for representatives who can reflect one's own view on life at each level of politics. In the organization of the economy, where the expansion of self-identity is much more constrained, generally limited to the workplace, the union, or the corporation, cultivating self-development means cultivating social (organizational) development between opposing sectors of the market, allowing for self-expansion.

The origins for this concept of the self developing in society can be found in the work of George Herbert Mead, who was also influenced by Hegel. Mead saw the self emerging through social interaction in the family and expanding through the incorporation of a "generalized other." This generalized other began to develop first in the family, as children identified with their parents and siblings and re-enacted their roles in games with other children; the interacting roles of others were then appropriated as their own, and this generalized other was expanded to the neighborhood and the community. Growing up meant expanding still further, to comprehend the roles of people in the larger society, and finally finding the largest identity of all, one's own humanity.[17]

Self-development in the marketplace is thus closely related to the roles people take there. A person's self-identity is first associated with the workplace but usually ends with the corporation whose own self-interest (an expansion of one's self) is related to its competition with others. Under this competitive structure, an individual's self-identity cannot expand from the corporation to larger identities; executives would say that it is enough of an effort to get employees to identify with the "corporate family."

But the structural basis for this expansion of the self beyond the individual firm is essential to the social development of the market. As people's roles become linked representationally through their relations with others in various roles in trade associations and the wider market economy, they will grow in their own capacity to identify with others and will thus assume responsibility for their place in the larger economic order.

The meaning of this concept of self-development in the marketplace was first brought home to me while I was talking with laborers in conflict with the United Fruit Company in Honduras and Guatemala in 1970. They could not identify with that corporation and kept stealing its tools and equipment, thefts that seemed to them quite legitimate because they believed that the company had stolen from them in the larger market. Another example. In 1977, when a new co-determination law went into effect in West Germany allowing workers 50 percent representation on boards of directors of all major corporations, union leaders with whom I discussed the change expressed their shock at its implications, saying, "Now we are going to have to take responsibility for the whole corporation." Previously, their identity had been solely with the union that had been in conflict with the corporation; they now had to struggle for a new self-identity and a new responsibility that went beyond their union, incorporating the role of being an executive into their minds. I also watched workers struggle with the expansion of their sense of responsibility to the whole corporation and then to the larger industry. That struggle continues.

The development of the self in connection with the market structure requires careful study. The search for self-identity reaches from laborers at the workbench who struggle over their relationship with a quality circle, to trade association executives who struggle to bridge the conflict between their corporate members in an industry, to the managers of a multinational corporation who must find a place for themselves in the global market. Research on the development of self-governance—as it connects the individual and the self-governing structure of the market—should become a critical part of socioeconomic studies in the future.

Social analysts like Erich Fromm and David Riesman, who saw character, personality, and self-identity as closely related to the historical structure of the market, knew that the roles people take in the marketplace generate a sense of selfhood. They were not far from Hegel's idea that the development of the individual is social, that is, related to "the other" and dependent on the capacity to understand the social whole. [18]

Let us now apply the categories discussed in this section to a model of how the economy is changing today, perhaps transforming itself into a significantly different social order.

A Model of Oppositional Trends at the Organizational Level

Many of the changes taking place in the American economy today are in opposing directions. We see the decline of traditional industry and the growth of a service sector side by side with an interest in reindustrialization. We see a movement toward centralization and bureaucratization side by side with a movement toward decentralization and self-management. And we see growing calls for protectionism side by side with an expansion of multinational corporations and international trade. Many other examples could be cited.

The model of change to be presented here focuses on a set of latent trends within the economy that are autonomous and yet related to each other in certain ways, moving in the same general direction. These trends may or may not become predominant in the future, but they appear to show the greatest potential; I believe they are indicators of a future that will be characterized at one and the same time by greater humanity and greater efficiency and productivity. They point to an economy that will be socially ordered through mechanisms of self-regulation in the public interest, rather than through government regulation and control. This model of trends, or sociological interpretation of the directions in which the market is changing, is set out in Table 1. It presents changes taking place at the level of organizations (Merton's "middle range"), grouped by the major categories in transition: the general *orienta-*

TABLE 1

The Evolving Market Economy: Current Developmental Trends
at the Organizational Level

Category in transition	Manifest traits	Latent traits
General orientation	Economic	Social
Process (interaction)	Competition	Cooperation
Organizational system	Corporation	Association
Phase	Production-oriented	Service-oriented
Goals	Maximizing	Optimizing
Motives	Self-interest	Public interest
Charter	Profit	Nonprofit
Ownership	Stockholder	Member/Stakeholder
Governance system	Command	Mutual
Authority	Centralizing	Decentralizing
Administration	Labor/management	Social management
Structure	Bureaucratizing	Federalizing
Investment criteria	Financial	Ethical
Norms	Government	Voluntary

tion of organizations, the *process of interaction* between organizations, and the *types of organizations* and *types of governance* in the market economy.

The *manifest traits* in this model are the characteristics we are trained to see every day, the popular picture of the economy that we read about in the newspaper and business magazines. According to this view, the market economy is typified by (1) an economic orientation; (2) an exchange system based on competition; (3) organizations called corporations, characterized by (a) an accent on production, (b) a goal to maximize profits, (c) motivations of self-interest, (d) charters for profit, and (e) ownership by stockholders; and (4) a corporate system based on command governance, a type of governance that has (a) centralizing tendencies, (b) an administration divided between labor and management, (c) a tendency to bureaucratize, (d) investments based on financial criteria, and (e) norms set by government agencies. In more popular terms, the manifest economy is based on money and is bottom-line oriented.

The *latent traits* in this model are those aspects of the economy that are less recognized yet nevertheless present. The latent economy is typified by (1) a social orientation; (2) an exchange system based on cooperation; (3) organizations called associations, characterized by (a) an accent on services, (b) a goal to neutralize or optimize profits, (c) motivations of benefiting others and serving the public interest, (d) charters for nonprofit, and (e) ownership through membership; and (4) an associational system based on mutual governance, a type of governance that has (a) decentralizing tendencies, (b) an administration based on social (self-) management, (c) a tendency to federalize, (d) investments based on ethical criteria, and (e) norms set voluntarily by jointly determined agreements.

I noted earlier that the profit sector is the same as the manifest economy; the latent economy includes part of the profit sector but much more. (The child of the future is much larger and more potent than its parent.) The latent economy crisscrosses into the profit sector while still remaining hidden, unobserved by most people or not yet fully developed.

The theory behind Table 1 is that for each category (or subcategory) in transition, the latent traits are in the process of becoming manifest. Some of the changes are already well advanced (although they may not be widely recognized by the public); others are just beginning to develop. The pace and manner in which each latent trait becomes fully manifest should be determined by two things: (1) the way the latent and manifest dimensions intersect for that particular area to create innovative and desirable new forms in the economy; and (2) how public policy promotes each of these changes.[19]

Each category in this model changes as its opposing traits intersect. For example, we have already noted how profit corporations are beginning to look like nonprofits in their new public orientation, and nonprofits are beginning to look like profits in their quest for money; we shall also describe how corporations like hospitals are today choosing to go either way, profit or nonprofit. Furthermore, new corporate creatures are being created that synthesize socioeconomic factors, such as community development corporations, community development finance corporations, and community land trusts. Although not depicted in Table 1, they represent the unpredictable creative intersection between the social and economic orientations. They do not fit into traditional categories because they are a sort of hybrid: they are profit-oriented in the interest of the whole community.

The model is therefore only suggestive of general directions. We cannot expect these categories to follow some linear development from latent to manifest, because new creations will emerge in the process. Indeed, these opposing traits are not wholly separate and not always in conflict with one another, but rather are in different stages of development, sometimes appearing side by side in complementary fashion, sometimes appearing simultaneously at times at different levels of organization.

In other words, I see a trend toward a matching of opposing traits: competition with cooperation, profit with nonprofit, command with mutual governance, maximizing with optimizing profits, self-interest with public interest, financial standards with ethical standards, an economic orientation along with a social orientation, and so on. These opposing traits are becoming more equal in importance today, and in some ways are mutually reinforcing. In this current transition of economic organization, they are coming toward what might be called, crudely, a complementary coexistence.

As the opposing traits are becoming more interdependent (rather than conflicting), they are sometimes being integrated formally into new legal contexts. Yet, as I have emphasized, the latent traits should not be idealized, for they also contain the potential for misdirection and destructive tendencies as they become a more important part of the system. This makes the process all the more complex and important to understand through research.

As an example of this downside dimension, consider the contemporary experience with worker-participation in corporate management. This new step from command governance toward social (self-) management often results in higher productivity and worker satisfaction, but in the short term, an experiment may not work because union leaders may see it as a management device to destroy unions, and management may see it as a basis for greater worker resistance. Some corporations have canceled their quality circles for such reasons. It is only in the long term, after many experiments, that we can see that this trend toward worker participation is of lasting value.[20]

This theoretical model suggests that as a result of these oppositional forces, the capitalist system is moving beyond its accent on corporate competition based on a system of command governance and beyond the simple maximization of profits rooted in corporate self-interest. The market is not losing these traits; they will no doubt continue as a basic dynamic of the economy for some time to come, but they are losing ground as other, opposing traits show a capacity to contribute to greater productivity and a better use of human resources.

This model is both related to, and different from, other well-known interpretations of the changes currently taking place in the market economy. For example, the sociologist Daniel Bell anticipated a major transition as modern society moves from an industrial to a postindustrial (service and information) economy, a pattern of change, he said, that cuts across such contrasting societies as the United States and the Soviet Union:

Industrial society is organized around the axis of production and machinery, for the fabrication of goods; pre-industrial society is dependent on raw labor and the extract of primary resources from nature. In its rhythm of life and organization of work, industrial society is the defining feature of the social structure—i.e. the economy, the occupational system, and the stratification system—of modern Western society. The social structure, as I define it, is separate analytically from the two other dimensions of society, the polity and the culture.[21]

Bell, writing in 1973, advanced the thesis that the next thirty to fifty years would see the emergence of a postindustrial society with a fundamentally different social structure. My thesis of the social market differs from Bell's forecasting tradition in the sense that I am looking specifically at the shape of the market as a social organization, and I see the developing trends as dependent partly on public policy.

Bell's forecast is relevant here because many scholars would argue that the service economy has already become a manifest part of the market economy. But I think that is premature because so much of what "services" mean remains to be revealed. Part of the development of services comes through the intersect of the profit and nonprofit sectors with the changing culture. We will look later at the power of religious insitutions, universities, and pension funds to buy stock in business and then allocate capital on the basis of social (noneconomic) criteria. If this trend continues, the whole concept of "servicing" societal interests and human values will become a part of this future, but such an idea does not exist in current concepts of a service economy. Also, later chapters will discuss the possibility of trade associations acting as a "service" to their members in realizing societal values in their own self-interest. This is also a latent part of the social transition depicted in this model, although it is not included in most concepts of a service economy. The role that trade associations have already taken in setting technical standards for the market (e.g., the American Standards Associations) and for setting ethical standards for their own industries (e.g., the American Society of Newspaper Editors, the National Association of Broadcasters, the National Association of Realtors) represent what could be the beginning of a larger service role for such associations in the future.[22]

If the entire transition depicted in Table 1 is made—that is, if all the latent traits shown become manifest—we would see a market system of a fundamentally different order. So sweeping a change will have altered the very basis of business itself, and could also challenge the foundations of the undesirable system of excess government control commonly known as the "welfare state."

The categories in Table 1 are too general to lend themselves directly to operational research and thus to be predictive of exactly when these changes will occur, but the advantage of this model rests in its coherent picture of change at a middle-range level of analysis. The problem today is that we lack such a model of social areas of change and therefore lack the overall capacity to orient research and policy that will bring a better future. The model points to where research should be focused, namely, at the intersections of each opposing trait.

We will now look at specific examples of how the latent traits depicted in Table 1 are emerging in the market today. We will examine changes in the market's "social process" as its dominant trait of competition becomes challenged and balanced by cooperation; changes in organization as corporations become challenged and balanced by associations; and changes in social governance, as the market's features of centralization and command governance become challenged and balanced by decentralization and mutual governance.

Social Process: The Emerging Balance Between Competition and Cooperation

Economists have modeled the market on the principle of competition, but our projection of the future suggests that the market system will be based significantly on the principle of cooperation. This means that sociologists ought to set to work as soon as possible on a model for a market based on this principle, recognizing that the key to self-regulation depends on how firms cooperate in the public interest. Our discussion here is suggestive of this need to shift professional modeling in that direction, a matter to be taken up in more detail in Chapter Six.

The Model of "Perfect Competition"

In the late 1800's, Léon Walras defined pure economics as a "physico-mathematical science" whose essence was the "theory of the determination of prices under a hypothetical regime of perfectly free competition."[23] This concept of perfect competition dominated early thinking in economics and became the basis for judging the relationship between producers in the market.

The perfect-competition model posited three conditions: First, a market characterized by perfect competition must have numerous small buyers and small sellers. Each firm should be small so that no one firm could affect the market price either by altering its volume of purchases as a buyer or by altering its output as a seller, and the total number of firms should be large—including thousands of buyers and sellers—so that conditions would not change if one firm left the marketplace. The idea was that the whole group should affect the price, and that none of its members individually could do so.

Second, the product of any one seller would have to be a perfect substitute for the product of any other seller; in effect, all products should be standardized. Buyers need not care who supplied the product, since all that mattered was the market price. And finally, all participants in the market must have full knowledge of the economic and technical data relevant to their decision making: all buyers must be aware of the price and product offerings of sellers; all sellers must be able to figure product prices, wage rates, material costs, and interest rates into their calculations. It was assumed that all actors in the market would act rationally in their own self-interest with this knowledge.[24]

Adam Smith and succeeding political economists believed that such a competitive market would operate in the public interest. But if the perfect market ever occurred in reality, it did not last long. There were no "thousands of sellers and buyers," all goods did not become standardized, and no perfect knowledge was ever realized for all the participants.[25]

Not only did the perfect-competition model fail to address the differences in power among the various actors in the market; it had no room for the socially variable modes of competition that emerged, such as the power of brand names, advertising, style variation, and location advantages. Nor could it accommodate cooperation through trade associations, which often had a very strong effect on market behavior. To economists, such cooperation smacked of collusion in the competitive system, and they eliminated it from economic models; Congress saw it as conspiratorial because it affected prices adversely for the consumer and legislated against it. There was no room for the idea expressed by such social visionaries as Peter Kropotkin that cooperation was the most critical process of "natural exchange."[26] Nor was there room in the model for what the sociologist Lewis Coser has described as the "functions of conflict." According to Coser, social conflict is an important process that takes place in every institution, and its valuable effects cannot be denied.[27] But the market could be modeled only for competition.

The nineteenth-century picture of the economy and the market became not only a scientific outlook but also a public ideology—one that remains firmly rooted in the United States today. Consider the following statement, drawn from a study of the American business creed:

Although our system is a unique creation, it corresponds to fundamental and eternal laws of human nature, presumably valid for all societies. . . . The great American invention rested on the recognition of "a principle as inexorable as any law of physics." The inevitable failings of other systems are rooted in the fact that they are not in accord with these inexorable laws of human nature.[28]

The public came to see the economy as the economist saw it, as a natural system of competitive markets. All other social processes, such as conflict, accommodation, adjustment, acculturation, and cooperation, were either less desirable or simply wrong. This belief penetrated all major institutions, including the religious sector, government, and schools. A twenty-first century anthropologist looking at this phenomenon would have to conclude that the concept of a "natural economy" based on competition was the major myth of the preceding century.

The Government as Creator and Regulator of the Market

Karl Polanyi always insisted that there was nothing natural about laissez-faire; free markets could never have happened by allowing "things to take their course." Establishing a labor market in England's rural society, for example, required the wholesale destruction of the traditional fabric of life and necessitated legislation to force the bulk of the population to work for wages. Likewise, the competitive market we know today could never have materialized without government enablement.

For well over a century, the competitive market in the United States has been shaped by government decree. Government has set the rules on market concentration, fair competition, the disclosure of information, product standardization, product safety, the conservation of resources, and dozens of other aspects of market relations. By creating the market system called laissez-faire, government has also become as much a part of the market as business itself.

We can briefly illustrate how government shapes market competition through laws and enforcement by looking at the area of public disclosure. The government entered this field in the early nineteenth century with the National Bank Act of 1863. There followed the Interstate Commerce Act (1887), the Sherman Antitrust Act (1890), the Food and Drug Act (1906), and a vast stream of similar legislation. Successive laws in a single area suggest the increasing complexity of the regulatory effort and the difficulties of enforcement. The Wool Products Labeling Act of 1939, the Fur Products Labeling Act of 1951, and the Textile Fiber Products Identification Act of 1958 all call for the disclosure of the component ingredients in fur and fiber products. The last act requires labels to show the generic names and percentages of all fibers that go into a fabric except those constituting less than 5 percent. Products like Dacron that are marketed under a trade name, must be identified by their generic names (polyester in this case), and the over 700 other trade-name fabrics must be identified as belonging to one of seventeen generic families specified by the Federal Trade Commission. With this growth in complexity came a predictable growth in the size and complexity of government, bringing ever more red tape, restrictions, and higher taxes. Similar examples of government regulation could be given for many other areas, including most notably the food and automobile industries.[29]

In a similar vein, government determines the extent to which a market is monopolistic or oligopolistic. The tariffs and quotas used to restrict the free flow of imports affect the level of domestic concentration. And licensing sets the level of concentration in numerous industries: finance companies, taxis, liquor stores, barbers, beauticians, landscape architects, to name just a few. Government franchises granting monopoly rights to bus lines, athletic stadium concessionaires, utility companies, and other businesses operate similarly, as do patents. The competitive market is morally regulated by the government, not manifestly by the firms themselves. In the process, the market has become a heavy burden that is costly for the government to maintain. This fact cannot be overemphasized because technology is expected to double in complexity in the next decades; unless some major changes occur, we can anticipate that the problems compounding government regulation and enforcement will do the same.

*Balancing Competition and Cooperation
in the Public Interest*

In a search for alternatives to government regulation, we will look in Chapter Six at systems of social regulation through business co-operation in Europe and the United States, to see how cooperation works selectively through trade associations for self-regulation in the public interest. This formation of social norms is part of the latent economy. Later, I shall explore how self-regulatory norms can be improved and enforced in the private sector within the framework of the U.S. Constitution.

At present, cooperation is not only a latent value in the market system; it has a bad name, often interpreted negatively by business and political leaders as opposed to the values of competition, and often defined by the courts as "collusion." But it appears that business itself is changing: increasingly, cooperation is matching competition in importance. And it is not only increasing *within* firms through labor-management programs and quality circles, but also increasing *between* firms as competitors collaborate in R&D projects, partnerships that are held to be legal as long as they do not lead to conspiracy to defraud the public or monopoly.

Cooperation is also becoming more valued as business works with nonprofit corporations and governments. One example may be mentioned here: Boston's Transitional Employment Enterprises (TEE), a nonprofit-supported work project designed to reduce risks for companies that hire disadvantaged people. In what is called "transfer diversion," income maintenance programs like Aid to Families with Dependent Children are relied on as incentives for employers to hire disadvantaged workers. The beneficiaries of such programs continue to receive their benefits for a few months after they are employed, which reduces the employers' wage costs, enables a period of training and support, and gives the workers a chance to prove their merit. When a TEE worker is permanently hired by the company, the transfer benefits stop, and he or she receives the regular wage. The TEE is only one of hundreds of new cooperative partnerships developing between the government, nonprofit, and profit sectors.[30]

Let us end this discussion of social process by noting the negative possibilities that might occur as cooperation becomes manifest. As cooperation grows in importance in the economy relative to competition, matching competition's relevance to explain the direction of the market, it might eventually become a leading characteristic for describing market activity. If this does happen, then competition will become a shadow factor, a latent dimension of the economy. This process of reversal from latent to manifest, and vice-versa, is important to understand, for if unwisely introduced, cooperation could function worse than, or at least no better than, competition. In certain cases, competition's becoming a latent factor may not be the best thing in the short run. It depends on the social process.

Today we can see examples of competition operating as a latent factor in organizations that are legally designed to be cooperative, such as nonprofit confederations, democratically constituted fraternal associations, trade unions, and religious institutions. In such groups, although competition is latent, it can still act subtly on exchanges without people being fully conscious of it; it can even cause such organizations to fail in their missions. Many trade unions have experienced this phenomenon, where competing leaders are disputatious. In religious denominations, such competition, which often centers around biblical dogma, has actually split denominations apart. Thus, competition—although not designed manifestly as part of such nonprofit organizations—can lead to conflict sharp enough to cause their downfall.

In order to avoid such problems from either direction, both competition and cooperation must become visible. The market can then operate more productively and creatively in everyone's interest. But as cooperation becomes more and more manifest, becoming a defining trait of the system, the business economy will inevitably begin to change its character.

Social Organization: The Emerging Balance Between
Corporations and Associations

Associational life in the market, although still largely latent, is vital to observe because of its crucial role in shaping market behavior. Associational life is observed through customs, fashions, fads, etiquette, traditions, folkways, and mores, and through the nonprofit associations—all outside the manifest economy. We shall explore both how the informal rules of human association in the latent market system interact powerfully with the more highly formalized corporations and how the particular form of social organization called "associations" is becoming more manifest in the economy today.

The Impact of Associational Life on the Market

The institutional economist John Commons asserts that the reason why people act in the market as they do is based partly on "the degree of organization" existing on a continuum from "custom" to "corporation," and that the probability of someone's behaving in a certain manner in the market is dependent on "the kind of sanction, the precision and publicity of the standards, and the degree of organization for enforcing the sanctions." As he sees it, the "Custom of Association" is an important market variable that controls

individual action by working rules, according to the *degree of organization* from loose to centralized. It is this custom of association and rule-making that we name Going Concerns, in their exercise of moral, economic, or physical sanctions. Formerly the corporation was looked upon as a creation of sovereignty, existing only in contemplation of law. But charters of incorporation now are known to be only the more precise and formal addition of the physical sanctions of sovereignty to the universal custom of association. What were stigmatized as conspiracies become corporations or other lawful associations in manifold variety when the custom of association is sanctioned by officials who guide the use of physical force.[31]

In other words, the behavior of the market is determined by customs and various other informal types of human association that become ever more formal and more centrally organized, until they become corporations with the power of state enforcement behind them. Although Commons is not insisting on a linear progression of formalization from custom to corporation, he is pointing to the power of influence in this variety of human association.

The broad concept of human association thus ranges from the most informal interactions and folkways of people to the more formal "associations" that become chartered as either democratic nonprofits or command-based business corporations. In either case, corporations are grounded in an associational life that goes beyond their formal organization.

Furthermore, business corporations in the profit sector are taking greater account today of their informal organization, that is, their associational life. It is in the informal life of the factory and the administrative office that executives find the stimulus for (or the inhibition of) productivity; indeed, the creation of a friendly, informal atmosphere in the social life of the corporation has become an important goal for many executives today because it pays off. Paying attention to it makes money. Thus, the informal life of the corporation—or in terms of our theory, the integration of the social factor into the economic factor—is increasingly being cultivated.

The concept of "association" is critical to explaining the transition taking place in the market economy, partly because formal organizations in the nonprofit sector, including various fraternal, religious, artistic, recreational, and business-oriented groups, generally describe themselves as "associations." When you belong to one of these associations, you are a "member" rather than a stockholder or an owner, and you are given voting rights attached to your membership. So it is significant that as today's executives look at the Japanese corporation, with its quality circles and lifelong membership for employees, they have begun to replicate it, describing their own employees as "members of the family." Furthermore, many employees in the growing numbers of employee-owned firms in the United States now think of themselves as "members" of their own firm.

The Multilevel Character of Associational Life in the Market

Exchange theorists have said that a major attribute of the market is its multilevel character, pointing both to micro and macro levels and to the interdependent relationships between the informal patterns of interaction among people in the marketplace and the larger associational life that determines the nature of the market.

There is a close interdependence between the associational life of workers and the effective operations of the formal corporation—for example, between the standards set by the nonprofit National Association of Security Dealers and the actions of its members in the profit sector, which eventually shapes their investment in other business corporations. This interdependent relationship between the manifest profit sector and the many other informal and formal associations that are intricately involved with it in the market marks all ranges of the market, from the local to the global.

The impact of this multileveled social organization of the market can be seen, for example, in the setting of prices. At the local level, consider the activities of a retail corporation with its labor, consumer, and capital markets operating together. It is worth noting again that economists do not study the associational aspect of this local market because social variables do not fall within their scope of inquiry. Theories of price, for example, do not account for either the *style of leadership* expressed through the local union or the *attitudes* of local management that determine the direction of collective bargaining, even though these phenomena clearly affect prices: if wages rise as a result of the style of labor-management leadership in collective bargaining, prices could rise as a consequence. The informal life of people in association with one another is thus important in predicting the price system.

In other ways, too, a network of social exchange among people in associations shapes local prices and market behavior in regard to the local retail corporation. This network is defined by the stratified power of dozens of nonprofit associations. The Chamber of Commerce is a trade association outside the profit sector, yet it influences the local government widely, for example, on zoning. Perhaps the local store, through its membership in the chamber wants to heighten demand by offering increased parking; plainly, it can create a level of customer demand in ways that go quite beyond utility models and consumer preference surveys.

Many variables in the associational life of the community determine the behavior of the local market. These include the association of churches concerned about retail sales on Sunday, trade association standards on ethical advertising, the retailer's access to supplies that are affected by accounting practices of wholesaler associations, the banker association's policies in making loans, and the associational life of ethnic groups in the neighborhood, to name a few. In other words, the determination of market prices is an intricate intertwining of associational life with corporate life. The local market is clearly affected by the systems of social exchange in the community, and the social organization of the market is critical in determining supply and demand and price behavior.[32]

Changes in the Social Governance of the Market

Numerous other aspects of social organization reflect the changing nature of the corporation. One reason why the corporate economy appears to be moving from a system of strict command bureaucracy to a system of mutual governance is the search for "excellence" in management today, which is interpreted in part as bringing the formal structure of the corporation in line with associational life. Thus the organization of companies has been shifting from straight-line hierarchies toward more horizontal and multilateral systems of communication as management experiments with "flattened hierarchies" and new modes of worker participation. The next chapter explores how such developments are signaling a new type of business association governed cooperatively by social (self-) management in the long range; the interim changes are already visible.[33]

In this transition, some scholars see the business corporation in trouble. R. W. Boyden, for instance, argues that the corporation has passed the zenith of its development. Comparing modern corporations with medieval corporations, he observes troubling similarities and common crisis symptoms. Just as medieval corporations failed to perform the task for which they were designed, suffered from a failure in beliefs supporting their existence, and grew on a scale having no connection with their original function, so Boyden sees modern management plagued by entrenched hierarchies, and unwilling or unable to control exorbitant expense accounts, confront semimonopolistic pricing, and construct a new culture for the corporation. He believes that the corporation will adapt as an organization only if people become more important than the institution, something that can only come about by separating the legislative and executive powers of the corporation and developing corporate law on internal affairs, with courts to administer justice. In effect, he sees the successful corporation becoming a more socially governed entity in the private sector.[34]

At the same time, the concept of association is gaining favor in connection with trade unions. Charles Hecksher argues for the development of "association" in the labor movement, as opposed to the old principle of "formal organization," which refers to the labor union that has become like a business corporation with a command hierarchy. Hecksher's new concept of "association" refers to a more informal and decentralizing mode of union organizing, closer to the participatory governance of workers. His "associational unionism" would "be based on universal rights guaranteed to all workers, . . . provide mechanisms of multilateral negotiation to work out agreements among these diverse claims, . . . encompass concerns about work structure and 'the quality of work life' on one hand, and about general policy issues on the other, . . . reduce the government's role as administrative judge of disputes, encouraging instead local negotiation, . . . provide ways of resolving difficult disputes, [and] enable those concerned to work out interpretations of rights."[35]

The concept of associational unionism is the more noteworthy for suggesting what the new mode of organization in business might look like. Participatory experiments in corporate management often use the term "association" to refer to a more cooperative, decentralized system of work, a style of social organization that is more typical of the nonprofit sector.

Finally, let us look at trade associations, democratic organizations in the latent organization of the market. They provide systems of information that help members raise the level of productivity and learn about new products, technology, markets, accounting practices, labor policies, and so on; all this gives them a rather powerful position in the new information economy. They are both the "information providers" and the basis for intercorporate communication. I shall explore later how they can serve as the social agency through which rivals may cooperate in the private sector to compete more effectively against foreign firms. These associations, which operate at the broad level of whole industries, often keep industries productive while serving as a buffer against too much government intervention, and they have the potential to match the power of the corporation as the primary unit of the future market system. If this were to occur, they would represent a linear shift from the latent to the manifest. In the process, they might also change their structure significantly by adopting social constitutions that specify their democratic practices (e.g., "due process") in more concrete terms, as we explore later.

The Growth of the Federative Principle and the
Intersection of Profits and Nonprofits

In his classic textbook *Society*, the sociologist Robert MacIver brilliantly discusses associational life, describing the "federative principle" by which organizations are built of local or regional units, "each possessing as much autonomy as is compatible with the ends of the association."

It should . . . be noted that the degree of effective localization varies with the type of group interest. Interests pursued by certain organizations can be fulfilled only by means of face-to-face contact and personal communication. This is why colleges, for example, must be in essentials localized, and why fellowship organizations, such as Rotary or Kiwanis or the myriad fraternal orders, must be composed of local groups. A church, no matter how highly centralized its government may be, depends for its life on the local assembling of its members.[36]

It is significant that much of the nonprofit sector is composed of democratic federations based on systems of mutual governance in which formal authority is decentralized, as opposed to the systems of command governance that currently characterize business corporations. Nonprofits range from confederations in which the autonomy of corporate members is maximized (e.g. trade associations) to more centralized federations (trade unions). Religious institutions also vary markedly in their governance, from the centralized order of the Catholic church to federative structures like the Presbyterian church, the more decentralized federation of the Congregational church, and the highly decentralized confederation of Quakers.

We should keep in mind that formally democratic nonprofit associations may not always be so democratic in reality; many trade unions have become like dictatorships, and trade associations and religious groups also vary in their practice of formal democracy. Yet there is a qualitative difference between the tendency to organize democratic structures in the nonprofit sector and the tendency to organize command structures in the profit sector.

The federative structure of nonprofit organizations becomes significant for researchers of this social transition in the light of the changes implied by Table 1. I believe that big corporations in the profit sector will take steps in the direction of "federalizing" in the future, and the profit and nonprofit sectors will thus show new intersects in their different types of organizations. For example, the federative organizations of Presbyterians and Congregationalists have long disputed the question of whether local congregations should own and control their own churches, as opposed to control by higher authorities in their organization. Such an issue of control can apply to the governance of joint ventures between business corporations. The issue of decentralized authority can also arise because of pressures from employee-managed subsidiaries to own their own companies while contracting commercially with their parent companies.

The characteristics of the nonprofit sector, such as social orientation and democratic forms of governance, are increasingly affecting the nature of the profit sector as the two sectors become more and more intertwined. For example, reliant as the profit sector now is on the investments of nonprofit institutions like universities, churches, trade unions, and pension funds, it must respond to the growing tendency among them to use social criteria in allocating their capital.

This practice of social investment has now stimulated banks and other fiduciary insitutions to make investment decisions on the basis of social issues because "there is a market out there." Trade unions, religious institutions, universities, and wealthy individuals who are conscientious about where their money is invested have all transferred large sums to such fiduciaries specifically for "social screening." Social screens include such issues as the quality of life in the workplace, the safety of the goods produced, environmental protection, energy conservation, nuclear power, and involvement in South Africa. The growth of social investment will probably lead to legislation that makes the process more public and legitimate in business law.

This growing interdependence between the profit and nonprofit sectors is also making it difficult to distinguish one sector from the other. Profit-making firms are beginning to look more and more like nonprofits. Business scholars talk about the shift away from maximizing to optimizing profits as executives' increased awareness of their interdependence with labor, creditors, suppliers, governments, consumers, and communities accents the importance of these groups to them as political "constituencies" of the corporation. A popular management theory uses the term "stakeholders" to refer to these constituencies. The corporation is becoming responsible to groups that have a "stake" in its growth and thus have some say about the proper conduct of the business affecting them.[37]

Meanwhile, some nonprofits are beginning to resemble profit-making firms in their attempts to maximize their income. The Metropolitan Museum of Art looks like a business when it sells goods ranging from posters and mugs to expensive reproductions. The goods are intended to stimulate interest in art, but like many other nonprofits, the museum relies heavily on such merchandising to support itself. In 1987, it earned $9.2 million, or 17 percent of $53 million in revenues—more than triple the pretax average for ten major department store chains. More than half of those sales came from mail orders; most of the rest came from the museum's 17,000 square feet of shopping space. The museum also operates an outlet in Macy's flagship Herald Square store, shares a store with the New York Public Library, and has its own shop in a mall in Stamford, Connecticut. In addition, it receives royalties ($3 million in 1987) from retailers and other museums that sell products based on the works in the Met's collections.[38]

Yet like other nonprofits that look increasingly like businesses, the museum pays no income taxes and is not legally required to do so as long as the business is "substantially related" to its charitable and educational purposes. But nonprofits like the Met are on the borderline, and this borderline is what we are talking about as needing socioeconomic research.[39]

A Society in Opposition and Evolution

Nineteenth-century social philosophers like Marx, Saint-Simon, Comte, and Spencer depicted society as evolving through powerful forces of change that were both creative and destructive in nature. From this perspective, conflict between the state and the market economy can be interpreted as part of an evolutionary process. This book suggests how this process is unfolding today as society evolves new mechanisms of conflict resolution and consensual patterns to handle these conflictual forces.

The meaning of this modern separation between the state and the economy and the evolutionary forces acting within them have been described by twentieth-century sociologists like Robert MacIver. For example, the state has evolved mechanisms for handling the oppositional forces of society through parliamentary bodies, judicial systems, and constitutions that mediate the conflict and guide political life, and has also helped the economy in particular evolve through legal mechanisms for corporate competition, collective bargaining, and rules of trade. But the state and the market economy are in a process of change and evolution, as an interdependent aspect of a changing order of society.

The contemporary attempt at resolving the conflict between the state and the economy can be seen in the uneasy balance of the welfare state, a system that could be defined as the prototypical "political economy" of the twentieth century. The term welfare state first emerged in the early 1940's to differentiate wartime Britain from the "warfare" state of Nazi Germany; it quickly entered the wider vocabulary to designate the idea that the state had become responsible both for the welfare of people displaced by the market and for the welfare of the economy overall. The state's role was to modify the play of market forces by guaranteeing minimum income for families through welfare services, and intervening in economic affairs to remedy inequities and injustices that occurred in the market.

But the welfare state has many problems of its own. In its welfare role, the state has been a protector of the poor but also a protector of the powerful and a maintainer of the status quo. And its role as the regulator of the economy has been criticized as contributing to a restriction on the optimum development of the economy.

This book suggests that because of the evolutionary forces at work in the market today, we may move beyond the welfare state as the economy itself expands its mechanisms for reducing state intervention. The market economy—as a part of society—has already been modestly building its own private mechanisms of conflict resolution (e.g., private mediation boards), corporate accountability systems (e.g., social auditing), and new countervailing powers (e.g., consumer federations). Likewise, the federative principle that operates in the latent economy may indicate a new basis for self-government in private markets.

In the rest of this book, we look at how forces within the market economy itself are bringing about this change. The basic proposition to be explored is that social and economic factors are already becoming integrated to provide a foundation for a new societal order of markets, and that the state's new role should be to foster that development through scientific studies and new public policies. We shall see how this evolution is taking place in the labor market, the capital market, and the interorganizational life of corporations. We will also look at how a new legal structure is emerging to support these changes, and at the role that scientific research and public policies can play to facilitate this evolution. Finally, we will look at the processes by which the welfare state may be transcended through a growth in the capacity of the market to regulate itself in the public interest.

PART II

The Emerging Social Orientation

Everything, which up to now has been considered as inalienable, is sold as objects of exchange, of chaffering. It is the time in which objects, which earlier have been conveyed, but never exchanged, have been given away but never offered for sale, have been acquired but never been bought: virtue, love, conviction, knowledge, consciousness and so on, the time which, in a word, everything has been transformed into a commercial commodity. It is the time of general corruption, of universal bribery or, in the language of economics, it is the time when each object, physical as well as moral, is put on the market as an object of exchange to be taxed at its correct value.

Karl Marx
The Poverty of Philosophy

CHAPTER 3

The Labor Market:
The Growth of Social Management

UNDER CAPITALISM, Karl Marx said, workers are bought and sold on the market like commodities. This was the early Marx, the philosopher whose writings still carry the sting of truth. Workers were merely factors of production, manipulated in the interest of higher profits, the price for the use of their labor determined in the market, which in turn was controlled by big capital. This process was a major source of modern alienation. When workers sold their labor power to an employer they became separated from a basic part of themselves. At first they would not feel this separation because it was a pattern of everyday life, understood as part of a natural system. But alienation was not simply a personal psychological problem; it was also a sociological problem that was part of the collective unconscious of society, a latent part of the structure of capitalism that could not easily be seen or felt. As workers became aware of being exploited each day, this fact would eventually break through into their social consciousness, and they would react against the system.[1]

Put another way, the sale of one's labor power involved exchanging it for money (wages), with the understanding that employers then had the right to dispose of the results of that labor on the market and keep the surplus. Since workers had sold their labor power, they did not have any right to participate in making decisions on production, but lacking control over their work and their products, they could not experience a sense of purpose and self-direction, which is the essence of human alienation.

For Marx, true labor was a process of self-creation, a voluntary activity that provided workers the opportunity to re-create themselves in the material world. But the capitalist system repressed this natural capacity. The only logical way out of this alienation was to gain control over the whole system of work through a class-wide effort to win collective power for self-determination.[2]

However, for Marx the problem of alienation went still further. To embody the product of labor in an object that became a commodity sold in the marketplace was to objectify labor. Once workers had sold their labor and all their products were appropriated by the employer, these products stood opposed to them as alien beings independent of their producers.[3] When employers appropriated labor power, they also appropriated the product of labor, or the "surplus value"—the difference between the value of the product on the market and the value of the workers' labor power. But once the product was released to the public, it took on its own power in the marketplace. Firms sold their commodities through marketing institutions, and these in turn acquired a separate life outside the control of their creators. The market system thus took on independent powers that became threatening to both the worker and the employer. In this way, alienation began with the modes of production and continued far into the marketplace of products.

The capitalist system became even more far-reaching as materialist values were conveyed into the larger culture, teaching not only the marketing of labor but also the marketing of any subject that could be made into an object and bought for a price. People began to quantify everything for the market. This process Georgy Lukacs and other Marxists called "reification." Social relations were no longer an end in themselves but instead gained the status of thinghood, and people evaluated and used each other for their own self-interest in the same way they used objects, no longer knowing each other for their own sake. In the end, human relationships became prostituted in the drive to advance self-interest and profits.[4]

This reification of human relationships too was unconscious, because it appeared only "natural" and normal for people to use each other for their own ends. People thus become culturally alienated from one another without realizing it, not even knowing that the problem was caused by an exchange system they themselves had created. So failing a breakthrough in consciousness, people would have no desire to change the system.

These nineteenth-century arguments have been debated for over a hundred years. Many scholars would rightly claim that Marx's theories of alienation and surplus value are not really applicable—that the notion of alienation is far more complex than he conceived, and overcoming labor's alienation would not result in overcoming all human alienation. Such scholars argue that the philosophical concept of alienation—which Marx drew from Hegel—is not reducible to a concept of political economy, but is a much deeper issue concerning the meaning of life itself and must thus be understood as part of the evolving spirit of humankind on earth.[5]

At the same time, many scholars would agree that Marx's original thesis—that labor is treated as an object in the marketplace—still has merit as a relative truth. It continues to explain the dynamics of the system, and for some Marxist scholars it is the basis for a future unraveling of capitalism. In other words, the labor market is still recognized as an economizing system with major human consequences, and resolving the basic problem of the labor market—the objectification of labor—is still required to resolve the larger philosophical question of alienation.

The Labor Movement and the Problem of Alienation

The effort to overcome the alienation of labor, which has been a major struggle of the last century and a significant part of modern history, now becomes part of our study of the social market. Alienation can now be seen as not only the plight of the labor class, but also a plight of the capitalist class caught in the tangled web of an economistic market. The problem of alienation extends also to the organization of capital, its mode of allocation, and the competitive relationship between firms operating in the context of society. Nevertheless, steps toward resolving this complex problem begin in the workplace.[6]

Some good studies have examined the problems of alienation in corporate life. Harry Braverman has demonstrated how the workplace is "deskilled" by management, eliminating labor's power to think; the power of thinking is monopolized by management.[7] Michael Buroway sees work inside the capitalist factory as necessary to obscure and secure surplus value. Work is organized as a game to earn "incentive pay," but what really motivates workers is that playing the game breaks the monotony and reduces tedium. In place of the coercion of earlier forms of capitalism, today's capitalism has "manufactured consent" from the workers.[8]

Richard Edwards has shown how U.S. capitalism has created three types of hierarchical control over the means of production: "simple control" through the petty tyranny of the workplace, "technical control" through the machine, and "bureaucratic control" through the administrative structure of the corporation. The "working poor" tend to serve in the "secondary [labor] market," the area of the petty bourgeoisie, the small shops and businesses where "simple control" is common; the "traditional proletariat" is mostly found in "the subordinate primary market" dominated by "technical control"; and the "middle layers" of workers are found in the "independent primary market," composed of big corporations, where "bureaucratic control" is most pervasive.[9]

The concept of a labor market through which capitalists impose a hierarchy of control over labor in order to maximize profits is central to neomarxist thought. The basic idea is that segmented labor markets have been a critical part of the development of the working class.[10] While this concept can lead to a disillusionment over the direction of the labor movement and a critique of its leadership, it can also provide a basis for seeing a reality behind the state of affairs in the labor market today. Our problem is how to take account of these studies and at the same time recognize the ground for public policies in this tradition.

If we can assume that change has a polar quality and remains complexly dynamic, with negative and positive poles representing directions toward which people can choose to go, there are at least two alternative interpretations of where labor stands today and where it will be in the future. One position is that the system has continued to worsen, dominance has become more subtle and insidious, and conditions of exploitation will be even worse in the future because the labor force has become unconscious of "manufactured consent." The other position is that labor has increased its participatory role in the economy both through the union movement and through new involvement in management and has thus advanced its capacity to become more potent, which could mean steps toward greater degrees of worker control through labor-management experiments, new forms of co-determination in corporate organization, and effective worker takeovers of firms.

This is the basic question in public policy today. On one side, there is the possibility that any measured increase in worker participation in management will allow continuing exploitation through subtle consent and bring even worse forms of dominance, for example, through more complex computer technology that can give management greater control over the production process by recording a worker's every movement. On the other side there is the possibility that continued vigilance and leadership from labor unions and participation in ever higher levels of management, control, and ownership in the future market can eventually overcome the problem of labor alienation. Our task requires that we look realistically at where labor and management are now in the twentieth century, as the basis for shaping public policies that will lead toward the most probable and effective alternatives in the future.

The Changing Relationship Between Unions and Management

The movement for greater worker control has been advancing gradually in both the United States and other nations around the world, but in ways that the nineteenth-century philosophers never anticipated. The problem can be understood in the twentieth century only if we include all working members of society—housewives, engineers, lawyers, minorities, managers, farmers, executives, shopkeepers, and government employees—as well as the traditional category of unskilled factory labor, even though these groups were not seen as suffering from alienation in the nineteenth century.

At the time Marx and Engels wrote *The Communist Manifesto* (1848), there was no homogeneous industrial working class, not even in England, the most developed country. The power of Marx's theory may be seen in some part in its having been written before the proletariat had actually been born as a class. As he predicted, a class consciousness developed among workers who were sweating together under factory roofs through the organization of trade unions.[11]

But the trade union movement in the United States never grew in proportion to the total labor force as it did in Europe and elsewhere. In a work force in which (by 1969) more than 80 percent of all adults were nonmanagerial wage and salary employees, or in Marxist terms, sellers of their labor power, union representation has remained relatively low. Moreover, by the 1970's the movement was in decline, embracing less than 16 percent of the work force, and labor leaders began seriously reviewing their purpose and direction.[12]

Charles Hecksher argues that there are two competing visions for the direction of unionism today. They are related to whether we see unions as formal organizations competing against management at the top (especially as in Europe) or as more decentralized associations that concentrate on issues of immediate concern in the workplace. "In fact," he writes, "they are and must be both. Yet these poles—spontaneity vs. discipline, democracy vs. control, community vs. bureaucracy, breadth of vision vs. narrow interest—have defined many of the structural problems and changes in the labor movement since its birth."[13]

Hecksher believes that the legal framework for collective bargaining under the Wagner Act of 1935 is obsolete. This law gave unions a source of power in the corporation by granting them the exclusive right to represent all workers. But the rise of foreign competition, the institutionalization of work rules, squabbles over grievances, and the successful efforts of business to undermine this structure make it no longer tenable as the single framework for planning labor's future. Part of the reason for seeking a new direction is that with less than 16 percent of the work force, unions no longer control the market in many basic industries and are having difficulty organizing employees in the growing service sector, yet nonunionized workers need support and protection. A new type of labor organization must be developed to continue labor's struggle for self-development.

Hecksher argues that collective bargaining is still important to establish competitive wages and working conditions, but it must be placed in an entirely new legal and structural framework in order to avoid the rigidities of the past. The alternative is what Hecksher calls "associational unionism." Here workers would not be forced to choose between exclusive representation by one union and no representation; instead, unions and other interest groups could speak for various fractions of the work force. Bargaining for wages and other matters would be determined through multilateral negotiations among management and different groups of employees, as well as perhaps such outsiders as environmentalists and consumers. Hecksher sees associational unionism as a decentralized form of multilateral decision making that will enable both labor and management to move much more flexibly to meet the demands of the market.

In effect, Hecksher is saying that while the union movement over the years has been beneficial to workers in protecting their rights and reducing the degree of their alienation in the workplace, it has now reached a point of bureaucratic stagnation. Reorganization along the decentralized lines he recommends should paradoxically strengthen the labor movement. In fact, the AFL-CIO and some affiliated unions have already embraced a form of "associational unionism" in ways that suggest the direction of Hecksher's concept. Instead of limiting membership to workers under bargaining agreements, for example, they offer group insurance plans and other services to "associate members," such as retirees and unorganized workers.

Hecksher points to the specific example of the Shell Canada plant in Sarnia, Ontario, now co-managed by the Oil, Chemical, and Atomic Workers Union. The new system emerged partly in response to pressures from well-paid workers for more opportunity to develop their skills and to have a greater degree of control over their work, and partly in response to the desire of engineers to have workers optimize their skills and increase their commitment to the new technology employed at the plant.

The details of this Sarnia operation are worth summarizing for readers unfamiliar with this trend as an intermediate model for labor. It offers a building block for still greater degrees of social management in the future:

A wholly new work arrangement was brought into being at Sarnia. The union agreed to forgo detailed job classifications and seniority-based promotion in return for the opportunity for meaningful work and job control. Work is now organized without job descriptions, and teams are made responsible for the overall operations and the rotation of tasks among team members on a daily basis. Each team of eighteen members (and a coordinator) operates the entire process including the labor work, shipping, warehousing, janitorial work, conflict resolution, administration, and many other aspects of maintenance. Each team rotates over the various shifts in innovative ways. The only nonrotating team is "craft instructors" who not only do basic maintenance work but teach such skills to all teams. It is therefore a relatively flat organizational structure in which only the plant superintendent and operations managers exist in addition to the worker teams. The premise of the plant design is "organizational learning" that promotes individual learning with a system of open progression. Grade levels are based on skill, measured by exams and performance tests.

Each member is expected to acquire all the knowledge and skill modules for process operations. Beyond this, there are different specialty areas, the combination of which define distinct career paths within the plant. There are no quotas as to how many can progress through these career paths and the expectation is that everyone will reach to top level, though there are no time limits placed on this, and workers are not forced to advance if they do not wish to do so. This type of organization clearly represents a profound shift from conventional plant design and suggests something of the future in labor-management relations.[14]

The Sarnia organizational model sought to increase learning and shorten the response time to disturbances as they arose. An offline computer facilitated learning through the use of computer software that responded to queries posed by the operators but left decision making in their hands. In order to make informed decisions and respond quickly, workers had to be supplied with technical and economic data conventionally made available only to technical staff. This learning model treated the entire plant as the relevant unit for all workers so that plant-wide learning took place.

The Changing Role of Labor Law

A second avenue for protecting workers from oppressive management and for overcoming the effects of alienation has been through legislation. The legal movement to protect workers has grown enormously in the twentieth century and will likely continue to grow in the coming years. During the early 1960's, for example, a number of laws began to express employees' rights in the corporation. Title VII of the Civil Rights Act amounted to a guarantee of due process, so that today minority employees can legally be disciplined and discharged only for reasons of work performance. (In 1975, 66,000 formal charges were filed with the Equal Employment Opportunity Commission in addition to the uncounted charges filed with state civil rights agencies.) Due process protection has also been extended to people facing a whole array of other problems. People over the age of forty are now protected by the Age Discrimination in Employment Act. The Vocational Rehabilitation Act has prohibited discrimination based on physical handicaps or mental limitations among federal contractors, and the Occupational Safety and Health Act enforces safety standards in the workplace. Before 1974, a company could fire employees to prevent them from vesting in pension funds, but the Employment Retirement Income Security Act ended this practice. The Clean Air Act Amendments of 1977 declared that corporate executives could no longer punish employees for blowing the whistle on pollution. At least thirty-five states have their own civil rights enforcement agencies, and thirty-one have restricted employers' use of lie detectors; at least eight states have passed provisions protecting whistleblowers.[15]

Other issues, too, have come under legal attention, such as the threat of being fired arbitrarily at any time by an employer, always a major fear of workers. The legal doctrine of "employment at will," which since its articulation in 1884 had allowed employers to dismiss employees without cause, began to be questioned by the courts in the 1970's. In West Virginia, a bank officer who was fired for questioning an order that he illegally boost customer service charges won substantial damages in court. In another crucial court decision made in 1974, the judge argued: "The employer's interest in running his business as he sees fit must be balanced against the interest of the employee in maintaining his employment *and the public's interest in maintaining a proper balance between the two.*"[16] Other decisions have begun to draw on the constitutional provision for free speech, which until now has been inapplicable to the private sector of corporate life.

Legal strategies involve the formulation of general rules, applied universally, stating exactly what conditions of work are permitted, and the process of government regulation involves matching facts to rules in the manner of a judicial proceeding. But the limitations of rule-based strategies have become apparent, and the right of workers to participate—for example, in the process of making workplaces more safe—is being recognized. Rule-based strategies for job safety require too many experts, overextend the state in the inspection process, and overemphasize medical and technical research at the expense of behavioral research and the study of social factors. Medical research is limited to identifying technical threats, but the social organization of work may also pose serious threats. This aspect of the workplace is increasingly coming under scrutiny.[17]

To reduce the need for more laws and court decisions in a declining period of unionism, many labor leaders are now pressing for an Employee's Bill of Rights to guarantee workers due process, freedom of speech and association, the right to information about corporate affairs, and the like. But another alternative is to strive for greater employee self-management.

The Trend Toward Social Management

By social management in the current practice, I mean a system of work that aims to increase the satisfaction and well-being of employees, develop their personal resources, and cultivate their self-management skills, while at the same time increasing productivity and profits. It means that management has found it important to integrate social and economic goals in order to become more competitive in the marketplace. But the term has also come recently to signify a trend toward increasing employee participation in managing work teams and overseeing work systems.

The process of increasing employee participation can be traced as far back as the 1920's, when employers found it profitable to put suggestion boxes on the factory floor so that workers could contribute ideas on improving production. Worker participation continued to grow with the establishment of labor-management committees that jointly determined rules on production and safety in the use of machines, and advanced further with Scanlon Plans and other profit-sharing plans instituted by management with labor participation. Today it includes quality circles, quality of worklife projects, autonomous work groups, labor-management committees, and the like. Social management has been a process of experimenting with increasing degrees of worker participation in running the operations in the firm, including recent experiments with labor representatives on boards of directors.[18]

European companies have taken big steps in this direction and found the practice quite valuable. The West German practice of co-determination has been so successful in fact that the European Economic Community at one time recommended it as a model for all member nations. Each European nation, however, has special problems of its own, and none can realistically serve as a simple model to be replicated by other nations. According to critics, one of the macro problems they all exhibit is state "corporatism," with big organizations—labor, capital, and government—ruling the nation. Both big unions and big business are now seen as too powerful, collaborating at the top, and the state is seen as too much involved in mandating changes. For many scholars of self-management, there is still much to be done beyond the European scene to decentralize and de-statify economic life.[19]

Two different trends are emerging in the United States. For one thing, American corporations have been emphasizing experiments in giving employees a greater degree of control over their conditions of work. The last two decades have been marked by a concern for the quality of worklife, including job rotation, job enrichment, job enlargement, and most recently, work time.[20] And for another, recent years have seen a growth in employee-owned corporations, a development that has been promoted through Employee Stock Ownership Plan (ESOP) legislation. Both trends show strong signs of continuing.[21]

This double trend toward increased worker participation and ownership is so important to the future of the American economy that we will now take time to examine how this movement has strengthened in the last few decades. The promotion of self-management may offer a way for the business society to develop a new economy that is both decentralized and humanized.

The Growth of Self-Managed Firms

By the mid-1980's, over 10,000 firms with more than 11 million workers had ESOPs or the equivalent. Most of these workers were employed by companies with less than 15 percent worker ownership, but about 1 million were employed by companies with 15 to 50 percent worker ownership, and about a half-million worked in the some 1,000 companies with 51 to 100 percent ownership.

At that time, *employee ownership* characterized companies like Science Applications (6,000 employees) and W. L. Gore Associates (3,000 employees), and a significant proportion of employees in such key industries as airlines and trucking had ownership interests. Employees were majority owners in many large companies, such as Davey Tree (2,600 employees), Life-touch Studies (4,000), and Parsons Engineering (7,000), and owned 100 percent of the stock in several others, including Avondale Industries (10,000 employees), Weirton Steel (7,000), Pamida (5,000), and OTASCO (3,000).[22]

The trend toward *employee participation in management* has increased in tandem with this trend toward employee ownership. In 1982, in one of the first studies of U.S. corporate experiments with human resource programs, the Stock Exchange estimated that about 14 percent of the 49,000 companies studied had such programs as job enlargement and rotation, employee participation in management training, labor/management committees, autonomous groups, and quality circles, and fully 70 percent of the companies with over 500 employees were seeking to involve workers in new forms of decision making. Significantly, just 3 percent of the managers interviewed believed that participative management was only a passing fashion.[23]

The two trends are taking place because they are productive and profitable, and public opinion research suggests that they will continue in the future. A U.S. Chamber of Commerce poll in the mid-1980's revealed that 84 percent of the work force wanted greater participation in management decisions, and a Peter Hart Associates poll showed that 66 percent of the work force preferred to work in an employee-owned firm.

It seems likely that employee ownership and management will merge and become an integral part of corporate life in the next few decades, but the process is not without pitfalls. While many observers suggest that both trends have positive long-term advantages (e.g., they contribute to a more productive economy, augur a significant advance in the capacity of corporations to become fully self-managed, increase the level of enterprise autonomy, and foster the economy's becoming a self-regulating system), others see them as mere fads that actually complicate the problems of free enterprise.

How can we evaluate these trends? Is there a need for legislation to promote them? What do studies suggest about the future? To try to answer these questions, let us look at some studies of what scholars describe as *relatively self-managed firms*, companies in which close to a majority of employees are involved in management and ownership and that seem to be heading in the direction of full self-management.[24]

The Performance of Self-Managed Firms

Although relatively self-managed firms seem on the whole to contribute to both social and economic development, they still have problems to solve in becoming the most effective enterprises for the future. They contribute toward social development insofar as they cultivate greater human resources, and add to the quality of life in the firm and to the well-being of local communities, and they contribute to economic development by their ability to increase the level of efficiency and lower the costs of enterprise management. But the manner in which they develop is critical to their success. They require a favorable legal environment and management consultation if they are to avoid the pitfalls that some have faced in the last decade.

There are at least ten potential benefits deriving from the unique nature of self-managed firms. Let us take them up one by one, looking also at the problems that may arise and possible methods for solving them.

1. *Self-managed companies help prevent plant closings, reducing the need for welfare and government intervention.* There are many possible reasons for shutdowns. Top executives may want to move a firm to where labor is not organized, or move overseas to save labor costs. They may close a plant because a subsidiary—purchased as part of a conglomerate deal—is found to be incompatible with the parent organization, or they may decide that it is more profitable to cease operations as a tax write-off. A firm can shut its doors at the choice of its owner. But especially when earnings do not match the expectations of top executives, shutdowns become a way to increase profits. In other words, even in highly profitable firms major lay-offs are deemed necessary simply to increase the level of profits.

Such was the case with the Library Bureau, a furniture factory in Herkimer, New York, that was taken over by Sperry-Rand in 1955. In 1976, even though the factory had yielded a profit in every year but one, Sperry-Rand decided to close it down, declare a tax loss, and sell its valuable machinery. Although the plant was making money at the time, it did not meet the standard of 22 percent on invested capital expected by Sperry-Rand executives. Furthermore, it had no organic connection to the main lines of Sperry-Rand's activity in electronics and machines. The executives looked on it as a liability that only complicated smooth management operations and felt it was more trouble than it was worth to the parent corporation. A shutdown was averted by alert employees who, initially against the wishes of management, collected money among themselves and with the help of the community purchased the firm at the last minute.

A firm's shutdown for whatever reason is always harmful in some measure and can sometimes devastate a community. The Library Bureau case and others like it are so significant because the workers kept themselves and a host of local institutions and small businesses from going under or from being detrimentally affected, and prevented a drain on the public coffers for welfare and unemployment compensation.[25]

Whether the reason for a business shutdown is cheaper labor elsewhere or a tax write-off, executives know that the state will assume responsibility for welfare payments to the newly unemployed. The costs of such shutdowns have been significant, not only in terms of government welfare payments, but also in terms of the struggle required by local communities to find additional resources to cope with the deterioration and problems that inevitably crop up when there are not enough jobs to go around.

The degree to which plant closings and relocations are destructive of community life is difficult to measure, but it is commonly recognized as a significant problem. The city of Detroit used to try to determine the number of plant shutdowns by asking Detroit Edison how many factory electricity cutoffs had occurred in a given year! Fully 278 plants shut down in Detroit between 1970 and 1976; the city staggered under the subsequent problems of family instability, crime, and drugs. The Ohio Bureau of Economic and Community Development ascertains plant closures by equating them with the number of companies that stop filing franchise tax forms. An acceleration of shutdowns so measured in 1981–82 appeared to push state job-loss figures close to 70,000.[26]

Buyouts by employees are an important method for saving jobs. According to a Senate Select Committee on Small Business in 1979, no employee buyout failed during the 1970's, and the total number of jobs preserved was estimated to be between 50,000 and 100,000, a considerable plus in terms of job preservation. Because of this positive experience, some analysts have suggested that government could provide a better environment for worker buyouts; they could be facilitated as a protection against plant closures, especially those that threaten vulnerable localities. It has also been suggested that firms whose employees have a greater say in management decisions, for example, ESOPs with pass-through voting rights, have special value in helping to stabilize the local economy. Encouraging the development of self-managed firms, therefore, should reduce the likelihood of shutdowns that carry so dear a social price.

Yet some recent worker buyouts have failed, seemingly for two reasons: (1) lack of careful feasibility studies to determine a firm's capacity to compete; and (2) lack of knowledge among employees about how to organize a self-managed company so that it cannot be bought by outsiders after it becomes successful. Consider, as an example of the first case, Rath Meatpacking of Waterloo, Iowa. Rath, which had not modernized its equipment under its conventional management, sustained a loss of $14.6 million in 1972 and was consistently in the red from 1975 through 1978. In 1979, the workers decided to provide the equity capital to keep the plant afloat, and they were able to buy it in June 1980. Although the union and workers cooperated energetically to turn the business around, the effort failed; the meat-packing market is extremely competitive, and Rath required not only top management skills but modern technology to survive. The lesson: industry overcapacity and a turbulent market can thwart even a highly motivated and skillful attempt to save a company.[27]

The experience of the Vermont Asbestos Group teaches a different lesson. The original owner, General Alkaline and Film (GAF), announced it would close the Vermont mine because it was worried about the remaining reserves and the need to install antipollution equipment required by the Environmental Protection Agency—a $1.25 million outlay. Within ten days, the president of Local 388 of the Cement, Lime and Gypsum Workers Union called a meeting to discuss a buyout. The final financial package included a mix of state and federal guarantees, a GAF mortgage, and 2,000 shares priced at $50 each, and in 1975 the workers took possession. They experienced quick financial success but were soon quarrelling over board representation and access to information from the board. The new firm had been organized as a conventional business, with shareholder power based on the amount of money invested at the time of purchase rather than on the principle of one person, one vote; since these amounts differed for each individual, voting rights were unequally distributed. A wealthy local contractor was subsequently able to buy out the company because some disaffected employees were willing to sell him their shares. In this case, the initial employee buyout could be described as an economic success but a social failure, since the employees succeeded in averting a shutdown but did not have adequate instruction on how to organize and operate a self-managed firm, and consequently ended up back where they started from.

Both problems can be resolved by private (or state) agencies providing employees considering buyouts with professional consultant assistance in making feasibility studies and in organizing a self-managed company that can operate in both their short- and long-range interests.

2. *Self-managed companies maintain local stability and keep capital flowing to the community.* Although plant closings by absentee-owner corporations are especially noticeable, they are only one element in the relationship that such corporations have with localities. Absentee corporations also tend to exploit the financial resources of the community and to draw capital away from it. Self-managed firms can stop this outflow and become a positive force for community development.

The capital outflow problem can be exacerbated and even spell disaster when a plant closure has a ripple effect, as happened in Youngstown, Ohio, where the local steel and tube company shut down. Apart from the 5,000 jobs eliminated, there was an additional loss of 11,199 jobs connected to the steel business. The whole process began with a parent company that did not update its technology and took the loss of its subsidiary as a tax write-off.[28]

But the capital outflow problem goes beyond shutdowns. Absentee-owned companies draw income excessively away from a community and distribute it elsewhere, causing a loss of circulating capital at the local level. Floyd Agostinelli has demonstrated how the export of profits from local chain enterprises in poor city neighborhoods (e.g., McDonald's) results in a major loss of investment capital to the locality; he argues that the pattern is unfair, and that localities with a high incidence of absentee ownership tend to deteriorate. The diminished financial autonomy undermines community cohesion, which permits social ills to proliferate.[29]

The presence of a *significant number* of relatively self-managed companies means that the local government has dependable tax revenues and that other enterprises can gain from the intralocal free flow of capital. Also, as suggested above, companies with high degrees of employee ownership and participation in management are less likely to shut down arbitrarily (or run away to another country or terminate a subsidiary for a tax write-off) and are more likely to maintain a continuing presence in the community, to keep capital circulating there.

In sum, there is reason to believe that higher levels of local employee ownership and control preserve the stability of community life. Policies supporting the growth of self-managed firms could have enormously favorable cost-benefit ratios for the state, not the least element of which is the possibility of reducing taxes.

Still, an overemphasis on employee ownership and participation in management can have its drawbacks; an overemphasis on local control could be regressive and lead to provincialism. The task is to find the right balance between outside and inside controls over the local economy. Many factors are important to consider in developing self-managed firms so that they are able to maintain a healthy commerce with the outside world: for example, recognizing that self-managed companies can be large (nationwide) and yet decentralized in a manner that yields autonomous local controls; making contacts through trade associations; using government resources for overseas marketing and production opportunities; and developing arrangements (e.g., community land trusts) that permit multinational corporations to operate locally in such a way as to protect local interests.[30]

3. *Self-managed companies tend to be highly efficient and productive.* Increasing levels of worker participation in management have greatly profited hundreds, and probably thousands, of companies in the United States. Job-enrichment and participatory-management experiments at Harwood Manufacturing Company, involving 1,000 employees, raised productivity by 25 percent. At the Monsanto Corporation, 150 machine operators and maintenance personnel began a "participatory experiment" that led to a 75 percent increase in productivity. A study of nine companies representing Scanlon Plans showed an average 23.1 percent rise in productivity. There is no question about the overall value of such ventures for companies, even though some have failed and others are controversial. The fact is that companies that have been sincerely interested in collaborating with workers and unions in these experiments have greatly benefited in social and economic terms.[31]

Studies also show a notable improvement in productivity among companies with high degrees of worker participation. Samuel Bowles and his colleagues demonstrate most persuasively at the national level a causal relationship between the structure of labor and management and productivity: an adversarial structure is associated with low productivity, and worker participation at high levels of management correlates with greater productivity. Hence, they argue that a new social contract is needed to include labor in the governance of corporations.[32] Other scholars have also stressed the causal connection. Robert Reich, for one, asserts that increasing labor participation in corporate governance is an important route to higher productivity; this same issue has figured in many studies on Japanese management.[33]

Employee ownership also correlates with increasing productivity. One of the first studies to demonstrate a positive correlation compared 98 fully or partially employee-owned companies with non-ESOP firms. Not only were the employee-owned companies 50 percent more productive than the other companies, but the more of the company the employees owned, the higher the productivity.[34] A larger study, based on a list of 1,400 firms compiled by the U.S. Department of Labor, revealed the same phenomenon: ESOP firms were more productive than non-ESOP firms. The ESOP managers overwhelmingly believed that the plan improved company performance. The most significant finding was that the productivity of the ESOP companies grew at an average annual rate of 0.78 percent, compared with a falloff of 0.74 percent a year for comparable conventional firms.[35]

The ESOP studies have convinced Corey Rosen that employee ownership not only correlates with higher productivity, but also provides many more advantages for a company than worker participation alone. Among other things, employee ownership can attract and keep high-quality, experienced employees in ways that short-term worker-participation experiments cannot, an advantage of considerable importance to some industries. As he sees it, worker ownership can provide an essential synergy without which other factors would not work in leading to higher motivation and productivity. Worker ownership keeps motivating workers; worker participation motivates them for only the life span of the experiment. Moreover, a company's success may depend on introducing new technologies (implicitly, a willingness to forgo short-run earnings for long-run benefit), something that workers may fight against, but that employee-owners can embrace because they see a longer term payoff for themselves.

Various other studies have demonstrated that both employee ownership and employee participation in management are associated on the whole with an increase in productivity.[36] In sum, the evidence is persuasive. What remains to be demonstrated, however, is a causal link between employee ownership and productivity. Some studies suggest that the motivation of employees is increased by a sense of ownership, but show only a statistical correlation with no real proof of a causal relationship. Also, measuring productivity is technically more problematical for firms in the services sector, restaurants, real estate offices, insurance firms, and the like, although such firms are coming to constitute over 50 percent of the enterprise economy. Still, failure to show direct causation between ownership and productivity does not invalidate their correlation.

Another problem is that productivity has a fascination for economists and business leaders because of its relation to the bottom line—that is, profits. This emphasis, as opposed to other values, such as free speech for employees, self-direction on the job, personal development, and social justice, has been questioned extensively by liberal scholars, some of whom conclude that while the accent on productivity as the basis for judging the value of corporate life may be part of the advantages of a business system, it is also a part of the problem.

4. *Company steps toward self-management tend to reduce absenteeism, turnover, sicknesses, and tardiness among employees.* In 1971, when General Motors announced that its Tarrytown plant was about to be shut down, the plant manager approached union leaders to work with him to keep it open. Initial skepticism gave way to joint planning, resulting in a complete turnaround in operations: over the next several years, absenteeism dropped from more than 7 percent to between 2 and 3 percent, and by late 1978, there were only 32 outstanding grievances, down from 2,000. The key to the change was a plan that accented new values: decentralized responsibility, authority, decision making, and accountability.[37] Similar benefits of self-management are evident in the celebrated studies of Japanese firms, which continue to challenge American management today. One of the explanations offered for lower absenteeism and labor turnover and better product quality is that higher levels of self-management within the Japanese work force develop a sense of purpose, belonging, motivation, and meaningfulness in work.[38]

Yet union leaders sometimes resist a company's efforts to develop a harmonious work force as a threat to union solidarity. In their view, getting workers to "identify with their corporate family" diminishes their identification with the union, and the effort to establish good "human relations" is merely a subtle way to destroy union power and maximize profits. And there in fact have been instances when union solidarity declined and unions were destroyed.[39]

Business and labor leaders have suggested that this situation could be ameliorated by improving the resources for consultation (respecting both sides) on the development of self-managed firms; establishing an informational center to gather facts on how both labor and management can benefit in the long run under the right conditions; and devising a long-range plan of cooperative development in constructing self-managed companies. In addition, the government might consider lending its agencies that are engaged in arbitration and conciliation to this process.

5. *Full self-management reduces the likelihood of pilferage by employees and other losses inside the firm.* Before a change to employee ownership at the Saratoga (New York) Knitting Mill, pilferage was a major problem, serious enough to require a guard service. After the employees purchased the plant, the service was terminated, and the incidence of pilferage dropped to zero. Other cost savings were also observed, for example, the reduction of fabric loss. Under conglomerate ownership, apart from pilferage, fabric had been lost predictably through trimming and damage; 1 percent of the total manufacturing cost was regularly budgeted to cover the loss. During the first year of employee ownership, an amount equal to only 0.25 percent of net sales was attributed to loss of fabric, a figure management itself considered significant.

Still other types of savings were documented by the employee-owners. In the textile industry, an average of 20 percent of batches have to be re-dyed because the color is incorrect or inconsistent. Earlier Saratoga management allowed for this with a budget allocation of 3 percent of manufacturing costs; after the employee takeover, the re-dye costs for the first year amounted to only 0.25 percent of sales. In the words of one foreman, "Now that they own the plant, they take care of getting the colors closer."[40]

Business leaders in the United States have been seeking to stop pilferage through legislation that would give their top managers the right to investigate employee lockers and to institute criminal charges against employees suspected of thievery. Pilferage is enormous, but the evidence suggests that there is a better alternative to taking away employees' privacy: providing incentives for the development of self-managed enterprises.

Although these positive effects of employee ownership can be observed in individual cases of self-managed companies, there has not yet been a carefully conducted survey to support a cause-and-effect conclusion. Besides, pilferage could also be a problem in a large worker-owned and -managed corporation, especially if workers have no sense of being personally hurt thereby. For this reason, self-management consultants emphasize the importance of an employee plan for setting aside a portion of the profits for the workers themselves. When employees know collectively about the desirability of an efficient and honestly managed plant, corporate norms are established, and internal surveillance is more easily accomplished.

It is well known that employees in newly formed self-managed firms have a flush of excitement about their new status, behaving for a time with extra care toward one another and with extraordinary motivation. In a later phase, they come face to face with everyday reality, and the old habits return. But based on observations spanning many decades (e.g., of the plywood cooperatives and the Mondragon system mentioned below), which suggest that positive values are maintained, self-management consultants conclude that even with the known fall from initial grace, employee concern for honesty and efficiency holds over time. In any event, additional studies would allow us to estimate more accurately the long-range impact of ownership on inside pilferage and quality control.

We should note, finally, that conclusions about employee honesty and the special care given to the quality of products and services are drawn from observations of only fully self-managed firms. It is likely that they would not hold for big firms with small proportions of employee ownership (without voting rights) or with short-term quality-of-working-life (QWL) projects.

6. *Self-managed companies help foster employees' personal growth and community values.* The experience of democratic participation in the workplace can positively alter people's attitudes and values as well as improve the quality of their work, and some researchers maintain that it can even make a positive change in self-identities. Although this is not universally true, there is a structural tendency for self-managed firms to cultivate a greater sense of personal autonomy and a broader set of human values than are usually found in other firms.

Raymond Russell noticed this tendency when he studied the

worker-owned and -managed trash-collection firms in San Francisco, demonstrated in a high level of teamwork among the workers. Interviews substantiated that the cooperation was based on a sense of mutuality in ownership and of common responsibilities in management that was not present in workers in conventional firms. For example, partners in self-managed firms were more likely than other respondents to agree with the statement, "In my company (or department), if each crew doesn't do their best, we all suffer." They were more likely to say they make an "extra effort" and to describe their relations with co-workers and customers as close and cooperative. A study of an employee-owned and -managed health company likewise revealed that the employees' sense of autonomy and competence increased along with their sense of social bonding.[41]

Indeed, the very symbols of work can change in self-managed companies. At Consumers United Group, an employee-owned and -managed insurance company, the president put his desk in the middle of all the other desks; he said he had no need for special perquisites. The president of W. L. Gore Associates insists that there are no "employees," only "associates," and refuses to give out job titles. At the employee-owned Frost Company, a Michigan manufacturer, every employee was put on salary, replacing the wage structure. At Quad/Graphics, management leaves the plant one day a year to let employees run it, symbolizing their responsibility as owners. The Herman Miller Company's annual report features pictures of all the employee-owners. At American Trust of Hawaii, a special employee ownership day was established to celebrate the employee-owners. Many companies symbolize worker ownership by abolishing special parking places, executive lunchrooms, and other pleasant but often unnecessary management privileges.[42]

At fully self-managed firms, these new structures go further to guarantee constitutional principles, usually attributed to a democratic government, such as free speech and free assembly, sometimes including tribunals in which all employees in the corporate work system are represented on a panel to hear grievance cases. At John Lewis Partnership in London, an employee-owned and -managed firm of 24,000, the company newspapers allow employees to question management anonymously, and specific managers must promptly answer them. These John Lewis employees believe that they can be whistleblowers without fear of reprisal;

free speech and free assembly are considered part of the governing principles of the company.[43]

There is reason to believe that an employee's experience in a firm that encourages democratic participation in the workplace can lead to a greater degree of political efficacy and community responsibility. Carole Pateman, a well-known scholar of worker self-management, has argued that we "learn to participate by participating" and "feelings of political efficacy are more likely to be developed in a participatory environment."[44]

Although the change in corporate style seems to offer greater opportunities for personal development, it does not always work out. Some managements offer mixed messages to employees that create disgruntlement. Managers may tell employees they are owners and talk about common benefits, for example, but keep established perquisites in place, including granting executives special bonuses. Mismatch between talk and reality can result in unhappy returns.

The dramatic changes in performance accomplished by top executives like those at Gibbons and Gore are not simply a natural outcome of an altered structure of work and ownership; they are also a function of personality and leadership style. A departure from traditional roles and relationships can sometimes have untoward results or be detrimental to human relations in a firm. The process of organizational development is actually very complex, with many varied leadership styles emerging, and the transition to a more fully self-managed firm usually requires careful joint planning and thorough study by employees.

The critical point here is that a company in transition is living simultaneously in two competing worlds, and there can be varied negative outcomes. Employees can become overzealous in demanding rights, or management can refuse to recognize the momentousness of the change. Managers must fashion new relationships to workers, who in some cases can remove them from office. The new relationships are best supported by an educational program in self-management.

In certain respects, Edward Greenberg's study of the workers in the U.S. plywood cooperatives of the Pacific Northwest showed very little difference of attitude from that found in conventional plywood plants. There was a common interest in job security and financial gain, and a common complaint about stultifying work routines. "The rhythm of the machinery process imposes a kind of sameness to the actual work found in both kinds of plants." Yet Greenberg did find a difference in the feeling of mutuality and caring and in a concern for the operation of the whole plant.[45]

One final point: differences in attitudes and values among employees in self-managed versus conventional firms are extremely resistant to measurement. This is only partly due to the difficulty of comparing positions and employee experience. The working environment, after all, is only one among many major influences on employees' lives, and perhaps not even as strong as others, such as early childhood, current family circumstances, religion, and politics.

7. *Self-management tends to reduce strikes and a firm's costs of labor-market transactions.* Although studies are lacking on the correlation between degrees of corporate self-management and strikes in the United States, studies from the longer-term experience of European countries show a reduction in the number of working days lost through strikes when firms include worker councils and labor representation on boards of directors. This difference first became evident several decades ago.[46] The evidence suggests that when labor is trained and prepared to participate significantly at top levels of governance in corporations, labor unrest can be significantly reduced. This is one reason that the European Economic Community considered making the West German model of co-determination (50-50 representation of labor and management on corporate boards) a guideline for its members.[47]

Still, the lack of systematic studies on the U.S. experience and some variability in the data on other countries caution against conclusions about a positive connection between self-management and reduced labor unrest. Yugoslavia, where strikes are staged in self-managed firms much more often than in other European countries, could be a case in counterpoint. Yugoslavians assert that the significance of the numerous strikes is lessened by the fact that they last only a few hours, during which time management responds to worker complaints. It is also believed by some that lower levels of education, political requirements for labor participation in management, and government oppression are special reasons for these stoppages. The causes of the strikes are most often external to the life of the corporation.[48] Studies of the outbreak of strikes in the country during the late 1980's confirm this, indicating that most arose in protest against political policies. That finding may be suggestive of what the future holds for socialist states like the Soviet Union that are seeking to take serious steps toward worker self-management.[49]

By contrast, strikes are not a problem for the producer cooperatives in Mondragon, Spain, but it took one short strike at the 2,000-worker firm at Ulgor to awaken workers to the fact that they had to decentralize their pattern of administration. Leaders decided that large companies needed to develop a federal structure that allowed companies to maintain autonomy with their own boards of directors, and it was agreed that autonomous companies should remain at about the size of 500 workers.[50]

The evidence suggests that a reduction in strikes is likely among firms taking deliberate steps toward self-management in capitalist nations. But the continuation of stable labor-management relations may require employee training on how to work together under the new arrangements, and may also require the formation of administrative committees (e.g., a grievance committee or labor tribunal).

A strike in one worker-owned company in the United States illustrates how problems may develop in labor-management relations. In 1975, after five straight years of losses, the Chicago-based Amsted Industries decided to shut down its lathe-making subsidiary in South Bend, Indiana. It seemed inevitable that the 500 workers would be laid off, but union and management worked with federal and local officials to raise $10 million for an ESOP buyout. In the first year, productivity rose 25 percent, workers received bonuses, and the company won the largest contract in its history. A study conducted by the Economic Development Administration found that almost all the employees felt morale had improved, that people were more conscientious about their jobs and had a greater sense of community, and that there was less waste and absenteeism. Everything seemed to be operating perfectly. The union local even contemplated decertification from the United Steelworkers. Then problems arose.

The ESOP had been touted as a substitute for a pension plan, which was dropped in the buyout because of its costs to the company, but employees began to see that employee ownership could not be an adequate substitute. The union's international body filed suit in federal court to recover the conceded funds. Union members were already skeptical of the arrangement because it blurred the distinction between themselves and management, and the loss of the pension fund worsened their attitudes. Furthermore, the ESOP did not give workers the right to influence management policy by voting for the board of directors, and management refused to accede to the workers' request for pass-through voting. Workers were now dismayed by what they believed were half-truths given to them about the ESOP arrangement, and their union leaders began demanding an unlimited cost-of-living allowance, which the company said it could not afford. In 1980, the 300 members of the Steelworkers local struck for nine weeks.[51]

The lesson of this case is that the introduction of self-management into a company requires at minimum an educational program that tells workers the whole story and a structure that accommodates both their interests and management's needs in implementing changes.

8. *Self-management reduces the need for supervisors and thus eliminates many costs of middle management.* In the traditional firm, the foreman is expected to be a coordinator and work scheduler as well as a police officer, ensuring that people work properly. But many studies have shown that middle-level managers and supervisors become less needed in relatively self-managed companies. One of the first cases in which this reduction was noted was that of the Saratoga Knitting Mill. Under outside ownership, the plant employed three janitors. After the buyout, employees kept their own work areas clear and neat, so only one janitor was needed. Samuel Bowles and his colleagues, who have studied the phenomenon at the national level, find the associated cost reduction to be highly significant.[52]

The worker cooperatives Christopher Gunn studied "use significantly fewer supervisors than their conventional counterparts; the average in the co-ops is one or two per shift of 60 to 70 people as opposed to five to seven in conventional firms." He goes on to note that "owner-members are willing to take direct action to solve production problems, and they also perform some of the policing function that supervisors and foremen perform in traditional mills. There is considerable peer pressure among owner-members to perform a job well."[53] Similarly, Greenberg estimates that conventional plywood firms usually have four times as many supervisors as worker cooperatives of the same size. Eliminating middle managers in no way reduces productivity or product quality, for several studies have shown that the plywood cooperatives surpass conventional firms in both respects.[54] On the negative side, introducing self-management techniques can be disruptive. As John Simmons and William Mares report in connection with General Motors' QWL experiments:

> Democratization of the workplace threatens first-level supervisors and middle managers more than any other group. For years they have been taught to keep their noses clean and get the production out. Their rewards were promotions, money, prestige, and perhaps a chance to "kick ass and take names." . . . Increased employee participation strikes at the heart of middle management's professional identity—indeed their very jobs.[55]

General Foods' experimental organization of a new plant in Topeka, Kansas, produced one of the most participatory self-managed (flattened hierarchies) businesses in the United States, and one of the most productive and profitable, but when the company sought to reproduce the experiment in some of its other plants, it met great resistance from middle management. It discovered that this type of change raises a question of identity. Does the position of supervisor become equal to all other positions? If so, supervisors feel that they are moving from a higher status to a lower status. Some consultants have asked whether supervisors should be "kicked upstairs" or eliminated entirely as a job category. General Foods was never able to replicate its successful experiment in its old plants, thanks largely to this kind of resistance.[56]

The lesson of these experiences is that success in self-management is likely to be achieved most easily in new plants and offices. Although major experiments are possible in established concerns, their success may take more time; the process requires a careful review of changes in status among long-time employees. The positive outcome of such experiments, however, points to a largely untried way to reduce some business costs. Consultants recommend that the new practices require more public attention and support for maximum success.

9. *Self-managed companies are more likely to survive in times of recession or depression than traditional companies.* This argument has not been studied extensively, but special cases have been observed with interest. The Pacific Northwest plywood cooperatives are noted for their capacity to live through difficult times, while many of the conventional firms failed. Begun in the 1920's, the cooperatives survived the Great Depression because they made adjust-

ments that traditional companies could not easily make, collectively agreeing on pay cuts, time off, work rotation, and the like. Indeed, their survival helped them corner the plywood market and encouraged other plywood co-ops to develop following the Second World War. They still show higher productivity than conventional firms in the same industry, and their capacity to survive is stronger. Greenberg is one among many observers of this phenomenon.

[Interviewer: Did you ever think of getting out during bad times?] No . . . instead of giving up, you fight all the harder. I mean, if things get tough, you know, why you don't all of a sudden go to work and somebody says . . . notice up there saying plant shutting down tomorrow because we're losing money. Here if we got to that point where it's shut down or something, they call a stockholders' meeting. They'd say, now look if we take a 50 cent an hour cut in pay, we can keep going. Let's have a vote on it. So, we'd keep working. Everybody'd vote for it. We did that once before here a few years back when we had to.[57]

In contrast to the co-op workers, among whom a "strong sense of mutuality, caring, and cooperation seems to come strongly to the fore during crisis times, a seemingly recurrent state of affairs for all of the plywood firms, given the instability of the industry in general," the conventional workers Greenberg studied perceived themselves as almost powerless, being used for the advancement of others and subject to higher-ups' decisions.

10. *Self-management tends to reduce the level of command bureaucracy and to increase the capacity for flattened hierarchies to operate in the interest of employees as well as the firm.* The difficulties of managing excessively large or conglomerate companies have been widely discussed. Yet conglomeration continues apace. The slowly advancing trend toward worker ownership among U.S. firms works against this tendency to expand past the point of effectiveness for two reasons.

First, the fully self-managed company tends to eliminate outside stock purchases, since in most cases employees can only sell their stock back to the firm. In other instances the practice of purchasing companies and building conglomerate structures is slowed considerably by the fact that all the employees must vote together on the sale of a firm. Even where the one-person, one-vote principle is not a feature, high levels of employee ownership by means of ESOPs, in which pass-through voting rights are provided, go far toward stopping financial speculators' excesses.

Second, the organizational structure seems to be less bureaucratized in fully self-managed firms. Joyce Rothschild-Whitt found that in the conventional firm, authority resides in the office hierarchy and in expertise, with work administered through formal rules, direct supervision, a maximal division of labor, job specialization, and a maximal differentiation of income. In the fully self-managed firm, the opposite occurs: authority rests with the employees as a whole, with minimally stipulated rules, an accent on personal authority, limited reward differentials, a minimal division of labor, the generalization of jobs, and a demystification of expertise.[58] As companies move toward becoming fully self-managed, it is reasonable to suppose that they will shed levels of bureaucracy, along with its red tape, impersonality, and other negative trappings.

It seems unlikely that big ESOP firms, with widespread ownership and pass-through voting rights, will move toward conglomeration. A case that bears watching is the *Milwaukee Journal*, which has acquired several other companies and turned them into subsidiaries. When the employees of those companies complained that they were not included in the original ownership plan, the board of directors decided to admit them to ownership on the purchase of shares, which opened the door to their representation on the board as well. Whether the firm will continue to grow and develop a large command bureaucracy with subsidiary employees on the board is problematical.[59]

The experience of many self-managed firms suggests that their employees tend to limit their own numbers to about 500. Once some relatively self-managed firms grew sizable, for example, they were reorganized to provide greater accountability to the employee-owners. Although some of West Germany's co-determined corporations have 10,000 to 40,000 employees, they also have a highly decentralized system of divisional worker councils and shop-level ombudsmen.[60]

We have mentioned that the 2,000 workers in the democratically managed corporation of Ulgor, in Mondragon, Spain, found its swollen bureaucracy to be intolerable and decided to decentralize into a confederation of smaller firms. The new corporation, Ularco, retained centralized functions in marketing and budgeting, but key decisions involving work processes were made in the autonomous firms. We have also mentioned social inventions at the John Lewis Partnership (24,000 employees) in London, where employees can register their complaints anonymously in departmental newspapers and get a direct response from the appropriate managers. Employee-managed and -owned firms seem to have a creative bent when it comes to alternatives to command bureaucracy.

Again, for all the virtues of relatively self-managed companies in reducing excessive bureaucracy, stratification, and differential rewards, and promoting a more egalitarian managerial system, the transition is not easily done. Three problems are critical to consider in the transition process: time, homogeneity, and emotional intensity.

Employees not well trained in self-management can take too much time making decisions in meetings, can become too like-minded, and/or can embroil themselves in differences of opinion that might not exist in conventional companies. Regular two-way communication may be good for morale, but it can also use up more of the workday than memos and one-way commands. Employees in relatively self-managed firms have found that they need to streamline meetings, reduce the number of meetings, and provide representational systems to handle grievances. Some consultants believe that self-managed companies attract like-minded members and hence there is need to cultivate diversity in ethnicity and political opinion while maintaining a sense of corporate community.

The more familial face-to-face relations of smaller self-managed firms may be more humane than the impersonality of a bureaucracy but can also be more emotionally threatening. In a relevant parallel situation, a study of New England town meetings found citizens reporting headaches and developing anxieties in anticipation of the meetings' conflictual character. To alleviate these problems, townspeople resorted to various devices, such as concealing their critical thoughts and minimizing differences of opinion in seeking consensus.[61] One might assume that workers in self-managed firms who experience similar anxieties would likewise resort to avoidance mechanisms of this kind.

Transition toward greater degrees of mutuality in decision making has its risks. While the learning process has begun in conventional firms experimenting with autonomous groups, QWL projects, and quality circles, the next steps can be still more taxing. Today employees in QWL programs are learning how to conduct meetings that can be personally confrontational yet sensitively led. Higher levels of co-management require still more skill training.

The lesson for corporate and public policy is that, to guarantee successful outcomes, steps toward greater self-management in business will likely require more training in managing intergroup relations.

The Next Step

Both trends—worker participation in management and employee ownership—were featured in *Business Week* cover stories in 1989, with a positive outlook given to both. The magazine judged that employee involvement was "sinking into the core of Corporate America," and that employee ownership represented "a time of change that could take its place in history." Corporate America, it seemed, was "rushing headlong into something that was, only a few years ago, almost universally unthinkable in executive suites: giving up billions of dollars' worth of equity—and crucial margins of power—to their work forces." [62]

The eventual outcome of these two trends could be an entirely new democratic enterprise, called by some the "worker cooperative" and by others the "labor-managed firm." Experts may not agree on an operational definition for this ideal type, but it is clearly part of the logic of the future. Louis Putterman has defined this type of firm as

an enterprise in which ultimate discretion over all matters lying within its field of choice—e.g., what products to produce in which quantities (and at what prices) to produce and sell in a market economy; how to organize the production process; what contracts to enter into with suppliers, customers, lending institutions, etc.; how to allocate net revenues; and even what decision-making procedures to adopt—is in the hands of the firm's personnel, with each member having an equal vote regardless of what skills or managerial rank he or she may have. [63]

Many economists have challenged the capability of the producer cooperative (or the fully self-managed firm) to perform effectively because of its structure, arguing that cooperatives tend to degenerate over time into conventional firms. But there is much evidence to the contrary, some even indicating that cooperatives have a superior economic capability. If I were to suggest here that they also have a greater potential than conventional firms for reducing worker alienation and eliminating the necessity for state regulations, their future seems all the more assured.

It is important to take a look at why economists argue against the high performance of employee-managed firms in the market. Because the literature on this matter is too vast and technical to go into great detail here, I shall simply single out the major issues and how they have been resolved.[64]

First, some economists argue that democratic firms over time tend to employ increasing numbers of workers who are not owners (hired labor), which leads them gradually to degenerate into conventional firms.[65] Although this is true in some cases, many democratic firms have placed restrictions on the use of "hired labor," most notably the French, Italian, and Spanish (Mondragon) worker cooperatives. Indeed, the successful Mondragon system of producer cooperatives, which has been expanding for some 35 years, has managed to exceed the productivity and profitability of the conventional firms in Spain without introducing any hired labor at all.[66]

The way in which property rights are defined in a fully self-managed firm also has important effects on its ability to maintain its unique democratic character, and some economists have argued that there have been problems in those areas. Erik Furubotn and Svetozar Pejovich base their criticism of property rights on a Yugoslavian concept of social property, which recognizes property rights as bundles of rights that can be separated and held by different parties. In this concept, "society" holds the final right to ownership of a firm's assets and rents these assets to the employees. In return for paying interest on the firm's capital and maintaining the book value of the assets in perpetuity, employees have the right to use the assets and appropriate the income from their use without having the right to liquidate the firm. New investments must be taken through collectively owned reserves.[67]

This model of collective ownership fits the legal system of Yugoslavia but does not fare well in the framework of U.S. laws because of the pressures toward degeneration. Jaroslav Vanek has suggested two alternative models that might be more appropriate for the United States. One is a shelter agency for the ultimate ("basic") owners in a federation of self-managed firms. In this case, the ownership is divided: the federation is the basic owner (in place of Yugoslavia's "society"), with the right of ultimate disposal of capital goods; and employees are user-owners, with the right to use the property and appropriate any surplus in perpetuity after paying the basic owner the market rate of return on capital.

In the other model, the basic and user rights to property are combined in the same corporation but are legally separated. New employees of the firm purchase a membership share, and the money is used to set up an individual "savings account" in the firm. This account becomes a source of capital for investment by the firm and is returnable to the employee on retirement. The membership share simply establishes the employee's right to a share of the net book value of the firm's assets; employees' voting rights and right to a share of the surplus are separately vested in them as a function of their work in the firm. This structure eliminates tendencies to degenerate in certain legal environments, for example, the tendency to underinvest and reduce membership or to liquidate the firm when new members buy new individual accounts, and it has been supported by consultants and is operating most effectively in the United States. This does not mean that it is the only type that will be highly competitive with conventional firms, but it is already a proven success under current U.S. business law.[68]

Finally, some economists have claimed that the democratic firm is not as efficient as conventional firms. But these arguments are based on the theoretical assertions of economic models—as in some of the earlier cases we have discussed—that do not meet the tests of reality. For example, Oliver Williamson claims that the cooperative firm is based on a set of internal transactions among its subunits, and the most successful firm organizes these transactions with the least cost. He offers the model of collective ownership in which member income is an average of group output, and strategic decisions are made in a general assembly of employees. His model is also based on the assumption that the firm operates through an information network he describes as an "all-channel network." As the firm grows in size, the increasing number of members and quantity of information lead to higher costs for information processing, communication, and decision making. These costs reduce the "collective's" ability to respond to market changes and make quick decisions, thus contributing to reduced efficiency. Williamson assumes that a pyramidal structure permits a quicker response and reduces the cost of communications, and that the cooperative firm will therefore eventually degenerate and convert back to pyramidal form to compete in the marketplace. He also assumes that the democratic firm cannot fire its employees and has no management hierarchy.[69]

However, the economic model of a "collective" is entirely removed from the reality of worker-managed firms that maintain a "coordinating hierarchy." They are quite capable of firing their employees and meet annually in general assemblies to set basic operating principles, as well as to elect officers to the board. Indeed, worker-managed firms continue to resemble ever more closely the decentralized firm that modern management is finding most effective in the current marketplace. This is another reason why they are likely to fit the needs of the future business market.[70]

Conclusion

There are signs from the union movement, state legislation, and trends toward social (self-) management that the market is developing a solution to Marx's concern over labor alienation. One could also argue that "worker self-management" is a common frontier of change for both state socialism and capitalism, that changes taking place in socialist countries today appear to be moving in the same direction.

The empirical evidence strongly suggests the benefits that would be derived from new government policies supporting relatively self-managed firms. The evidence shows that support for worker participation and worker ownership will help to save jobs, maintain local flows of capital, and promote community development. Firms moving toward higher levels of self-management have the potential to be more productive and efficient, to reduce absenteeism and labor turnover, to curb the extent of tardiness and malingering among employees, and to reduce pilferage. Further, they provide the best structure for employees to develop a sense of purpose and meaningfulness in their work, and have the potential to save money and increase efficiency by reducing the corporate costs of middle management, and the multiple costs of bureaucracy. Finally, the evidence suggests that cultivating self-managed firms can help reduce local social problems with a consequent lessening of the financial burden on government and ultimately the taxpayer. New public policies in support of the trends toward employee-owned and -managed companies should be helpful to corporations, to their employees, and to the economy overall.

CHAPTER 4

The Capital Market:
The Growth of Social Investment

MOST OF US who live in a market economy identify "capital" with money. But at other times in history, capital has meant land, labor, minerals, even machines. For the ever-insightful Karl Marx, the very essence of capital is found in social relationships. In his view, money used simply as a means of payment is not capital; it qualifies as capital only when invested in the purchase of labor power. Similarly, the tool a peasant uses to build a cart to take his wheat to market is not capital but qualifies as such when a laborer uses it to raise tobacco for a multinational business.[1]

A social relationship has always been hidden in capital markets; in the terms of this book, the hidden relationship that Marx attempted to reveal as the true basis of wealth is a latent aspect of the market economy. Although the social character of capital is more complex than he assumed, his recognition that capital was defined by social relationships was the beginning of a revelation that continues today.

Marx's interpretation of capital stood in opposition to the views of the conventional neoclassical economists, who tried to explain the dynamics of capital in terms of a mathematical relationship between the various elements of the economy. Capital consisted of the factors of production—that is, capital (profits and interest), land (rents), and labor (wages)—and these factors were "variables" in a larger model of how money flowed through the system. These economists assumed that under the existing system, everyone received his or her "due": entrepreneurs got their profits, landed gentry got their rents, and laborers got their wages. The prices of land, labor, and capital itself could be explained by their "marginal utility," a formula based on the assumption that no one, capitalist or consumer, will buy a new unit of anything unless its utility exceeds (or is seen to exceed) its cost. In this neoclassical model, the prices of all the factors of production together determined the prices of commodities and the distribution of income.[2]

In the theory of marginal utility, the market mechanism is a natural phenomenon whose allocations can be analyzed mathematically without reference to any other factors. Capital is a homogeneous thing—which is to say, there is something called "capital" that changes and moves about the market while all other factors are constant. In other words, marginal-utility theory assumes that capital can be abstracted and treated as though it were a valid and reliable representation of reality.

Marginal-utility theory is still widely accepted by mainstream economists, and its assumptions may be seen in the behavior of investors and business leaders who each day must make decisions about what to do with their own or their firm's capital. However, the theory has two major flaws. First, abstracted capital cannot be found in reality except as it appears concretely in different stages of product development. The argument that capital cannot be abstracted requires a detailed analysis of economic theory, a task we need not undertake here because it has already been so well accomplished elsewhere. Joan Robinson, for example, has demonstrated that a quantity of capital has no meaning apart from the rate of profit, and therefore the assumption that the "marginal productivity of capital" determines the rate of profit is meaningless.[3]

The other great flaw of marginal-utility theory is that its assumptions do not fit the organizational reality of a market. In particular, the authors of marginal-utility theory ignored the social organization and the independent social processes of the market. As many of the economists today still do, these neoclassical economists ignored the fact that the market functions on the basis of social stratification and such factors as power and prestige, as well as profits and productivity. Capital circulates through the power structure of society just as it seems to circulate through the commodity system, abstracted from society. Furthermore, capital is allocated according to noneconomic as well as economic principles, as we shall see.

The Social Aspect of Capital

Marx and his sympathizers made the point that capital is essentially social power, which in the system of free enterprise of their day they saw as an expression of dominance. But the use of capital for dominance and exploitation is only one of its social aspects. Once we acknowledge that capital is rooted in a social context, we may assume that it evolves differently in each political stage of society.

In feudalism, for example, power resided in the social organization of land, and in industrial capitalism it resided in the social organization of labor and machines. In the postindustrial transition, capital is coming to reside in the social organization of knowledge and in new systems of information.[4] There is also an increasing recognition today that capital can be used to advance the higher ends of society. Indeed, the ideal concept of capital could be compared to Marx's ideal concept of labor. For Marx, labor was a creative activity whose highest purpose was to transform things into products of use and value to society (not the state). Through such labor, workers could express their own humanity. Similarly, capital can be idealized as the creative potential that exists in things, a potential that when used constructively enables the creation of products or services of use and value to society.

Applying these two idealized concepts together, we can say that the market at its best becomes a method of exchange in which labor (an activity) creates capital (a thing) as an expression of society. Thus, labor is potentially a creative activity, and capital potentially a thing of value (or "means"), both of which can be used for the fulfillment of higher values.[5]

At the same time, the reality of the market today must be acknowledged. Capital remains very much as Marx originally conceived it; it is often organized to dominate labor and perpetuate class dominance for the accumulation of private material wealth. Even as we recognize that capital is knowledge, which may be used for a higher end, we must also recognize that knowledge, too, may be used to gain dominance over others. It is important to recognize both the destructive and the constructive uses of capital in whatever form it may take during each period of history.[6]

Thus capital has many purposes, only some of which are utilitarian, measured through greater productivity, efficiency, and material well-being. It can also be used both to advance products and services useful to society and to advance the larger values inherent in a culture, including in our own case such values as individual self-expression, human dignity, freedom, democracy, justice, and equity, and, indeed, the values of self-management and self-regulation. These larger values represent the culture, the hidden wealth of the United States, and capital can be directed toward the fulfillment of these broader values in the corporate structure and in the marketplace in ways that integrate them with the economic values of productivity and efficiency.

But the use of capital for societal ends depends on the way the market is organized. Our knowledge of how capital is socially organized to achieve societal ends therefore makes a difference on how it is allocated in the reality of the market today. In this chapter we will explore how the current allocation of capital leads on the one hand toward destructive ends (in the very sense that Marx once claimed), and on the other hand toward the integrating of utilitarian and societal values in the marketplace. In particular, social investors are beginning to allocate capital with this integration in mind.

In this sense, *social investment is the allocation of capital based on the knowledge of how the market is organized to express societal values.* Although the nature of societal values is still being defined in the practice of social investment, it can be seen as investment in the environment, the earth's resources, world peace, social justice, the quality of worklife, cooperation, and many other broader values that social investors believe must be expressed in the marketplace today.

Yet much money is also being invested badly, because it is going for unproductive purposes and destroying the underlying structure of wealth. Many investors today act as though money alone were the nation's wealth, to be used to make the most money in the shortest time, ignoring the impact of their investments on all other sources of wealth, such as the environment, knowledge, and social organization, while also disregarding the potential of these other resources to advance the larger ends of society. In addition, many companies think they will do better if they spend their money to buy up other companies and expand vertically, even though such large, command-structured companies have been shown to be inefficient.

The relationship between money and the outcomes of its investment in various forms of social organization is crucial to follow. First, the social organization of the market itself is a crucial determinant of what happens to capital as money; the social organization of the investment system itself, for example, can affect how money is invested or misused. The right kinds of social organization can make more money with higher productivity, by decentralizing intracorporate and intercorporate levels of the market. Money, in turn, is itself a determinant of social organization through the manner in which it is allocated. For example, when capital is socially allocated, it shapes the market to create not only more money (one value), but also a different type of corporate system that more fully expresses human values.

Put another way, the creation of new sources of wealth depends not only on the economic organization of the market, but also on its social organization. Knowledge about how the social organization of the market works for and against the fulfillment of values becomes the new capital, and the basis for selecting social criteria to allocate money to improve that organization. This proposition has two assumptions:

1. Knowledge about the way capital is *socially organized* (not merely economically organized) can create more wealth. The social organization of both corporations and investment determines how capital is allocated and thus determines the efficiency and productivity of both individual companies and the economy as a whole.

2. Knowledge about how investment is made on the basis of *social criteria* (not merely economic criteria) can create more wealth and at the same time express societal values directly in the marketplace. The way capital is allocated and invested, both by a company and by outside investors, must go beyond the strictly economistic principles of conventional utility theory. By structuring and allocating capital according to social as well as economic criteria, greater economic and social returns can be achieved for both company and investor.

In short, the wise use of capital depends on its social organization, and the way capital is allocated makes a difference in how the economy functions to increase the wealth of a nation. We shall now apply this interpretation of capital to illustrate how it is used both unwisely and wisely.

The Social Organization of Capital for Inefficiency and Economic Decline

It is increasingly being recognized that the basic problem of the U.S. economy today is the misallocation of capital, or "decapitalization." The subject began surfacing in daily papers and journals

in the 1980's and is now widely discussed in public circles. Economists and business leaders alike declare that the inefficient allocation of capital to nonproductive uses has led to the "defunding of
America," with serious consequences.

Although many examples could be cited, we will focus here on
two major trends that are furthering the wasteful and destructive
allocation of capital in the United States: the whirlwind of investment for short-term profit rather than long-term productivity and
the continued agglomeration of companies into excessively large
centralized firms.

The Rising Investment in Nonproductivity

The primary problem with the investment system in the United
States today is that money is no longer being invested to support
long-term business productivity, but instead is going to whatever
financial deal promises to produce the largest profits in the shortest time. Thus, in every corner of the economy, investment is characterized by a frenzied process of mergers, acquisitions, spinoffs,
leveraged buyouts, buy-backs, and recapitalizations.

Edward Hyman of the Cyrus J. Lawrence investment firm claims
that takeovers and other similar deals cost the economy 0.5 percent
to 1.0 percent of the GNP in 1987 (or 30 percent of our 2.5 percent
growth in GNP). David Teece, a business professor at the University
of California at Berkeley, warns that the future impact may be even
greater. Capital spending and R&D expenditures are on the decline,
according to Peter Jordan, an analyst with Data Resources, who asserts that the downtrend in the latter is a sign of trouble. When
people simply try to prop up share prices by taking on new debt
and doing a lot of financial paper shuffling, they are not engaged in
real production.[7]

In *The Next American Frontier*, Robert Reich noted that in this
spate of "paper entrepreneurialism," vastly more money is spent
on buying existing businesses than on creating new ones. In 1977
American companies spent $22 billion acquiring one another, and
by 1979 they were spending $43.5 billion.[8] Since the publication of
his book, conglomeration has continued at a breakneck pace.

In a related trend, a greater amount of short-term financing than
ever before is going to fund leveraged buyouts. In the first six
months of 1984, a record $6.3 billion was spent on leveraged buy-

outs, nearly five times the amount spent for this activity in all of 1981. By 1986, this record looked paltry: the eight largest leveraged buyouts alone accounted for $22.5 billion. In an attempt to prevent buyouts, companies began spending huge amounts of their reserves to buy back their own stock; from January 1985 through August 1987, $120 billion of stock buy-backs were announced. This trend is clearly impeding corporate growth: over that same period, corporate investment in plants and equipment declined 3 percent.[9]

Furthermore, private capital is increasingly being used for speculation rather than for productive purposes. From 1960 to 1979, financial speculation of all kinds grew from 6 percent of all investment to 33 percent. This phenomenon is considered to be a major cause of the loss of an estimated 38 million jobs in the United States during the 1970's.[10]

Many economists today are wondering whether the current organization of the money market may actually destroy the foundation of the investment system itself. Business executives no longer have the power to determine how their companies' funds are invested, since corporations are increasingly owned by Wall Street firms. Under the leadership of these professional money managers and investment houses, which control more than $1 trillion in holdings (an estimated 60 percent of all corporate stocks and bonds), the historical focus on cornering the market or investing for long-term productivity has shifted to an emphasis on breaking up companies in order to maximize short-term stockholder value.

In the past, clients used to evaluate money managers by their long-range performance; the pressure now is on money managers to outperform the market average every three months, and the new goal is to get the highest returns in the shortest time. Although the usual standard is quarterly earnings, some mutual funds have begun to report earnings *hourly*. Nor does it matter whether these returns reflect the firms' performance or simply come from premiums accompanying their takeover or breakup. Ten years ago, institutional money managers averaged a 21 percent annual turnover in their stock portfolios; the rate is now over 65 percent. Since it seems unlikely that the fundamental worth of so many companies can change that rapidly, money managers must be basing their actions on something else—the hope of making a quicker dollar elsewhere.

This widespread obsession with short-term performance is also affecting corporate executives, who have begun to shape their companies according to this criterion, with detrimental results. Companies are now forced to shorten their internal investment timeframe and adopt tactics that will lead to immediate increases in their stock prices, regardless of what the longer-term effects on their companies will be.

For example, General Motors and Hewlett-Packard, two companies in highly competitive markets, have bought back some of their own stock rather than using that money for internal development that would strengthen their ability to fight U.S. and foreign competitors. Boeing, the Seattle-based aircraft maker, reduced its research and development spending in order to fight a potential takeover by one of the 1980's highest flyers, T. Boone Pickens. Despite its excellent sales and order backlogs, Boeing was considered a good takeover prospect since its concentration on R&D had kept its earnings cyclically low. Cutting those costs allowed its earnings and stock prices to go up, which stopped Pickens but also reduced Boeing's long-term ability to compete against its European counterparts.

Some economists have begun to admit that the investment system in the United States today has become a money game no different from the kind of thing that goes on in Las Vegas. But at least in Las Vegas the house always wins. The tables on Wall Street are not perfectly rigged: not only do small stockholders, workers, and managers lose; big stockholders often lose too—sometimes in huge amounts. The game is much riskier, since its winners have no interest at all in fundamental issues such as the productivity of the firms they so blithely buy, sell, dismember, and recombine, much less in whether those firms are providing society with any socially useful products or services.

The Growth of Large, Centralized Firms

Corporations today are being shaped by two opposite trends—a movement toward greater centralization and a simultaneous movement toward greater decentralization. One reason for the increase in large, centralized firms is the threat posed by foreign competition. Many business leaders believe that their firms must expand in order to advance the technological knowledge so essential to gaining a competitive footing. However, studies suggest that although the trend toward centralization has been important and useful in certain respects, it also brings major problems.

This trend is most evident in the common phenomenon of corporate mergers and the conglomeration of firms. Conglomerates tend to be cumbersome and bureaucratic, bogged down by red tape and often stifling to the very innovation their creation supposedly encourages. Another problem occurs because conglomerates tend to cover a broad spectrum of industries and have no real sense of identity with any one industry area.

The absentee ownership characteristic of conglomerates also carries with it costly consequences. Conglomerate executives in central headquarters are not likely to have empathy for the citizens who live and work in the various localities where their subsidiaries are located. But as we have seen, the decision to close down local subsidiaries that, though profitable, are not making enough profits to fit the conglomerate master criteria can be devastating both to the employees and to the larger community. Moreover, such shutdowns mean added costs to government, which must shoulder part of the burden of repairing the damages.

Still another harmful result of centralization can be seen in the effects of centralized computer systems that contribute to dangerous fluctuations in the stock market. But I do not want to dwell here on the way capital is badly organized and misused. My interest is in clarifying how it can be properly organized for increasing the physical wealth of the nation and promoting the still higher ends that include the advancement of culture.

The Social Organization of Capital for Efficiency and Economic Growth

We have seen how both the misdirection of investment and the growth of large, centralized firms contribute to the inefficient and even destructive use of the nation's capital. Happily, an awareness of social factors and relationships is emerging as a countertrend to guide investment toward more productive ends. We will look first at how the social organization of business can enable it to make the most of its resources and operate more productively and profitably. Then we see how new forms of social organization for investment, as well as new social criteria for investment, can lead to an economy that is better able to allocate its resources in the public interest.

New Forms of Corporate Structure

Improved productivity in a corporation cannot be brought about merely by better equipment or even simply by bringing in new people. Researchers are beginning to discover that productivity and profitability are related to the way in which firms are socially organized. Some economists have even developed the term "organizational capital" to refer to the benefits that result when such structural changes are made.[11] As John Tomer describes it:

Investment in organizational capital refers to changes which are vested in the organization of the firm which are substantially independent of the capabilities of its employees; such changes are expected to result in lasting increases in productivity. This capital formation is brought about by efforts to establish or change the firm's organization, the formal and informal social relationships and patterns of activity within the enterprise. Thus, organizational capital is what an organization has embodied in it in terms of systems, procedures, structure, and interpersonal and intergroup relationships which have been developed in the organization to insure its effectiveness and efficiency.[12]

In other words, the mere bringing together of labor and machines says nothing about a corporation's ability to produce, nor does the amount of money a firm has mean much in terms of results. It is the way people organize to make use of this capital that makes the difference in productivity and profits. Different types of social organization yield different degrees of productivity.

Intracorporate Decentralization and Cooperation

An early example of intracorporate decentralization in the United States was studied by Alfred Chandler in connection with the administrative centralization of several major corporations beginning in the 1920's. The significance of Chandler's work was that the later decentralization of General Motors turned out to be quite effective and productive, and began to serve as a model for other corporations.[13]

It should be noted that the most productive changes are not made through a simple linear process of decentralization. Although decentralization may lead to higher productivity and a better coordination of resources, this most often happens successfully with an appropriate parallel process of centralization. Chandler first noted this interdependence in the efforts of GM President Alfred Sloan to decentralize the company. In 1918, Sloan inherited a "loosely knit federation" made up of Chevrolet, United Motors, and General Motors of Canada. He proceeded to centralize them through an executive committee that formulated long-range policies; then he strategically divided the corporation into autonomous units, each with "decentralized administrative control." This decentralization required a new commitment to the administrative center in order to ensure effective coordination.

Peter Drucker has called today's decentralizing of corporations "federalizing," finding their pattern of transferring greater powers to separate divisions, while retaining a certain degree of authority much like the federal government's relationship with the separate states.[14] The potential of federalizing becomes more real as firms take steps toward allowing departmental and worker representatives from the decentralized divisions to participate at higher levels of management or to sit on the parent firm's board of directors.[15]

The principle of federalizing can apply as well to whole industries. Some social economists have suggested that the corporate system can best be served by a model based on the concepts of a "republic" with "constitutional law." Scott Buchanan, for one, suggests that the analogue of states' rights and the federal principle will provide a useful guide to the future of the U.S. economy. He wants to see the private sector maintained, but with more attention paid to its democratic foundation.[16]

One aspect of decentralization within a corporation is the encouragement of greater worker participation and ownership. As we have seen, this trend has been growing over the last few decades. It began with the setting up of such organizational structures as quality circles, autonomous work groups and labor-management committees; its strongest manifestations appear in companies that have established ESOPs, particularly those that also give their employees voting rights or provide other mechanisms through which workers have some say in the direction of the company.

With regard to increased productivity, we may note that in a 1988 study the National Center for Employee Ownership found that productivity rates increased at a rate of approximately 3.9 percent a year among firms owned by a majority of their employees.

Even a sample of thirteen "publicly traded firms that were at least 10 percent employee owned" outperformed their rivals by 62 percent to 75 percent on such measures as sales growth and return to equity. And in a sample of thirteen once-failing firms that had been bought out by their employees, employment rates grew twice as fast as in comparable conventionally owned firms.[17]

From such evidence, we can conclude that the form of social organization of worker self-management is an example of more effective capital formation. *The capital lies in the social organization of work that yields higher levels of productivity and higher levels of management capacity.* In other words, greater worker participation and ownership are examples of capital formation made possible through social power, that is, the sharing of power.

Intercorporate Decentralization and Cooperation

Competing firms, past and present, often seek to become more efficient and profitable by buying up competitors and integrating vertically. But as we have seen, these vertical giants have not always been as successful as expected. We now look at alternative forms of intercorporate organization that can increase productivity. The place to begin is with technological change, which as Ralph Landau writes,

has been central to U.S. economic growth, both directly (in which case it can be said to account for perhaps 30 percent of economic growth) and through its positive effect on other factors of production (which can be said to account for perhaps another 40 or 50 percent of economic growth). Although scholarly research has not yet provided conclusive evidence, my colleagues and I believe it is in this broad sense that technological innovation is the key to viable strategies for future economic growth: it can raise the factor productivity of the economy at an accelerated rate.[18]

Although many corporations still believe they must become larger in order to improve their degree of technological development, there is increasing evidence that when small firms develop cooperative relationships, they can become equally competitive.

Landau and his colleagues note that the principal sources of technological change and innovation are the R&D units of corporations, trade associations, and universities. They recommend that the manufacturing sector be made a major focus for investment in R&D, because of that sector's continuing importance to the U.S.

economy, and that new technology be connected to market needs, keeping in mind the need to reduce production costs and to improve quality and reliability. They conclude that if innovation is carried out wisely, capital investment can be recovered before competitors begin to imitate the new product.[19]

In view of these considerations, a 1986 study on the competitive advantages of small firms is highly relevant. Walter Adams and James Brock reviewed hundreds of studies that demonstrated the inefficiencies of big corporations and the value of small-sized businesses. For example, noting that the new market realities demand flexibility and speed, they cite a study by the National Science Board showing that firms employing more than 10,000 people produced only 34 percent of all major technical innovations in the United States—proportionately far less than their share of industrial output. They further noted that the smallest firms produced about four times as many innovations per R&D dollar as middle-sized firms, and 24 times as many as the largest firms.

Nor do giant firms display any appetite for undertaking more fundamental and risky research projects. That is, contrary to the image that bigness is conducive to risk-taking, there is no statistically significant tendency for corporate behemoths to conduct a disproportionately large share of the relatively risky R&D or of the R&D aimed at entirely new products and processes. On the contrary, they generally seem to carry out a disproportionately small share of the R&D aimed at entirely new products and processes.[20]

Although economists have long argued against joint R&D because they believe it can lead to organizational difficulties and to collusion that harms the consumer, smaller firms have begun to realize that collaboration can not only pay off, but is a legal method of rallying against foreign competitors. Moreover, such cooperation allows firms to remain small and retain their autonomy.

One reason firms are collaborating more often today is that inventions are so quickly absorbed in the market. Today's inventions constitute "intellectual property" that leaks easily to competitors, and the high cost of being the first innovator is often not worth it. A second reason is that business collaboration and cooperation is characteristic of Japanese industry and an essential ingredient in Japan's competitive success. As a result, U.S. firms that have been hurt by these Japanese practices are now adopting them as useful practices for themselves.[21] Discussing this trend, William Ouchi and Michele Bolton conclude that "a society which fails to fully provide for the creation of multi-firm industry collaboratives will, in a world market, suffer in competition with a society which does."[22]

The value-adding partnership. Up to now, most intercorporate R&D has taken the form of the kind of vendor-customer relationship that has a long history in the United States. For example, a manufacturer of a photolithography tool will work jointly with a manufacturer of semiconductor devices, and the semiconductor firm will then purchase the tools that were developed through the collaboration.[23] But a distinctive new form of cooperation among decentralized small firms, the "value-adding partnership," or VAP, is growing and showing signs of especially successful efficiency and productivity. The VAP idea is based on the concept of the "value-added chain" developed by micro-economics to describe the steps that a product or service goes through as it moves from raw material to final consumption. For example, in the area of packaged foods, a value-added chain would go from farmer to broker to processor to distributor to retailer to consumer. A VAP is composed of a set of independent firms that work together closely to manage the flow of goods and services along the entire chain of production, from supply right through to retail sales. VAPS can occur in any sort of industry or product or service area.

The VAP form of intercorporate organization is especially relevant for the postindustrial economy, since it is based on new communication and information systems. For it is essentially thanks to the development of new low-cost computers, specifically, making it easy to communicate, share information, and respond quickly to shifts in demand, that this new type of organization is possible, and farsighted business leaders are taking advantage of the opportunity. It should also be noted that structures such as VAPS are a central issue of social development, as discussed in Part III, since the balance of power between firms in the value-added chain is critical to developing the power of self-regulation in the market.

Russell Johnston and Paul Lawrence, who have studied the development of VAPS, conclude that they are part of the future. As one example of a VAP, they describe the recent history of the McKesson corporation, a $6.67 billion distributor of drugs, health care products, and other consumer goods. Once a conventional wholesale distributor threatened by vertically integrated drugstore chains, McKesson has transformed itself into the core of a value-adding partnership that is now outcompeting the chains.[24] This transformation began with an entry-order system at McKesson's warehouses based on data-collection devices wheeled around customers' retail stores in shopping carts. By expediting the checking of inventory and the calling in, recording, packing, and shipping of orders, the system dramatically cut the costs of processing orders. In addition, since the system could also specify how to pack orders so that they coincided with the arrangement of customer's shelves, restocking became more efficient.

This use of information technology soon led to other applications. For example, managers realized that the computer could manipulate data to help each retail customer set prices and design store layouts to maximize its profits. They also began using computers to perform accounting services such as producing balance sheets and income statements. Then they discovered that the system could be used to warn retail stores of potentially harmful drug combinations by tracking prescription histories.

McKesson thus offered the independent drugstores many advantages of computerized systems that no one store could afford by itself. The drugstores were able to offer their customers better prices, a more targeted product mix, and better service, all of which helped them stand up against the chains. Still, the drugstores maintained their autonomy, so they could be responsive to the needs of the local area and form lasting ties with the community. This actually gave them an advantage over the chain stores, whose managers had to answer to headquarters and could be transferred from one location to another.[25]

Everyone benefited from the arrangement. McKesson benefited from the success of the independents; the user fees covered the cost of service development plus a return on the investment. The more efficient ordering systems allowed McKesson to reduce its warehouses from 130 to 54, eliminate 500 clerical jobs devoted to taking orders, strengthen its customer base, and reduce the number of shipments per customer while lowering its own and customers' inventory costs. In addition, after the system was introduced in 1976, sales to pharmacies soared from $900 million to over $5 billion in 1988.

But the extension of cooperative ties did not stop with retail store customers. McKesson recognized that the up-to-date information on sales had great value to suppliers (consumer goods manufacturers) as well and began to sell it to them. Suppliers used this information to schedule production more efficiently, streamline their inventories, and make more timely shipments to McKesson. Computer-to-computer ordering from suppliers then permitted McKesson to cut its staff of buyers from 140 to 12. The system gradually grew to the point where McKesson's total network included the manufacturer, distributor, retailer, consumer, and a third-party insurance supplier.

From this example, we can see how the VAP model adds value through the cooperative network and points toward a new type of vertical structure that can successfully compete with the conglomerate. The VAP is both more decentralized and more effective than the command system of a large bureacratic firm.

VAPS are also becoming more evident in other countries. The textile industry of central Italy, for instance, has many successful VAPS. Over the past 25 years, the large, vertically integrated textile mills of the Prato area have been transformed—with one exception—into 15,000 to 20,000 smaller companies. The successful decentralization of this industry began when Massimo Menichetti took over a large, vertically integrated textile mill from his father. At the time, labor costs were rising and foreign competition was intense. To reduce labor costs and match the competition, he needed to be able to create new designs and a greater product variety more quickly and efficiently, which required the capacity to shift production from one product to another without wasting time or materials.

Menichetti believed his company had become too big to adjust to the new demands and proceeded to break it up into eight independent organizations. With considerable vision, he sold between 30 percent and 50 percent of the stock in those companies to employees, allowing them to make the purchases with company profits without putting up their own money. In the meantime, he started a marketing company in New York with the stipulation that it could represent no more than 30 percent of the production volume of the cooperative group he had organized. Within three years, business was both effectively decentralized and highly profitable. Because of its success, other mills began to model themselves after the Menichetti chain of autonomous firms, and small companies with cooperative relationships now cover the entire Prato area.

The ties among this new array of decentralized, closely coordinated independent firms exist not only vertically, with suppliers and customers, but also horizontally, with what would usually be direct competitors. A set of folkways based on reciprocity has emerged in the process. For example, a weaver who underestimates his orders during one season might receive overflow orders from a competitor who guessed right, since they both understand that next year their roles may be reversed, and they know that if they help each other through tough times, they can avoid building overcapacity that could eventually hurt all of them.[26]

These are not isolated examples. Book publishing in the United States has developed the VAP model, its leading competitors having divested themselves of various operations that were formerly vertically integrated. Typesetting, graphics and artwork, and printing are contracted out, and the core function is now brokerage and marketing. The movie industry has been moving in a similar fashion. Gone are the big movie studios that once held exclusive long-term contracts with actors and directors, a full-time staff of composers and scriptwriters, and fully equipped production lots. The new-style studios, which act like brokers who negotiate a set of contracts for a film production, have proved to be more effective than their predecessors. Japanese trade associations also have VAPS that arrange for the buying and selling of goods at every step of the chain, ranging from mines to household consumers and reaching across continents. They are decentralized and never involved in management operations.

Advantages and disadvantages of VAPs. The present competitive structure of the market has many potential drawbacks. For example, firms in a vertical line of competitive selling and buying are generally suspicious of each other's motives. Any firm at any time can engage in some opportunistic behavior and leave the others in the dust. A company may ship poor materials, delay payments, steal employees, start price wars, capture a vital resource, or do a hundred other things that show a lack of concern for both competitors and customers. Since competing companies tend to share as little information as possible, managers often lack important information along the value-added chain.

The typical solution of the capital-rich company in this situation is to buy out its competitors and create a vertically structured conglomerate. This leads to problems we have already discussed, resulting in government regulations. In essence, the conglomerate becomes a liability because of its bureaucracy. It can develop many different troubles, including an incapacity to respond effectively to the market because its bureaucracy has too many functions.

But smaller autonomous firms can divide up these multiple functions and deal with them more creatively. In a VAP, since each small company performs just one step of the value-added chain, it overcomes many of the disadvantages of the conglomerate. It can tailor all aspects of its organization to this single task, leading to low overhead, lean staff, and few middle managers, and it can make and execute decisions quickly without suppressing creative ideas. Each company is free to be different in ways that create the diversity needed for innovation.

At the same time, VAPs have some of the advantages of a conglomerate. Managers take an interest in the success of other firms in the chain because they have a common goal. They share information throughout the chain, coordinate their activities with their trading partners, and secure the benefits of economies of scale by sharing agreed-on services like purchasing, warehousing, R&D centers, and market information.

However, as currently constituted VAPs also have disadvantages, particularly with regard to issues of control. VAPs still exist in a competitive system in which even the advantages of a cooperative network are not enough to guarantee that they will not regress into destructive games with each other. Nor is there is anything to stop a VAP from moving toward anarchy or again becoming a vertically controlled giant corporation. Given these possibilities, Johnston and Lawrence believe that the partners in a VAP must adopt a set of ground rules that generate trustworthy transactions and must establish a climate of working together. Their studies of VAPs suggest that member firms should limit relationships to two to six suppliers of critical items and two to six customers, since too many partners means few repeat transactions and no time for close ties to develop. But partners should also avoid becoming overdependent on one relationship. A company can keep potential partners "on reserve" through occasional transactions so that its welfare will not be harmed if a regular player fails to cooperate. The authors recommend that businesspeople take counsel from social scientists like Robert Axelrod, author of *The Evolution of Cooperation* (1984), who has identified norms that allow cooperating players to be successful in their relationship over the long term.[27]

The value of a business confederation. One especially interesting point for our purposes is that the VAP functions almost like a trade association. As described in later chapters, the trade association is a confederation of firms in which each member has full autonomy, but the association maintains certain constraints by virtue of common needs and disciplines members when necessary through its democratic organization. Since the VAP is only an informal alliance of firms rather than a chartered confederation, its structure can lead to problems. Without the protection of formal norms or written agreements, the system can easily disintegrate. Or if some firms in a VAP have exclusive control over technology, like McKesson, they can come to dominate the organization.

I suggest that an alternative structure that would help strengthen this new VAP pattern of cooperation is a confederation based on a form of mutual governance. In such a model, control over selected aspects of the market organization, such as the use of shared technology, would be maintained jointly by the member firms. The confederation could also set norms for their doing business cooperatively, and establish a tribunal with rights to limited punishment for offenders—the punishment not being so severe as to destroy the offender's capacity to do business but severe enough to persuade members to observe the norms.

This is exactly what is done in trade associations, as we shall see in some detail in Part III. The development of such an associative system, which maintains the independence of member firms while allowing cooperation, constitutes the frontline of development in market organization and points to needed research, since it holds great potential for increasing productivity while at the same time maintaining stable growth in the market economy.

The success of VAPs points to a paradox that must be resolved in the social development of a market. If firms want to find greater independence in the market, they must become closer to one another through cooperation. By sheer competition, firms create the conditions for self-destruction and government regulation. It is a fact of social existence that in order to become more independent as human beings, people must cooperate and become closer to one another.[28]

This reconciliation between seeming opposites among firms can come about through the proper balance between competition and cooperation in market relations. VAPs are delicate structures, like spider webs. Although under their present structure they may easily be torn apart, they nevertheless show potential strength and more real promise for the future than traditional patterns of competition. They are creating norms of cooperation that allow them to compete together with justice for all participants. In Part III, we will explore how these norms based on cooperation can be enforced socially without destroying the autonomy of the member firms.[29]

Social Investment: New Structures and Motives for Investing

According to the manifest definition of the economy, capital is invested toward economic ends, in particular the goal of making the highest profit. However, the economy's latent social traits are beginning to affect the investment of capital, a change that is essential if we are to prevent the cannibalization of the entire economic system.

These new structures for investment are shaped by social as well as economic ends and are characterized by the emergence of workers and nonprofit organizations as owners and allocators of capital. If all goes well, the result may be the increasing investment of capital for the greater benefit of the public interest and the economy as a whole, as well as for the greater self-interest of the particular investors and the firms in which investments are made.

The Stock Market

Because of its recent inefficiencies and damaging impacts on the economy, many observers have offered proposals for how the stock market might be reorganized. Among the most interesting are the revolutionary reforms suggested by Louis Lowenstein, professor of finance and law at Columbia University. Lowenstein says that institutional investors, who control the major portion of the stock market, are excessively speculative; less than 10 percent of stock trading, he estimates, reflects long-term judgments. Most investors behave more like traders than owners and care only about short-term stock-price fluctuations. As a result, stock prices bear little relationship to the actual circumstances and prospects of a company or an industry, and market transactions send very few helpful signals to corporate managers.

These problems have been worsened by the rapid growth of indexing (which encompasses almost 40 percent of all institutional stock investments) and of futures and options. These methods of allocating capital are in opposition to business values, and hence Lowenstein finds the market totally wasteful. As institutions try to outperform one another, trading turnover has reached levels not seen since the turn of the century. Although traders insist that this provides liquidity, Lowenstein counters that the market has too much liquidity and estimates annual trading costs at more than $25 billion.

For Lowenstein, the solution to short-term speculation is to impose a 100 percent tax on all capital gains on securities held less than one year; and the solution to the blatant disregard of investors for the companies themselves is to offer shareholders exclusive rights to nominate a significant share of the company board. The shareholder-selected directors would, it is hoped, be more responsible than today's institutions. Lowenstein's goal is to create a cadre of interested parties who would "act like owners of a local factory rather than holders of a parimutuel ticket." [30]

Although these suggestions are a step in the right direction, I believe they do not go far enough, since they focus almost exclusively on the economic aspects of the stock market and do not look carefully enough at the social aspects of the problem. To restructure the investment process more effectively, both in the public interest and in the interest of individual investors and the companies in which they invest, we must also look at the people who make decisions about how money is invested and at the criteria by which money is invested. If we turn our attention to these social aspects of the investment process, we will discover that several new trends suggest that the latent dimensions of the economy are beginning to emerge here as well.

Employee Control of Investment Funds

Not only is the current organization of capital unproductive, but the ownership of stock is not all that it is claimed to be. The ownership of stock and investment funds is not widely held by the public, as touted by some stock analysts. In 1983, according to one study, fully 80 percent of U.S. households did not own any stock, and less than 10 percent owned portfolios of any value. [31] These statistics demonstrate how stock ownership, the "showpiece" of democracy, is only a façade for a structure in which institutions actually hold the power.

But making the ownership of stock more widespread for consumers is not the solution. A stock market based primarily on individual ownership is anarchic; individuals acting separately cannot exercise real control through voting, because they have no organization through which to communicate their shared values and come to conclusions about how their decisions affect the society as a whole.

More important, we have seen the problems that result from the fact that the stock market has now become largely a gambling place. A way must be found to reorganize the structure of investment so that owners of stock are once again seriously interested in the welfare of the companies they own and are not just using investments to make quick money for themselves and their beneficiaries by selling and buying at the right time.

The majority of funds in the stock market today are held by such institutional investors as banks, mutual funds, insurance companies, and pension funds. Pension funds alone, which even today represent one of the largest sources of capital in the world, are expected to reach over $4 trillion in the mid-1990's. It is significant that these funds have been declared "delayed wages" by the courts. But in fact, control over the allocation and direction of this money is for the most part separated from the workers who are their true owners.

Some writers argue that this institutional separation of pension funds from the influence of the employees who own them causes inefficiency and the misallocation of capital. Although they do not advocate full worker control over these funds, which would represent simply another class bias not necessarily in the public interest, they advocate much more employee participation in decision making, for two reasons.

First, in one of history's great ironies, corporations have become heavily indebted to the institutions that control this worker-owned capital. Consequently, they are especially vulnerable not only to market fluctuations but also to labor conflicts, since when workers slow down production or go on strike their actions reduce corporate income and make it more difficult to pay off corporate debts. Another irony is that now when workers strike, they are often acting against themselves, because the debt payments ultimately go toward their own retirement. But the connection between workers' capital and corporate performance is so hidden today that most labor leaders do not take it into account when planning job actions.

If employees were more actively involved in making decisions about pension fund investment, these connections would become clearer to labor.[32] Further, giving employees more say over how their pension funds were invested would broaden the basis for making investment decisions in the public interest, since they represent a broader spectrum of the public than bankers and other fiduciaries acting alone on purely economic principles.

The issue here is whether the allocation of capital in the interest of the beneficiaries (workers) should be integrated with the allocation of capital in the public interest. The argument for making this integration legal can be illustrated in the well-known case of U.S. Steel. Professional fiduciaries acting on behalf of the steelworkers invested their pension funds in Japanese steel companies, rather than investing to modernize U.S. Steel itself, because the Japanese investments showed the highest promise of economic returns. This action, although proper and legal, nevertheless strengthened the Japanese steel industry as a competitor with the United States; as a result, the fiduciaries unintentionally helped to destroy the U.S. steel industry and caused the loss of retirement income for thousands of steelworkers.

Many other such cases testify to how the allocation of capital can no longer be justified solely on the basis of highest returns on investment, but must rest on a larger socially based set of criteria that takes into account the public interest. Because of these cases, the AFL-CIO became alarmed enough in 1981 to investigate the possibility of gaining greater control over pension funds and recommended that a tripartite commission made up of representatives of labor, management, and government be set up to make investment decisions.[33] Although this has not happened as of this writing, the national Council of Institutional Investors was organized in January 1985 as an association of investors representing about 30 public and union pension funds, with more than $100 billion in combined assets. Now a peak organization of pension fund managers, it develops and reviews the use of common criteria for allocating funds, and asserts the rights of pension fund shareholders around such issues as the election of corporate boards, "golden parachutes," money managers' fees, and the performance of investments. Social issues are a part of the agenda of this organization.[34]

The need for workers to participate in the control of investment capital has been supported by such business scholars as Peter Drucker. In *The Unseen Revolution* (1976), he projected that by 1985 workers in the United States would own over 50 percent of the nation's corporations through their pension funds. Drucker thought that workers therefore had a right to participate in corporate decision making, and further, that adjustments would have to be made in the "prudent-man rule," which requires that the sole criterion for the allocation of capital must be the maximizing of economic returns on investment on behalf of the beneficiaries.

Drucker could see that pension funds had reached such prominence in the system of investment that they were no longer just one part of the capital market, but in fact *were* the capital market. As a result, if pension fund trustees operated solely on economic principles such as the "prudent-man rule," the economy would soon run out of steam. Instead, Drucker said, pension trustees must become responsible for stimulating new businesses and industry even as they tried to preserve the old. These funds must be invested in the larger interest of the economy as a whole. The first step toward this reform, he suggested, should be the appointment of a board of directors of sufficient public standing to be independent of corporate management. This public and community relations board, which would administer the pension funds, would have strong visible representation by consumers, employers, and the "owners"—the nation's employees themselves. Drucker cited the Teachers Insurance and Annuity Association, which is governed by a board of distinguished citizens elected by the beneficiaries, as one model of an industry-wide public and community relations board. The correct model, however, would require a "radical restructuring of the institution of governance."[35]

The fact that many workers now belong to ESOPs also bears on the investment picture. These worker-owners need to be involved at the national level in making decisions about their pension funds. Some writers suggest that they could be represented on the Council of Institutional Investors and on the tripartite commission recommended by the AFL-CIO, if that is ever established. Beyond this, there is some question of how much of the stock of employee-owned firms should be removed from the public arena. Though some analysts believe that all the stock should be gradually returned to employees in their own corporations, there are two major arguments for keeping some of it on the market. First of all, such stock is purchased by universities, religious institutions, and other nonprofit organizations as a source of income, and they should be allowed to continue supporting themselves in this manner. (At the same time, these nonprofits are learning to make money themselves through entrepreneurial ventures of their own, reducing their dependency on this source.) More important, even employee-owned firms need the larger perspective of outsiders, particularly social investors. People with concerns more far-ranging than the firms' profits need to have influence on their boards, for employee-owned firms are just as capable as others of producing unsafe products and exploiting the environment in their own self-interest.[36]

The transition toward higher levels of social management suggests new roles for trade unions, trade associations, and investors who can aid the development of self-managed firms. Strong trade unions can defend the interests of employees who have not yet obtained voting rights in labor-management councils or corporate boards; strong trade associations can influence their members to establish codes of conduct and safety and to establish tribunals for the codes to be enforced in the public interest; and shareholders can exercise their influence over, and perhaps be represented on, the boards of directors of the self-managed firms. Some consultants have proposed that the employees of such firms should control over 50 percent of the boards of their companies, and that outside investors should have the remaining minority voting rights for their own purposes (e.g., receiving dividends, dealing with social concerns). As with all the proposals mentioned here, new socio-economic and legal research can help to clarify how such issues can best be implemented in public policy.

Socially Responsible Investing

Perhaps one of the most important new trends today is "socially responsible investing," also known as "ethical investing" and "social investing." This field has grown rapidly in the last decade. In the words of *The Social Investment Forum*, the organ of the professional (trade) association of investment managers interested in the practice:

For years, individuals and institutions have reconciled their principal and their principles—with investments that yield financial and social returns. Increasingly, investors express their concerns for peace, human rights, the environment, economic development, occupational health and safety— through investment portfolios that are socially and financially sound. As

Social Investing matures as a discipline, professionals are providing a growing range of positive investment options, from widely traded stocks and bonds to innovative community development strategies. Today, social investment is practiced by the broadest spectrum of the investing public—large and small institutions, state and local governments, individuals of modest means and wealth, and private and public agencies. *Over $450 billion of such "social investments" are now under professional management.* This number includes investments that have been affected by either divestment or legislative action limiting investment in South Africa, and increasingly, investors seek reinvestment options that are socially positive. Interest in the movement is growing rapidly, and funds under professional management with social criteria are experiencing dramatic growth.[37]

Although there was some small interest in social investment in earlier years this social movement began significantly in the 1960's, during a period of unrest in metropolitan areas. Charitable foundations, religious institutions, universities, and other nonprofit institutions began to shift their attention to solving problems in the corporate economy while keeping in mind their own interest in maintaining returns on their investments. Gradually, mutual funds, pension funds, and banks began to enter into the field of social investment by taking ethical and social concerns into account along with financial concerns for themselves.

A major legal concern initially was the "prudent-man" ruling, which came out of a Massachusetts court in 1830 and still influences legal decisions in the field of investment. This historic ruling asserted that trustees of funds must be guided primarily by the economic interests of the beneficiaries and the safety of the money. Many state statutes provide lists of permissible investments (e.g., government securities, first mortgages on land, high-quality bonds) for public monies, limiting the options of trustees. Nevertheless, much research has accumulated around this legal issue, with the result that cautious investors of public monies can now proceed much further than the regulations seemed to suggest.

Social investors employ "social screens" to identify companies that meet the criteria of their clients. They tend to favor companies with good records in occupational safety and health, good product quality, good labor-management relations, QWL programs, fair treatment of women and minorities, employee ownership, contribution to community development, protection of the environment, and the like.

Franklin Research and Development Corporation, an independent investment advisory firm, is one of many dozens of companies that deal exclusively with clients having social concerns. Franklin manages assets totaling approximately $160 million for 230 clients and publishes a newsletter called *Insight*. It is cooperatively owned by its employees and distributes profits in the form of equal sharehold dividends. Table 2 illustrates a "social screen" Franklin uses to allocate funds. It rates companies on a 1-to-5 scale in seven key categories: community impact, products and services, energy sources, employee relations, the environment, South Africa, and weapons. In addition, the company provides special screens for clients who have other concerns.

Firms like Franklin are not alone in this field. Banks and mutual funds are increasingly supplying staff to meet their clients' demand for social investing, and *Business Ethics, Catalyst, Good Money*, The Clean Yield, The Council on Economic Priorities, The Data Center, The Interfaith Center on Corporate Responsibility, and many other "information providers" supply fiduciaries with the wherewithal to create social screens for their clients.

Aside from satisfying investors because it appeals to their ethical principles and moral or social concerns, socially responsible investing is profitable. This has no doubt helped the field to grow as fast as it has. Between 1974 and 1982, the Dreyfus Social Fund Third Century returned 373 percent, compared with 110 percent for the Dow Jones Industrial Index. The Pax Fund's net asset value per share rose approximately 61 percent between 1975 and 1980, a bad period for mutual funds, and in 1983 Pax provided a total return (capital gains plus income) of 22.9 percent. The social accounts of Franklin Research were up over 50 percent from mid-1982 through mid-1983; the Dow was up only 44 percent.[38]

An article on social investing in *Barron's*, the conservative business weekly, noted with great surprise that in the stock market crash of October 1987 ("Black Monday"), three social investment funds did noticeably better than the Dow average. The Calvert Social Investment Fund's Managed Growth Portfolio dipped just 8 percent, as opposed to the Dow's 24 percent plummet in the first week of the crash; the Pax World Fund was down only 8 percent during the period October 15–30, compared with the Dow's overall dip of 15 percent; and on November 4, 1987, the New Alternatives Fund showed a 1.5 percent return for the year.[39]

TABLE 2

Franklin Research & Development Corporation's Criteria for Social Investing

Area of concern	#1 rating	#2 rating
Community	Excels in at least three of the named citizenship areas and thus provides a model for the corporate community	Excels in at least one area of citizenship, participating in programs that meet substantial social needs
Products and services	Markets quality products with an exceptional degree of social usefulness	Has quality products and a demonstrated concern for consumers
Energy	Is non-nuclear and leads in conservation and promotion of alternative energy sources	Is non-nuclear and has taken moderate conservation and efficiency measures
Employee relations	Has no recent major controversies and excels in at least three of the named areas	Has no major controversies and excels in at least one employee relations area
Environment	Takes exceptional initiatives and goes beyond peers in pollution control and hazardous waste reduction	Has a demonstrated strong concern in limited environmental areas
South Africa	Has a formal policy of not conducting business in South Africa	Has no current involvement, either through direct ownership or licensing
Weapons	Has no weapons-related contracts and significantly promotes peace	Has no nuclear weapons contracts and not more than $1 million in other weapons systems

Supporters of social investment suggest that this record of success is due to the fact that social investors pay more attention to the corporations in which they invest.[40] Instead of working with the computer simulations of market data and formulas so favored by most institutional investors, social investors tend to examine each case with great care, which is rewarded by greater accuracy and predictability. But the fact that social investors are making money is not even the point, since anyone who knows the volatility of the

TABLE 2

(continued)

#3 rating	#4 rating	#5 rating
Has a record of active participation, but with no outstanding initiatives	Has only occasional community involvement	Has a poor record, often including insensitivity to community concerns
Product quality and utility are average	Has demonstrated disregard for product quality or safety	Markets products that are arguably harmful to society or individuals
Is non-nuclear and has no record, positive or negative, on energy conservation	Relies on nuclear power for up to 25% of its energy generation	Relies on nuclear power for more than 25% of its energy generation
Has a mixed, average, or indeterminable record on employee relations	Has performed in a negative fashion or substantially below peers in at least one employee relations area	Has poor performance in three or more employee relations areas
Has a mixed record or is not in an industry with substantial environmental challenges	Has a record which includes occasional major environmental controversy or litigation	Has a consistent history of pollution control or other environmental problems
Has no employees or assets but sells non-strategic products through licensing or distribution agreements	Operates with a positive employment record in South Africa but is not a part of a strategic industry	Operates in a strategic industry in South Africa
Has non-nuclear contracts less than $50 million or 5% of sales	Has nuclear contracts less than $10 million or non-nuclear over $50 million, equal to 5% to 50% of sales	Has more than $10 million in nuclear contracts or has more than 50% of sales from weapons activities

stock market knows how easy it is to lose. The point is that investors are *not losing money* when they use social criteria and invest in accordance with what they believe to be in the public interest as well as their own. In sum, combining social and economic criteria can produce a synergy for both social and economic development.[41]

CHAPTER 5

The Private Market:
The Growth of a Social Sector

OBSERVERS TELL US that the market economy is no longer characterized primarily by agriculture and manufacturing, but rather by services and nonprofits. While the terms "service" and "nonprofit" are overlapping and each alone does not connote a major change in the structure of the economy, together they appear to represent a significant new development within the private sector; that is, they represent the first stages in the growth of a "social sector."

The private sector is popularly distinguished from the government sector by being based on individual self-interests. But these "private" interests rest on a social foundation, and nonprofit and service firms are beginning to manifest that fact as a latent dimension of the economy.

I use the term "social sector" in its analytic meaning to refer to the private sector as grounded in symbolic interaction and human organization, that is, assuming that the private market has a social orientation. The degree to which the private sector has this orientation is not yet fully understood by the public because of long-standing popular beliefs that business is grounded in an economically oriented system ruled by profit making, subject to the natural laws of competition, and needing government regulation. But as the nonprofits and services expand, I think "social sector" will become a more appropriate term than "private sector" and will slowly enter the everyday vocabulary. I am therefore using this analytical (social) perspective of the private sector as a basis for interpreting its future.[1]

As we shall see in later chapters, much of the private sector has already become socially regulated without government controls, through folkways, customs, mores, corporate contracts, organizational norms, interorganizational agreements, trade association ethics, nationwide standardization practices, collective bargaining, and norms that encourage the development of countervailing powers. Although many social relationships between organizations control the market apart from competition, few people see this fact because of the common belief that government regulation of the market is the only way to achieve control in the public interest. One reason for examining the private sector as a social phenomenon is to clarify how the market may become a more self-regulating system.

We will see how the nonprofit and service sectors of the post-industrial economy are changing the market in ways that can help develop new grounds for social self-regulation. For example, the exchange relationship of *professionals* and *clients* in the post-industrial economy tends to be closer and qualitatively different from that which existed between *manufacturers* and *consumers*, just as the relationship between the nonprofit corporation's *staff* and *members* is fundamentally different from the profit corporation's *labor* and *management*. This sector offers the potential for closer interpersonal connection, and less hierarchy and dominance between these opposing roles. These changes do not necessarily mean that things will get better but, through them, people may have greater opportunity to observe the market as social rather than as based primarily on economic laws, as a system created by their own actions, a system of human design that is susceptible to social governance through their own organizations.

That we are in transition to a postindustrial economy is hardly in dispute, thanks to the work of Daniel Bell and other scholars.[2] The changes have not meant that competition is reduced or that the operative economic factor is diminished, but they do suggest that the values of competition and the role of the producer, so singularly visible in the industrial economy, must now share visibility with those of cooperation and the role of the consumer. I believe the new structures require these changes in visibility. Furthermore, in the postindustrial economy, people should become increasingly oriented to noneconomic values, again not all for the better, although some values (e.g., health, safety, nutrition) can become a basis on which people can begin to compete directly in the interest of the consumer and also begin to cooperate in the public interest.

The Nonprofit Sector

If you do not like the profit sector, David Rados observes, it is possible to fill most of your life's needs by relying solely on non-profit organizations.

You can be born in a non-profit hospital that is managed in turn by another non-profit hospital chain, receive medical care from a non-profit health maintenance organization, bear all your education in non-profit schools or at the hands of the state, and be buried by a non-profit burial association in a non-profit cemetery. It is possible to eat at non-profit restaurants; buy food, clothing, furniture, auto repairs, and appliances from consumer co-operatives or thrift shops; buy gas, water, and electricity from municipal utilities; talk over a cooperative telephone system; ride on city-owned buses and subways; live in apartments owned and operated by housing associations or in a commune that has organized itself as a non-profit corporation; relax at public beaches and in public parks, visit historic sites, borrow books from a library, and attend concerts, plays, operas, ballets, and lectures given by or sponsored by non-profit corporations. Should you run afoul of the law, you may be represented in court by a legal aid society; and should you lose, other organizations stand by to help you return to society. If you are interested in correcting a social wrong through the courts, non-profit organizations may provide lawyers and money. It is not prudent to purchase equities in non-profit organizations because they cannot pay dividends to their owners; but you can have a buy or sell order executed on a non-profit stock exchange, buy insurance from mutual insurance companies, and place your savings in mutual savings banks. Your credit may be rated by a non-profit credit bureau. You can borrow money from a credit union. You can watch non-commercial television and listen to non-commercial radio, read news from the wires of a non-profit news service, subscribe to non-profit magazines and newspapers, watch sports provided by the schools, play golf at a non-profit country club or on a city course, and fly to an overseas vacation on state-built airplanes on government-owned airlines. You can drink at social and fraternal clubs and gamble at church bazaars. And, of course, you can work for non-profit organizations, which taken all together are diverse enough to need and find room for almost every skill and inclination. If you choose to work in the profit sector, you may join a non-profit trade or professional association, and you may contribute money or time as a volunteer to charity.[3]

No one knows the actual number of nonprofits. The national list in the *Encyclopedia of Associations* runs to almost 1,500 pages. Howard Oleck estimates that, in 1971, Ohio alone had 30,000 charters for nonprofit corporations and 100,000 for business corporations, and suggests that a ratio of one nonprofit to every two or three profit corporations seems to hold for most states.[4] But the nonprofit *corporation* is only one of five legal forms that a nonprofit organization can take. Adding in the other legal forms, Oleck concludes that there may be almost as many nonprofit as profit organizations. Because Ohio is in many ways a typical state, his figures may apply nationwide.

Nonprofit organizations come in all sizes. Some are huge, like the Teamsters Union with 2 million members and the Boy Scouts with 3.9 million; many are middle sized, like the National Woman's Christian Temperance Union with 250,000 members and the American Civil Liberties Union with 275,000; and others are very small, like the American School Band Directors' Association with 982 members, the United States Deaf Skiers Association with 150, and the American Catholic Esperanto Society with 53.

The nonprofit sector continues to increase its share in the U.S. economy. In 1929, the sector (including government institutions) accounted for 12.5 percent of all goods and services purchased; by 1963 it accounted for more than 27 percent. In the same period, its share of the labor force climbed from 9.7 percent to about 20 percent.[5] Since then, these organizations have simply proliferated. By 1980, those in the private sector alone accounted for 5.5 percent ($123 billion) of national income, 7.5 percent ($116 billion) of total income, and 9.2 percent of total employment. In constant 1972 dollars, their per capita operating expenditures increased 70 percent from 1960 to 1980.[6] The private nonprofit sector is clearly growing faster than the rest of the economy.

Experts on nonprofits suggest, however, that their significance is not to be found in employment and income figures so much as in their impact on people's lives and their vital role in shaping the values of society. Although this argument is hard to evaluate because of the difficulty of measuring the sector's intangible factors, what is interesting for our purposes is to see the relationship between the profit and nonprofit sectors: they are like brothers and sisters within the larger family of social exchange in the social market. It is clear that *the business system could not survive without the nonprofit sector to support it.*

The Different Classes of Nonprofits

According to Oleck, nonprofits take five forms: the *individual enterprise*, where a person makes charitable contributions and receives tax deductions; the *partnership* of two or more people (although this form is rarely seen among nonprofits); the *association* (or *society*), which does not have a charter but is still formally organized with a united purpose; the *nonprofit corporation*, which operates with a charter and tax benefits; and the *foundation*, which organizes an endowment and receives contributions to carry out the plan of a founder and give away money.[7]

It is hard to draw a line between profit and nonprofit corporations because the legal definitions differ from state to state, but in general the distinction is based on two criteria. First, the nonprofit corporation cannot share its profits the way a business does. There are usually no owners, or shareholders, there are never any dividends, and managers and workers do not have an exclusive claim on residual products—that is, the current money flows and nonmonetary benefits—that are otherwise available in business firms. The law permits "reasonable compensation" to members, officers, managers, and employees. The concept of profit, although critical, is difficult to define. One definition refers only to direct tangible monetary returns on investment or payments from income; another includes indirect monetary benefits such as savings on food expenditures by members of a consumer cooperative, the appreciation of works of art owned by museums, and the monetary benefits gained for a firm in the toy industry made possible by its trade association.

Second, nonprofits are defined by their purpose and activities. Certain activities are prohibited. Nonprofits cannot devote any substantial part of their activities to political lobbying and can avoid taxes only on income generated in pursuit of their specific social purposes. When they are dissolved, they cannot liquidate their assets and pay their owners; the assets must be given to another tax-exempt organization. These prohibitions are important to keep in mind as we distinguish this sector as a part of the social foundation of the economy manifestly different from business.

The nonprofit organization's purposes are described under various legal categories—charitable, scientific, educational, recreational, social, cultural, political, civic, governmental, trade, professional, and religious—thus differentiating it from a corporation organized primarily for economic reasons.

These legal categories seem clear enough, but the line can blur in specific cases, as for example when a church receives great economic benefits from its bingo games, or when a university reaps profits from its football program. This leads us to the thorny issues of latency in our theory of the social market.

Social and Economic Differences Between Profits and Nonprofits

The nonprofit and profit sectors are legally designed to keep distinct what I describe conceptually as socially oriented and economically oriented corporations. The socially oriented (nonprofit) sector includes all corporations whose incorporators set forth noneconomic reasons for organizing. That would seem to be sufficient demarcation, but close examination reveals an intricate relationship between the social and economic factors as latent and manifest dimensions of the emerging economy. Careful scrutiny will be the task of future researchers, but let me suggest some preliminary points to look for here.

Interinstitutional relationships. The popular focus on the economy as only the profit sector prevents us from seeing the interlocking relationship that the economy has with the nonprofit sector, a relationship that is important for assessing the latent and manifest dimensions of the market system. In fact, *business is supported and maintained by the nonprofit sector.* Most experts on the economy would say that business could not operate without nonprofit trade associations; without them, the economy would become chaotic, like a political system without political parties. Labor historians also note that it would be difficult for the business economy to function without nonprofit labor unions protecting the interests of working people, since labor unions are responsible for the wage structure, safe working conditions, pensions, and a hundred other factors that have become a standard part of the business economy.

Furthermore, most people still do not realize that the nonprofit sector owns a huge share of the country's corporate stocks, which is to say, a huge share of the profit sector; or that the control of the greater part of these holdings, in the form of pension funds, now lies partly in the playing field of workers. This still-latent power to influence the business economy is sure to become manifest, or public, in time.[8]

The nonprofit sector is rooted latently in economic foundations, just as the profit sector is rooted latently in social foundations. Although nonprofits are socially motivated, economic motives play a vital role in their operations. Consider some of the economic advantages they count on from government: they pay reduced postage for bulk mailings; are sometimes granted the power of eminent domain and freed, in some jurisdictions, of the obligation to contribute to unemployment compensation funds; pay no customs on art imports. Under common law, they are free of tort liability. And under Public Law 480, a nonprofit organization can even obtain surplus farm commodities free for distribution overseas, with the federal government paying the shipping costs. In forty states, nonprofit hospitals can issue tax-exempt bonds to finance construction. It is important to understand that *corporations have economic incentives to become socially oriented.*

The formal and informal structures of nonprofits. All of this does not overrule the fact that the nonprofit organization's primary motivation is social—in principle, at least. The formal structure of a nonprofit appears in its legal charter and written statements, where the economic factor is latent. Yet even this formal difference is difficult to assess in specific instances.

Take the Mormon Church, which owns a newspaper, eleven television and two radio stations, a department store chain, and an insurance company, and has a controlling interest in the Utah-Idaho Sugar Company. Or consider the Smithsonian Institution in Washington, which has eight retail shops, a catalog sales operation that grossed about $5.5 million in 1976, and a magazine that earned almost $3 million that year. Such a mix of social and economic structures is evident in many nonprofit corporations.

When does a nonprofit become a profit corporation? Crossovers from a manifestly social to a manifestly economic operation are increasingly being tested in the courts. In a not untypical case, the Internal Revenue Service investigated a hospital in Sweetwater, Tennessee, that first leased and later bought its premises from a doctor whose clinic shared the building. The hospital and clinic bought supplies together, paid each other's utility bills, and sent joint statements to patients. Employees of one also worked for the other, and the hospital lent more than $200,000 on easy terms to a nursing home owned by the doctor. At this point, the U.S. Tax Court ruled that the hospital must lose its tax-exempt status.[9]

The social and the economic may be just as thoroughly mixed in an institution's informal structure. The officers of a nonprofit, for example, may be primarily motivated by salaries and profits, but how are we to measure the strength of these motives in relation to statements about formal purposes? What are fair salaries for the faculty of a private school whose primary interest is research and teaching? At what point does the economic motive exceed the noneconomic motive?

The last question is fairly easily answered in the case of the non-profit corporation organized as a front for a person's own self-interest and profit. Many tax authorities see certain foundations as nothing but tax-exempt personal holding companies. In the 1930's, there were 240 nonprofit foundations. By 1969 the figure stood at 30,000–50,000, and in New York they were increasing at the rate of 100 a month.[10] Clearly, the primary drive for profits has not died with the rise of the nonprofit sector.

The multilevel structure of nonprofits is critical to assessing what role social and economic factors play in the lives of their employees. Say church secretaries and janitors unionize in order to raise their wages. Identifying their motives as primarily social or primarily economic is partly a subjective judgment, that is, dependent on comparative standards. What does custom say is the proper income for janitors or secretaries? Is the judgment made on norms in church beliefs? (The Jesuits take a vow of poverty but may drive collectively owned Cadillacs.) Is it made by comparing church income with the income of other organizations?

In a hierarchically organized institution like the church, the emphasis may well differ at different levels. For example, all branches compete for income, and a foreign branch may or may not be fulfilling its religious mission in the light of the cost to the main office. The concept of a social sector clearly does not eliminate the economic factor's playing a critical role in shaping institutional life.

The balance between social and economic motives. The latent economic motives of a nonprofit organization may vary from mild to intense. The leaders of a church may not be as altruistically inclined as their flock would expect; indeed, they might act in conflict with the organization's chartered purposes, moved by a search for personal power, a quest for corporate prestige, jealousy, or a myriad other things. Thus, the profit and nonprofit sectors can look very much alike at the informal level of organization. Ironically, a profit-based newspaper might be responsible for unmasking the profit motives of the leaders of a putatively nonprofit church.

Put another way, leaders in the informal life of nonprofits are not necessarily more idealistically motivated than leaders in business firms simply because their institutions are formally designed for charitable purposes. In some cases, profit corporations might even function more directly in the public interest than nonprofit corporations. The public perception that the one is based on self-interest, and the other on social interests is not universally true or a simple conclusion.

Moreover, the social and economic factors need to be looked at separately as well as together, since at times the social motive can operate with a destructiveness that may even exceed the destructive potential of the economic motive. For example, the motive force driving some business executives to build monopolies and conglomerates may be power, not profit. The drive for power, an expression of the social factor, can be hidden by the legitimacy of striving for profits. In other cases as well, the profit motive may be incorrectly blamed for exploitation when the power motive is actually responsible. The close connection between these two factors therefore becomes an important part of research in the social market.

The time-frame during which a nonprofit corporation is studied can also make a difference in ascribing dominance to one motive or another. Some observers believe that nonprofits seem to be more economically oriented today than they were some decades ago. Each nonprofit corporation has its own history, which may show periods of rise and decline in the realization of its social goals.

Interfirm competition and cooperation. While nonprofit corporations are latently competitive with other corporations in their field of activity, their manifest emphasis is cooperative. Put another way, it is legitimate, moral, and appropriate for nonprofits to cooperate with one another in the interest of the community, unlike the profit sector, where firms are evaluated for how well they compete. We have already noted that cooperation between business firms is often interpreted as collusion. On the other hand, nonprofit service corporations like the Boy Scouts and the YWCA act together in community councils and community chest drives to raise income jointly, and though religious institutions may compete latently for members, they usually formally work together and avoid open competition.

Membership–ownership–income structure. Nonprofits also differ from profit corporations in their membership, ownership, and sources of revenue, and ultimately in their allegiances. The business corporation legally owes its allegiance to its stockholders— its owners. The nonprofit corporation owes its allegiance to customers, members, and clients. We can illustrate the differences through three distinct types of nonprofits: those that operate in the public interest but function like a business with a need to make their income in the marketplace; those that operate purely as a service to fill members' needs; and those that operate in the interest of society as a whole.

The *public-business nonprofit* receives donations or loans for its public purposes from backers who then have no legal control over the money. Loans are repaid from any surplus or profits, the assumption being that the organization will function in the market like a business and become economically self-reliant. Examples of this type are community development corporations, the Tennessee Valley Authority, Amtrak, the Cleveland Municipal Lighting Company, and the University of Chicago Press. Customers are the primary source of income.

The *common-benefit nonprofit* supplies the special needs of its members, who support it with fees and sometimes services. Examples are bridge clubs, burial associations, consumer cooperatives, and buying clubs. The association is not open to outsiders, and members are the primary source of income.

Examples of the *public service nonprofit*, which fulfills the needs of people in the larger society, are the Red Cross, the American Cancer Society, and the local foundation for the blind. Donations are the primary source of income.

In sum, the rise of the nonprofit organization challenges the idea of a private sector based solely on economically oriented, self-interested enterprises. While it does not follow that nonprofits will operate automatically in the interest of their members or the public since we noted earlier that the social factor can sometimes be an expression of dominance and power over others, and moreover, although nonprofits are not formally designed to operate for profit and may actually emphasize profits in their informal structure, I believe the character of the market will inevitably change as the nonprofit economy continues to develop. The social factor will become more manifest in the private sector, not merely a latent part of the exchange system.

The Service Sector

In the years after the Second World War, with less than 50 percent of the employed population active in agriculture and manufacturing, the United States became the world's first service economy. By 1980, some two-thirds of U.S. workers were in the service sector, with distributive and social services accounting for most of that. Western European countries are making the same transition, with 52 percent of the workers in the European Economic Community and 48.6 percent in the larger set of countries represented by the Council of Europe engaged in services by 1977.[11]

The Definition of Services

Most writers make the service sector part of a three-sector model, along with extraction (agriculture and mining) and manufacturing, but there is little agreement on exactly what is and is not a service. Broadly speaking, "services" refers to exchanges that do not involve tangible objects like machines or furniture, but center on intangibles, like broadcasting news and professional counseling. For most economists, however, the notion of intangibility is not sufficient, because it defines the field by what it is not. They would define services as an activity of one sort or another.

G. B. Thomas finds services characterized by three tendencies. First, their product tends to be "immediately provided" and, incidentally, hard to measure because of its intangibility. Second, the labor tends to be professional, requiring more "social" than manual skills. And third, organizations providing services tend to differ from those in the industrial sectors, since there are nonprofit firms among them, and they tend to be smaller, with more self-employed workers.[12]

Some economists, like Victor R. Fuchs, exclude transport, communications, and public utilities from the list of service industries because their reliance on expensive equipment and complex technologies makes them more capital-intensive than other services.[13] Others suggest that a service is any economic unit that performs an activity for the benefit of another economic unit. A service is thus defined as a "change in the condition of a person, or of a good belonging to some economic unit, which is brought about as a result of the activity of some other economic unit, with the prior agreement of the former person or economic unit." In this definition, services are seen as social, other-oriented, that is, consumer-oriented or consumer-intensive.[14] Still others divide services into two types: consumer and producer services, or what are called final and intermediate services. Final consumer services incorporate entertainment, leisure, personal services like hairdressing, and such nonmarketed services as public education. These services are "final" in the sense that they go directly to the consumer and are not related to the making of a material product. Examples of intermediate or producer services are office cleaning, legal and financial consultancies, and technical design.[15]

The question of distinguishing between producer and consumer services is debated because all services actually exist on a continuum in this regard. G. J. Stigler says that at one extreme, consulting construction engineers serve only business, and at the other, teachers serve in a nonbusiness capacity, with independent lawyers falling somewhere in between, receiving income from both business and nonbusiness clients.[16] But H. I. Greenfield argues that most analysts make this distinction only because it "will facilitate both the description and analysis of an advanced economy."[17]

Because Marxists focus on production as critical to understanding the economy, services seem less significant to them. Indeed, Ernest Mandel declares that services are unproductive. Yet as J. I. Gershuny and I. D. Mills argue, Marx himself made the distinction between productive labor, which produced surplus value, and unproductive labor, which did not. For Marx, domestic labor as traditionally constituted would be unproductive, whereas cleaning services organized as capitalist firms would be productive.[18]

Still another categorization divides services into four groups: distributive services (e.g., transportation and storage, communication, wholesale and retail trade); producer services (e.g., banking, credit, insurance, real estate, engineering, accounting, legal services); social services (e.g., medicine, education, welfare and other government services); and personal services (e.g., hotels, repair, dry cleaning, barber shops, entertainment, recreation).[19]

Not all analysts agree with Daniel Bell's thesis that the rise of the service sector is a postindustrial development. J. Singelmann, for example, claims that the Canadian and U.S. experience was different from that of Western Europe and Asia, where labor moved into services before moving into manufacturing. In Singapore over 60 percent of the population was employed in services as far back as 1920, and services have accounted for over 70 percent of GDP (in constant prices) since 1960, the first year for which reliable data are available; the same shift of labor moving to manufacturing after services has been documented for West Africa. There are historical questions about the interpretation that services followed industry when one realizes, for example, that shipping and retail trade formed central portions of the economies of England, the Netherlands, and Portugal as far back as the eighteenth century.[20]

Dorothy Riddle argues that the Industrial Revolution did not occur in a vacuum but grew on a service foundation. She notes that very large-scale manufacturing was possible only because of transformations in capital markets that made it possible to obtain funds from impersonal sources and to pool investment capital. The timely acquisition of raw materials and distribution of finished goods could not take place without major developments in such service industries as transportation and communication. Of primary importance were the changes created by the services in using the products of manufacturing as opposed to changes in the manufacturing process itself. Thus, services actually fueled the development of manufacturing and continue to fuel the growth of the economy.[21]

Critics have sought to dispel a number of myths about services, for example, that they are less valuable to society than agriculture or manufacturing. Riddle declares virtually the opposite: services are more critical to the survival of society than the other two sectors. Nations can survive relying solely on imported agricultural products, as Hong Kong and Singapore do; and nations can thrive by importing most of their manufactured products, as Egypt does. But no nation can survive without a service sector; there would be no transportation or communications, financial markets, or government structure. Even agricultural economies need the services of public administration, trade, transport and credit.[22]

Another myth is that industry provides a sturdier base for growth and productivity in an economy than services do. This belief lies behind arguments for re-industrialization as the route to restoring the U.S. economy. Some scholars contend, however, that it is just the opposite, that services are leading the economy in new productive directions. Information technology has become a spur to manufacturing, and new design concepts are emerging in the service sector that will return industry to its former growth status. We will explore these issues further in our review of how social factors are embedded in the economics of the service industries.

Social and Economic Differences Between Industry and Services

The service sector's market structure differs from the manufacturing sector's in three important ways. First, manufactured products tend to be produced at a single point in time and consumed at a later point in time—sometimes much later. They also tend to be produced well away from the point of sale. The consumption of output in services, by contrast, tends to be immediate and close by; this increases the importance of the interpersonal factor in the market and also begins to change the picture of productivity compared with industry. Economists say that it is difficult to conceive how to hold a space on an airplane if the service is not consumed or used immediately; it is lost forever, and the waste of the service inevitably repeats itself. A service cannot be observed as a material good waiting at a distance to be consumed, and services that fail to be used immediately add to the overall cost of production. This difference in distance and time also bears directly on questions of customer satisfaction in the immediate market.[23]

Second, because the consumer tends to be close to the producer in the service sector, the exchange relationship is unlike that in the manufacturing sector. The delivery of services often requires direct personal contact between an entrepreneur or employee and the consumer. It is reasonable to assume that this contact increases the level of social consciousness between producer and consumer, and to miss this pivotal role of social interaction is to miss the essence of many service organizations. Furthermore, the activities of service entrepreneurs as producers transcend the mere production of a service, since the service industry tends to produce and sell the service at one and the same time.

The personal interface between producer and consumer suggests that the consumer (client or customer) is active in a transaction in which information is exchanged. Consumer information is the raw material of most service organizations, and key information is often secured directly from consumers. Insurance agents must secure information from clients to provide the best coverage; financial planners must obtain information from clients about income, family composition, age, style of living, and so on. Many service organizations are actually information-processing entities.[24]

Finally, service firms tend to be smaller than industrial firms. Over 60 percent of all service workers are employed in organizations with fewer than 100 employees, compared with just 30 percent of workers in manufacturing. This tendency, which far from being unique to the United States, is pervasive throughout developed economies,[25] also helps bring producer and consumer closer together, though the development of information technology can in some cases create more distance between producer and consumer. Computerized medical testing allows a patient to be at one site and the diagnostician to be elsewhere, and automated banking certainly represents a loss in close human interaction.

Information systems add to the differences between the manufacturing and service sectors. The one is based on persons-to-things, the other on mind-to-mind. As a result, some writers forecast a basic change in the economy. From a historical perspective, the land-based power of the feudal period was replaced by the more powerful machine power of the industrial period, and machine power is now being replaced by the information power of postindustrial society. The information-power market requires a social foundation.

But there is no guarantee that service corporations will remain characteristically small and decentralized. They can be centralized and global as well as decentralized and national. Examples of large centralized service corporations that play a powerful role in world trade include transport, tourism, financial activities, insurance, and business services in such domains as engineering, the law, R&D, and advertising. The structure of the larger of these corporations seems no different from that of the industrial corporation, and the owners of multinational corporations and people in developing nations in particular are not just geographically distant, but a world apart from one another.[26]

Some writers suggest that a service activity itself has a socializing impact on global marketing, since the multinational service firm seems to provide greater attention to the consumer than does its counterpart in manufacturing, even though it is under the same requirement to operate primarily in the interest of the owners. The attention is brought about by customization, local or domestic (host) staffing, and host controls over the branch corporation. These are only preliminary observations, however. Service firms operating overseas have not been studied either systematically or comparatively with industrial corporations in similar circumstances.[27]

In sum, service corporations tend to be closer to consumers than industrial corporations, and have a tendency on the whole to be smaller and more decentralized. There are of course service organizations that are neither; the Bank of America has 91,000 employees, Citicorp 64,000 domestically and internationally, and Sears 450,000.

But large service corporations like these appear to be the exception to the rule. The question is how services can be studied to assess whether their development will create a greater consciousness of a social sector.

Future Directions for Research

Since corporations in the service sector have a special orientation toward solving problems with consumers, it is reasonable to propose that the consumer will become the focus of attention and self-organization in the future, in the same sense that the worker was the focus of attention and self-organization through trade unions in the industrial period.

If this notion is translated into research, it suggests that *in special cases*, human interaction (the social factor) in the service industries should play a more powerful role in the consumer market than the economic factor. A key function of research in this service era could be to determine the extent to which the character of social exchange may affect the economic exchange. Put another way, human interaction in the micro-markets of the service sector (including service producers and their customers) should lead toward greater consumer authority, much as the interaction of manufacturing producers and labor led to a drive toward worker authority in the union movement. Social exchange (rather than economic exchange) then becomes an independent variable defining market behavior in the service sector.

This broad hypothesis can be studied through an analysis of exchange in service markets. For example, researchers will want to know how social relations, as opposed to purely economic relations, shape market prices, demand, and the like. We can suggest hypotheses about what may be found and point in the direction that studies can be made.

The nature of the service act varies markedly, depending on whether the service is related primarily to people or to things and whether the exchange is based on tangible or intangible actions. An increase in services designed to alter the condition of people's bodies (e.g., health care, massage, beauty salons, exercise clinics), for example, would suggest an increase in the frequency of social interaction between producers (as entrepreneurs) and consumers. Some market analysts are beginning to see the social significance of this shift toward services as based as much on the "laws of social exchange" as on the "laws of economic exchange." We may recall, in this connection, the social exchange propositions of George C. Homans (mentioned in Chapter One), who found that the higher the frequency of interaction, the greater the attraction, the greater the likeness of sentiments, and so on. The social factor is latent (unseen) in a market defined formally by economic factors, but this interpersonal relationship should affect the economic laws (e.g., price-supply-demand) in the market.

The extent to which a high social-skills market may lead toward mutuality and greater human reciprocity, rather than to new forms of stratification, must be investigated. We should also investigate whether such a development might introduce new forms of equity between producers and consumers by decreasing the distance between them. Most important to our thesis, we must investigate the degree to which the emphasis on the value of *efficiency and productivity* may be reduced as more weight is put on the social factor, or in other words, how the broader concept of effectiveness (rather than simply efficiency) may be evaluated.

In sum, we must examine the degree to which social relations influence the economic relations that determine market behavior. How might demand, for example, be affected by the interpersonal relationships in certain activities? Will an increase in the businesses involving "people's minds"—in education, human-resource counseling for companies, information services, and the like—intensify types of social exchange as a determinant of market behavior?

An increase in service businesses related to *things* requires the specification of market types to know how social exchange affects the market. The type of social interaction here depends on the way businesses organize their relationships to consumers in such areas as landscaping, banking, and securities. We can expect that services related to things through people directly would exhibit higher degrees of personal interaction determining market outcomes.

An increase in those services that emphasize the customizing of products and services also changes the character of the market. The marketability of services rests in how well they can be tailored to meet individual needs, counteracting the tendency toward standardization in the industrial period, determining and restricting customer options. Furthermore, the standardizing of products was closely associated with geographic distance from the consumer, as well as with corporate power to stimulate demand through mass advertising. In other words, the social organization of many businesses in the provision of services shifts the power to create demand from the corporation back to the customer or the consumer. This tends to create more of a mutuality between buyer and seller, and more consciousness of the social nature of the relationship. I think customization tends to be more characteristic of the service sector as a whole than of manufacturing, though it is also on the increase there.

Customization proceeds along two dimensions: (1) the extent to which services can be customized economically, and (2) the degree of judgment exercised by customer-contact personnel in meeting individual customer needs. The group of services found in the legal and health care fields represents high customization and a wide latitude for service personnel to exercise their own judgment in diagnosis and prescription. In this category, the locus of control shifts slightly from the customer to the supplier (producer) because of the expert role of professionals. Here researchers should find relatively more social distance and imbalance in the relationship because of the power of professionals to determine the outcome. Although some professionals in this category may find it difficult to adopt the client's view or to understand his or her human needs, even within this variable of professionalism the character of the social interaction should still be a significant determinant of market behavior.

I am dealing here with the micro-market and not the governing organizational structure of the service field acting on it. For example, I am not evaluating the ability of the American Medical Association to affect the health market. The AMA's decisions on the number of students to admit to professional schools (supply) and its norms on the propriety of professionals competing through advertising (demand) can have a major effect on prices and other market variables. Such macro-organizational forces can have a greater effect on the market than the structure of social action in the immediate marketplace. However, let us simply note that the micro-level market suggests a shift toward social exchange as an influencer of market behavior that requires empirical study. Services tend to be decentralized, and the producer-customer relationship should become increasingly significant in this market sector, while at the same time the growth of trade and professional associations may assume a greater significance in the macro-economy.

Conclusion

If the nonprofits and services continue to develop a significant presence, they can change the character of the market in the United States. The nonprofit sector contains organizations of a wholly different type, organizations that are manifestly socially oriented, with closer connections to members and clients, and that emphasize cooperation in interfirm relations, and the service sector contains organizations that on the whole tend to be closer to the consumer than industrial corporations, and that are generally small (even though this sector also has some of the largest corporations).

Through the ever-increasing growth of these two sectors, the social orientation of the American economy should gradually become more integrated into public awareness. It should become more apparent that the private sector is actually organized for both social and economic purposes.

However, this development has a dangerous as well as a promising side. The struggle for corporate power is a driving force when corporations compete without rules, and such a struggle will not abate in the social sector without intercorporate rules. Indeed, the struggle for power can become more subtle as it mixes with religious beliefs and political ideologies. A nonprofit religious institution, fraternal organization, trade union, or trade association that seeks to expand its power and dominate others in the name of a social goal can be no less dangerous than a mammoth business seeking only profit. The rise of the social sector therefore means that we must take a new look at the social purpose and structure of the corporation, lest the struggle for power and beliefs become the culture of the postindustrial society.

These observations about the development of the market lead in two research directions. First, research is needed on how the market is governed not merely by profit, but also by its social motives and types of organization, norms, and processes of social exchange. Second, research is needed on how the market can become self-regulating, requiring fewer federal and state laws. Increased knowledge about how the market can regulate itself through nonprofit (trade and professional) associations that bridge corporate self-interest, making it possible for corporations to compete in the public interest, is critical to the further development of the social sector.

Since the market is a system in which social and economic factors coexist, the increase in nonprofits does not eliminate the significance of the system's economic orientation, but it does increase the significance of its social orientation. Although the corporate charters of nonprofits are designed for people to pursue social values, the shift from latent to manifest dimensions in the private sector is subtle, and future researchers can record how these dimensions alternate in their expression in the whole, profit and nonprofit, economy.[28]

The changes in the labor market leading toward more worker participation and ownership demonstrate that the manufacturing sector is also cultivating the social factor. Thus it is becoming increasingly evident that interpersonal relations, human organization, and cooperation are all important in getting the job done throughout the whole economy: producing or buying an automobile is no less a social activity than obtaining the loan needed to pay for it. Furthermore, as fiduciaries increasingly recognize ethical factors in their decision making, the social foundation for the allocation of capital is also becoming more visible.

Viewing the nonstatist sector of the economy as "social" rather than "private," both in professional references and in daily life, can make a world of difference in influencing public policy. As people recognize that cooperation, human organization, and culture constitute a central part of this "private" sector, the creation of societal norms and self-regulatory structures in the market economy should be increasingly legitimated.

The social sector, as the next stage of the private sector, is not simply a visionary construct; it is a fact that can be witnessed by everyone. We know that the market system is grounded in social exchange and norms that operate outside government controls, and that its workings cannot be explained by economics alone.[29] Furthermore, the norms of social exchange that shape the market are constantly changing. In the capital market, private firms constantly generate social norms, such as the organizational rules that govern the stock exchange and the professional rules that govern accounting practices; corporations and unions continuously create social norms to govern the labor markets; corporations continue to create industry-wide norms (standardizing products, formulating ethical principles, etc.) through trade associations that impact the consumer market; and in the international market, global corporations and world banks continue to establish new norms through corporate contracts and professional criteria for investment. This is the social reality that defines the market today for professional observers.

But although the whole market system is social in an analytical sense, it becomes publicly social when people realize that the system is guided by their own norms and not simply by pure economics, government, or natural law. The question for the future is whether this consciousness will extend beyond professionals and be translated into public policy.

PART III

The Social Governance of Markets

Aside from the difference between despotic and libertarian governments, the greatest distinction between one government and another is the degree to which market replaces government or government replaces market. Both Adam Smith and Karl Marx knew this. Hence, certain questions about the government-market relation are at the core of both political science and economics, no less for planned systems than for market systems.

Both political science and economics have been to a degree impoverished by pressing the study of these questions on each other, consequently leaving the questions to fall between two stools. Thus, when political science turns to institutions like legislatures, civil service, parties, and interest groups, it has been left with secondary questions. The operation of parliaments and legislative bodies, bureaucracies, parties, and interests depends in large part on the degree to which government replaces market or market replaces government. Charles Lindblom
Politics and Markets

CHAPTER 6

A Pattern of Cooperation:
Trade Associations

WE HAVE SEEN how the latent social factor is slowly becoming manifest in several key areas of the market economy: in the role of labor, the allocation of capital, and the character of corporations in the private sector. In this part, we will examine another major area in which the social factor is becoming manifest: in the relationships between corporations as they both compete and cooperate with each other, and the ways in which they jointly develop mechanisms through which societal norms begin to influence their actions in the market.

Despite the popular picture of the market as guided totally by economic ends, the fact is that it functions within society, which means that it always serves a broader purpose than the limited goals defined by its own economistically based system of exchange. Society is concerned about what goods and services will be produced, and in what amounts, how they are to be produced, who gets them, and how the market meets the changing conditions of the times. Society also has a set of values by which the market is expected to operate as it carries out the above activities.

Values are what a society considers to be important and desirable for everyone. Although different institutions and subcultures within a society may have some conflicting values, there is an overall consensus on certain values, which tends to hold the society together. Thus, values are the broadest interests guiding the actions of people, in the market system as well as in all other parts of the social system; they are the ideals motivating collective conduct. It was once said that values are like heavenly stars: they are unreachable and untouchable—nonempirical—and yet they enable navigation.

Since values are broad directional principles, they must be translated into concrete norms so that they may be applied to specific areas of society. If the market (like any of society's institutions) does not make sure these overarching values and specific norms are followed in its operations, then some outside entity (or entities) assumes the task. That entity is usually the state.[1] This brings us to the crucial question of how a market can become self-regulated. In other words, how can the market's participants themselves ensure that the norms and values of society enter into and shape their actions?

As we have seen, leaving the competitive market completely to its own devices, governed solely by the principles of economic gain, can and does result in the exploitation of labor, consumers, minorities, and the environment. Where this occurs, government must step in to protect the public interest. But this has its own disadvantages: excessive control and the stifling of initiative, excessive bureaucracy and red tape, and wasteful expenditures on regulatory agencies and personnel. What is wanted, therefore, is some means by which individuals and organizations can themselves bring about the expression of the public interest in the marketplace—a model of social governance in short.

There is a whole range of groups through which the market can be socially self-regulated. These include not only nonprofit trade associations, but also trade unions, consumer associations, environmental organizations, and many other types of voluntary associations, all of which are normally ignored by the classic picture of the competitive economy, although people regularly cooperate through them to make the market operate in their common interests. We will focus in the following chapters on the role of the trade associations (also called "industry associations"), since they offer the most direct and most developed route through which corporations that naturally compete with each other in the market can also work together in the public interest.

Taking as our thesis that *a self-regulating market is one in which people participate through their firms as members of democratic trade or industry associations to set the norms and determine the course of exchange in the market, apart from state regulation,* we will begin by examining how these associations are achieving various degrees of market self-regulation at the present time. Our ultimate goal is to understand how they might be able to bring about even greater self-regulation of the market in the future.

The Historical and Current Role of Trade Associations

Some scholars suggest that trade associations emerged to replace the functions of the merchant and craft guilds of the late medieval period. These "new guilds" had neither the same solidarity and strong norms controlling member behavior as the old ones, nor the deep sense of fraternity. A part of the new culture of free enterprise, they were looser in structure and more permissive of independent action by their members. Admittedly defensive, they provided a means for acting collectively against such outside threats as unions and governments; yet they were also individualistic.[2]

The first trade association in the United States may have been the New York Stock Exchange (1792), but trade associations did not really flourish in this country until the second half of the nineteenth century, when hundreds came along. By the late 1980's there were over 3,800. Today the average U.S. industry association has a staff of twenty-three and a budget of $1.2 million, but many have well over a hundred employees and budgets ranging between $10 and $20 million.[3] Although they are less cohesive in the United States than in Europe, they function powerfully on both continents.

We will examine a set of industry cases from both areas, not to compare their success, but to emphasize the variety of ways in which the market can be regulated through cooperation. The comparison is vital since interfirm cooperation has much more legitimacy in Europe than in the United States, where—as was pointed out earlier—cooperation has a bad name and is often legally tagged as collusion. But even in the significantly less hospitable climate of the United States, there are elaborate patterns of cooperation. One reason we lack documentation on those patterns, I suggest, is that researchers have not yet seen their significance for the future. Indeed, I would argue that the widespread but not always recognized practice of cooperation in the market is the answer to the "mystery" of how an economic system characterized by competing firms already operates to some degree in the public interest. It is the "invisible hand" of cooperation that governs the market in the public interest; cooperation is the latent dimension of the competitive market economy.

Our case studies are the dairy industries of Switzerland, the Netherlands, and the United States and the pharmaceutical industries of the Netherlands, Great Britain, and the United States. In particular, we will look at how industry self-regulation through trade associations combines with government monitoring to re-solve problems relating to prices, output, product quality, advertis-ing, and other areas. But before we turn to that subject, we need some general background on the social organization of industry associations.

The Structure of Trade Associations

Trade associations can be organized in a variety of ways. We will see examples of each type of organizational structure in our case studies. At the simplest level, there are *horizontal trade associations*, which embrace all the members who participate at the same level of an industry: all the milk producers, all the cheese manufacturers, all the grocery retailers. Through horizontal associations, members formulate rules and regulate the market in order to reduce the dele-terious effects of their ongoing competition with each other and protect themselves from outsiders.

Next there are *vertical trade associations*, which embrace all the members of an industry at certain levels (or all levels) of the chain from producers to processors to distributors to retailers. A vertical association in the optical industry would include eyeglass manu-facturers, wholesalers, and retailers. Some vertical trade associa-tions include only some of the levels of the industry, such as pro-cessing and production.

Finally there are *peak associations*, which not only embrace all stages of production, but also include more than one industry. Some peak associations are confederations of horizontal associa-tions and vertical associations in related industries. Others link trade associations in different industries, creating a pyramid of as-sociated industries. The National Association of Manufacturers (representing all U.S. manufacturing firms) and the U.S. Chamber of Commerce (a federation of corporations, trade associations, and local Chambers of Commerce) are peak associations. A peak asso-ciation may also organize to settle problems around a common problem. An example is the American Standards Association, which seeks to standardize products in the interest of both its com-peting members and the larger society.

Some industries have also developed interassociation committees and tribunals to deal with conflict between the territories mapped out by the parent associations, as has happened in the U.S. phar-maceutical industry, where conflicts over such issues as generic labeling between manufacturers (sellers) and retail druggists (buyers) are settled by committees representing both parties. Also, trade associations composed of small firms may settle conflicts with a big corporation through private mediation committees. General Motors and the automobile dealers' trade association, for example, have established an independent tribunal to hear local dealers' complaints and determine whether GM has discriminated unfairly against them according to their contracts.

Trade associations as they exist today should not be idealized as democratic associations acting in the public interest. Despite their democratic charters, they can be dominated and controlled by big corporations in pursuit of their own interests. And in any case, they always advance the "territorial interests" of their own constituencies or industries. Both corporate and trade self-interests are legitimate ends and important to maintain. The critical question is how to do that while also serving the public interest. Later we will discuss how the system can be improved through appropriate public policies. For now, let me simply propose that these associations provide a potential for organizational development in the private sector that serves the public; when properly balanced, the system will work efficiently and reduce the need for government regulation.

The Structure of Competition and Cooperation

Patterns of competition and cooperation in the market exist in all countries. The question is not which pattern is better, but how the two mix in the public interest. An essential factor affecting the nature of this competition and cooperation is the degree of centralization or decentralization that characterizes the way firms are organized.

Table 3 schematizes the various possibilities. In this model, each social process—competition or cooperation—has a "pure form" or "ideal type," which represents the most decentralized possibility. All other forms of the process can be seen as modifications on a continuum that moves to the most centralized form. In the competitive pattern, the "pure form" is the decentralized ideal of "pure competition," the model of thousands of presumably autonomous, competing firms against which the market is studied by mainstream economists. In real life, this model is approximated in markets that are relatively decentralized and in which many unassoci-

TABLE 3

Competition and Cooperation in the Market by Type of Social Organization

Social organization	Social process	
	Competitive pattern	Cooperative pattern
Highly decentralized	Pure competition	Confederation
Semi-decentralized	Monopolistic competition	Multifederations
Semi-centralized	Oligopoly	Federation
Highly centralized	Monopoly	Statutory federation

ated firms compete. Moving toward the semi-decentralized form of competition, we see what the economist Edward Chamberlain described in 1933 as "monopolistic competition": fewer firms than in pure competition, but great differentiation of products in the product line. For example, many stores sell photographs, but each specializes in (monopolizes) a particular kind of photograph.

As we move on to the semi-centralized form of competition, oligopoly develops. The number of firms decreases, and a few dominate the market. Here we begin to see such phenomena as administered pricing and price leadership, which in the United States are considered forms of monopoly or limitations on free enterprise and are monitored by the Justice Department. Finally we reach the highly centralized pattern of monopoly, in which only one firm operates in the market.

The interesting fact is that the social process of cooperation follows the same developmental continuum, but cooperation in the market is largely ignored. Let us follow the pattern of cooperation through its various levels. Here the "pure form" is represented by the completely decentralized trade association, which is actually a democratic confederation of many autonomous businesses organized to advance their common interests. Although member firms still compete, they are also mutually governed to some extent through the association, which acts on their behalf to bargain, negotiate, and sign contracts in selective ways. The association sets norms by determining such issues as fair competition among members, equitable voting arrangements, rules in consumer warranties, and fair employment practices.

Like pure competition, this pattern of pure cooperation only approximates reality. Some confederations are relatively democratic and decentralized, others centralized and controlled by large corporations. In any case, U.S. trade associations rarely bargain centrally with labor unions, as their European counterparts typically do. Nor do they centrally negotiate contracts vertically or regulate their markets in certain areas (e.g., output or price), as some European associations do. Indeed, trade associations in the United States could be taken to court if they engaged in some of the practices of European associations.

Moving to the semi-decentralized area, we find that certain trades have more than one confederation; multifederations often develop around specialized fields. In the United States, the insurance and shoe industries have a number of overlapping confederations operating simultaneously. Each association has a different focus or specialty, and firms are allowed to belong to more than one competing association. Thus, a shoe manufacturer might belong to several different associations, each emphasizing a different and essentially competitive type of shoe. The shoe manufacturer may see its business interests as cutting across these specialty trade areas.

In the semi-centralized pattern of cooperation, we see the pattern of the federation, which has more centralized control over its member firms than the confederation. The decision-making authority on key issues rests in its top board, in the same sense as in a federal government. Finally, in the most centralized (monopolistic) pattern of cooperation, we have a statutory federation—a democratic organization of competing firms that is government-monitored and bureaucratized, and is the only such association allowed in its industry.

Here we see clearly how centralized tendencies differ in the United States and Europe. The competitive emphasis has led toward oligopoly and monopoly in private markets in the United States, but toward centralized associations and statutory federations of trade associations in Europe. In either form of centralization, however, the consequences can be command bureaucracies that become monopolistic, inefficient, and inhumane.

Like the competitive pattern, the cooperative pattern by itself can become oppressive when it becomes part of a bureaucratic state. Associations have sometimes increased their control over the market with government support, moving from confederations to federations to statutory federations, and centralizing their power over member firms through their administrative control at the top. Again, the irony is that a statutory federation can function in a manner similar to a corporate monopoly despite its formal designation as a democratic association.

In short, the thesis to be presented through our cases is that cooperation is a pattern of exchange in the market whose role must be recognized along with that of competition. The unit of study in cooperation is the federative model, while the unit in competition is the single firm. Adding the cooperative pattern to our picture of the market is important for three reasons. First, the model of pure competition does not work by itself; the unregulated market composed of many firms results in high birth and death rates of firms, in cyclical behavior in prices, production, and predatory pricing, and in feudal behavior through conflicts, buyouts, mergers, and finally market concentration, which eventually leads to government control. Second, the competitive market in any case results in confederations of firms that cooperate to advance their shared interests. Third, these confederations of firms, which already exist—weakly or strongly—must be recognized for their potential. They can become new monopolies, or they can become the basis for social self-regulation. We refer to these cases later in a theory of social self-regulation.

The Dairy Industry

Switzerland

Milk is highly valued in Switzerland both for reasons of personal health and for its importance to national economy. Nearly half of all raw milk is processed into cheese (more than half of which is exported); the rest is turned into fluid milk (18 percent), butter (15 percent), cream (13 percent), and other products (less than 10 percent.) About 80 percent of Swiss cheese and almost 100 percent of hard cheese are manufactured in 1,500 or so village dairies, often family enterprises employing only a few people.[4]

The Swiss dairy industry is organized into a variety of categories and levels of association. Swiss milk producers are organized into more than 4,000 local cooperatives, thirteen regional associations of cooperatives, and the Central Association of Swiss Milk Producers (zvsm), a confederation of associations representing all milk producers and, hence, a large share of all Swiss farmers.

In addition to milk production, the local cooperatives and the regional associations are active in milk processing. The local cooperatives, which normally own the buildings and machinery of the village dairies, generally lease the dairies to independent cheese-makers, although about 20 percent are run by the cooperatives themselves. The regional associations operate industrialized dairies that manufacture the whole range of milk products, as well as fifteen factories that account for more than 80 percent of domestic butter production. Most recently, the milk producers' organizations have grown to the extent that they act not only as interest associations but also as business firms. All of these producer associations are democratically organized.

Milk processors are organized into six business associations divided into two large groups. One consists of the cheese manufacturers, with more than 1,000 members in all, organized into a complex system of three interlocked associations, two of which represent independent cheesemakers (the Association of Milk Buyers, composed mostly of village dairies, and the Association of Soft Cheese Manufacturers). The other group, with about 10 to 20 member firms, consists of industrialized dairies: the "Milk Group" of the Association of the Swiss Food Processing Industry, which includes the entire dairy sector, and other associations with rather specialized domains, such as the Association of Box Cheese Manufacturers and the Association of Ice Cream Manufacturers.

Because of its wide and dispersed memberships, the cheese manufacturers' association is divided into many regional subgroups and employs a full-time professional staff. The industrial dairies are more simply structured and delegate official affairs to a lawyer. Both types of organizations—the cheese manufacturers and the industrial dairies—are also democratically organized.

In addition to the above, two leading food retailers, the consumer cooperatives MIGROS and COOP (with market shares of 24 and 15 percent, respectively), engage in milk processing. MIGROS manufactures practically all its milk products in its own dairies, and COOP runs a dairy with a regionally limited trading area.

All these democratic associations represent different interests, often competitive. Producers are interested in high prices for raw milk; processors are interested in a high margin between the prices of raw milk and milk products; and retailers are interested in low prices for consumers. They want to regulate the system as a whole in order to satisfy their interests, and they have agreed to collaborate with the government in regulating certain dimensions, although this has not precluded their competing on specific matters such as the prices of products.

The regulation of quality. The system by which quality is regulated in milk processing illustrates how the Swiss government plays only a limited role in market operations. Milk processing is overseen by four semipublic bodies. The Special Commission on Milk oversees the functioning of the system as a whole, and three Regional Programme Commissions implement it: the Käseunion (Cheese Union), which is charged with quality control and promotion in the domestic and foreign markets; the BUTYRA, which controls the import of butter; and the Milk Commission, which issues binding quality regulations for milk and milk products.

It is significant that the voluntary sector is represented in the semipublic bodies, although somewhat unevenly. For example, the Central Association of Milk Producers is represented in all four regulatory bodies and thus has a unique position in the regulation of milk processing because it has a legal responsibility for administering the system as a whole. The Association of Milk Buyers is represented on all but the Milk Commission. The federal administration—mostly represented by the Office of Agriculture—participates in these bodies in an advisory capacity. Interestingly, both the Käseunion and the BUTYRA are business firms; the former is a joint stock company, the latter a cooperative. They are given exclusive right to buy the products they market from the manufacturers and are thus able to control their respective markets comprehensively.

The powerful role of the private milk producers' associations in the regulation of milk processing is controversial. From their point of view, they are simply acting democratically to represent the interests of their members. Some people accuse them of favoring their own processing plants in the allocation of raw milk, a charge association officers deny, pointing to the right of appeal from their decisions to the high monitoring functions of the Federal Office of Agriculture.

The regulation of prices. Because the milk producers' associations collect virtually all the raw milk, cheese manufacturers have to buy their supply from the associations, with quantities, prices, and terms of delivery set by contracts. This organization of the milk market operates on three levels. At the national level, a long-term skeleton agreement between the Central Association of Milk Producers and the Association of Milk Buyers regulates general conditions in the raw milk market. At the regional level, annually renewed collective contracts between the regional associations of milk producers' cooperatives and the regional sections of the Association of Milk Buyers regulate prices and set various levies to be paid by milk buyers. At the local level, annually renewed contracts between local producer cooperatives and buyers regulate delivery schedules, rent for cheesing facilities, and the like.

The processors' most important contracts are said to be at the regional level. In addition to general rules obliging the parties to observe the legal prescriptions, the contracts are concerned with economic issues contested between sellers and buyers, such as the price of raw milk. In order to become legally binding on both sides, local contracts have to be approved by regional associations of producers' cooperatives. The associations also determine whether the contracts are in line with the regulations of the processing program. New entrants into cheese production first have to go through the producers' associations to get the amount of raw milk they need, and since priority is normally given to existing contracts, the best way to enter into cheese manufacturing is to lease an existing outlet from a retiring contract holder.

The regulation of output. Individual cheese manufacturers are subject to the control of the democratically organized milk producers' associations. All buyers, for example, are contractually obliged to furnish the associations with comprehensive production statistics. On the basis of these statistics, the Central Association of Milk Producers can require processors to reduce their output in response to excess production (e.g., the Käseunion reports that a particular kind of cheese can no longer be marketed at justifiable prices). Dairies are not allowed to change their products without notifying the association, and the association has the final word.

Cheese retail markets vary in degree of regulation from strong to virtually none; the less valued the type of cheese, the less regulated the market. The traditional hard cheeses are marketed exclusively through the Käseunion, and producers are legally required to sell all their output only to it. For other cheeses, some separate marketing organizations also buy up the entire production but without legal mandate; still other varieties have their own marketing agencies, but without monopoly arrangements; and some varieties, mainly specialty soft cheeses, are completely unregulated.

Critics allege that the milk producers' associations curtail the freedom of action of both the individual cheese manufacturers and their associations. They concede that the manufacturers can take part in the administration of regulations as members of the regional commissions and semipublic boards, but in practice, they say, there is little way they can withstand the power and information advantages of the milk producers' associations.

Conclusion. The Swiss milk-processing system secures a continuous supply of milk and milk products irrespective of seasonal variations in production and consumption. Milk regulation, which cost about 800 million Swiss francs in 1985, is covered by state subsidies. Although there have been some complaints about this expenditure, there have as yet been no proposals for a basic change.

The main feature of the system is the central role of private interest organizations and their participation in the implementing of public policy through government agencies. The advantage of the system is the security it provides for producers and consumers in maintaining a dependable supply. One disadvantage may be the loss of freedom evidenced by the imbalance of associational power among participants, and another may be the government outlay for the system, something difficult to evaluate without more detailed comparative studies.

The internal structures of the marketing organizations vary widely and should also be examined further. For example, in the Käseunion, which has a 24-person board of directors, the processors' associations are a small minority, with only two seats, against ten for the Central Association of Swiss Milk Producers. Clearly, studies are needed to determine the extent to which the internal bureaucracy in these associations affects the market, but it is clear that interorganizational cooperation is central to the determination of prices and level of supply in both the domestic and the export market.

The Netherlands

An important distinction in the Dutch dairy industry used to be made between farmer-owned cooperatives and proprietary firms, with each holding roughly equal market shares around 1910. But cooperatives now account for 90 percent of all production.[5] The dairy industry is organized into twelve cooperative trade associations. These cooperatives have four regional dairy unions, which combine with a few individual cooperatives to form a national trade association, FNZ. The small private industry has one national organization and six product-specific associations made up of both private and cooperative firms. Rules are binding only on members in the respective domains, but almost all firms have been organized, so in effect, they apply to the entire industry.

Self-regulation through cooperatives. The most persuasive case for strong overall self-regulation is offered by the Frisian dairy union, one of the four regional unions. It has the largest number of binding rules, and it actively enforces them, for example, by regulating competition for raw materials in regard to price and supply.

All Dutch cooperatives pay members a weekly advance on sales, and at the end of the year, the final price is determined and members calculate their dividends for tax purposes. The cooperatives reportedly developed because processing factories had vigorously competed for suppliers by paying exceptionally high advances. Most regional dairy unions tried to reduce competition by introducing binding rules on calculating advances. The Frisian union has gone so far as to determine the advance centrally every two weeks, and even has the power to determine which farmer should supply which factory. The Frisian union (and other regional unions) also prescribe bookkeeping practices, monitor the accounts of member firms, and regulate their investments. All these social regulations are formulated and enforced privately; at no stage does the government intervene. However, the state charters the private associations, requires them to satisfy a civil code, and supports their internal rules by private-contract law.

The need for such social regulation is explained by the history of the industry, developing as it did out of the fierce competition of factories for milk suppliers, and the lack of trust between the cooperative farmers on the one hand and the factories' directors on the other. The farmers' distrust was due in part to their own lack of expertise and their need to rely on factory managers for knowledge of the trade. In these circumstances, the cooperatives turned to regional associations to control their books and their directors for them.

In addition, a vital sense of social solidarity developed among the farmers, which was strengthened by the possibility of self-regulation. The very strong organization in Friesland can be explained in part by a deep-seated sense of regional identity growing out of the separate culture of the Frisians and a conflict of interest with other regions. State intervention was not necessary in this case because regulatory arrangements were stable and accepted by members.

The regulation of product quality and safety. The need to regulate product quality gave voluntary associations the opportunity to participate more widely in industry self-regulation. In the late nineteenth century, adulteration had become a serious problem in the dairy industry. Some merchants and factories, for example, mixed margarine or water into their "butter." As the industry's reputation began to suffer at home and abroad, the voluntary associations tried to curb these practices. Some of them formed for just this purpose; members would have their products stamped with an identifying mark, guaranteeing content. But competition continued to interfere with these private regulatory efforts, and finally the Butter Act of 1889 brought the state into the picture. State butter regulations, however, were not binding, merely offering state-guaranteed trademarks as an alternative to private trademarks. The industry responded by establishing formally independent Butter and Cheese Control Stations throughout the country, which issued trademarks to firms that voluntarily submitted themselves to the stations' quality control.

Because milk deteriorates rapidly and is easily polluted, factories voluntarily introduced payment based on quality; in 1958, the state made this private arrangement compulsory nationwide. Quality-based payment made testing inescapable, and the regional cooperative dairy associations assumed responsibility for quality control. But once the state had mandated quality-based payment, it wanted more control; the industry opposed transferring authority, and a battle ensued. Preemptively, the dairy associations established a private control arrangement independent of themselves; the state consented to this arrangement and delegated the necessary rule making to representatives of the industry's trade association.

Almost all regulatory functions are now in private hands. Only the regulation of quality-based payments is a semipublic responsibility, but even this is managed by the private agencies registered with the state, and thus the state plays a passive role. All other regulations are created by the industry's voluntary associations.

The statutory trade association. The most important organization in the Dutch dairy industry is probably the statutory trade association (STA). This was created under the 1950 Act on Statutory Trade Associations, which covered a variety of industries. Two types of associations are provided for in the act: those organizing a market sector horizontally and those organizing a market sector vertically. Forty-two horizontal and fifteen vertical associations have been created since 1950, mostly in agriculture, food processing, mining, leather, and shoe making. The dairy industry's trade association is vertically structured.

The legal status of the STAs is somewhat like that of a municipality. Both bodies function under law, can "tax" members with their consent, and may enact, within limits set by a charter, rules that have the force of law. In both the municipality and the association, the central government is represented through its appointment of the chair, but apart from this each is governed wholly by its members. A difference is that the municipal council is elected by the citizens from among candidates nominated by political parties, while the executive board of an STA is made up of representatives nominated and appointed by its component voluntary associations (somewhat like political parties). Since it is the associations that participate on the board, the affiliated individual firms are only indirectly represented. In other words, the STA has a monopoly in its domain and, in the case of the dairy industry, is officially affiliated with all dairy farms. It can collect fees and make binding rules through member consent, and its decisions become public law. In turn, its status is regulated so that it cannot change its structure without formal state approval. The state is represented on the governing board by a full-time chair and a number of civil servants who have the status of observers without voting rights.

The regulation of welfare. Other regulatory activities in industry in general, though not directly related to milk production, are noteworthy for our purposes. For example, all sectors of the Dutch economy have sector associations involved in social security programs, including managing worker's compensation plans. Although rule making in this policy area rests with the state, the private-sector associations have the authority to issue rules, conditions, and prescriptions on implementation that are binding on every employee in their domain.

The Netherlands also has works councils composed of representatives of employers' associations and trade unions, and sector committees mediate when an employer declines to establish such a council. These sector committees are organized by the semipublic Social Economic Council at the request of the relevant employers' association and trade unions; there is one committee for each sector, and the state is not represented on it. Decisions are made autonomously but the committees' financial affairs are controlled by the Social Economic Council. The committees' activities are paid for by the employers' associations and the trade unions.

Conclusion. Regulations within the Dutch dairy industry were instituted at private initiative, arising from the need to reduce destructive competition. Observers suggest that the self-regulation has been effective. Quality control and market rules governing competition for raw materials seem to have improved the industry's economic position. Critics assert that modernization may have been retarded by reduced competition, but supporters of the system argue that thanks to efficient, large-scale production, high quality, tight organization, and effective private-market agreements, the industry has improved its position in the world market. In addition, self-regulation has unburdened the state. Supporters claim that without the private organizations, the state bureaucracy would be much more extensive than it now is. Still, a complex private bureaucracy has also evolved around the state, so that there are almost as many regulatory organizations as there are firms in the industry. So thoroughly tangled are their relationships that the government is pressing for a simplification in structure. Furthermore, as the years have passed, there has been a growing concentration of property and trade. Four firms now dominate the dairy industry, and some quality-control stations essentially work for only one large firm. Critics contend that if this trend continues, the interorganizational system will become untenable.

The United States

Farmers in the United States have a tradition of assisting one another through mutual-aid societies. The entire U.S. dairy industry is characterized by cooperatives, encouraged in part by the Capper-Volstead Act of 1922, which granted agricultural cooperatives partial immunity from federal antitrust laws. Today cooperatives handle 80 percent of the milk produced. J. M. Williams, who studied the Dairymen's League in New York State, a typical dairy cooperative, noted that a feeling of powerlessness because of unaddressed grievances against middlemen and dealers in farm products, led the state's farmers, about 75 percent of whom owned their farms, to organize to improve their lot.[6]

The U.S. dairy cooperatives act like trade associations. They lobby legislators, provide member insurance, advertise to increase demand for dairy products, and disseminate information. They also bargain with milk processors on the price to be paid to producers, represent dairymen at hearings on federal milk marketing orders, and provide for the transfer of milk from farm to factory. Some even take on the processing job.

The regulation of prices. The Agricultural Act of 1949 directed the Secretary of Agriculture to support the price of dairy products by purchasing supplies at a minimum price. For each milk marketing year, the secretary announces what the U.S. Department of Agriculture's (USDA) Commodity Credit Corporation will pay for milk products:

USDA purchase prices are set at levels expected to support the annual average price which plants pay to farmers for manufacturing milk equal to the announced support price. In determining these purchase prices, consideration is given to developments in average processing and marketing margins, relative market prices, production, stocks, consumption of different dairy products, results of recent price support operations, relative volume of purchases, CCC stocks, and utilization in available program outlets.[7]

The USDA reports that farmers are generally "price takers," with manufacturing plants setting the price based on their returns. Smaller manufacturers primarily consider the prices paid by competing buyers. Furthermore, the price system is not the basis for competition:

Plants compete vigorously for raw milk but price competition is generally deemphasized. Rather, competition is through the assembly functions. Examples of competitive practices used occasionally are subsidized hauling, patronage refunds, premiums based on fat solids or a combination of fat solids and nonfat solids, farm supplies sold at a reduced cost, money advanced against future milk checks, group insurance plans, fieldman service for physical improvements such as bulk tanks, market information, and integrity (prompt payment of the milk check over time). The manufacturer offers these advantages in assembly services to help earn the goodwill of producers and assure a steady supply of milk to the plant.[8]

The government influences milk prices by issuing federal marketing orders, under which milk processors are required to pay dairy farmers through their cooperatives a specified price for their unsold milk; it is then processed into such items as ice cream, cottage cheese, skim milk, and powdered milk. By a marketwide pooling agreement, producers receive the same price for their milk whether it is classified as Class I fluid milk or goes into a manufactured milk classification. The government also supports the dairy industry by agreeing to buy cheese, nonfat dry milk, and butter at designated prices. Because the prices of these commodities are tied to the price of milk through the marketing orders, the net effect is to support the price of all dairy products.

It is said that because of government action, the U.S. dairy industry is highly stable, and producers and processors have maintained relatively high returns on investment. Indeed, this agricultural sector stands in contrast to most other sectors, such as livestock, poultry, corn, and potatoes, where cooperatives are not well developed.

Corporate-state controls. Over the past fifty years, fluid-milk processing has shifted from being carried out in thousands of small plants to being carried out in a few large plants. Processors now number only about 1,000 (about one-tenth of their number in the 1930's), and the average plant processes 25 times as much milk. Cooperatives have gained great prominence in the processing field. Similarly, the marketing of packaged fluid milk has shifted from three-fourths home delivery in 1929 to less than 7 percent today, and the supermarket chains now have 13–15 percent of the market. Of course, supermarkets have changed the entire food retailing picture, supplanting the small distributors who were still dominant into the 1960's.[9]

Many critics of the dairy industry declare that big cooperatives and government supports have led to monopoly power. The corporate-state monopoly was facilitated by widespread mergers between 1967 and 1970, when over 170 local cooperatives with some 70,000 members became four multimarket regional supercooperatives. The largest of these, Associated Milk Producers, Inc. (AMPI), was formed in 1969, when fourteen Chicago-area cooperatives merged with Milk Producers, Inc., itself the result of a 1967 merger of six cooperatives from Kansas, Oklahoma, Texas, and Arkansas. AMPI continued to add cooperatives, until by 1972 it controlled over 75 percent of the raw milk supplied to Chicago,

Madison, Indianapolis, Houston, Dallas, San Antonio, Memphis, and Oklahoma City.

Mergers led to the control of the milk supply in other states as well. The second largest regional cooperative, Mid-American Dairymen, Inc., formed in 1968 from thirty-one cooperatives, had over 24,000 members in mid-1971; Dairymen, Inc., formed from eight cooperatives, had over 10,000 members by 1972; and Milk Marketing, formed in Cleveland, Akron, Toledo, and Pittsburgh, continued merging until 1978 and now has over 10,000 members in Indiana, Ohio, New York, Pennsylvania, West Virginia, and Maryland. "As a result of these merges, seven cooperatives can now speak for one-half the U.S. milk supply . . . in contrast to more than one hundred co-ops speaking for the same volume of milk in the same number of markets five years ago." [10]

Critics contend that these associations are now in a position to manage prices in two principal ways. One is *price alignment* across markets. When prices are high enough in a market to bear transportation costs, lower-priced milk will move into that market. Once cooperatives in various markets succeed in aligning or fixing prices in this manner, it is difficult for processors to find lower-priced milk, and cooperative monopoly power is strengthened. The other price-setting mechanism is the *full-supply contract*, by which processors agree to buy their entire supply of milk from a single cooperative. As cooperatives tie up all the major milk processors in such contracts, the ultimate effect is to dry up the market for independent producers. This puts pressure on these farmers, too, to join the cooperative. As the number of independent farmers in a market dwindles, they lose their viability as an alternate supply source, and processors become increasingly dependent on the cooperative for their milk. Processors who thereafter refuse to enter into full-supply contracts or pay monopoly prices can find their milk supply from a cooperative literally shut off overnight. [11]

Conclusion. Critics charge that the USDA has become an empire supporting the monopoly created by these mergers. They argue that federal regulation artificially increases the price of milk, adding anywhere from $500 million to $800 million annually to the consumers' milk bill. Furthermore, federal regulation produces disproportionately large benefits for the wealthiest and largest dairy farmers, and little if anything for the small family farmer. (Big dairy farmers average over $2,000 a year in federal benefits, small dairy farmers only

$135.) Such regulation unnecessarily wastes resources.[12] The USDA response is that it has stabilized milk prices, increased farm income, maintained an adequate milk supply, and improved the farmers' bargaining power.

The Pharmaceutical Industry

The Netherlands

The Dutch pharmaceutical industry has some 70 firms of diverse size, but its 5 multinationals account for 90 percent of production capacity and 80 percent of the 11,600 pharmaceutical workers.[13] The multinationals also do the bulk of R&D on new drugs. Though the industry produces drugs for animal use, we will limit our discussion to drugs for human use and the associations related to them.

A government body, the Ministry of Public Health, is responsible for overseeing both prescription and over-the-counter drugs and regulating their producers. Prescription drugs are dispensed largely through health insurance organizations and closely regulated by the state. (About 70 percent of the Dutch population is covered by the Health Insurance Act; its implementation is delegated to private organizations under the supervision of the government's Health Insurance Council.)

Until 1975, the Dutch pharmaceutical industry had two separate associations, NEPROPHARM for domestic producers of pharmaceuticals and BIPA for importers, both of which were organized together with business associations from other industrial sectors in a legally registered private-sector cartel, the Pharmaceutical Wholesale Trade Union, or PHC, which had considerable regulatory powers.[14] PHC was founded in 1925 because of a pressing need, in the words of the president, "to put an end to the chaos in the pharmaceutical sector . . . there were no norms for the lay-out of factories and for manufacturing standards, there was no control of manufacturing processes and no control of the chemical and therapeutical quality of drugs."[15] PHC was responsible for the approval of drugs, quality control, the regulation of price margins and advertising for the whole trade, and many other issues.

In 1975, BIPA and NEPROPHARM merged into a new association, NEFARMA. When the PHC cartel was dismantled two years later,

NEFARMA developed a new code of behavior to compensate for its loss. NEFARMA is also integrated into a broader associational network, as a member of VNCI, the peak association of the Dutch chemical industry, and as both a direct and indirect member of VNO, the national peak association for all industry. It also belongs to international business associations such as the International Federation of Pharmaceutical Manufacturers Associations (IFPMA), the European Federation of Pharmaceutical Industries' Associations (EFPMA), and the European Association of Major Public Specialty Items (AESGP). To represent their interests as employers, NEFARMA members are also indirectly organized in a separate employer association, WV, via VNCI.

Neither the domestic producers nor the importers of generic drugs are organized into formal interest associations, nor are they involved in private quality regulation; and because of conflicting interests and competition, they are not allowed to join the above-mentioned associations. The two groups have occasional informal meetings to defend their interests against the producers and importers of specialty pharmaceuticals.

Private vs. state regulation. Several critical events and long-range trends led the state to step up its regulation of drugs over the years 1952–83. One important event was the Thalidomide scandal of 1959–62; the use of this narcotic sedative by pregnant women resulted in severely deformed babies in many countries, including 80 in the Netherlands alone. Meanwhile, the European Community was moving toward more restrictions on cartels; in the 1970's, the European Commission found the PHC cartel in violation of the Treaty of Rome. Finally, the arrival of a public system of health care in the Netherlands, as part of the trend toward a welfare state, brought greater state scrutiny.

At the same time, manufacturers were evincing an interest in self-regulation. NEFARMA, which quickly developed into a strong business association with a great influence on public opinion, succeeded in continuing some of the self-regulatory activities of PHC and in introducing self-regulation in new areas, reducing the need for state oversight. By 1980, 92 manufacturers and importers of industrial drugs were members of the association, it had a professional staff of 11, and its budget amounted to about $1.25 million. In 1982, it added a full-time paid president. NEFARMA underwent considerable centralization in this period. For example, subunits for particular interests (e.g., manufacturers and importers) were abolished a few years after its founding, suggesting that organizational unity was more important than differentiation. The association also devised a number of binding rules regulating the business behavior of its members.

The regulation of advertising. Advertising is an important element in the competition of brand-name products, especially where only small differences exist between labels or between new and old products under the same label. On the positive side, advertising can promote superior quality; on the negative side, it can generate misleading information and unfair competition.

Since 1926, advertising for over-the-counter-drugs (as opposed to advertising intended for professionals) has been regulated in the Netherlands by business associations rather than the state. Associations of manufacturers, importers, advertising firms, and publishers of periodicals and newspapers agreed on an advertising code, and set up a private association, KOAG, to enforce it. Any manufacturer or importer of drugs who wanted to advertise had to present copy beforehand to KOAG. It was practically impossible to place an advertisement without KOAG approval because the participating associations obliged their members not to accept advertisements that lacked such approval.

An interesting countervailing power developed in a group of outsiders, the manufacturers and suppliers of "alternative drugs" (i.e., herbal medicines). Since these companies do not belong to any interest associations of the pharmaceutical industry, KOAG could not take any hand in their advertisements; nor could the state, because alternative drugs are not legally recognized as drugs, and consumer organizations concluded that they had little or no therapeutic effect. In these circumstances, the pharmaceutical industry has favored state intervention in this area.

In 1958, when the state moved to regulate overall pharmaceutical quality, it also outlawed misleading advertising and provided for a state inspection board. However, the board was never set up for several reasons. First, there was a constitutional problem; its purview could have been considered a form of censorship, contravening freedom of the press. Second, the European Community was at the time trying to harmonize its members' regulations on advertising, and the Dutch government was waiting for its conclusions. (In the end, the national governments could not come to an agreement.) Third, KOAG was functioning very well in this department, according to public opinion, and was thus best left to carry on.

In 1973, manufacturers and importers introduced a new advertising code that banned misleading advertising and required meeting prevailing standards of good taste, and created the Council for Medicines Communication (RGA) to implement it. The development was not received kindly by KOAG. Among other things, as an initiative of only the manufacturers and importers organized in BIPA and NEPROPHARM, RGA regulation was fully paid for by those interest groups, whereas KOAG regulation also represented the interests of advertising and publishing firms, and the importer-manufacturer contribution was limited to 25 percent. (It makes a difference who pays.) That year, NEFARMA published complaints and recommendations about RGA in its final report.

In 1978, NEFARMA introduced a "Code of Behavior" containing still more disciplinary rules. It combined all the self-regulatory measures of the industry into one set of rules (unlike the separate KOAG and RGA regulations). This was followed in 1983 by the organization of a code committee to handle all complaints about the pharmaceutical industry.

The new code was drawn up only in part because of a need for uniformity among the rules of the various associations and the likely possibility that the state would act on its own. The industry was also reacting to pressures from the international community. Multinationals were selling certain specialty drugs directly to the public in the Third World that were available only on prescription in the West. Furthermore, the multinationals felt free to use simple and misleading advertising overseas (e.g., omitting mention of negative side effects). Criticism of such marketing practices by international consumer organizations and the World Health Organization led to the development of an international code for the pharmaceutical industry.

Conclusion. This case is instructive on several counts. First, we see how "chaos" develops when competition is unregulated; some sort of association must set standards that apply to competing firms, or the state will become the regulatory body for them. Second, we see that although standards can be established, they are most effective when applied to issues of mutual concern among competing members. Third, standards that protect outsiders must then include them in the standard making.

The peak associations sometimes provide the basis for setting up committees that require interassociational monitoring. The extension of NEFARMA's membership into the peak association of the Dutch chemical industry—as a cooperative countervailing power—offers the opportunity to set standards for the chemistry profession. Such professional standards would not normally be created from within the pharmaceuticals themselves. Further, their association with other peak associations, such as the employer association (WV) and the international manufacturers (IFPMA), broadens their responsibility to act with public accountability.

These connections undoubtedly have an indirect effect on conduct, but specific committees are required to implement a code effectively. Even though KOAG did such a good job regulating advertising in the view of the public that the state could not interfere because of constitutional limitations on free speech, it did not apply the same rules in the Third World, so that the World Health Organization and international consumer organizations had to step in. The establishment and enforcement of international codes is currently under review by the United Nations.

This case shows how self-regulatory activities reduced the need for state regulations. But it also suggests that the democratic trade association may be subject to strong enough pressures of centralization (e.g., NEFARMA's subunits were abolished as it grew in size) to impel the government to take a look at whether the association has lost touch with the membership. In the Dutch case, when the government finds such private associations not operating in the public interest, it does not assume a position of command, but simply plays a countervailing role, with limited authority but effective means of enforcement through public policies.

Great Britain

The British case shows how government stepped in to regulate the pharmaceutical industry when the industry itself was unable to do so. We focus on the Pharmaceutical Price Regulation Scheme, which seeks to control the profits made by the prescription-medicine industry on sales to the National Health Service (NHS). The scheme assumes that a "reasonable level of overall profit on sales" to NHS will produce a reasonable level of overall prices for the medicines supplied. In operation since 1958, with variations in practice and the law since that time, the shape and workings of the scheme have often been the subject of negotiation between the government and the Association of the British Pharmaceutical Industry (ABPI).[16]

Negotiations between the government and the industry. The scheme provides a framework within which individual suppliers can negotiate with NHS on profits and prices. The government's justification for the scheme was that, since the Exchequer was the main purchaser of the drugs, in effect a monopsonistic buyer, it should have something to say about the profits. It proposed that profits should fall within the range generally accepted as appropriate in other fields of government trading—in 1958 7.5 percent to 15 percent on "capital employed," that is, capital calculated on a historical basis. The industry, for its part, was concerned about profit levels in a field where rapid obsolescence means costly R&D. The government stated that its intent was not to fix prices but simply to negotiate them to reasonable levels.

A negotiating committee was formed, with representatives of ABPI's Division B (manufacturers of medical, veterinary, and dental specialty products for home and export trades) and representatives of leading pharmaceutical companies such as ICI, May and Baker, Glaxo Laboratories, and the Wellcome Foundation. The manufacturers agreed that there were excesses in the pricing and profitability of certain prescription medicines and were therefore willing to accept an external check on payments made for their products out of public funds. But they also insisted that the abuses were the exceptions to the rule.

ABPI's constitution did not permit it to bind members to a pricing policy, a restriction fully in line with the British noninterventionist tradition that trade associations should be voluntary organizations. The government had to rely on the hope that the negotiating committee had a sufficiently high level of Division B representation to ensure the ABPI members' compliance with the final agreement.[17]

ABPI was later able to make adjustments in its constitution, but its inadequacy in decision-making procedures and its failure to represent the industry became apparent in the process. Not all the companies were willing to abide by the agreement, notably the subsidiaries of large Swiss corporations, which did not belong to ABPI. And though two Swiss corporations did join ABPI, their market power overbore ABPI's attempts to bring them into compliance.

One case, in the 1970's, can illustrate how this failed attempt at self-regulation brought government enforcement. Roche Products, the British subsidiary of the Swiss multinational Hoffmann-LaRoche, was required to reduce its prices for librium and valium. When it resisted, the government permitted other firms to manufacture and distribute equivalents under Section 412 of the 1949 Patents Act. Roche Products thereupon withdrew from the Pharmaceutical Price Regulation Scheme; the firm was then referred to the Monopolies Commission and became subject to penal sanctions. The commission found that in 1970 the Swiss parent company had charged its British subsidiary £570 and £922 per kilo for librium and valium, respectively, while the active ingredients of these products were available from other manufacturers at £9 and £20. In the light of its findings, the commission adjusted the firm's international transfer price, recalculated the firm's financial statement, and declared Roche's profits "quite unjustified"—the result of excessive prices due to its monopolistic position. The company was ordered to cut the 1970 prices for librium and valium by 60 percent and 75 percent, respectively.

Negotiations between the government and individual companies. In the first three months of the fiscal year, companies doing at least £200,000 of business per annum with NHS must provide the Department of Health with forecasts of their anticipated profits. The department sets target profitability levels for the pharmaceutical industry as a whole, based on Treasury guidelines that assume a rate of profit for government suppliers in line with the average for British industry, and then constructs a "merit league table" of profitability targets for individual companies, calculated on the basis of their forecasts. The department may make adjustments to a company's profit statement after considering, for example, its sales-promotion expenditure, its reported stock levels and capital, and the exchange and inflation rates it has used in its calculations. At the same time, the department observes a "tolerance level" when a company exceeds its forecast profits to avoid penalizing it for effort and thus lessen the industry's incentive to increase productivity and returns. Over-target profits will be allowed if they are imputed to effort rather than incorrect or misleading data in the company's financial report. In addition, the department permits companies to offset shortfalls in profits one year with proportionate excesses in the next.

Should the department find a company's profitability record unacceptable, or a company regard its profitability target as unacceptable, the two sides meet to discuss price changes. When a company's overall range of price increases or decreases has been agreed on, the department will often ask for a settlement giving details of how the company expects to distribute the price raises or cuts among its products. The department evaluates the acceptability of price increases for individual products relative to the retail price index. If it is not satisfied with a proposed change, it may encourage the company to adopt alternative measures; if necessary, it can coerce the company. In fact, the Minister of Health can fix the price of individual medicines if the company and the department cannot come to an agreement.

Conclusion. Because the government is dependent on the goodwill of the prescription-medicine industry for the successful operation of NHS, it relies on ABPI to act as an intermediary during the negotiations for state purchases. However, this case illustrates the complexity of relationships between the government and the pharmaceutical industry in price control. The government became a major party because the industry's own modes of competition and cooperation were not working in the public interest.

The United States

The Standard Industrial Classification Manual puts U.S. drug manufacturing into three categories: biological products, medicinal chemicals and botanical products, and pharmaceutical preparations. The pharmaceutical-preparations industry alone accounts for about 97 percent of all shipments of finished drug products, including both the products of the ethical drug industry, which sells only to the medical profession, and those of the proprietary drug industry, which sells to the public.[18]

Governmental control of drugs dates back to the 1906 Pure Food and Drugs Act, aimed at preventing food adulteration; legislation and Congressional hearings on the growth of pharmaceuticals have been continuing features ever since. Interest has focused not only on dangerous drugs and "medical quacks," but also on prices. In 1959, Senator Estes Kefauver's Antitrust and Monopoly Subcommittee found that the public was being duped with "nonefficacious drugs" and high prices, because corporations were taking advantage of a combination of patent protection, consumer and physician ignorance, and "minimal incentive for physicians" to consider patient drug costs.[19] One approach to the price problem has been shortening or eliminating the patent protection monopoly producers enjoy. Once other suppliers are free to manufacture and distribute these products without concern for patent infringement, prices are driven downward. Mandatory cross-licensing— the granting of manufacturing rights to competing firms with little compensation to the patent holder—also reduces monopoly.

Studies suggest that the federal government also plays a major role in shaping the size and concentration of drug firms. The 1962 amendments to the Food, Drug, and Cosmetic Act, for example, seem to have inadvertently provided an advantage to larger firms by requiring companies to spend more on developing and introducing new drugs. The huge increases in R&D costs make it difficult for small firms to innovate and develop in the field.[20]

Distributive conflicts. The distribution of ethical and proprietary drugs has led to a number of conflicts that have been resolved in ways of interest to our study. The normal channel of distribution for drug products goes from manufacturer to wholesaler to retailer, and then to the ultimate consumer. But the pattern has slowly changed, thanks in part to the growth of chain stores, with the result that the competition between individual firms is not as significant as the competition between associations of firms. Herein lie the major problems of conflict-resolution that must take place outside the government.

Manufacturers dispose of a majority of their products through their own wholesale outlets, but also make direct sales to pharmacists. The bulk of final sales is made primarily through two types of consumer outlets; the independent retail drugstore and the chain drugstore. Independent druggists have objected to the chains' competitive advantages in volume purchasing and their capacity to spread losses over multiple units. If the chains charged the same price as the independent and pocketed the difference there would be no problem, but when they charge less and put the independent out of business, the latter's trade association cries "monopoly."

Independent druggists had been accustomed to setting the norms for retail prices. For example, in the 1960's certain major brands of drugs were produced and packaged at a cost of about 1.5 cents a tablet, sold to druggists for around 18 cents, and retailed at a suggested price of 30 cents. This retail markup of about 33⅓ percent was considered standard.[21] The appearance of chains on the scene caused great dismay. As bulk purchasers, they have the purchasing power to set distributive policy for the industry. This includes eliminating wholesalers by absorbing their functions through backward vertical integration toward the manufacturers.

Three other actors have arisen to muddy the conflict: the retailer-owned aggregate wholesale organization, a cooperative buying venture formed by independent retailers, who use its concentrated purchasing power to force manufacturers or wholesalers to offer quantity discounts; supermarkets, although they have not constituted as serious a threat to the independent druggist as the chains because they mostly sell proprietary drugs; and pharmacies owned by physicians. Independent druggists are concerned that doctors with financial interests in particular retail outlets may direct prescription business to those outlets, and the American Pharmaceutical Association's Committee on Professional Relations has stated that "there is an inherent conflict of interest, whether exploited or not, in physician ownership."[22]

Conflicts between trade associations. The business society can no longer be characterized as composed of independent firms competing against one another, because trade associations are both regulating competition between firms and regulating conflict between themselves. The pharmaceutical industry has four particularly strong associations that are sometimes at odds.[23] There is first of all the National Wholesale Druggists' Association (NWDA), founded in 1876 and headquartered in New York City. One of its prime objectives is to coordinate the activities of manufacturers and retailers, and its Manufacturer Relations Committee and Retailer Relations Committee work with channels of distribution. NWDA helps manufacturers make contacts at meetings; counsels on distribution policies, trade practices, government regulations, operating costs, packaging improvements, and labor relations; and recommends new marketing and promotion methods.

The two principal retail organizations are the National Association of Retail Druggists (NARD) and the National Association of Chain Drug Stores (NACDS). NARD has traditionally and mostly successfully opposed discriminatory practices by manufacturers and suppliers, such as secret rebates, hidden discounts, and privileged allowances to selected retailers. It has also opposed methods of competition believed to be unfair, such as loss-leader selling, sales through nonretail outlets, and discount operations. Because of the countervailing power of these associations, the government does not need to expand its staff and regulating power over the industry in these cases.

Finally, there is the American Pharmaceutical Association, dating back to 1852 as the first national pharmacy association. APA's house of delegates is the primary policy-making body, and it has a council or board of directors and eighteen standing committees. It has been active in helping to resolve distributive conflicts.

A major conflict over "fair markups" serves as an example of a failure in the system. (It also illustrates how an issue of social justice enters into the marketplace.) NARD has continually sought to ensure the traditional one-third markup margin for its members. It successfully maintained that practice by collective agreement for many years, until it was challenged by NACDS and other associations. NARD then turned to Congress and succeeded in getting "fair-trade legislation" passed. Fair-trade laws transfer price competition from the retailer to the manufacturer and force the discounter to sell a fair-traded product at the same price as all other retailers. In this case, the government had to settle the dispute and regulate the market.

Conclusion. We have seen that the U.S. pharmaceutical market is highly regulated through its trade associations; they are collective actors who must be taken into account as much as (if not more than) individual firms. They hold a great power for shaping markets either from the negative standpoint of their monopolizing market sectors or from a positive standpoint of showing a capacity to act together as a self-regulatory system.

The negative side is seen in the fair-trade legislation in which Congress was lobbied to shelter weaker actors in the market by law. In this case, not all parties in the pharmaceutical industry were represented in NARD's agreement for a 33⅓ percent markup, and complaints continued about the legislation from wholesaler and consumer associations. This congressional action tells us how *not* to approach self-regulation in public policy—that is, actions that respond to pressure from just a single trade association are doomed to failure. A better result can be achieved by reviewing the social organization of the whole industry and then establishing a joint committee among all relevant associations (including consumers) to settle the issues. Only the government can play this third-party role in some cases, to demand that solutions be found within the associative system itself. But the associations have shown their capacity to resolve conflicts themselves; they must solve other thorny problems, too, if they do not want to fall under government control.

The positive side is that associations have managed to solve a host of problems on their own hook (discriminatory practices by manufacturers, secret rebates, hidden discounts, privileged allowances to selected retailers, unfair competition, loss-leader selling, counseling on operating statistics, safe packaging and many others). Government could use its powerful role to help peak associations organize to go farther in this direction. Instead of accepting the "collective markup agreements" of one trade association, for example, Congress could respond to such lobbying efforts by demanding that the parties find their own solutions. To do so requires a new political philosophy in which government assumes a larger role in creating a basis for self-regulation in the public interest.

But is it possible to increase the capacity of an industry to regulate itself in the public interest? To what extent can trade associations—competing with one another as well as cooperating with one another—regulate markets without government controls? In the next chapter, we will consider how our case studies suggest a theory about the social governance of markets.

CHAPTER 7

A Guiding Model: Self-Regulation

THE PREVIOUS CHAPTER introduced the question of how the values of the larger society can be brought into the market through the actions of the participants themselves and presented a series of case studies that demonstrated how private trade associations, sometimes in combination with and sometimes apart from the government, helped to shape the market. Before we attempt to develop principles from these cases that can help us build a model of market self-regulation, we must look at a deeper issue: that is, the relationship between the social and cultural structures of society. Our particular interest is in the disjuncture between cultural values and the structure of the economic system, and we shall begin by examining several ways in which the structure of the economy is readjusted so as to express society's larger values.

The Conflict Between Social and Cultural Structures

Sociologists suggest that the disjuncture between a society's social and cultural structures can be a major force for change. The social structure is conceived as the network of positions and corresponding roles that mark a society's institutions, associations, and systems of stratification, the cultural structure as the network of valences that give directions to these structures, including values, norms, folkways, and systems of knowledge. The two structures—the social and cultural—do not always coincide; indeed, they can even be in contradiction. For example, it is hard to imagine how a social structure like a private business or an absolute monarchy, both of which are organized without electoral mechanisms, could express democratic values. And yet democratic values may find some measure of expression when a firm's president sets up worker councils with considerable autonomy or a king sets up a court of nobles with rights to dispense justice in the land.

Each institutional structure in society—each religious, political, economic, educational, or whatever institution—has its own sub-culture, a set of specific norms and values that orient it toward the world, and these various subcultures can stand in tension with one another as each emphasizes its own guidelines for behavior. The values emphasized in the subculture of a religious institution, such as charity, sacrifice, and selflessness, can stand in tension with the values emphasized in the subculture of economic institutions, such as self-interest, profits, and efficiency. At the same time, there is an overall consensus on certain values; and though these shared values may not be fully realized in every institution, this consensus is what tends to hold a society together.

Daniel Bell describes the government as the arbiter of "crescive, unplanned change in the character of society, the working out of the logic of socio-economic organization, and a change in the character of knowledge." When change occurs, people have to decide, politically, whether to accept the trend, accelerate it, impede it, or redirect it. Consequently:

Politics, in contemporary society, is the management of social structure. It becomes the regulative mechanism of change. But any political decision necessarily involves some conception of justice, traditional, implicit, and now increasingly explicit. [People] accept different principles of justice, or different hierarchies of value, and seek to embody them in social arrangements. . . . Capitalism was not just a system for the production of commodities, or a new set of occupations, or a new principle of calculation (though it was all of these), but a justification of the primacy of the individual and his self-interest, and of the strategic role of economic freedom in realizing those values through the free market. This is why the economic function became detached from the other functions of Western society and was given free rein.[1]

In this chapter, we will look at three different ways in which the social structure of the economy can become adapted to a society's cultural structure, focusing on how the organization of business connects with these larger values and integrates them into its economic order. In the United States, we will see how the broad values of society are introduced into the economy from the outside by the government, and how government agencies, representing the larger consensus in society, regulate corporate behavior. Then we look at Japan, where the government plays a powerful role in the economy through an agency that works closely with corporations and trade associations to advance both their interests and the country's national purposes. Finally, we will assess the cases discussed in the last chapter, to see how European trade associations are able to be relatively self-regulating in specific areas of the market without government controls, and investigate what makes such self-regulation possible.

Let me point out that none of the cases, here or in the last chapter, represents the ideal. I am abstracting from all these examples to suggest a new course for government policy. My goal is to formulate a model that emphasizes the virtues of each case, to suggest a public policy that allows a close working relationship between the government and private associations aimed at encouraging greater self-regulation. Specifically, I believe that a government can work intimately and effectively with trade associations to promote the national interests, as in Japan, but that this can still be done while remaining separate and independent of these associations, as is relatively true of the United States.

The descriptive features of the cases that follow are therefore highly selective of what goes on in these countries. They serve as models to allow us to develop a social logic, a basis from which to develop public policies. So if I emphasize the way European associations regulate their own conduct in the market, one should keep in mind that European governments also intervene in their economies in many ways. Similarly, if I emphasize how the U.S. government regulates the economy from the outside, one should keep in mind that in many market sectors, trade associations are also relatively self-regulating. And if I emphasize the way that government policies in Japan effectively integrate societal values into the organization of trade associations, one should keep in mind that from an ethnographic perspective, much more alienation exists in the larger Japanese culture.

Government as Regulator: The United States

Freedom, equality, justice, welfare, and democracy are among the deepest-seated American values. Since the market itself does not always live up to these ideals, the government has regularly

TABLE 4

Examples of Societal Values Entering the Market

Value	Market norms
Freedom	Open competition in every industry; free entry into the market; plurality of choice in buying and selling
Equality	Diffusion of power; equal opportunity; limited equality of income
Justice	Fair competition; fair labor standards; fair disclosure of information
Welfare	Employment opportunities; health and safety; concern for the environment
Democracy	Equal voting rights for association members; electoral processes in associations; due process and challengeable elections

acted as an external entity, using both legislation and enforcement activities, to try to ensure that it does. In some instances, these efforts actually limit the role of government, but more often, they have led to ever-increasing layers of government regulation and control. Table 4 shows some of the ways the market is expected to express these particular values.

Freedom. This value is at the very root of capitalist culture. Freedom means the absence of restraint, the ability to act according to one's own volition unencumbered by outside controls. Indeed, the norms reflecting this value are symbolized by the master belief in free enterprise. A key norm of free enterprise is the opportunity to enter into a market at any time, to buy and sell openly without either monopoly or government restrictions. Freedom of entry into a market is therefore a legal norm backed by the government. When the market limits this freedom—through monopoly or price fixing, for example—the government acts to remove such barriers; the Department of Justice is mandated to prohibit price fixing and exclusive dealing, and the Federal Trade Commission to monitor price discrimination.

Another aspect of freedom deals with the degree to which corporations are free to control employees on the job, or to fire them, as opposed to the contrary freedom of employees to work without such restraints. The most recent issues of employee freedom are found in the norms of entitlements, including the right of corporations to search employee lockers as opposed to the right of employees to be free from searches. In the United States, freedom is a condition formally granted to all persons, regardless of attributes, including their relationship to modes of production.

There are numerous freedom norms. Ironically, an important one concerns the free enterprise system itself, in the prohibition against government's interfering with corporate life. This legal norm, which was established by the Supreme Court in 1819 in a Dartmouth College case, originated in English law but was applied creatively because of the American experience with British oppression. This norm interacts closely with the norms of equality in the marketplace.

Equality. The value of equality is especially relevant when one party's freedom to act in the market encroaches on another's. Ideally, such conflict should be resolved according to freedom norms through equality, or its derivative, equity, which means that each party's interests are given the same weight. The freedom of one corporation to act in the market is restricted when it interferes with the freedom of another corporation to act, and the solution is made in terms of equity. Among the more important equity norms generated from the larger culture and integrated into the subculture of the market are a wide diffusion of economic power, equal bargaining power on both sides of an exchange transaction, equal opportunity regardless of race, religion, sex, or national origin, and limited inequality in the distribution of income.

Limited inequality among firms is a legal norm, mandated by the Justice Department. A major debate among antitrust economists turns on what constitutes inequality in the distribution of power among competing firms. The current thinking is that a four-firm concentration ratio of 70 percent is the limit of inequity. Congress determines the basic norm of equity, and economists help set the precise quantitative figure for market concentration that represents the public interest.[2]

Justice. The value of justice generates norms of fairness. The unrestricted competitive market has led to numerous and varied injustices, such as restricting supply, securing monopoly profits, misleading and deceiving consumers, exploiting labor, and using inferior and dangerous materials. As a result, the government has introduced laws requiring full disclosure, prohibiting unfair practices, and the like. Such matters as false advertising and deceptive practices are monitored and controlled by the Federal Trade Commission.

Welfare. Welfare, especially as it relates to public health, has been a major focus of government regulation ever since the passage of the drug and cosmetic laws in the early twentieth century. Most recently, many environmental laws have been enacted on the basis of the public's health and welfare; the ban on the burning of sulfur-laden coal is just one example. Many other specific norms for health and safety have developed in the past forty years; most states now mandate the use of seat belts, and collapsible steering wheels may be required for all cars in the near future. The Supreme Court has expressly prohibited government from exercising control over private corporations, but exceptions are made when it comes to people's welfare: corporations are not permitted to maintain unsafe workplaces. In fact, the government has the right to enter the workplace without prior notification to investigate safety violations. The value of freedom is thus counterbalanced by the value of human welfare with its own legal norms.

Democracy. This major value is applied only selectively in the market economy. Many nonprofit corporations and trade associations are required by law to operate according to democratic principles. Trade unions must abide by the norms set out in the 1959 Labor-Management Reporting and Disclosure Act: democratic voting procedures, the secret ballot, a constitution, and by-laws governing the amount and use of funds. Significantly, though democratic practices figure large in the co-determination schemes of European firms, they have never been imposed on U.S. corporations.

Further comments about values in the market. Value aspirations contain the potential for change; they express the latent possibilities for business evolution. Freedom of entry into a market is a social norm, not a part of animal nature. It had to be socially constructed and realized. This leaves room for the creation of new norms in the future. Under the right conditions, for example, the norm of free entry into a market might change to one that adds the requirement "without class distinction," that is, that gives access to any group of people apart from the amount of capital they possess, dependent only on their imagination and leadership, as well as the per-

TABLE 5

Government Enforcement of Societal Norms and Values in the Market

Norm	Freedom and equality (market structure)	Justice (corporate conduct)	Welfare (corporate performanc
Maintenance of competition	Monopolies (DOJ); mergers (DOJ, FTC)	Price fixing (DOJ); price discrimination (FTC); exclusive dealing (DOJ, FTC)	
Establishment of the plane of competition	Disclosure of information, truth-in-lending (FRB, FTC); grading and standardization of agricultural product (USDA); general weights and measures (BOS); trade marks and copyrights (DOC)	False advertising, deceptive practices (FTC)	Health and safety di closures (FDA, FTC, OSHA, PSC); health and safety of products, in transportation, etc. (DOT, PSC pollution (EPA, S&LC)
Public utility regulation		Prices in transportation, utilities, banking, and insurance (CAB, FHLB, FRB, ICC, S&LC); abandonment of service (CAB, ICC); credit availability (FRB)	Profits in transporta tion, etc. (CAB, FPC ICC, S&LC); service requirements (ICC, S&LC); safety (DOT FAA, FPC, NRC, S&LC); innovations (ICC)

SOURCE: Adapted from Douglas Greer, *Industrial Organization and Public Policy* (New York: Macmilla 1980).

KEY: BOS, Bureau of Standards; CAB, Civil Aeronautics Board; DOC, Department of Commerce; DC Department of Justice; DOT, Department of Transportation; EPA, Environmental Protection Agency; FA Federal Aviation Agency; FDA, Food and Drug Administration; FHLB, Federal Home Loan Bank Boa FPC, Federal Power Commission; FRB, Federal Reserve Board; FTC, Federal Trade Commission; ICC, Int state Commerce Commission; NRC, Nuclear Regulation Commission; OSHA, Occupational Health a Safety Administration; PSC, Product Safety Commission; S&LC, State and Local Commissions; USDA, L partment of Agriculture.

suasiveness of their product's marketability and the logic of their business plan.

Table 5 shows how each of the societal values we have discussed has been introduced as a market norm through government legislation, monitoring, and enforcement activities. Obviously, a staggeringly large bureaucracy has been built up to enforce these norms, at the taxpayers' expense.[3]

Put in terms of our theory, one could say that some of these values, although manifest in the society at large, are still latent, so far as the market is concerned. They have been made manifest only by means of government action. But there are numerous disadvantages to this situation. At the very least, business has to pay for an outside entity to monitor its behavior. It would be much more advantageous and economical for all concerned if corporations and business leaders themselves were to acknowledge that these values should guide the shape and behavior of the market.

Government as Integrator: Japan

Japan is the outstanding example of a concerted, state-propelled effort to integrate cultural and social structures in the marketplace, a policy that has much to do with its current eminence in the world economy.[4]

The Ministry of International Trade and Industry (MITI). The Ministry of International Trade and Industry can take credit for the "miracle of Japan" in the postwar period. MITI's primary mission is to determine how well the personnel, capital, and plants of the various Japanese companies supplement one another, and how these resources can best be combined in the interest of the society as a whole. Through MITI, the government views the market from a single, overall perspective that, among other things, has enabled Japan to set its sights on pioneering new technology. Beginning in 1975, for example, MITI financed one-third of the development costs of very large integrated circuits, a stage required for the evolution of semiconductors. MITI sees to it that new technologies are diffused rapidly into the economy and incorporated into commercial products.

MITI's aim is not to reduce competition among Japanese companies; it is, rather, to create the strongest possible companies with the greatest competitive potential. It accomplishes this by promoting cooperation in the public interest. "Perhaps the nearest American analogy," according to the sociologist Ezra Vogel, "is the National Football League or the National Basketball Association":

League officials establish rules about the size of team, recruitment, and rules of play that result in relatively equally matched teams of great competitive abilities. They do not interfere in internal team activity or tell a coach how to run his team, although they do try to provide information that would enable the coach to improve. MITI is divided into branches corresponding to the major industrial sectors, and firms generally specialize in a particular industrial sector. In each sector, the MITI branch tries to create the most effective league of competing companies. Through these branches, MITI considers the overall prospects of an industrial sector and the potential of companies within that sector. It helps to ensure that the promising companies get the necessary capital, land, foreign exchange, technological know-how, and access to resources and markets to make best use of their potential.[5]

MITI goes much farther than any U.S. government agency in helping firms to profit from pursuits consistent with the nation's goals. It helps arrange funding for private businesses from the Development Bank and the Export-Import Bank, and encourages private banks to give loans. Its officials sell reclaimed or refilled land not to the highest bidder, but to companies that can make the best use of it in the national interest. In many ways, MITI is an integrator for the competitive market system at home so that the system can become a strong competitor in the world at large.

At the same time, MITI deals with the risks of domestic monopoly by setting up roadblocks for companies that control too large a share of a given market. To contain damage to small shops and prevent their rapid decline, it decrees how large a department store may be and where it can be located. When pollution becomes an issue, it decrees whether the economic benefits of a given factory outweigh potential harm to the environment before allowing expansion, and new plants with the potential to pollute cannot be built without MITI approval. MITI also controls some research expenses, and it approves licensing agreements and affiliations with foreign companies. For all its power, however, MITI is still limited by Japanese law, and when its efforts to expand its own authority seem to go too far, they may be rebuffed by the business community and the Diet.

But MITI's success derives not just from its own power, but also from the business community's voluntary cooperation with its aims. According to Vogel, MITI achieves this cooperation by making it clear to companies that the government is interested in their welfare. MITI officials and company executives meet constantly, formally and informally, developing an understanding of what is needed in the market. (A mid-level MITI official commonly spends three or four evenings a week informally with appropriate business representatives.) Company officials know that when they request licenses, permits, choice locations, or tax breaks, MITI is more likely to respond favorably if their companies cooperate in the national interest. MITI works to obtain consensus in an industrial sector in the interest of the business community as a whole.

In order to set feasible goals, MITI officials regularly collect an enormous amount of information. They keep up with foreign developments in technology and basic financial statements and reports of developments of firms at home and abroad. The agreements they promote among companies in a market sector require a higher level of trust than can be achieved simply through formal contacts with individual firms. Business leaders often convene parallel meetings of their own to reach understandings that will be presented in later meetings with MITI officials.

In the case of a declining industrial sector, intensive cooperation between MITI and the affected companies results in critical planning for recovery. When companies cannot solve their problems alone, MITI officials think with them about appropriate mergers or breakups but do not have the power to require changes. For example, MITI tried to reduce the present six major auto companies to two or three, without success. MITI can help to arrange tax breaks, capital funds, and technology transfer for companies that cooperate, but there are still limits to how far it can go.

MITI may propose specific regulations for approval by the Diet, but such regulations serve only as guidelines for standards and procedures and do not greatly restrict the scope of corporate decision making. MITI wants to avoid too many minute regulations that might hamper its effectiveness and distract attention from its major issues and larger purposes. Whereas in the United States, regulatory functions are independent of the Commerce Department, in Japan the combining of regulatory and advisory functions in MITI helps ensure that regulations are administered in a way consistent with the ministry's overall purpose.

The role of trade associations. Japan is divided into nine "large regions," each of which has a trade association of large business enterprises to promote regional interests. These associations meet both to work out concrete plans for regional development and to engage in social activity that reinforces the sense of community, especially among regional leaders. Over the years, these leaders have developed a set of informal rules to ensure the success of their associations. For example, the head of the association must not use the post to advance his own company's interests and must not be from a prominent regional company with competitors of comparable size; yet he should be a respected person, capable of mobilizing support for the association's undertakings. Regional leaders tend to be from companies without regional rivals or from small locally based companies.

Since each of the regions plays a major national role, leaders of these business associations regularly see politicians and Diet members on an informal basis. In this context, they are more statesmen than businessmen, since they cannot speak for their own company's interest. They are selected because of their sense of responsibility to the region as a whole. Regional business leaders work with regional labor leaders, newspaper and television representatives, and university faculty in pursuit of regional interests, and regional and trade interests are therefore represented together.

Unlike American conglomerates, which spread over several sectors, major Japanese firms specialize in a single sector, such as electronics, banking, trade, real estate, or textiles. The government encourages this specialization because the expertise developed as a result becomes an advantage in the market. These companies may belong to trade associations based on their specialty or be organized instead into "groups" consisting of one firm from every industrial sector. There is still another type of organization, affiliating all firms of a given size in all sectors. For example, the Japanese Federation of Employers deals with labor problems of all large firms, and the Federation of Economic Organizations and eight regional associations deal with all issues other than labor that confront big business.

The Chamber of Commerce speaks particularly for small business, since membership in Japan (unlike the United States) is mandatory. Every company is by law a registered member of the Chamber of Commerce, and the majority of companies are small. At the prefectural level and below, there are few large company headquarters, and so the chamber branches commonly serve as the focus for the entire local business community. In this sense, they are like their American counterparts, though on the whole they work more closely with government officials in planning the development of their region, taking an active part in things like landfills and reclamation projects.

The Federation of Economic Organizations, composed of the 700 or more largest Japanese companies, is similar to but much stronger than the U.S. National Association of Manufacturers. All major corporations, regardless of their location, belong to it, and their top leaders work closely with its large professional staff to forge agreements on behalf of big business as a whole. The federation occupies a fourteen-story building in the heart of Tokyo, where dozens of meetings are held each day for leaders of the largest companies to study and discuss issues of interest to their sector or the entire business community. It sponsors meetings with foreign business leaders and sends specialized missions of business leaders abroad to find solutions to trade problems. Because the federation represents so many diverse companies, it cannot be partial to any single group or any industrial sector, although it does give aid to needy sectors. It concentrates on issues common to the business community as a whole and must make arguments in the broad terms of the public interest.[6] Nevertheless, it has received its share of press criticism for slighting small business and the public at large.

Both trade associations and alliances of companies in a sector oversee a range of interests impossible for U.S. associations because of antitrust laws. The Japanese associations discuss virtually every issue considered by MITI in their sphere, and in declining industries they help solve the problem by apportioning quotas for reduced production. When the United States demands limitations on Japanese exports, these associations, in cooperation with MITI, also apportion quotas for reducing exports, although ironically the kind of restraint the United States demands of Japan would be illegal under U.S. antitrust laws. Similarly, when the economy threatens to become overheated, the associations work out with the appropriate MITI branch a fair system for restraining expansion.

Sectoral trade associations sometimes develop and directly administer special projects. The banking association, for example, developed and operates the system that permits deposits to be transferred by a centralized computer, from any regular commercial bank to any account in any other commercial bank. The steel trade association, interested in keeping down the cost of electricity and fuel, takes an active role in securing stable sources of energy for the entire nation and in lobbying within the Federation of Economic Organizations to limit the inflationary pressures of electricity and fuel costs. The automobile association seeks to keep down the cost of steel, as well as electricity and fuel, so the industry may continue to compete internationally.

Neither MITI officials nor trade association executives want strong anti-monopoly legislation, and they are regularly in conflict with the Fair Trade Commission, which breaks up trusts. MITI officials believe that in the short range, gaining the cooperation of companies in a sector is the best way to cushion economic fluctuations and reduce disruptions in specific industries, in the lives of their employees, and in the economy as a whole. They are confident that with their centralized guidance, plus the sanctions at their disposal, they can contain the dangers of oligopoly, and believe that cooperative practices among trade associations will avoid the dangers of sudden layoffs and unemployment.

Vogel notes how the foreigner is struck by the paradox of extraordinarily competitive business leaders who nonetheless genuinely enjoy each other's company when working for their sector as a whole.

Officials who fight to increase their company's market share can seem totally relaxed in the camaraderie of drinking with counterparts in rival companies. Sector association leaders at times fight almost as arduously and effectively in the interest of the sector as a whole as the individual company leaders fight for the good of their own businesses. Indeed, they cannot understand how Americans can keep their individual companies abreast of modern developments without the kind of cooperation that American antitrust practice forbids.[7]

Vogel suggests that "justice" has different meanings for Japanese and Americans. Americans equate justice with "fair play." There are certain rules, and if the game is fought fairly, the loser congratulates the winner, who gets the whole pie. But in Japan, people look at the pie and see if it can be expanded, how many ways it can be cut, and what acceptable rules can be devised to apportion it more evenly. They are interested not only in the rules but in the results, and rules may be changed to accord with a sense of "fair share." After the contest, everyone must receive some share. If there is any doubt about how one contest was decided or if an indivisible pie is given to one party, the disadvantaged party has a standing claim to a larger share of the next pie.

Thus, when the national budget is apportioned, there is an assumption among interest groups that each will in some way receive its fair share. Income distribution statistics for Japan indicate that the gap between the highest and the lowest quintile is among the smallest in the world. This includes keeping a balance in salary and price increases between different sectors of the population, the government, industry, small business, and agriculture. The government is concerned primarily with issues of unequal distribution because of price increases, and handles these issues through subsidies, tax policies, and the like, but deliberative councils composed of well-known private citizens also consider important issues of equity confronting the country and serve as a check on government practices.

The social and cultural structure of Japan is thus much more integrated than in the United States. Because of the cooperative working of the Japanese economy, U.S. government officials and business leaders have often felt at a great disadvantage in negotiations; for example, U.S. government officials are relatively uninformed about American companies, which only reluctantly share information with those whom they suspect of being more interested in regulating than assisting them.

Does this extraordinary pattern of cooperation offer a model for the United States? I must conclude that certain features of the MITI model look like a corporate state, which in a time of crisis could move toward becoming a fascist state. But it also has features that could be adapted to give the United States a more self-governing system. We will return to this subject in Chapter Eleven.

Associational Self-Regulation: The European Cases

Our European cases in the previous chapter showed how associations, whether of horizontal, vertical, or peak structure, introduce societal values into the market. We saw social—nonstatist—regulation in many areas: price setting, product quality, output, advertising, and welfare, among others. We also saw how much more far-reaching the associational structure is in some European countries than in the United States.

The regulation of prices. Price regulation in our cases was accomplished either through private agreements and negotiated contracts among competing/cooperating trade associations or through government statutes and mandates.[8] In the United States, the National Association of Retail Druggists set price markups by members' collective agreement, but not all parts of the pharmaceutical industry were represented in NARD. When associations representing other segments of the industry complained, NARD obtained federal legislation to protect its own retail members, a solution that was still unsatisfactory to wholesaler and consumer associations. The NARD example suggests how *not* to approach self-regulation.

A more successful type of private price setting was accomplished through vertically negotiated contracts between groups of horizontal associations in Switzerland. The long-term agreement between the Central Association of Milk Producers and the Association of Milk Buyers enabled the two groups to jointly regulate the general conditions of purchase between buyers and sellers of raw milk, and regional and local associations of milk producers and milk buyers negotiated contracts that regulated both prices and various services. In this case, self-regulation in the dairy market operated through the entire vertical chain of associations, from supply and processing to distribution and consumption. Since the two retailers, MIGROS and COOP, are not ordinary retail businesses but consumer cooperatives representing the consumer directly and together owning 39 percent of the market, a relative balance of power has begun to emerge among the major business associations at all levels of product development. The system is depicted in Table 6.

In a system *where all parties can pursue their interests as fully as opposing interests allow, and where conflict can be mediated through interassociational committees, the result is significant self-regulation.* The benefits of such a counterbalanced system can be seen throughout the Swiss dairy industry. Although trade associations set the primary pattern for governing the market, there is still free competition outside the negotiated contracts, along with some government involvement. This has some advantages, leaving room for firms to operate independently in the private sector but under a degree of government surveillance. This countervailing force keeps the two consumer cooperatives from becoming a consumer monopoly over firms in earlier stages of processing and supply. In short, the system offers flexibility for competition and cooperation to work together in the public interest. It is an important example of self-regulation to which we shall return.

In other cases, prices were regulated through government controls. One example was the British government's direct negotiation with industry associations on the pricing of the pharmaceuticals it consumed. Another type of government control was exemplified by the U.S. government's price-support programs for the dairy industry. Neither of these systems matched the power of self-regulation in Switzerland.

The regulation of quality and safety. Two social facts are important to see in our cases. First, market norms were generated within the

TABLE 6
Balance of Power Through Competing Associations
in the Swiss Dairy Industry

Association	Trade-Interest Motive
Suppliers (producers)	Seek to sell high-priced milk
Processors	Seek to buy low-priced milk; and seek to sell high-priced cheese
Retailers (consumer cooperatives)	Seek to buy and sell low-priced milk products
Individual consumers	Seek to buy low-priced milk products

private sector, sometimes out of sheer necessity, as corporations sought to avoid destructive conflict and maintain peaceful relationships with competing firms. Second, firms cooperated to synthesize their interests with the larger public interest.

The case of the Dutch dairy industry demonstrated how *corporate self-interests and societal values became integrated* through the trade associations' efforts to solve problems arising in the competitive system. To maintain milk quality and avoid public health problems, private Dutch factories agreed on the principle of prices based on quality and safety. The state later found the principle so important that it mandated its application but delegated the relevant rule making and monitoring to the trade association. It was in the private interest of the factories to maintain standards and sustain their business.

Furthermore, *associational norms on product quality and safety can be established and enforced in the public interest in the absence of government laws or regulation.* We can again cite the Dutch case. Recall that when the dairy industry was ineffectual in maintaining the quality controls established in 1890 because firms persistently found ways to circumvent them, the state sought to do the job, and that the industry associations then set up their own control system using a special trademark. These "private rules" (social norms) were obviously in the public interest because the trademark guaranteed product quality, but they were obviously also in the industry's self-interest.

Our cases revealed a range of regulators of product quality, from private associations, to government agencies such as the U.S. Department of Agriculture, to semipublic corporations like the Käse-union, a private democratic association operating with government support that develops rules jointly with the Swiss dairy corpora-tions. In sum, the cases revealed many possibilities for regulating product quality and safety, as well as for generating rules and providing for the enforcement of norms. *Rules can originate and be enforced in the public interest at any point along the continuum from pri-vate associations to a central government.*

The regulation of output. We saw how individual Swiss cheese manufacturers controlled output through their own milk associa-tions. Such a system of private governance is legitimated in each country as long as the associations involved are democratic and properly managed. There is some criticism that the Swiss Milk Producers' associations are too strong and tend to curtail the free-dom of action of individual cheese dairies, although the producers reply that those businesses have recourse to regional tribunals when they feel they have been unjustly treated.[9]

Control over product output in our Swiss example is relatively nonstatist, formally democratic in the private sector, and relatively decentralized in its vertical structure. *A pattern of self-regulation therefore operates most effectively in the public interest when a balance of power is maintained from supply to consumption.*

The regulation of advertising. In the Dutch pharmaceutical indus-try, an advertising code and an enforcement body (RGA) were es-tablished by business associations representing wholesalers and importers. But the code's limited origins caused problems. Then a KOAG regulation became a joint venture of four interest groups, and finally NEFARMA, *representing the entire industry,* established a code of behavior that combined all the self-regulatory measures for the industry into one set of rules, and also established a code commit-tee in 1983 to handle all complaints about the industry.

The lesson of this development is that *it is important for a peak as-sociation to represent the whole industry—to represent not only competing firms but also competing stages of product development and sale.* To be sure, no consumer associations were involved in this instance, but their involvement appeared unnecessary, partly because the op-posing interests of the trade groups were so various that normal consumer complaints were resolved in the process of resolving in-ternal conflicts. Furthermore, the power of the peak association to settle differences worked well in reflecting the public interest, and the state's readiness to act if necessary was sufficient for the self-regulatory pattern to operate acceptably in the public mind.

Going beyond the cases. The European cases point toward a basic principle of self-regulation: *if self-regulation is to be effective, all parties affected by a corporate activity must be represented through their associations.* We can also extrapolate from them to project two directions of development. One path is suggested by the Frisian case. As we saw, the Frisian union is deeply involved in social regulatory activity apart from the state; it sets rules to allocate supplies from farmers to specific factories, regulates prices, teaches accounting techniques, monitors firms' accounts, and regulates member firms' investments. Its unique capacity to do these things may derive from its ethnic and regional cohesion, but that attribute also carries the potential for an association to become provincial and bureaucratic. To avoid the potential for monopoly, *it is important that the state keep an eye on an association's democratic polity to ensure that individual members are free to operate independently within the larger market.*

On the other hand, associations could act in the public interest to a greater extent than they do now. In European countries, trade associations and unions typically deal with welfare issues, including such matters as labor-management conflict, pensions, work safety, and health insurance. We noted that Netherlands work councils composed of representatives from both employers' and employees' associations deal with labor-management problems and oversee workmen's compensation. The associations, not the state, underwrite the councils' activities. The extent of the self-regulatory activity carried out by associations suggests that they are capable of assuming responsibility in still more areas of the market economy under the right conditions.

A Theory of Social Self-Regulation

Our underlying interest in the cases in the previous chapter was to learn how the market can regulate itself in the public interest and government intervention can be reduced. We can now see that the market is not only shaped by competition but also socially constructed through the actions of both private trade associations and the government. In other words, the market is socially governed through the power of (1) intercorporate associations (not only individuals and firms); (2) common values (not only self-interests and utilities); and (3) cooperation (not only competition). Indeed, these cases suggest that cooperation should be considered the "invisible hand" in the market. Cooperation explains how the market survives and becomes effective in the modern world.

We are now ready to draw conclusions about the conditions under which trade associations would be most effective in self-regulating the market. These cases suggest that advances in that direction can be made only if trade associations meet four specific conditions: they must maintain an internal democratic polity; must maintain both a horizontal and vertical balance of power among corporations; and must have established independent mechanisms for conflict resolution. Let us examine each of these conditions in more detail.

1. *A democratic polity must be maintained within the internal organization of horizontal and vertical associations in order for them to be capable of self-regulation.* Trade associations are chartered as nonprofit democratic organizations, but the actual practice of democracy becomes critical as they are given more authority to become self-regulating. These democratic principles are set out formally both in the charters of trade associations and in the law, as we shall see later.

2. *A balance of power must be maintained within horizontal trade associations.* The balance of power should allow competition to take place while members are cooperating to control it; the strength of competitors must not be too unequal. This is the traditional assumption behind current U.S. policy, which requires the Antitrust Division of the Justice Department to investigate and take appropriate action whenever firms become too concentrated. Compliance with this principle remains essential to self-regulation. The degree of concentration that is permissible becomes a function of whether a trade federation is authorized to act as a production unit, about which more will be said later.

3. *A balance of power must be maintained among associations acting across stages of unit development.* The strength of buying must be comparable to the strength of selling between each phase of the supply-production-distribution-retail-consumption continuum, and the vertical purchasing power of buyers at each stage of development must be roughly equal to the selling power of sellers in the marketplace. The Antitrust Division also acts on this issue, although there are less specific norms guiding its decisions here

than in regard to the equitable balance of power between sellers horizontally. New legislation is needed to specify more concretely what constitutes vertical monopoly.

4. *Effective methods of conflict resolution must be established within and between trade associations at different stages of unit development.* Although trade associations have already gone some distance in this direction, the system needs to be strengthened if they are to assume more responsibility for the conduct of their members. The associations especially need to be prepared to negotiate conflicts between vertical stages of buying and selling. When serious conflicts occur that the associations cannot mediate, government may intervene, and self-regulation loses. The quarrel between the U.S. retail druggists and distributors over price markup was finally settled by Congress, as we saw. But we also saw an instance where retail druggists and manufacturers were able to settle their disagreement without recourse to government intervention. Studies show that interassociation mediation is already being practiced in many vertical stages of product development; it simply needs to be encouraged.[10]

These conditions are not entirely unrelated. An association dominated by a few large companies is unlikely to be all that democratic. Currently, only antitrust legislation and the government's determination to enforce the law maintains what balance there is among firms in an industry. How to handle the problem of unequal size without government intervention would become a crucial issue if trade associations move toward greater self-governance. Because market self-governance is predicated on the principle that all parties affected by actions in a political system should be represented in the key decision making, an equally crucial issue is ensuring that affected parties are actually heard and represented in private polity, lest a monopoly develop.

The Integrating of Cultural and Social Structures in Associations

If trade associations are to integrate the values of the larger society into the market, they must first integrate them into their own internal structures and into the policies they establish for their member firms. And before they can attempt that they must overcome the disjuncture between the cultural and social structures in their own operations.[11]

TABLE 7
Horizontal and Vertical Social Structures
of Government and Trade Associations

Government	Trade association
HORIZONTAL STRUCTURE	
Citizens	Firms
Taxes	Dues
Congress: laws	Board of directors: rules
Courts	Tribunal boards or committees
Chief executive, agencies	President or CEO, staff/committees
VERTICAL STRUCTURE	
Levels of government	Levels of market
Town	Producers
City	Processors
State	Distributors
National	Retailers
	Consumers

In order to understand where American trade associations stand today and in what directions they need to go, let us compare their political structure and process with those of the formal political system (Table 7). At the horizontal level, the two are much alike. Under a democratic government, citizens vote; in a trade association, firms vote. Under a democratic government, the sources of income are mainly taxes; in a trade association, the sources are mainly dues. Under a democratic government, a legislature promulgates laws for the citizenry; in a trade association, an elected board of directors establishes norms by which firms compete in a market. Under a democratic government, a judicial branch composed of courts interprets the law; in a trade association, tribunals (or grievance committees) interpret the norms. Under a democratic government, a chief executive and the executive branch carry out the legislature's mandates; in a trade association, a president and staff (or committees) carry out the board's mandates and run the organization.

Vertically, there are also some parallels. Under a democratic government, there are towns, cities, counties, and states (or their equivalents), and a national government; in the trade associational order, there are producers, processors, distributors, retailers, and consumers. Each level (or stage) has its own democratic organization, and interassociational bodies resolve conflicts that develop between levels. Further, each political level must establish some measure of community, a sense of unity and purpose. Both a town and the nation require a sense of togetherness; producers and retailers must likewise maintain that sense of community. Indeed, the entire vertical structure must itself maintain a sense of cohesion in a symbolic community in order to function adequately.

However, there are also important differences between a democratic government and a trade association, the most notable being that the modern democratic government tends to be a federation and the trade association a confederation. In the United States specifically, political power is relatively centralized: the citizenry elects a legislature, which provides the administrative basis for state jurisdiction; in turn, each state authorizes cities and towns to govern themselves. Each level of the polity is authorized by a higher central body. But the elected board of an association cannot create firms or authorize their right to exist. The full authority for firms to act independently in the marketplace rests at the bottom of the organization, even in a vertically structured peak association. If firms do not want to abide by the codes of conduct that constrain them, they have the option of leaving their association and joining a neighboring association or "going it alone" in the market system, without legal reprisal. Power is thus maintained primarily by consensus (bolstered by a need for mutual aid and defense) within a noncoercive system of interaction (customs, rules, mores).

In addition, the state can physically enforce its laws and put people in prison. While the association is often successful in enforcing norms and can issue penalties, it cannot destroy a person's ability to be free and do business. The state also differs in that its statutes tend to be legal specifications of misconduct, whereas the association is more prone to set broad rules and principles guiding conduct. Finally, it is significant that citizens do not have the trade association members' option of dropping out and creating a new organization.

For these and other reasons, the private associational system seems to exemplify greater freedom and individuality in certain respects than the democratic state. But this freedom has its limitations and is partly an illusion. For one thing, trade associations must always operate within the framework of the state, and thus have final recourse to coercion. More important, the associational system is actually a *latent* structure still in the process of emerging; that is, trade associations have not fully evolved to represent the manifest economy. Still more important, since the manifest economy is characterized by concentrated capital, corporate self-interest, profit making, corporate oligopoly, bureaucracy, and command governance, as part of that economy, they are necessarily shaped by these characteristics.

In sum, the visible government of the modern state is being compared here with a relatively "invisible government" in the economy, which although developing as part of the legal system, does not always perform as democratically as its charter supposes. It remains to develop as part of a manifest and purposive economy. The continued evolution of these self-governing associations depends both on their becoming more visible to people and their being guided into a stronger position in the economy by public policies. At the same time, public policies must stimulate the corporate economy to become more decentralized and more efficient in the national interest. If this latent system of associations continues to generate its own growth and is supported by public policies, it may then take more responsibility from the state and regulate the market more fully through its blend of balanced power and accountability. It will then become a part of the manifest economy, a main characteristic of the future market economy.

Associational Community and Autonomy

The "community" is as important a value in the federative structure of exchange as "competition" is in the traditional market. A sense of cohesion and common purpose at each level of associational life is essential for effective administration and survival. Most trade association executives are especially conscious of the need to cultivate this sense of community as key to the success of their own operations. Similarly, if associations are to operate in the public interest, they must work together with shared purpose and find grounds for cooperating in various activities on a regular basis. The next chapter suggests what can be done to steer them in this direction. At the same time, the purpose of public policy is to enable trade associations in the United States to operate in the public interest relatively free of government control. Even now, as we have seen, European governments collaborate with associations and corporations in a much tighter fashion than is favored or even legally permissible in the United States. European associations tend to tie in their activities with government planning in anticipating supply and demand and remedying inflation, and some even have statutory authority to regulate a market on behalf of the state. Trade associations in Japan also have a much closer relationship with their government, as we have seen.

On the other hand, some U.S. associations are inevitably influenced by the close interdependence between government and the industries they represent. We saw this in the dairy and pharmaceutical industries, and it can be documented in many others. The defense industry in particular is so intertwined with government via contracts that it is sometimes impossible to distinguish what is owned by government and what is owned by defense contractors.

To my mind, the importance of the trade association's independence from the government cannot be overemphasized. However tempting it is to envision a close collaboration between the two, the dangers of such collaboration far outweigh its competitive advantages. Perhaps the most frightening instance of this arrangement was the incorporation of trade associations into the fascist state of Italy. The self-regulation of the market can only be carried out when trade associations are able to follow a decentralized and independent pattern of development.[12]

Conclusion: Building a Model for Self-Regulation

The structure of democratically organized voluntary associations holds the promise of the type of governance about which the nineteenth-century philosophers dreamed: a decentralized confederation of firms operating under the aegis of society. (These scholars also added the notion of worker ownership, which we discussed in Chapter Three as a trend in the United States.) In very broad terms, the federation offers a foundation for the economic orders that twentieth-century theorists of capitalism and socialism have imagined. On the one hand, the business scholar Adolf Berle has described and supported the idea of the "economic republic" that seemed to him to be developing within modern business. On the other hand, the socialist G. D. H. Cole vigorously promoted the "guild socialism" that he saw emerging in Great Britain.[13] From their two very different perspectives, both writers were advancing the idea of an associational order that is responsible for acting in the interest of the larger society. Thus, the concept of a federally organized economy continues to find its way into each new half-

TABLE 8
The Social Governance of Markets Through
Voluntary Associations: A Model

Cultural structure:
Societally-accepted norms and values enter the market through the organization of voluntary (trade and professional) associations

Social structure:
Horizontal and vertical associations express democratic systems of governance relatively independent of the state

Structural integration:
Cultural values and norms are integrated in the market through voluntary associations that (1) develop a sense of community among their independently competing firms and (2) maintain autonomy from government controls through systems of social (self-)accountability that function in the public interest

---

century. As the market economy continues to evolve at its own pace and in its own direction, these ideas continue to find their advocates and spread their influence.

We have seen how trade and professional associations have been developing a normative order that integrates societal values into the market through such mechanisms as their own democratic principles and structures, their development of ethical codes for member firms, their use of "due process," and their establishment of professional tribunals. If they continue in these directions, their ability to regulate the market independent of government influence will increase.

The capacity for the economic order to become more self-regulating depends on the degree to which (1) voluntary (professional and trade) associations can integrate more societal norms and values into the market; (2) associations can ensure democratic participation at every level, both horizontal and vertical, of organization; (3) a sense of community can be developed within and between all levels of trade associations; and (4) associations can remain autonomous from government controls. These criteria are summarized in Table 8.

Let me point out that our discussion in this chapter of the way decentralized trade associations develop into a self-governing system bears only on the first step in the development of the latent economy. Table 8 refers to voluntary associations in general, not simply trade (business) associations, since I foresee the fully self-governed economy as being shaped by all kinds of associations. This model, therefore, could refer to the process of integrating the structure of any kind of private association—religious, political, recreational, economic, artistic, scientific, or whatever—with the larger cultural life of society.

Finally, it should be noted that although trade and professional associations have been developing a significant basis for market self-regulation through their own cooperative structures and activities, there is a limit to how far they can go in introducing societal values into the market without changes in the legal climate and supportive public policies. We will therefore need to look into these matters in the succeeding chapters.

CHAPTER 8

A Method of Measurement: Social Indexes

TO GUIDE the policies of regulatory agencies, economists have formulated a set of indexes to measure *competition* through such concepts as degree of concentration, amount of assets, and market share. Now we must also think about the degree and type of *cooperation* that could guide public policy relative to the public interest. My purpose here is to raise the issues that must be dealt with in any set of social indexes purporting to measure the capacity of firms to cooperate both for self-regulation and for competition in the public interest. Again, we will confine our discussion specifically to trade associations.

One important measure would be the ability of associations to control the conduct of their members while respecting their rights to freedom, individuality, and fair competition, since such a capacity would help a market sector remain independent of government regulation. Another key measure is the ability of associations to influence members to become organizationally viable, that is, to help them meet the welfare needs of their own constituencies while developing effectively within the framework of their democratic organization. And there are many other things to weigh.

Referring back to the model of self-governance through associations presented in Table 8, we will consider the development of such social indexes in relation to how (1) the values of the culture become translated into norms in the American marketplace; (2) the politics of U.S. trade associations are shaped by these norms; (3) trade communities are formed through these associations; and (4) associational autonomy may be interpreted, in light of our model.

Social Values and Trade Association Norms

Social issues for which government control is now sought, such as product quality, safety, full disclosure of facts, warranties, and environmental protection, can also be dealt with in the market through the normative life of trade associations. New developments in public interest law are increasing the legitimacy of trade associations to take on this task.

Business law began in part in the United States out of the concern that trade associations might interfere with fair competition,[1] but the courts and regulatory agencies have started to approve greater regulatory activities by trade associations *when associations are operating in the public interest.* This was the gist of the message the Federal Trade Commission conveyed to a trade association in 1967. Expressing its concern that the association did not expel shippers' agents who had repeatedly ignored the association's ethical code, the FTC observed that there "is a greater public interest in protecting shippers from dishonest shippers' agents than there is in condemning the minimal restraints that might result from application of the code." Additionally:

Undoubtedly unreasonable, and therefore unlawful, restraints might result if an association member is arbitrarily or improperly expelled from membership, but the Commission believes that there is ample public interest in effectively encouraging association members to refrain from the clearly pernicious practices condemned by the code.[2]

Support of public responsibilities for trade associations seems to have gained momentum in the early 1970's. One of the first indications of this trend came from Virginia H. Knauer, President Gerald Ford's special assistant for Consumer Affairs, who told members of the American Society of Association Executives at its 1970 convention that "there is a great need on the part of many associations for an effective self-regulation process." That same year, Congress gave jewelry trade associations the authority to enforce their own codes—the first legislative recognition that codes could operate in the public interest.[3] It represented a slight movement toward the level of control that is more typical of European associations.

Two other codes have been given legal standing through court cases, although not with the same enforcement authority. One is the code of the National Association of Broadcasters. American Brands, Inc., sued NAB, charging that the three major television networks had violated the Sherman Antitrust Act by refusing to run its cigarette advertisements on the grounds that they did not conform to the NAB code. In denying American Brands an injunction, the court commented that there "is a substantial if not compelling public interest in having a meaningful, full, specific and adequate disclosure of the relevant facts in cigarette advertising," and that to prevent NAB from implementing the code pending the outcome of the suit would be "contrary to the public interest."[4] The second code was the system the trade associations in the motion picture industry adopted for rating films unsuitable for children; it was held to be in the public interest and not per se a violation of the Sherman Antitrust Act.

In the past decade, the FTC on its own authority has selectively approved codes of ethics in the public interest. On January 17, 1983, in a letter to the American Bar Association, the commission endorsed certain revisions to the ABA's Model Rules of Professional Conduct. Specifically, the FTC hailed plans to discard the more subjective criteria prohibiting attorney advertising considered "self-laudatory" or "undignified," in favor of the more objective criteria of "false" and "misleading." The FTC also authorized the use of the code for communicating information to the public.

Later that year, in June, the FTC expressed its approval of the American Academy of Ophthalmology's proposed code of ethics. In its letter one finds a shift in official recognition toward the more subjective side of codes of ethics. The code states, for example, that ophthalmological services "must be provided with compassion and integrity," and further, that "confidence must be maintained through continued study, confidentiality of patient communications must be respected, fees should not exploit patients or others, patient's welfare must be the ophthalmologist's primary consideration, and ophthalmologists deficient in character should be reported to the proper authorities." The FTC did not find any significant threat to competition posed by these guidelines; in fact, it ruled that the adoption of the proposed code for the purpose described by the academy would violate neither the Federal Trade Commission Act nor any other statute enforced by the FTC. The FTC letter also stated that the code did not raise significant antitrust issues, referring specifically to proposed rules that would "assure to patients such important protections as informed consent, careful pre-operative evaluations, and appropriate consultations." Likewise, the academy's banning of false or deceptive advertising, including both affirmative representations and misrepresentations arising from "the failure to disclose a material fact," did not pose an unreasonable threat to competition or consumers. Indeed, the

FTC said that the rules served "to enhance the competitive process and provide valuable consumer protection."[5]

The growing trend to look favorably on associations' codes of conduct as being in the public interest stems from the recognition of the importance of norms (customs, folkways, traditions, and mores) that develop within the market itself, rather than being imposed by the government. Such norms are approved on the basis of public values that are held not only by the private parties in the trade association, but also by society at large.[6]

In the light of these developments, we are now ready to suggest specific social indexes to measure the capacity of trade associations to take on even more public responsibility.

The Social Structure of Horizontal Trade Associations

In the United States, most trade associations are organized as democratic confederations in which all members have an equal vote in the governance, but each business retains full autonomy to operate as an independent entity. Thus we need social indexes that enable us to determine the degree to which members are free and independent participants in the governance of an association.

Legislative Branch

The legislative branch of a trade association is concerned with rule making, not in the sense of laws enforced by courts but in the sense of norms enforced by association tribunals without the coercion implied in laws. Here we are concerned with the way power is exercised by a body that has neither powers of police nor militia. We can assess its power by looking at voting procedures, sources of income, and the formulation and enforcement of rules.

Voting procedures. The members of a nonprofit association must have equal voting rights in electing the board of directors, which in turn is responsible for appointing staff. Still, surveillance is often required in assessing equity in the political structure, notably in "providing detailed voting rules, . . . preparing and distributing copies of the voting rules, providing the right to vote by proxy, avoiding higher-than-majority voting rules, providing detailed rules for balloting," and so forth.[7] Associations customarily lay out the rules covering the election of directors and the annual meeting in their bylaws. Model bylaws also detail what to do about challenged votes, challenged elections, and the like. Some state statutes provide for inspectors of elections to oversee the conducting of a vote. A member's demand for inspectors must ordinarily be honored even when not backed by the bylaws.[8]

Proposed index: *To what extent do members of an association have equal voting rights in decision making?*

Sources of income. A trade association usually draws its income from members' dues, the structure of which can often express a power differential not reflected in the voting structure. Sales figures are the most popular basis for a dues structure, but some associations prefer units of production or number of employees or total corporate assets. To avoid the problem of larger corporations exercising undue influence over association policy because of their contributions, it is recommended that an association set maximum limits on dues.

Another potential problem, setting dues at a size that may exclude would-be members, has already come before the courts.[9] In 1975 the Supreme Court approved a federal district court decision that the imposition of a minimum fee schedule by the Fairfax County Bar Association and the Virginia State Bar Association violated the Sherman Antitrust Act. The court ruled that the schedule, though purportedly only advisory, was in effect a "rigid price floor" and hence constituted price fixing. In another Virginia case involving minimum fee schedules, a federal district court held that a realty multiple listing service's enforcement of a minimum commission schedule violated Section 1 of the Sherman Act.[10]

Proposed index: *Does an association's income structure avoid discrimination in members' rights to participate fully?*

Judicial Branch

Unlike the judicial branch of the U.S. government, which works within a normative framework established by Congress and state legislatures, the judicial branch of a trade association is responsible to two kinds of legislatures: both those legislative bodies and its own legislature. Issues to be indexed under this area include membership and expulsion policies, due process, and sanctions.

Membership and expulsion policies. Some trade associations have become monopolistic by excluding certain competing firms from membership. Exclusion means that nonmembers do not have the special privileges and market advantages that would otherwise be theirs through association activities. Since being barred from such benefits as participation in trade fairs and receiving trade magazines can be devastating for some firms, exclusion practices can be illegal. When the Associated Press blocked certain newspapers from joining, it was found to be in violation of the Sherman Antitrust Act.

Trade associations do not have the right to compel firms to join if they do not wish to do so. In fact, forcing membership has met with judicial disapproval in a number of cases. But they do have the legal right to expel members, even when this eliminates competition, where there is a serious breach of public norms. Expulsion has passed court scrutiny, for instance, when it involves outright dishonesty or an action that critically disrupts an association's legitimate goals. The important requirement is that there be a "fair and impartial hearing" with a notice of intention to proceed in the expulsion process.[11]

It is in this delicate balance between the full invitation to membership, the refusal to compel firms to join, and the reluctance to expel members except for the most serious breaches of broadly accepted norms that extremism is avoided. A proper balance begins to be defined by keeping in mind both the utilitarian tradition and what Durkheim called social solidarity.[12]

Proposed index: *To what extent are proper membership and expulsion policies followed?*

Due process. Constitutional due process guarantees mean that any provision of an association's code can be subject to court review. For example, a court found that the Angus (cattle) Association's expulsion procedure was inadequate in several respects: "the bylaws of the association did not provide an opportunity for cross-examination or for adequate confrontation of witnesses, formal provisions for notice were lacking, and there were no express provisions governing the conduct of any hearing at which a member violation is at issue, or the rights of any party involved in such a hearing."[13]

The use of boycotts to enforce industry codes is unlawful, and an agreement by the association as a whole to stop doing business with code violators violates the Sherman Antitrust Act. However, *unilateral* decisions to withhold business from companies that violate codes or standards are wholly legal, voluntariness of action being the test.

Because disciplinary proceedings by an association are quasi-judicial, such procedures must satisfy the "elementary requirements of any judicial proceeding." Government courts have held that there must be

1. Reasonable notice of charges;
2. Notice of a hearing;
3. The right of confrontation and cross-examination;
4. An opportunity to refute all charges; and
5. A hearing before an unbiased tribunal.[14]

To fulfill the due process requirement, the judicial function of the association must be independent of any external influence. When a subcommittee of the committee that initiated charges against a member of a bar association handled its own disciplinary hearing, a state court voiced its disapproval because of the possibility of external influence. Once the judicial body is designated, the court said, the members must avoid becoming involved in any other phase of the disciplinary procedure, including preliminary investigations or the formulating of charges. However, the combination of the investigative and adjudicative function in one body does not, by itself, violate due process. These examples show that the courts are gradually infusing the model of a democratic government into the polity of the trade association.

Proposed index: *To what extent does a trade association follow the legal tradition of due process?*

Sanctions. Many associations make the observance of rules of conduct compulsory by making them a condition for admission to membership. Fines, suspension, and expulsion are frequently imposed to compel later adherence, along with such other penalties as ostracism, the withholding of business data, and economic boycotts. But judicial review has made it difficult to enforce codes when they appear to violate the principle of fair competition. For example, the New York Dental Society's code declared that it was unethical to publish or broadcast technical material for a lay audience without first securing the society's approval. Although the intention was to curb unprofessional advertising, a court barred the society from enforcing the code as violating the right of free speech.

Other cases are instructive. The Ladies Professional Golf Association suspended a member for cheating during tournament play, but a court held that the suspension excluded her illegally from being a competitor in the market. In the American Angus Association case, the association suspended a firm that had violated a blood-typing rule; a court ruled that the suspension represented monopoly power, since it placed the firm at a severe competitive disadvantage.

The legal restrictions on trade associations in the interest of maintaining fair competition can be complex. For example, a code of conduct cannot require members of an association to refrain from advertising below-cost prices because advertising can be a legitimate method of competition. But as we have seen, it can also be an illegitimate method of competition. So there is a delicate line to walk among the various opinions rendered at different times.

Proposed index: *To what extent do enforcement sanctions interfere with free competition?*

Norm Making

The law recognizes that trade associations represent entire industries and have a responsibility, if not a duty, to encourage ethical conduct in a wide range of areas. It is further assumed that such codes of conduct will be periodically examined so as to keep pace with changing circumstances and conditions.[15] We examine some of these areas below.

Product quality and safety. We saw how the cheese makers' associations in the Netherlands, threatened by government intervention, undertook their own program to guarantee the quality of their products, issuing a trademark that became highly valued. In the United States, questions might be raised about a practice of that sort. Could nonmembers sell their cheese without the trademark? Must a firm be a member of the association to obtain the trademark? Such questions highlight the fine balance that must be maintained between freedom of enterprise and the trade community's power over member firms in the market.

The Southern Pine Lumber Association faced the same dilemma of maintaining quality when its members began selling inferior lumber. It was a public issue because construction companies needed to rely on the quality of the lumber. The association set up a trademark to guarantee quality, but barred nonmembers from using it. This action made the association a monopoly, because nonmembers could not compete without the trademark. In a test case, courts found that the trademark (a marketable item) had to be available to everyone, and that all firms in the industry had to be represented on the board regulating the trademarking activity.

Proposed index: *Are all firms in the industry represented on trade association boards that control the safety and quality of a product?*

Price control and output. We noted in our European cases (e.g., the Dutch Frisian Union) that output was controlled through trade association agreements based on the assessment of consumer demand. This practice is important to study because it counterbalances tendencies in the capitalist system toward cyclical overproduction and underproduction, a not uncommon problem for U.S. farmers particularly.

Although U.S. courts have prohibited trade associations from controlling prices, federal agencies have "permitted" oligopolies to "administer" prices for lack of solid (witness) evidence, along with a lack of staff to monitor such practices. Let us look at this problem and its alternatives in public policy. In a 1921 case, the hardwood flooring trade association required each of its 365 members to submit six reports: (1) a daily report of all actual sales; (2) a daily shipping report, with exact copies of the invoices; (3) a monthly production report; (4) a monthly stock report; (5) current price lists; and (6) inspection reports. In turn, the trade association supplied detailed reports to its members based on the submitted information. This exchange was supplemented by monthly meetings, where speakers urged cooperation on reducing production because of expected low demand. The Supreme Court concluded that this was "not the conduct of competitors." [16] In subsequent cases, the court showed its displeasure with trade association programs that involved the elaborate standardization of sales conditions, reports of future prices, and requirements that members must adhere to their reported prices. In general, the court has shown approval when associations limit price reports to past transactions, preserve the anonymity of individual traders, make data available to buyers as well as sellers, and permit departure from prices filed. [17]

This legal tradition raises two issues relative to a theory of self-regulation. First, the democratic practices of the trade association must be indexed in order to determine the extent to which the control of prices and output is voluntary among member firms. Such indexes have already been discussed in terms of polity. This issue goes to the heart of the way corporations organize to market their products through vertical structures. This issue also includes a debate about giving oligopolies, with their direct command over mass production, the right to control production on the basis of their market forecasts, while denying that right to a democratically constituted body of small firms. On the other hand, in a low-demand market, small firms can destroy one another through competition unless they are able to maintain their production rationally through cooperative action. The legal questions here rest on the current presumption in the United States that the *enterprise*—not the trade association—is the more legitimate unit in judging freedom to make decisions in the marketplace. In the perspective proposed here, the nonprofit trade association should be recognized as having its own legitimacy and constitutionality. Furthermore, recognizing trade associations of small firms as legitimate *production units* in the economy could provide a social basis for small enterprise to survive in a market field of conglomerates. Such a development, which is discussed in detail in Chapter Eleven, would require new legal bases.

The second issue concerns the extent to which production may be controlled to raise prices improperly. Let us say that producers plan to curtail production with the specific goal of causing a scarcity of product that will push up prices. In this case, professional judgment about propriety rests on the extent to which production is being controlled in a monopolistic manner. A political judgment must also be made on whether the distribution of other firms in the vertical line (wholesale, retail, and consumption) are balanced in their power against the power exerted by producers. This includes the freedom of firms (and associations) in other sectors to enter production in the event of such monopolistic practices.

We noted that the MIGROS and COOP cooperatives in Switzerland not only represented the consumers in balancing the power of producers and distributors, but also maintained some production of their own, which provided the added balance against monopolistic measures taken by a producer's association. In the United States, distributors can engage in modes of production that offset the threat of a producer's association attempting to create scarcity for the purpose of raising prices. We will discuss this matter in detail later, but the decision about the right to control production levels through a trade association rests on whether a balance of power exists vertically.

Agricultural markets illustrate the relevance of this issue. Farm cooperatives argue that the FTC unfairly compares their marketing power with that of business corporations. They point out that, unlike an auto or steel manufacturer, which can control production according to predicted demand, the agricultural marketing cooperative has no control over the production of its farmer-members and usually has contractual agreements to market everything they produce. Hence, a milk cooperative's control of 75 percent of the supply of raw milk does not confer the same power as a single firm's control of 75 percent of steel production. That firm expects to sell all its output at a certain price; the coop's clients buy only as much as they want and often specify the price as well as the quantity. Cooperatives assert that it is critical to understand such variations in organizational structure in assessing the balance of power in any industry.[18]

Now, one could counter this argument by pointing out that statisticians today can pretty accurately forecast demand, so the dairy farmers *could* control production to match anticipated sales by reorganizing their cooperative. However, if they did so, they would lose government support of various kinds. So one question to be resolved is whether individual farmers want to produce as much as they can without taking demand and the larger needs of the society into account. Furthermore, Supreme Court decisions have generally opposed the setting of levels of production by trade associations. If farm cooperatives were actually to seek to control their production, they could be transgressing the law.

The self-regulatory solution to this paradox is to create a legal basis for farmers collectively to control their own production. The question for the courts is whether there is a balance of power in the stages of production of certain farm products that would permit such action. The question for farmers, in turn, is whether they want to exercise control through cooperatives and trade associations. The answers can be found in the way trade groups are organized in vertical structures.

Proposed indexes: *To what extent is control over prices and output a result of decision making by all members of an association? To what extent does a balance of power exist between levels of associations at each stage of production (verticality)?*

The Social Structure of Vertical Associations

Corporations and associations that join across market sectors from supply to production to distribution to retail have vertically integrated their markets. The degree to which firms vertically integrate is constantly changing in a system of dynamic markets. Corporations may decide to incorporate firms vertically at any stage of production. For example, the U.S. pharmaceutical industry in the nineteenth century had no supply enterprises; raw materials for synthesized drugs were imported from European sources. Then supply firms began to develop as autonomous firms while pharmaceutical manufacturers were simultaneously growing in number. Gradually, manufacturers began to see advantages in vertically integrating their activities, backward to supply and forward to wholesale and to other distribution systems.

Some trade associations in the United States also organize vertically—the Better Vision Institute, which is composed of U.S. manufacturers, distributors, and service people in the optical products field, is one—but this pattern is more typical of the European economy. We saw how the whole Swiss dairy industry is closely interrelated through associations of firms from supply to distribution to consumption, with local milk producers organized into regional associations, which are organized into a central association of all producers in the country. Although that central association regulates production and prices with the Association of Milk Buyers in a closely integrated system, neither is vertically integrated under a command system as in business corporations. The dairy associations are democratic and autonomous at each level and voluntarily contract with one another. In the United States, it is the business corporation that engages significantly in vertical integration; hence, vertical markets must be examined first.

The criterion of public interest. U.S. manufacturers launched into forward integration when railroads and the telegraph and telephone systems appeared in the latter part of the nineteenth century. With vast new territories to be served, it became crucial to devise a coordinated manufacturing and distribution network. Manufacturers could have remained specialized and built large plants, and specialized distributors could have provided the initiative for a distributive system, but in many industries the marketers were unable to sell and distribute products in the volume produced. "Once the inadequacies of existing marketers became clear, manufacturers integrated forward into marketing." [19]

Not all industries integrated forward, to be sure—some only forged advertising and wholesaling connections and left retail alone—but the significant development in this process was the emergence of the "multidivisional firm." The transformation of the corporation from a unitary command system has been documented by Alfred Chandler, and its success has been carefully studied by other business scholars. The multidivisional firm (M-form) removed the executives responsible for the destiny of the entire enterprise from the more routine operational activities and gave them time for long-term planning and evaluation, leaving the broad strategic decisions of allocating resources to a top team of generalists with little reason to favor one unit over another. [20] This change accomplished a number of things. It helped to tighten up corporate effort, provided more planning power, and decentralized administrative authority, with operating divisions assigned the status of quasi-firms and governed in a quasi-market fashion, and the central office assuming the functions of review and resource allocation ordinarily associated with the capital market. As a result, a measure of social development could be observed as more autonomous authority was divided among managers.

The emergence of the multidivisional corporation as an adaptation in the process of vertical integration is critical to our study of trade associations. The step toward the large size required to move vertically also requires greater decentralization, a process that corresponds to the effectiveness that a trade federation gains in overseeing whole industrial sectors. I am suggesting that total vertical integration may work most effectively through a decentralized federation of firms left to manage their own sectors with both profit motives and professional competence.

Indexing the capability of firms to move vertically is then associated with their effectiveness in performing their tasks in the public interest—actually in both the corporate interest and the public interest simultaneously. This order of development within market sectors is not easy to accomplish. The trade association waits in the wings to be considered as a legal alternative to fulfill the task under the conditions of indexing being reviewed here.

It should be noted that there are many social factors involving the motives and the power of manufacturers that are not fully answered in Chandler's analysis. For example, to what extent was "demand" created by the manufacturers (rather than by consumers) through their vision of the "potential" market? To what extent were the marketers' skills and marketing knowledge inadequate? Perhaps they were inadequate relative only to the more powerful and skillful manufacturers. Had the marketers developed comparable management skills and vision, could the distributive system have maintained its autonomy, as opposed to being integrated into the manufacturing companies' hierarchy? Is this process of takeover "natural" or socially constructed by the producers? Put another way, in a totally different environment of government incentives, folkways, and so forth, could the manufacturers have trained the marketers to become skillful in marketing techniques and then shared with them in the profits? If the U.S. Antitrust Division had been adamant about stopping vertical moves, could the autonomous division of ownership between manufacturing and distribution have been maintained, with no loss of efficiency in the marketplace? The answer depends partly on whether people believe an autonomous system of distribution is important and partly on the question of effectiveness. I suggest the answer can be found by applying indexes on trade polity along with indexes on what Oliver Williamson calls transactional costs (to be discussed later).

The concepts of both power and authority are critical to the social development of firms and market sectors. It is notable in this case that the decentralization of power and authority in the M-form coincides with what Williamson calls "bounded rationality" and Chandler calls efficiency. I would argue that, in assessing the capacity of markets to become self-regulating, power and efficiency both play critical roles.[21] Chandler's M-form suggests that the decentralization of authority works by increasing the firm's capacity to become both more efficient and self-governing. Hence, further decentralization is worth examining, especially from the perspective that a trade association is an important alternative in the productive development of markets.

Proposed index: *To what extent does the vertical integration of a firm require greater decentralized (federated) authority to operate effectively in the public interest?*

Measures of vertical integration. There is no such creature in today's economy as a vertically integrated firm whose operations are 100 percent owned and physically interconnected under a command system and supply 100 percent of the firm's needs. Vertical integration now varies in breadth, stages, degree, and form.[22] *Breadth* is determined by the activities a firm might perform in-house. For example, a television manufacturer is broadly integrated if it designs and makes its own electronic components, picture tubes, and power supplies, sells its sets through its own retail outlets, and maintains a service operation, while the less integrated firm simply designs and assembles its own electronic components.

The *stages* of vertical integration involve each distinct activity. For example, the stages of integration for a television firm that produces picture tubes, the glass envelopes that encase them, connectors, capacitors, and other ordinarily purchased components, are greater than the stages for a firm that merely assembles picture tubes from sourced components. A firm with more stages would behave differently under adverse competitive conditions from one with fewer stages. Furthermore, business units are typically concerned primarily with stages of activity adjacent to their central missions, but their parent companies may push the stages of corporate involvement much farther. Thus, the proper stage of integration is more an issue of corporate than business-unit strategy.

Degree of integration is a separate issue for each activity. The firm that is highly integrated performs nearly all of a given activity in-house; the firm with less internal integration purchases some part of the product and/or service needed from outsiders. Finally, the *form* of a vertical relationship affects the amount of asset exposure and flexibility a venture possesses. Although a firm may prefer an outright ownership of trading partners, there are situations in which joint ventures or local ownership may be more profitable.

The advantages of vertical integration, whether through corporations or trade associations, are apparent. First, integration saves costs by eliminating duplicate sources of overhead. Retailing one's own wares can save the cost of wholesaler advertising, for example. Second, arrangements between manufacturing firms' trade association and wholesaling associations may also reduce costs as long as the practice does not interfere with fair competition among nonmembers in the same product line. In addition, expensive and time-consuming tasks, such as price shopping, communicating design details, and contracting, can be circumvented through vertical integration if goods and/or services are purchased routinely. The economic benefits of integrating firms come from improved coordination of activities.

Vertical integration can be used by firms or associations to gain improved marketing and technological intelligence, develop a superior control over an environment, and offer product-differentiation advantages that competitors in adjacent lines cannot duplicate.

Proposed indexes: *To what extent is a market vertically controlled by a command system through measures of breadth, stages, degree, and form?*

To what extent does a vertical merger reduce transaction costs?

The balance of power among buyer and seller associations. This category needs little comment. Keeping in mind our theory of self-regulatory development among associations, we plainly need to ensure a balance of power among buyer-seller associations.

Proposed indexes: *To what extent does fair competition exist between associations?*

To what extent does a balance of power exist between associations at different stages of development?

Conflict resolution. We have not discussed the degree to which horizontal associations integrate vertically because this practice is not so widespread in the United States as it is in Europe. But because development can be expected in this direction with public policies based on self-regulation, it is important to consider the relevant features of verticality. The extent to which one trade association has the capacity to resolve its conflicts with another in the vertical market chain affects the ability of both to govern themselves. Issues of organizational bureaucracy also become more critical to examine here, especially because they become a part of future considerations. And it is critical to examine the extent to which vertical power reaches the organized consumer, as in the dairy market in Switzerland.

Vertical problems of fairness have been resolved in the United States through interassociational committees. The association of retail druggists has settled conflicts with manufacturers over a number of issues, such as generic drugs. The National Association of Automobile Dealers and General Motors have a tribunal to adjudicate disagreements over norms in distribution, and petroleum industry associations have settled problems between themselves through interassociational committees. Other vertically related trade associations have likewise established their own judicial arrangements outside the federal court system.[23]

Proposed index: *To what extent can vertical conflicts be resolved through interassociational committees or other means?*

Community Building Within Trade Associations

For firms to achieve a sense of community with each other, they must find a basis for cooperating regularly. Our case studies in the pharmaceutical and dairy sectors showed some efforts to create common activities. Here are five other examples from the United States:

1. By holding periodic meetings, the National Association of Pharmaceutical Manufacturers attempts to encourage a sense of community among its members. It considers problems arising from government laws regarding its sector; conducts educational seminars in cooperation with the Food and Drug Administration and the scientific community; organizes joint research; sponsors competitions; bestows awards; and conducts technical symposia.

2. At another level of market organization, the National Association of Chain Drug Stores sponsors recruitment programs for pharmacy students; holds conferences on such subjects as administrative operations, cosmetic and fragrance marketing, and merchandising; and publishes a monthly journal, a semimonthly newsletter, an annual almanac, and an annual calendar.

3. The National Association of Drug and Allied Sales Organizations provides employment services and health, accident, and life insurance to members; conducts surveys of sales skills; helps retailers and manufacturers in hiring; conducts specialized education programs; and publishes *The Traveler*, a monthly informational journal.

4. The United Dairy Industry Association conducts nutrition research and education programs for the National Dairy Council; provides telecommunications services; holds conferences; and publishes monthly newsletters plus an annual report.

5. The Wisconsin Cheese Makers' Association educates members in the art of cheese making and the care and management of

factories; works to curb incompetency; seeks to protect against imitations; offers short courses at the university level; holds biennial contests to stimulate interest in product quality; and publishes newsletters and journals.

Proposed indexes: *How often are meetings held* (monthly, annually)?
Attendance at meetings (20%, 60% of the membership)?
How often does the staff communicate with members through a medium such as a newsletter or journal (daily, weekly, monthly)?
Which common interests are represented in the activities (e.g., recruitment, accounting, sales, R&D)?
What is the ratio of staff to membership?
Are there conflict resolution committees?

To maintain viability, professional and industry associations must establish and enforce norms in both their own and the public interest. Hence, such indexes of community life should also be used by government agencies and the courts in measuring and cultivating a self-regulatory system.

The Need for Autonomy

The Case of Schechter v. United States

In the early 1930's, during the Great Depression, Congress enacted an experiment in industry self-regulation that is especially important for understanding how trade associations may develop autonomously in the public interest. I refer to the National Industrial Recovery Act of 1933, which authorized the President to approve "codes of fair competition for any trade or industry upon application from groups representing industry members," provided

(1) that such associations or groups impose no inequitable restrictions on admission to membership and are truly representative of such trades or industries or subdivisions therefore, and (2) that such a code or codes are not designed to promote monopolies or eliminate or oppress small enterprises. . . . The President may, as a condition of his approval of any such code, impose such conditions . . . for the protection of consumers, competitors, employees, and others, and in furtherance of the public interest, and may provide such exceptions . . . as his discretion deems necessary to effectuate the policy herein declared.[24]

Once a trade code was approved by the President, any violation of it was declared to be "an unfair method of competition in commerce within the Federal Trade Commission Act as amended."

A number of codes were quickly developed, approved, and put into effect, including the Live Poultry Code applicable to New York City and the metropolitan area. In *Schechter* v. *United States*, the code came before the Supreme Court in 1935, on appeal by a New York City slaughterhouse convicted of numerous violations. The court rejected the government's argument that because the code was written during an extraordinary emergency, it was legitimate.[25]

The Poultry Code was deemed unconstitutional on three grounds. First, because it became law through presidential authorization rather than congressional enactment, it represented a usurpation of power. Second, all of the infractions involved in the case occurred in intrastate, not interstate, commerce. Third, as a private code, implying voluntary compliance, it could not have the effect of a law to be enforced by government; law making is a state prerogative. The *Schechter* decision does not bar the self-enforcement of codes of ethics but does prevent giving the force of law to codes promulgated by a private group.

Later Experiments

Experiments in trade association self-management are being conducted today with the approval of the Federal Trade Commission. We saw some of them earlier in the chapter. Here is another example. When, in 1967, a group of magazine publishers became concerned about abuses in door-to-door sales of subscriptions, it secured FTC approval for a self-regulatory program to curb them. All subscription agencies employing sales personnel would be given the names of salespeople who used deceptive practices, and any agency that let the practices continue would be penalized by up to $5,000 per violation, enforcement to be handled by an independent administrator. The FTC declared that such fines would "not operate anticompetitively or in a confiscatory manner but [would be] sufficient to constitute a deterrent."[26] The FTC placed two conditions on the arrangement. First, compliance with the code by subscription agencies was to be completely voluntary, and second, approval was for only a three-year period, after which the program would be reconsidered. As it happened, when the time

ran out, no request for renewal was made, but in the meantime the
FTC had issued formal complaints against a number of agencies.

A Melding of U.S. and European Practices

According to our concept of social development, it is possible for
codes to be generated within associations, then enforced effectively and fairly by them without interfering with open competition, but this can be done only when public policy encourages it.

I believe that trade associations can become more autonomous,
as they tend to be in the American tradition, and at the same time
increasingly publicly responsible, as they tend to be in the European tradition, and that they can move in these two directions
while members simultaneously maintain their efficiency, productivity, and profitability. Both economic and social indexes must be
used to measure this line of development in order to determine the
extent to which associations can act on their own apart from government authorization and at the same time function responsibly
in society.

We have already discussed indexes designed to measure the extent to which associations are organized to reflect the public interest. Let us look now at their general capacity to operate independently of the government, indexing for autonomy in four areas:
statutory monopoly, state involvement on boards, government support systems, and constitutional authority.

Statutory monopoly. In the Netherlands, we saw trade associations that have a "statutory monopoly" to operate in given sectors.
The Dutch STA has the legal right to regulate market sectors on
both horizontal and vertical levels, and it is an autonomous democratic entity mandated to make enforceable rules. Such an arrangement is impermissible in the United States under present law. The
difference between the Dutch association and the U.S. association
is a matter of legal tradition, but it may also be a matter of business
evolution.

Because nonstatutory trade associations have developed a capacity to act responsibly in the area of product safety without requiring government authority, it is reasonable to believe they may take
steps in that direction under the advisement of federal agencies
without taking on this aspect of the European tradition. This means
that they may establish a broad set of norms without requiring stat-

utory authority, a practice that would maintain the principle of free competition and the right of groups to organize other trade associations as a changing market may require.

Proposed index: *To what extent can a trade association set social standards apart from the government?*

State boards. In the Netherlands, the government is represented on a trade association governing board by both a state-appointed full-time chairperson and a number of civil servants who have the status of observer without voting rights. In the United States, there is no direct government involvement in trade associations, although the activities of semipublic agencies such as utilities are monitored. Conceivably, similar monitoring could develop in strategically sensitive markets, but it is also conceivable that the monitoring function could be only temporary. The ultimate objective of trade development in the social sector should be autonomy in the public interest.

Proposed index: *To what extent should the state be represented in the governance of trade associations?*

State supports. In both the United States and our European cases, government is deeply involved financially in markets like the dairy and pharmaceutical industries. It is reasonable to believe that such government involvement could be reduced, or even eliminated; the degree of reduction can be indexed through government cost ratios or cost-benefit studies, as well as through the social indexes under discussion.

Proposed index: *To what extent should government be involved in the buying, selling, price setting, and subsidizing of products within an industry?*

Constitutional authority. Trade associations are in the process of social development; as nonprofits, they are related to what we have described as the "social sector." They formulate bylaws delineating the norms of democratic practice within the association and the equitable distribution of power among the members; and they establish social norms reflecting the fundamental American values (freedom, equality, justice, welfare, democracy, etc.) that were formerly channeled through the government's control over the economy.

Can these values and norms be incorporated into both the constitutions of trade associations and their administrative and judicial functions? Many matters that now fall almost entirely in the purview of government—health, environmental protection, conservation, labor relations, consumer protection, product quality, and full disclosure are a few—could enter the domain of the trade association. The incentive for this to come about is for the association to be given more power, provided that association executives and constituencies respond to the indexes of polity discussed here. The democratic constitution of the association may then become a basis for developing principles that in themselves generate public norms in the marketplace.

Fundamental in this connection is drawing a line between principles and procedures. A federal agency is plainly much more "controlling" over the market when it prescribes precise procedures by which associations must conduct their operations than when it simply sets down general principles guiding their conduct. While precise procedures are needed in certain cases because they are objective and provide a sense of security for association executives—they are exact on what is right or wrong—they are restrictive and inappropriate in other cases, since they can curb individual freedom and imagination.

It is important to draw a distinction as well between statutory and constitutional law. Statutory law is based on operational definitions of publicly unacceptable behavior (e.g., "burglary" is breaking and entering after 6:00 P.M.). This is different from constitutional principles that guarantee, say, the right to free speech, or due process, or the separation of church and state. Put more concretely, if government were to specify exactly which members of a trade association should be on a tribunal to enforce ethical codes, it would be limiting the association's freedom to operate independently, more so than if it merely set forth a principle ("a tribunal should be composed of parties not involved in the offense"). The same distinction applies to the development of a trade association's constitution. Constitutional principles reflect the basic values of a society; a legislative body translates them into norms. In turn, the judiciary interprets the norms and the administration enforces them.

It is possible to encourage the development of private (social) constitutions that would be the repositories of the values underlying American culture. Such trade association constitutions could then guide the formation of norms that would, in turn, direct association activity. If the norms failed to express the principles in practice, they could be brought into conformity. A trade association constitution would thus allow an association to be more self-governing as it acts to realize these values in the marketplace.

Proposed index: *To what extent can trade associations develop private constitutional authority based in the public interest?*

It is conceivable that the fragmented and competitive market economy described by Karl Marx as anarchic and by Emile Durkheim as anomic may find itself becoming organized by public policy in a new context of society, while building a new foundation on the principles of community. This chapter has explored how social indexes can be used to measure the development of trade associations that might move us in that direction. In the next chapter, we will look at the emergence of new legal rationales that may give them a strong legitimate basis on which to act in the public interest.

CHAPTER 9

A Legal Rationale: The Public Interest

WHEN ALEXIS DE TOCQUEVILLE VISITED the United States in the 1830's, he was struck not only by the ethic of "individualism," but also by the social orientation that seemed to him to characterize the new democratic republic. He speculated that the success of the new enterprise was linked to a moral life apart from government, which included the "mores" and "habits of the heart" that shaped the dispositions of individuals in action. But while he noted that the American republic was creating a tradition of public concern rooted in religious life and local politics, a public-spiritedness that enabled institutions to be self-governing, which was all to the good, he felt compelled to warn of the destructive drift of a commercial society and individual self-interest if left to develop unchecked. He also feared that the state's administrative apparatus might grow and intensify the breakdown of communal organization already taking place under the impact of commerce. To combat these tendencies, Tocqueville reaffirmed the importance of civic associations as forums in which an understanding of the meaning of citizenship could be developed. Associations could provide regular opportunities where opinion could be shaped publicly and public initiatives could be inspired.[1]

In fact, there is a growing public philosophy reflecting precisely the kind of "civic republicanism" de Tocqueville recommended, a development that has led some scholars to assert that a new concept of the "public" is appearing that goes beyond the state.[2] One of the most telling signs of this changing mood is the growth of what is called public interest law.

Public interest law has moved in two directions. The more publicly visible trend is toward serving the interests of minorities and other underrepresented members of society. But equally important is the development of public interest law that breaks tradition in business law. Both trends suggest new avenues through which the government can help the private sector work in the public interest.

The origins of public interest law go back a hundred years, but it has expanded spectacularly in the past two decades. In 1969, there were 15 nonprofit public interest law centers with fewer than 50 full-time attorneys in the United States; by the end of 1975, there were 92 centers with almost 600 attorneys. The numbers have continued to increase, and the spectrum of issues covered now includes consumer protection, environmental protection, land and energy use, tax reform, occupational health and safety, health care, media access, corporate responsibility, education reform, employment benefits, and manpower training.[3]

One aspect of public interest law that is especially relevant here, which is developing in conjunction with economic theory, is an attempt to integrate the opposing concepts of allocative efficiency and distributional equity. It assumes that the goals of efficiency and equity are not necessarily contradictory, and that their synthesis can be a basis for judging whether the market is operating in the public interest. We shall look first at this side of public law in order to clarify the equally nettling issue of combining social and economic indexes of development.

The Meaning of Efficiency and Equity

"Efficiency" in our context refers to the size of a society's output, "equity" to how the fruits of that output are distributed to people. The public issue is how these two concepts can be measured together in the marketplace, and then how they can be related to socioeconomic indexes.

Efficiency can have two meanings. There is "technical efficiency," which means providing a particular product or service at the lowest possible cost. And there is "allocative efficiency," which refers to the degree to which productive resources are put to their most valuable uses. Allocative efficiency is increasingly relevant in assessing market decisions in public interest law, because it is related to equity and what institutional economists have defined as a social welfare function, or "welfare optimality," an idea introduced by the sociologist Vilfredo Pareto.

"Optimum" means most favorable; it differs from "maximum," which means the greatest value attainable in a given case. The difference can be seen by comparing the speed sought by a dragster in a race with the speed sought by the driver of a family car; the dragster maximizes speed at virtually any personal cost while the driver of the family car varies speed to purpose. Social norms also enter into determining the speed of the family car. The father may want to conserve gas, and the mother may be concerned with the family's safety; the local government may be concerned with public safety and a gas shortage.

According to the principle of optimality, whenever free and voluntary exchange occurs with no adverse third-party effects, at least one person is made better off and no one is made worse off (as each party to the exchange understands his or her own well-being). This is not the world of oligopoly or monopoly, where consumers are given offers they may not be able to refuse. It is a world of free and voluntary exchange, and such exchange would simply not occur unless at least one person's lot is improved and no one else's is worsened. Pareto's optimal conditions therefore require at least two conditions of efficiency: consumption and production.

Consumption efficiency exists when goods go to people who want them most, as tea goes to tea drinkers and coffee to coffee drinkers. In other words, the goods are allocated properly to those who want them. Production efficiency exists when each desirable good is produced as resources permit, keeping in mind the production of other desirable goods.[4]

The theory of allocative efficiency follows from this concept of the optimum. It is based on the assumptions that (1) resource owners, including workers and households, know what they can earn in various uses of their time; (2) producers know the prices at which they can sell added output; and (3) the prices that producers can get are close approximations of the prices that consumers are willing to pay. Adherents of this theory argue that competitive forces can be expected to bring about allocative efficiency if all three conditions are satisfied.[5] If condition (3) does not hold, then too few resources will be devoted to producing the commodity involved. Thus allocative efficiency can be achieved only when consumers clearly transmit their demands to producers.

At the same time, there is a public interest in achieving a fair distribution of society's income and other rewards, such as the opportunity for people to improve their positions and to participate equitably in the corporate economy. In judging equity, some people emphasize the process by which income is divided and power exercised in the corporate system, and others emphasize the results of the process, the degree of inequality in income.

Efficiency and equity are not necessarily exclusive, since efficiency is not achieved by a narrow preoccupation with cutting costs. Legal economists assert that there is a public interest in both the efficient use of resources and the distribution of the fruits of their use. Even if the measurement of efficiency and equity results in the favoring of one or the other in a particular case, the calculation makes that evident in seeking a synthesis.[6] The assumption in this approach to public interest law is therefore that when programs are efficient and their distributional effects are deemed equitable, they are in the public interest. Decisions regarding the public interest are not judged solely on these dimensions, of course, but legal economists propose that they be factored in.[7]

The concept of allocative efficiency involves a comparison of the values to consumers and to resource suppliers of alternative uses, and holds that the social welfare is inseparable from the welfare of the individual. By definition, an action is not in the public interest if it makes everyone worse off. Thus, resources are allocated efficiently when consumers get the goods and services they want at prices sufficient to compensate workers and other resource owners for their voluntary supply of the resources required to produce those goods and services.

In addition to this concept of efficiency, public interest lawyers recognize another: that people decide not on the basis of whether one allocation of resources is more desirable than another, but on the basis of how certain allocations are arrived at, that is, on the basis of the process itself, not its individual workings. Thus a constitution can be viewed as an agreed-on set of rules for determining and restricting what is efficient. The U.S. Constitution, for example, provides for due process without explicit attention to its benefits and costs in specific instances. It can be argued that the costs and benefits of due process in a particular instance are so great that it would be inefficient to make such a determination. The constitutional guarantee can be thought of as reflecting a judgment that on average and over time the resources required to carry out the guarantee will bring benefits that outweigh the costs. In other terms, it is assumed that the political forms of democracy are the most efficient method of organizing government, as experienced over centuries, and given the historical costs of dissent and revolution.

Our model for the social governance of the market in the public interest can be assessed within this framework. The model is based on a structure of equity that has endured the tests of a century of trade association activity and that has yielded positive results in the employment of corporate resources within industries, since trade associations have organized themselves democratically with due process, and have established communities of interest that can operate responsibly within market sectors under specific conditions.

From the above discussion, we can now see that certain measures are available to government agencies to help them determine the public interest in cases brought to their attention. In addition to all the traditional economic measures of such issues as economic concentration, barriers to entry, price fixing, and technical efficiency, they can apply the measure of allocational efficiency based on known factors in the distribution of resources, and the measure of equity based on principles of democratic governance of trade associations.

Balancing Efficiency and Equity in Public Policy

Some legal economists have already begun to apply the concepts of allocative and technical efficiency and distributional equity quantitatively in assessing public policy. They observe that when the profit sector fails in matters of equity, the problem can be corrected through the distributional-equity capabilities of nonprofit organizations such as trade associations or government institutions, which are better prepared to achieve this value. Conversely, when the nonprofit sector fails in technical efficiency, the problem can be corrected through the more efficient capabilities of the profit sector. Either sector may succeed or fail, of course, in either area, so it is important to explore how success in one sector can correct failure in the other. We shall examine instances in which applications of this principle have been made, and add the concept of democratic polity (process equity), which is implicit in our associational model of market governance.

Safety

The Occupational Safety and Health Act of 1970, written "to assure so far as possible every working man and woman in the nation safe and healthful working conditions," provides for input by workers or their representatives at various stages of rule promulgation and enforcement. These employee rights are an important foundation for public interest litigation and other activities, especially since National Safety Council data show that thousands of workers are killed and millions injured each year in on-the-job accidents, and that the frequency is increasing on both counts.

In a very important study, Russell Settle and Burton Weisbrod assessed public interest law activities in this domain based on three recent cases, evaluating objectives, remedies sought, and outcomes in terms of both allocative efficiency and distributional equity. They saw a potential private market failure if workers have an imperfect understanding of the hazards inherent in jobs, if job safety and health hazards impose external costs on nonworkers, or if society's well-being is in part dependent on the continued safety and health of workers, potential in the sense that it may or may not be possible for collective intervention to bring about a more positive outcome. In response to this problem, they looked at the costs and benefits entailed in the operations of the Occupational Safety and Health Administration by analyzing efficiency in many areas, including workers' information about the law; the burden to workers of gathering sufficient evidence to protest a safety problem; the information available to workers on what constitutes a hazard; the job-loss risk in reporting a hazard; and union efficacy in providing information to 21 million members, as opposed to the 60 million workers covered by OSHA. Their conclusions, although tentative, were not optimistic in terms of efficiency.[8]

Settle and Weisbrod then looked for methods for increasing efficiency, such as union financing of the collection and dissemination of work-hazard information by safety and health experts, and pressuring employers for improvements in conditions. The associated costs would be enormous, they judge, requiring large union memberships and vast treasuries. For example, little is known about the ultimate effects of literally thousands of potential occupational health hazards; the 1972 Toxic Substances List identified over 13,000 hazardous substances, and another 25,000 to 300,000 may have been omitted.

Settle and Weisbrod also investigated the income-distribution effects of OSHA standards to determine how the poor might benefit from selective enforcement. Although there is no legal basis for that kind of enforcement, and no solid data that low-paying jobs are more hazardous, they found that OSHA has tended to focus on higher-paying jobs, due partly to its Target Industry Program, which concentrates on a small number of high-risk fields, such as roofing and sheet metal, meat and meat products, transportation equipment, lumber products, and longshoring, all fields where pay scales are higher than average. To relate efficiency and equity issues statistically is too complex a procedure to describe here, but the researchers concluded that the application of their measures would yield a basis for public policy. Further, although government can compensate to some degree for the failure of the private sector, both government and the private sector fail in certain respects to be fully efficient and equitable.

But the Settle and Weisbrod analysis is based on the concept of the market as made up solely of corporate units. By measuring the role of trade associations described in our model of social governance, we would add "process" (or structural) equity to distributional equity. Indeed, I would add still another equity measure, one that assesses the level of worker participation and worker management within corporations. Let us look at each of these issues separately in order to determine how job-safety problems might be better resolved in the public interest.

Settle and Weisbrod found that employers as well as workers have a concern for safety and health in the workplace, but may not maintain the proper standards consistently because of competitive pressures. Since firms act primarily on the principle of technical efficiency, seeking to reduce production costs, this means that the market of independent firms is partly responsible for unsafe workplaces. It follows that employers need *industry-wide safety standards;* but safety practices will become economically feasible only when *all competitors follow the same safety procedures and install similar protective equipment.*

In such cases, trade associations, in collaboration with unions, can share the responsibility and costs of taking on the critical role of setting standards and gathering information on hazards across an industry. With such industry-wide standards, competition would then take place on a level playing field, since an entire industry would be engaged, and rivalry in regard to matters of efficiency would be minimized.

Second, a government program encouraging worker participation in ownership and management should logically bring greater interest in maintaining safe workplaces. Where workers participate in management at high levels, concern for job safety should increase; information should be more readily communicated to workers; and workers would be more willing to point out unsafe conditions, since they would not worry about losing their jobs. Moreover, government could save money through the consequent reduction in OSHA expenditures.

The cost savings accruing to the government as a result of encouraging self-regulatory practices have been studied in Sweden, where employer and trade union associations participated in a successful self-monitoring system. Members of the trade association saved money (technical efficiency), safety and health standards were enforced more equitably, and government did not have to be a monitor. While all private interests therefore benefited, the new organization of employer/employee association monitoring within the industry was also in the public interest, because it was both more efficient and more equitable for everyone.[9]

Consumer Protection

In another important study, this one examining consumer problems, Arthur Snow and Burton Weisbrod found many failures of allocative efficiency that were measurable both in the private market and in government. The associated technical costs to government of such failures are extremely burdensome. In 1973, for example, there were some 20 federal and 2,000 state and local agencies engaged in providing consumers with information and other forms of protection, at a cost to the federal government alone of at least $1.2 billion.

The market fails when it does not give consumers adequate information to make rational choices, with damages to third parties the most deleterious effect: when a car with a high performance risk causes an accident, a third party is damaged; when people smoke, they pollute the air others breathe. Snow and Weisbrod estimated the costs of "third party" effects to be substantial. Focusing on the competitive system that produces the damages, the authors reasoned:

The existence of incentives that lead a manufacturer or retailer to misrepresent his product or to withhold information for which consumers would be willing to pay is a source of potential private market failure, and hence is a source of inefficiency and inequity. If firms or individuals responsible for "third party" effects were motivated by social responsibility or honesty, the market failure might be avoided. However, too much social responsibility or too much honesty might create problems of their own. It might be inefficient and it might be deemed inequitable for one man to impose his version of responsibility on another.[10]

The authors cannot conceive of this problem being resolved by the competitive profit sector and therefore recommend government controls. But I would argue that the problem of third-party damages could just as well be solved by altering the conditions of competition through the horizontal structure of associations. "Too much honesty" need not interfere with a firm's efficiency when competing firms are cooperating to solve the problem. Deceptive advertising becomes the exception when firms work together through their trade association to establish standards of honesty, and they can do this when they maintain the democratic polity that many associations have already put together.

The vertical structure of associations can also provide the solution. By way of illustration, let us look at a case where that might have worked fully as well as the chosen avenue—government. The Virginia Pharmaceutical Association Code of Conduct prohibited advertising, but with the help of the State Board of Pharmacy, the pharmacists had gone even further, lobbying for and securing a state law that prohibited the advertising of prescription drug prices. In 1974, the Virginia Citizens Consumer Council, a nonprofit consumer organization, sued the State Board of Pharmacy in federal court, asking that this prohibition be struck down on the grounds of unconstitutionality. The court found in favor of the plaintiffs on the basis of "the right to know" guaranteed by the First Amendment, and the Supreme Court supported this decision.[11] Although in this case the consumers seem to have won, the market situation remains unstable. The pharmacists had pushed for this law because they felt threatened by chain stores, which could conceivably lower prices until they put the independents out of business. I suggest that this problem could be resolved if the three associational levels competing in this case—the association of chain stores, the Virginia Pharmaceutical Association, and the Consumer Council—got together and worked to that end through joint committees or some other mechanism.[12]

Such committees could be mandated by legislators, who should also encourage outside mediation and private tribunals to deal with these cases if the contesting parties fail to come to agreement on their own. The formation of a private tribunal can be done on a democratic and professional basis, with each of the parties selecting a judge, and an additional judge chosen to chair the tribunal. Such a tribunal would be much closer to the problem than a federal court would be.[13]

The kind of struggle described here clearly does not redound to the long-range interest of the consumer. Although in this particular case, a balance of power between the pharmacists and the chains may or may not be achieved by the concerted action of the three associations involved, the arrangement has worked in many other cases of associational conflict, and it is an important mechanism. It can also be more efficient than the usual drawn-out lobbying, legislative, and litigation process so onerous to everyone.

Collective Goods

One more point should be mentioned before we examine the broader application of these measures through government agencies. Public interest law is concerned with what are called "collective goods." A lighthouse is a collective good, since all ships benefit whether or not their owners have contributed to its costs. So is the private spraying of mosquito-breeding areas, since many people benefit who have not paid for it; and so is the installation of devices in factories or cars to decrease air pollution, since everyone benefits from the actions of a few. To the extent that the cooperative actions of competing trade associations lead to the creation of collective goods, they should be vigorously encouraged by the government. Furthermore, such cooperative actions should reduce the costs of government in many ways, as we shall see.

New Policy Guidelines for Applying Social and Economic Indexes

Measures of social equity can be combined with measures of economic efficiency to evaluate market decisions. The institution of such practices would be a major new direction for public policy. Let us look at some key issues in which such indexes could play a joint role, suggesting new questions that agencies like the FTC and OSHA could ask in making judgments about the marketplace that will take the public interest into account.

When Should a Firm Vertically Integrate?

Since firms that want to integrate vertically are usually motivated by both social and economic reasons, both social and economic indexes are required to resolve the issues that such moves raise in the marketplace. When a firm proposes to integrate vertically, the FTC should specifically ask whether the change would destroy the basis for an industry to act democratically on its own behalf and in the public interest.

Power theory has been advanced as one explanation of the social motive for vertical integration. It suggests that a firm will seek to maximize not only its profits but also its power over the market. From this view, a firm will integrate as much of the vertical market as possible and be restrained only by government action. (It is assumed that corporate executives believe that in the long run power and profits reinforce each other.)

The economist Oliver Williamson rejects the idea of a social element like power entering into the decision to integrate vertically and argues that the decision should be based purely on profitability. To support his theory, he cites cases of vertical integration based on gaining power that later failed. For example, Williamson says it was unsuccessful (i.e., unprofitable) for Pabst (a beer brewer) to move backward into timberland and barrel making; for Singer (a sewing machine manufacturer) to move into timber, an iron mill, and transportation; for McCormick Company to move into timberland, mines, twine factories, and hemp plantations; and for Ford Motor Company to become a "fully integrated behemoth at River Rouge, supplied by an empire that included ore lands, coal mines, 700,000 acres of timberland, sawmills, blast furnaces, a glass works, ore and coal boats, and a railroad." Williamson argues that while management does make such mistakes out of misguided assumptions, they become corrected over time, as the unprofitability of these moves becomes apparent. He concludes that it is therefore critical for both a firm and the FTC to consider transaction costs in judging a vertical move, since whether to move vertically or horizontally is purely a matter of economic efficiency.[14] (For a more detailed discussion of Williamson's work, see Chapter Ten.)

I would argue that transaction costs are an important measure for determining the rightness of a vertical step, and Williamson's calculation of transaction costs should precede a decision on vertical integration not because his approach is correct as an overall theory of rationality, but because it carries its weight as one important factor to be considered. We should keep in mind, however, that this singular "rationality" about corporate behavior does not explain why one firm merges with another or takes a vertical step when to do so runs *against* its cost evaluations.[15]

Any judgment on a vertical merger should also take into account whether the trade association community would be destroyed by the prospective move. If a trade community is broken up through vertical moves by conglomerates, this can have a serious impact on the survival of an industry, since the breakup may mean that corporate self-interest wins out over the associational values. Those values, as we have seen, are created through the cooperation of competing firms in activities such as trademarks indicating product safety or product standardization, R&D, trade fairs, management training, and ethical codes, which are often essential to the public welfare. Yet the market is constantly changing, and trade communities cannot last forever. In the face of technical progress and organizational inventions, for example, it may be necessary to drop the wholesaling sector of a market like candy or steel; it may become more cost effective for the manufacturer to move directly to the retailer. Since new technology can radically alter the social organization of a vertical market, no single unit of analysis should dominate decisions on vertical integration or corporate mergers.

The new thinking in public interest law on the need to integrate efficiency and equity becomes important in judging whether productive resources are put to their most valuable uses in such a case. For example, Settle and Weisbrod's measures can help to ascertain whether information would continue to be made available equitably and efficiently to producers and consumers in a vertical move. It is important that this figure into a decision for or against, since the public interest is best served when all buyers and sellers can make decisions based on the optimum allocation of information. Furthermore, the concepts of polity and process equity broaden the base for determining whether a new level of efficiency may or may not be achieved. A federal agency should assess whether cooperation between firms, which may provide special opportunities to create collective goods, operates in the public interest.[16]

In sum, the indexes we have discussed can measure the effectiveness of vertical mergers, and they can combine with traditional economic indexes to broaden the base for decision making. When the FTC, then, legitimates a corporate merger, it can do more than prevent market concentration; it can also see that the corporations involved reduce government costs, protect the integrity of the industry, and add to collective goods.

When Should a Trade Association Act in the Public Interest?

Trade associations contribute to the public welfare by maintaining codes of ethics, interindustry mediation committees, product quality, pension funds, R&D committees, and labor-management training programs, and through a host of other responsibilities that go beyond the singular capability of their member firms. The extent to which each new activity serves the public interest requires individual evaluation. Let us look at one example. Assume that a trade association wants to add both a code of ethics and a job-safety program, activities that could require consultation with federal agencies like the FTC and OSHA. Key questions for these agencies would include the following:

1. *Does the association fulfill index requirements in connection with its procedures and processes?* Does the association have a tribunal with an explicit set of sanctions about which its members are fully informed? Does it have a clear statement about due process? Is there an adequate distribution of power (market concentration ratio) within the industry? Are the workers represented? Is there a labor-management committee to oversee the monitoring and enforcement of job safety or other issues relevant to labor in the code of ethics? In other words, is the association democratically organized?

2. *Do the new responsibilities add to technical efficiency?* Does establishing common standards for job safety or making ethical agreements against secret rebates to customers reduce the costs of competition for the association's members? Does the added activity reduce production costs for members? Can the measures of technical efficiency join with measures of social equity? For example, does improving on-the-job safety conditions for all workers in the industry also improve production efficiency?

3. *Do the new responsibilities reduce government costs and increase associational autonomy?* Does setting standards and enforcing job safety by the association in collaboration with unions reduce costs for OSHA (for example)? To what extent is the association able to

bear the costs? Does it need a subsidy that would still mean an overall saving for the government? How can the association best be organized to enforce the norms effectively with minimal or no monitoring from OSHA? Also, does the new code of ethics reduce FTC staff time in monitoring?

In short, OSHA and the FTC should review cases with an eye to determining whether an industry or professional association can take over some degree of agency responsibility and thereby reduce the cost of government. Under recent concepts of public interest law, can the trade association reduce government costs by self-monitoring?

4. *Do the new responsibilities add to the collective good?* In reviewing cases, a government agency may want to consider that an organizational innovation in the public interest can become a model for others to replicate, or a social innovation may enlarge the pool of potential ways to organize a market in the public interest. For example, if members of a trade association agreed to use equally effective pollution-avoidance devices in their factories so that they can compete fairly, the action becomes a collective good for residents of the communities where the factories are located.

5. *Do the new responsibilities contribute to the freedom of individual association members?* Additional responsibilities in the association can add to or detract from the freedom of member firms and from the quality of community life. Each new activity can augment associational power and reduce the power of the individual firms, or the contrary. Again, matters of cost efficiency and polity are critical. Do the firms retain equal rights and an equitable voting status in the association? And finally, does the new activity interfere with fair competition?

Conclusion: The Social Organization of Markets

We have explored how the market is organized socially, so that we can identify new policies and future steps that will enable it to operate more fully in the public interest on its own initiative. We have seen how trade and professional associations help bridge the gap between the corporate (business) and civic orders. Private greed can turn into "public goods" through cooperation between competing firms without resulting in collusion. The contradiction between self-interest and the public interest can be resolved, and business can plan to create "collective goods" while pursuing its own self-interest. We have also noted how peak associations might play even broader roles in promoting the public interest. However, in order for these nonprofit associations to bring the values of the larger culture into the marketplace, and to enforce related norms most effectively, they must be democratically organized at all levels, must represent all stages of the vertical chain of production, and must be autonomous from government control.

Furthermore, our discussion of the integration of equity and efficiency indicates that values prized separately by the government and business need not be in conflict. Attention to their integration helps us realize that the civic and the commercial order may move closer to each other in reflecting the values of society, particularly in regard to how markets operate in the public interest. A government that seeks to help both profit and nonprofit leaders integrate commercial and civic values in their markets could sponsor research with these leaders on this subject. There is a need to formulate indexes that will point the way to achieving greater economic efficiency along with greater social equity in the private sector. Such measures would also enable trade associations to act more fully in the public interest. Studies also need to be conducted not only on how local, regional, and national trade associations may help bridge the gap between equity and efficiency, but also on how peak associations can do this. Further suggestions related to these issues appear in Chapter Eleven.

Trade associations that cultivate job safety, product safety, service quality, consumer protection, environmental protection, equal opportunity, worker self-management, the conservation of resources, employee rights, uniform pension plans, and good labor relations can give an industry a competitive advantage that is ultimately measured in efficiency, reduced tax dollars, and the public interest. Business associations that help their members to solve problems while both creating social equity and optimizing profits are the ones that are likely to flourish in the future economy.

PART IV

The Social Development of Markets

[A] great part of that order which reigns among mankind is not the effect of government. It has its origin in the principles of society and the natural constitution of [people]. It existed prior to government and would exist if the formality of government was abolished. The mutual dependence and reciprocal interest which [people have upon one another], and all the parts of a civilized community upon each other, create that great chain of connexion which holds it together. The landholder, the farmer, the manufacturer, the merchant, the tradesman, and every occupation, prospers by the aid which each receives from the other, and from the whole. Common interest regulates their concerns, and forms their law; and the laws which common usage ordains have a greater influence than the laws of government. In fine, society performs for itself almost everything which is ascribed to government.

Thomas Paine
The Rights of Man

CHAPTER 10

Organizational Studies

IN THIS CHAPTER we consider studies that can illuminate the concept of a self-regulated market, looking at two aspects of this issue: current studies that foster the creation of a false community in which big corporations and the state take over the market, and organizational studies that stake out a new direction for policies that promote self-regulation in the public interest. These organizational studies complement the development of a field of law based on the public interest, which as we saw in the previous chapter is a bridge to public policy. I believe that a series of studies based on the findings of organizational research can be applied to public policies supporting self-regulation.

The Creation of the False Community

Many scholars have recently argued that the "free market" is less significant than it once was in explaining how the economy operates because it has been overruled sectorially either by private corporations or government, as one or the other has sought to overcome the frightening condition of normless anarchy noted by both Marx and Durkheim.[1]

Partisans at both ends of the spectrum go farther, claiming that the market has become self-destructive. Writers of the political Left argue that the market does not work because oligopolies (hierarchical communities) control it through "administered pricing." For them, the most outrageous fact is that this practice is defended in the name of "efficiency." Proponents of the Right argue that the market does not work because federal departments, regulatory agencies, and a multitude of laws control it, a practice that others would defend in the name of "equity."

The Efficiency Argument

Alfred Chandler, in a well-documented work, describes how the visible hand of big corporations began to replace the "invisible hand" that Adam Smith believed would lead small competing firms to operate in the public interest. Chandler's theme is that the "modern business enterprise took the place of market mechanisms" in coordinating the activities of the economy: "The market remained the generator of demand for goods and services, but modern business enterprise took over the functions of coordinating flows of goods through existing processes of production and distribution and of allocating funds and personnel for future production and distribution."[2] As business firms acquired functions previously carried out by the market, they became the most powerful institution in the economy, and their managers the most influential economic decision makers.

Chandler posits several propositions about this transformation. First, the modern multiunit business enterprise replaced small traditional firms when "administrative coordination permitted greater productivity, lower costs, and higher profits than coordination by market mechanisms." Second, the advantages of many units within a single enterprise could not be realized until a managerial hierarchy had been created. Whereas the activities of small traditional firms had been coordinated by market mechanisms, in the modern corporation, middle managers came to monitor and coordinate production and distribution, while top managers evaluated and directed their work, thus taking the place of the market in allocating resources for future production and distribution.

Chandler's third and fourth propositions are again drawn from history. He claims that modern business enterprise appeared for the first time when the volume of economic activities reached a level that made administrative coordination more efficient and more profitable than market coordination. Once a managerial hierarchy had been formed and had successfully carried out its function of administrative coordination, it became a source of permanence, power, and continued growth.

Chandler also emphasizes the concentration of professional managers and its implications for corporate policy. History shows that the careers of salaried managers who directed these hierarchies became increasingly technical and professional, the firm grew accordingly in size and diversity, corporate decisions became based more on motives of stability and growth, and very large enterprises then came to dominate major sectors of the economy and altered the structure of market sectors and the economy as a whole.

Chandler concludes that as technology became more sophisticated and as markets expanded, administrative coordination replaced market coordination in an increasingly larger portion of the economy. But critics have said that he is never explicit about how the market actually operates after management has controlled the processes from production to consumption.

In sum, the big corporations took the coordination and integration of the flow of goods and services over from the market, from the production of the raw materials through the several processes of production to the sale to the ultimate consumer. The "visible hand of management replaced the invisible hand of market forces where and when new technology and expanded markets permitted a historically unprecedented high volume and speed of materials through the processes of production and distribution."[3]

The political Left would observe that Chandler omits from his history the social impact of corporate dominance and monopoly, which in part generated government controls. But Chandler speaks convincingly of the trend toward corporate hierarchy in the name of efficiency, and he is joined by many other economists and organizational analysts who see corporate hierarchy as a functional substitute, often a considerably more efficient one, for much of market activity.[4]

The Equity Argument

Decrying corporate hierarchy and the competitive market, historians and economists of the Left recommend strong government monitoring and regulation to protect the consumer, labor, small business, and the environment. Although many neo-Marxists have become disenchanted with the performance of the state in socialist countries, and many liberals (now neoconservatives) have become disenchanted with the performance of the state in capitalist countries, most of them still look to the state as the only responsible agent to deal with problems in the market system.

But exactly what its role should be is sharply disputed. For example, Andrew Martin calls attention to the difficulty of maintaining a durable, countervailing influence by "political elites independent of business" in an economy that remains fundamentally capitalist. He notes that the power of business is such that even liberal U.S. presidents go through the ritual of appointing people to head the Department of the Treasury and the Federal Reserve Board who are reassuring to industry, and the litmus test of policies today is whether they are good for business. Martin suggests that the entrenched power of business in a market economy can be offset only if several conditions are present: a strong, ideologically coherent labor movement; very high voting participation by wage earners; and a labor or social democratic party that is generally the party of government. He concludes: "In short, democratic control of a capitalist economy is not likely to be possible under most conceivable circumstances."[5]

The political Left is aware of how business has used government controls to protect its own interests. When the social historian Gabriel Kolko looked at early-twentieth-century business, he saw the opposite of what Chandler saw: disliking the rigors of competition, business leaders sought government control over selected markets in order to protect their interests. Paradoxically, they also sought government support to secure their positions of market control. Kolko argues that the dominant trend in business at the turn of the century was not toward trusts, cartels, and monopolies, but rather toward greater economic decentralization and cutthroat competition. Unable to halt these trends by itself, big business turned to government for relief.

Despite the large number of mergers, and the growth in the absolute size of many corporations, the dominant tendency in the American economy at the beginning of this century was toward growing competition. Competition was unacceptable to many key business and financial interests, and the merger movement was to a large extent a reflection of voluntary, unsuccessful business efforts to bring irresistible competitive trends under control. Although profit was always a consideration, rationalization of the market was infrequently a necessary prerequisite for maintaining long-term profits. As new competitors sprang up, and as economic power was diffused throughout an expanding nation, it became apparent to many important businessmen that only the national government could rationalize the economy. Although specific conditions varied from industry to industry, internal problems that could be solved only by political means were the common denominator in those industries whose leaders advocated greater federal regulation. Ironically, contrary to the consensus of historians, it was not the existence of monopoly that caused the federal govern-ment to intervene in the economy, but the lack of it.[6]

Kolko believes that the regulatory laws of the Progressive Era were not initiated by liberal reformers, as is conventionally claimed. In fact, it was big business that first pressed for federal controls and then influenced the regulators. In virtually every case, government chose solutions advanced by business and financial interests; big business—Chandler's "visible hand"—continued its control over the market through government.

To clarify this difference in the interpretation of history, let us note that Chandler looks favorably on this development because he believes that managerial hierarchies could better accomplish what the market could not; the competitive small businesses and con-federations of businesses that were developing before the turn of the century could not compete with the efficiency made possible through hierarchical coordination of the market by the "modern business enterprise." Kolko, on the other hand, is sympathetic with the decentralization of business and dismayed at the corpo-rate monopolies that developed, since he saw that big business used the government to regulate competition in its own interest, to the detriment of small business, workers, and the public at large.[7]

Neocorporatism: Efficiency and Equity Through Tripartite Control

In answer to the continuing question of whether corporations or government should control the market, a synthesized version of market control, known as "neocorporatism," emerged. Seeking to integrate both efficiency and equity as values guiding market man-agement, neocorporate public policy results from the high-level collaboration of business, government, and unions in a regulatory state.

Although the neocorporatist approach had long been strong and overt in Europe, it has quietly taken hold in the United States as well. Robert Reich notes of this development:

Between 1920 and 1970 American business, labor, and government hewed to a new set of organizing principles in which tasks were sim-plified, ordered according to preestablished rules, and carefully moni-tored. These principles were put into effect by a new class of professional managers who controlled individual firms, coordinated investment and production across whole industries, and found their way into government. High-volume production, featuring long runs of standardized products, generated vast economies of scale and new levels of wealth.

The social vision that underlay this process was rooted in the ideals of large-scale efficiency and rules to constrain arbitrary authority—ideals applicable to curing social ills and to defending the nation against foreign aggressors. The principles were those of scientific management, symbolized by the well-oiled machine and suggesting a pattern of organization by which Americans' aspirations could be achieved without political rancor.[8]

However, Reich declares that pressures for a new approach beyond neocorporatism are now being felt, as rigid management-centered organization has proved inappropriate for a country so thoroughly linked to a world economy.

The Alternative: Efficiency and Equity Through Social Development

At the beginning of the twentieth century, it seemed clear that the future would be shaped either by corporate controls over the market based on the values of efficiency or government controls based on the values of equity. The actual outcome was that both sides won in some measure, resulting in the growth of both corporate and government hierarchies. But labor continued to gain power through its own union hierarchy, and neocorporatism now legitimates the power of labor to join business and government to help stabilize the competitive market. Yet many observers note that the big business–big government–big labor troika does not seem impressively different from the political-elite model that once led to the fascist state.

An alternative to the three positions of corporate control, government control, and neocorporatism is essential. I believe the path is through social developments within the market itself, along the lines suggested in the preceding pages. Let us probe further into the matter by looking at the findings of interorganizational studies of the social market, and then suggesting the kinds of studies needed to produce public policies that will promote the development of self-governing sectors in the market economy.

Economic and Social Perspectives in Organizational Theory

Sociological studies of organizations began in earnest during the late 1950's and early 1960's. Consisting mainly of case analyses exemplified by the work of sociologists like Peter Blau, Alvin

Gouldner, and Philip Selznick, they were carried out to refine Max Weber's theory of bureaucracy, to develop a taxonomy, and to learn about the impact of technology on organizational behavior through contingency theories. A central theoretical work in this period was James Thompson's *Organizations in Action,* which treated organizations as open systems subject to uncertainty arising both in the environment and in technology.

Organizational theorists began to consider the field of business seriously through the work of such scholars as Richard Cyert, James March, and Herbert Simon. The possibility of integrating economics and organizational theory grew gradually as Kenneth Arrow, Alfred Chandler, and Ronald Coase began to connect social and economic factors in business research; most recently in this tradition is Oliver Williamson's work in formulating a theory of markets and hierarchies.[9]

Williamson's conceptual framework is especially important because it provides a basis for evaluating antitrust cases. It provides a comparative institutional assessment of alternative means of contracting, using motifs of bounded rationality and opportunism and focusing on the nature of contract relations that become established between parties in the marketplace. As a theory of transactional behavior, it furnishes insight into business behavior, since it recognizes uncertainty, frequency of transactions, and the relationship between durable transaction-specific investments and least-cost supply as key features of the market. Williamson bases his transaction-cost analysis on the following premises:

(a) markets and firms are alternative instruments for completing a related set of transactions; (b) whether a set of transactions ought to be executed between firms (across markets) or within a firm depends on the relative efficiency of each mode; (c) the costs of writing and executing complex contracts across a market vary with the characteristics of the human decision makers who are involved with the transaction on the one hand, and the objective properties of the market on the other; (d) although the human and transactional factors which impede exchanges between firms (across a market) manifest themselves somewhat differently within the same firm, the same set of factors applies to both.[10]

Transaction-cost analysis can help a firm to decide such issues as whether to stay in the market to do business or to negotiate with its own divisions. It also addresses issues of vertical integration across successive manufacturing stages. Transactional studies in business so far have included assessments of the employment relationship, franchise bidding for natural monopolies, the efficacy of capital markets, oligopoly, vertical market restrictions, aspects of inflation, and contract law. We shall not pursue transactional theory further here except to note that it is based on principles of efficiency and is clearly applicable to decisions leading to the development of federations in the business market.

The transactional approach is complementary to the sociological approach. It differs from sociological theory in three respects. First, it views organizations as instruments of rationality and efficiency, goals that stem in part from the work of Weber, but more fundamentally from the culture of business itself. By contrast, sociologists see organizations as more culturally complex. As Gouldner wrote many years ago: "The rational model assumes that decisions are made on the basis of a rational survey of the situation, utilizing certified knowledge with a deliberate orientation to an expressly codified legal apparatus. The focus is, therefore, on the legally prescribed structure—i.e., the formally 'blue-printed' patterns—since these are more largely subject to deliberate inspection and rational manipulation." [11]

Sociologists would note that rationality and efficiency need not be primary among an organization's many goals; factors such as corporate loyalty, communalism, fraternity, familism, and patriotism may be latent in a business culture based on rational efficiency but still play a predominant role in guiding decision making. Recreational or aesthetic considerations or considerations of justice may also be primary goals. As a result, many organizational analysts analyze an organization on the basis of "organizational effectiveness"—that is, the ability of an organization to achieve whatever goals it defines for itself.

Second, transactional theory (as well as some organizational theory) dealing with business makes the economic factor primary and the social factor secondary. To quote one representative work: "The objectives of economic governance are efficiently and adaptively to co-ordinate the activities of firms and their 'relevant environments,' that is, customers, suppliers, competitors, labour, technology generators, government agencies, etc." [12] By contrast, sociologists see people's interdependence as the determining factor. Even when people in corporations seek to maximize their economic life, they must first become oriented to one another—they must first take account of one another, know what other people are doing in order to determine the course of their own conduct, and interpret the symbolic behavior of others. Hence, the social factor is analytically prior to the economic factor, apart from whether the profit motive or the efficiency motive is causal.

Third, transaction theory is guided by economic concepts such as measures of market concentration and unfair competition, while— following the sociological tradition—we have seen how social indicators can also be used to evaluate the social development of a market. Economic development, meaning the cultivation of material resources, can be indexed by such criteria as increases in profits, productivity, and the GNP, and also indexed instrumentally through measures of efficiency, transaction costs, and effective administration coordination. Social development, on the other hand —broadly defined as the cultivation of both human and economic resources—means the cultivation of a balance of power among corporations, the realization of societal values like freedom and justice in the structures of work, and the creation of equity and welfare in the marketplace, and can be identified by increases in effective authority and power among individuals in organizations. Such changes can be assessed through empirical studies that demonstrate a greater distribution of knowledge and skills among associations and their member firms, or studies on the fulfillment of public values in the private sector, such as quality of product, work safety, and environmental protection. But this type of development is still best measured in conjunction with indexes of economic development.[13]

In order for the study of organizations to be integrated into public policy, then, economic indexes such as productivity and efficiency need to be applied simultaneously with indexes of organizational and interorganizational development.

Interorganizational Studies and Self-Regulation

Although the connection has not been made explicit elsewhere, some interorganization studies are also connected to a theory of self-regulation. A brief review of the literature reveals the logic of self-regulation through studies that show (1) the problems of state regulation, particularly the inability of the state to represent the public interest in certain domains of policy; (2) the social costs of

conventional business; (3) the assignment of some government responsibilities to democratic associations that can do the job more
effectively; (4) problems with private-government funding, and (5)
the balancing of vertical and horizontal organization. Let us examine each of these issues.

The Problems of State Regulation

Three problems arise when the state tries to intervene in the
economy and control corporate conduct. The first is government's
ineffectiveness in legal regulation. There are many reasons for this.
Let us note just a few. The principal obstacle is that the system is
too big and complex; government simply cannot monitor all the
practices in market relations that need monitoring. Furthermore,
government tends to hire business people to monitor their own industries (who else has the expertise?), an awkward and obviously
unhealthy arrangement. Moreover, powerful businesses can afford
large legal staffs to protect themselves from government suits. And
not least, the effort to control corporations results in red tape and a
bureaucratic tangle.[14]

Second, government has an image problem. It must win the support of groups that are asked to sacrifice some of their interests in
favor of the general interest and legitimize its intervention.[15] Finally
and relatedly, it must defend the subsidies that result from lobbying and industrial self-interest. Although the costs of government
subsidies are shared by all taxpayers, the beneficiaries are the managements, workers, and customers of the subsidized sectors only.
Many equity issues could be raised in this connection. For example
why does government give $455 million in tax breaks to the timber
industry, but not the same breaks to the semiconductor industry?
Why are billions in loan guarantees channeled to industries like
footware and housing, when doing so diverts capital from emerging industries like specialized steel? Such decisions have yet to be
examined more carefully from the perspective of industrial self-
regulation.[16]

The Social Costs of Business as Usual

Research into the social costs of business as usual can be traced
to Thorstein Veblen, who wrote in 1917 that "it will be necessary to
investigate . . . in a convincing way what are the various kinds and

lines of waste that are necessarily involved in the present business-like control of industry."[17] The systematic study of social costs began with K. W. Kapp. Such costs, defined as "all direct and indirect losses sustained by third persons or the general public as a result of unrestrained economic activities," may take the form of damage to human health, the destruction or deterioration of property values, the premature depletion of natural wealth, or the impairment of less tangible values, such as the quality of life.[18]

Social costs come in various guises. Some examples. Direct costs occur when a company (or industry) passes on to the general public or third parties the expense of carrying out an activity that should really be borne by those engaged in it or benefiting from it. If through environmentally damaging practices, a company reduces its costs, the difference between its actual costs and those that would be incurred through acceptable practices are borne by the general public. Likewise, if a company manufactures a product more expensively than it has to, it imposes a penalty on the general public.[19]

The Assignment of Public Responsibilities to Democratic Associations

A number of observers have argued that democratic private associations, when properly organized, are better vehicles for exercising social control than either the state or conventional business. First, they note that since private associations are closer to their members, they can create norms governing their conduct and justify enforcement better than a more distant government agency. Furthermore, questions of enforceability enter directly into the decisions that create the norms; association members voluntarily make choices regarding norm support. Second, since the agents of enforcement—the association's professional staff—are closer to and more knowledgeable about members than state bureaucracies, courts, or the police are, they are better equipped to judge how to deal with offenders.[20]

Although the reverse of these arguments is usually used to support government control, they can also be marshaled against organizations that are not fully democratic or lack experience with self-regulation. The staff of an association may be "too close" to the members to be objective, may be unable to make highly discriminating judgments against offending members, may be biased in attitude or unprofessional in sanctioning. The differences between the state and nonprofit associations in their effectiveness in enforcing norms, therefore, must be studied very carefully.[21]

Gouldner's classic study of the making and enforcing of norms in a gypsum plant illuminates why a democratically constituted association may generally be a better alternative than either a corporate or a state hierarchy. The plant's many bureaucratic rules, imposed by a command management and the state, were neither consistently respected nor consistently obeyed. When a management rule was broken, the offender was assumed to have done so knowingly and malevolently and needed to be punished; when a state rule was broken, neither management nor labor cared because the state was an outsider. But when the rules were determined democratically by both labor and management, they were obeyed, and when a violation did occur, it was assumed that the offender was well intended and simply did not understand the reason for the rule. The offender was not punished, but "consulted" and "re-educated." In effect, workers generally believed the democratically determined rules were in their common interest.[22]

The separate literatures on corporate social responsibility, industry self-regulation, and economy-wide self-regulation are all relevant to the conceptual framework proposed in previous chapters. There are certain limited responsibilities, for example, social audits, that corporations can undertake when in competition with others.[23] There are also broader responsibilities that trade associations can assume (for example, ethical codes), recognizing the limitations of members' self-interest.[24] And there are still broader responsibilities that peak associations can take on, although they have their own limitations, depending on how they are organized.[25] Since much of the argument against self-regulation is confused by the fact that each level of business can assume only certain public responsibilities, studies at each of these different levels are vital to the determination of appropriate responsibilities in the public interest.

The Public Funding of Private Organizations

The nature of government funding of private organizations determines the degree to which they can become self-governing. Two major issues are involved here: whether the nature of the funding leads to more direct control or to more freedom and autonomy; and in the latter case, the extent to which government should retain key controls in selective areas, such as equity (e.g., affirmative action) and civil rights.

Pointing to the rapid growth of clerical and accounting systems within all types of organizations and the complexities involved in reporting data to the government, Harry Braverman notes that organizations must not only carry on the work they were designed to do, but must now develop ever more elaborate ways to keep track of what they do; for example, hospitals must not only admit and care for patients but also keep records on changes in status and location, all services rendered, controls exercised, justifications for departures from established norms, and so forth. Thus, organizations become more elaborated and extensive as external funding and regulatory sources require evidence of conformity to their requirements.[26]

Furthermore, federal and state controls can be extremely complex, specialized, and fragmented, since government programs develop at different times, with different agendas, and are administered by a bewildering array of agencies; observers have counted from 40 to 160 separate agencies engaged in regulating hospital activities alone. The associated requirements are bafflingly inconsistent, yet no single agency has sufficient authority to impose uniformity or rearrange jurisdictions. In the absence of a unitary system, government demands are made piecemeal and in contradictory fashion, all of which increases the burden on the private sector.[27]

Vertical and Horizontal Balance

Roland Warren developed a sociological model for examining how horizontal and vertical relationships connect organizations from the locality to the nation. Although the model differs slightly from horizontal and vertical trade relations among competitors, since it focuses on the patterned horizontal relationships among organizations within a community, as opposed to the vertical relationship each has with a national headquarters, it is still highly relevant to the issue of community building in both local and national markets.

Warren believes that localities have lost their sense of community (i.e., their solidarity, values, and strength) because the organizations located in them are linked vertically to distant headquarters where decisions are made. But this is so, in part, because localities have lost their horizontal connections to local organizations. As local leaders, concerned with economic stability and growth, increasingly direct their attention elsewhere, the long-range cumulative impact can be alienation, leading to crime, drugs, and suicide—just as Durkheim noted at the beginning of the century.[28] However, the opposite trend is dangerous, too, because excessively horizontal relationships can dim the larger vision.

Organizational studies show that similar problems develop when extreme levels of either centralization or decentralization occur in business. (Here, centralization refers specifically to decision making at higher levels within a market sector, not within a corporation.) Centralization is often sought because of the belief that it reduces uncertainty, yet the experience of traditional industries like steel has shown that this does not necessarily follow.[29] On the other hand, an emphasis on decentralization can lead to fragmentation, people working at cross-purposes, and a loss of vertical community; the medical-care and educational sectors are good examples of institutional markets that have become characterized by great fragmentation.[30] More research on the proper balance between centralization (verticality) and its impact on the locality are thus important to organizations taking steps toward self-regulation.

New Directions for Organizational Research: Societal Sectors

Richard Scott and John Meyer have defined a "societal sector" as a group of organizational units that are functionally interrelated, even though they may be geographically remote from one another. For example, medical care is provided by a variety of structures that do not come under one organization, nor are they necessarily related formally. Although this concept of sector builds on the economist's concept of industry ("all sellers of one type of product or service—or, more abstractly those firms characterized by close substitutability of product usages who as a consequence exhibit demand interdependence"[31]), it allows more room for social analysis than the economic concept.

The concept of the societal sector allows social scientists to focus their organizational research on markets that are composed of both profit and nonprofit associations, and introduces a new taxonomy of firms in highly interdependent markets, speaking directly to the interorganizational problems of business today. This approach, for example, yields insights into how markets differ from one another in their institutional and technical characters, rather than just in their products or their profit levels. Institutional markets are characterized by the elaboration of the rules to which organizations must conform if they are to receive support and legitimacy from their environment, and technical markets are defined as those within which a product or service is exchanged so that organizations are rewarded for efficient control of the work process.[32]

Studies show considerable sectorial variation along both dimensions. It is possible for a sector to be highly institutionalized, with little technical development (e.g., the educational market); highly technical and low in institutional development (e.g., retail-goods manufacturing); simultaneously high technically and institutionally (e.g., the medical care or banking markets); or simultaneously low in technical and institutional development (e.g., personal services). As these taxonomic differences are studied in detail, hypotheses can be developed about how sectors behave differently, which contributes to our understanding of the variety of ways in which markets can become self-regulating.[33]

J. Rogers Hollingsworth and Leon N. Lindberg have used the sectorial approach to typologize the U.S. profit sector by size of firm and level of technology (see Table 9). For each sector, we will first note key characteristics, and then consider specific issues affecting its capacity for greater self-regulation.

Cell 1, relatively small firms with low levels of technological complexity, distinguishes between producers of undifferentiated and differentiated products. The firms in cell 1 tend to exemplify "pure competition," as in certain agricultural markets (e.g., meat and vegetable sectors) where there are large numbers of sellers, and no single seller directly affects prices. Entry into the industry is fairly easy, and prices are relatively competitive. On the other hand, in agricultural sectors in which prices are very stable, notably the dairy industry, government intervention is extensive, and trade and cooperative activity are pervasive.

The organizational structure of each sector must be considered in determining how it can be encouraged to become self-regulated. In cell 1A for example, it makes a big difference when the American Farm Bureau Federation, the National Farmers Union, and

TABLE 9
A Typology of the U.S. Profit Sector

| Technological sophistication and rate of technological change | Size of firm, size of demand at the firm level, and level of investment | |
	Low	High
Low	A. Agriculture and other undifferentiated products B. Residential construction, printing, publishing, apparel, textiles, furniture, banking, savings, etc.	Autos, steels, fabricated metal products, canned foods, soft drinks, etc.
High	Pharmaceuticals, high-performance plastics, ceramics, specialty steels, radioisotopes, various electronics, etc.	Mainframe computers, nuclear energy, aircraft, telecommunications, etc.

SOURCE: Adapted from J. Rogers Hollingsworth and Leon N. Lindberg, "The Governance of the American Economy," in Wolfgang Streeck and Philippe C. Schmitter, eds., *Private Interest Government* (Beverly Hills, Calif.: Sage, 1985), p. 225.

trade and cooperative associations work closely with the Department of Agriculture. If new administrative policies to encourage self-regulation were introduced into this sector, the USDA could co-plan with all these groups on controlled output by marketing cooperatives, self-monitored cutbacks in production in certain low-demand markets, and the like.

In the small firm–low technology–differentiated products category, (cell 1B), the textile industry is typical: its firms have organized trade associations that engage in the standardization of products, testing of materials, promoting of markets, and development of ethical codes. But some subsectors are controlled by oligopolies. If greater self-regulation were sought here, these oligopolies could be examined more carefully by the Antitrust Division for more effective, decentralized planning. Government agencies are much more distant from these industries and trade associations than from those in cell 1A. Government is more likely to be involved in legislation protecting the industry from foreign competition; its use of protectionist Orderly Marketing Agreements (OMA) illustrates its primary connection to this sector.

In cell 2 (large firms with low technological complexity), many firms are vertically integrated to allocate capital, technology, and personnel across industries. Trade associations play a less significant role among these firms, compared with those in cell 1 since gigantic firms carry out their own technical research, advertising, and cost-benefit analysis. Business elites are more active in informal networks through service on corporate boards and through organizations that cut across many sectors of the economy, such as the Conference Board, the Council on Foreign Relations, and the Committee on Economic Development, and executives are more concerned about public policies that affect the larger economy, such as interest rates, foreign competition, investment tax credits, trade union legislation, and antitrust laws. In this section of the economy, the federal government could work more closely with business (as Japan's MITI does) to help firms compete against foreign invasions into their markets, but this should be done by strengthening trade associations, as described in Chapter Eleven.

In cell 3 (relatively small firms with high technical complexity), we find firms in the early stages of the production life-cycle, in which trade associations are only beginning to be developed. The semiconductor industry is a good example of how the market is governed here; in contrast to agriculture or aviation, it has been relatively independent of government. Government involvement has been very selective. Apart from the specifications to be met in electronic components procured by the Defense Department, research supported by the National Science Foundation, and the pharmaceutical industry's regulation through patents, Food and Drug Administration oversight, and consumer protection laws, these firms are still relatively free of direct government control. Trade associations have not played a major role here, although they might do so in the future if government encouraged inter-association committees to adjudicate industry conflicts. There is also a need to develop consumer organizations in relation to the pharmaceutical industry and for conflict-resolution among its retail, distributive, and manufacturing associations. The creation of interassociation committees could lead to the elimination of fair-trade legislation in this field.

Finally, the technical complexity of the cell 4 firms' markets means that a considerable amount of borrowing takes place. All these industries are highly interdependent. The aircraft corporations especially operate through close informal networks with subcontractors from adjacent industries. Since the government is closely allied with the industry, and neocorporate tendencies are high, it is especially important to study firms in this sector to determine the degree of market concentration and barriers to entry. The telecommunications and nuclear power markets are especially closely interlocked with government policies.

However, this interlocking also means that under new administrative policies, government would have more power to encourage self-regulation in this sector. For example, at the time of the breakup of AT&T, the government could have considered the alternative of a publicly oriented confederation of firms in telecommunications, with an administrative center and a federation of independent firms organized in the manner of a trade association. Such a plan would have avoided a great deal of the public confusion that resulted from the process of dismantlement.

In sum, sectorial market typologies are probably the most promising dimension of interorganizational studies today. As a field of research, they offer a promising foundation for developing policies that can lead the private economy to function in the public interest.

CHAPTER 11

Public Policies

GOVERNMENT has always played a role in the market economy, but its proper role has continually been debated, and its purposes have often been contradictory. For example, government supports business with loans, contracts, and subsidies, and then regulates it to protect consumers, workers, the homeless, the jobless, the poor, and the natural environment from its harmful effects. Assessing government's purpose for intervening in the economy is therefore central to determining the direction of future public policies.

We have seen that government regulations are required because business is not adequately structured to operate in the public interest. Put another way, since business does not fully reflect societal values such as social welfare, freedom, democracy, justice, and equity in its daily operations, the government must see that business abides by those values; government must do what business does not do by itself. The irony, of course, is that first business acts against the public interest and then pays taxes to have itself regulated—a most inefficient way of doing business.

From the perspective of this book, government's main purpose should be to support business in organizing a market that regulates itself. It can do this by encouraging business to express the values of the larger society, to build ethical codes into the process of doing business, to mediate conflict, and to monitor itself in the public interest; overall, to develop a market system that is efficient and self-regulating. Although government must protect people and the environment when leaders in the private sector cannot or will not do so, the state's main function should *not* be to set ethical and technical standards, provide subsidies, or control the market on behalf of the public, but rather to create conditions for the market economy to do these things by itself. In this chapter, we will consider what kinds of public policies would help stimulate a more self-regulating market.

Policies to Promote Self-Managed Firms

If the trends of worker participation in management and worker ownership continue, the overall result should be greater efficacy in corporate self-management. But the continuation of those two trends depends in part on future public policies. The question is, is it proper to institute public policies that will encourage a development that runs counter to the conventional organization of business?

As things stand, conventional corporations receive public support in numerous ways. Traditions and mores determine what is right and wrong in business. Families and public schools teach young people about the way to organize a business; conventional management training is supplied persuasively by graduate schools of business; the legal system sets the precedents and the framework for business to operate "as usual"; lawyers are trained to work only on conventional stock ownership and are unequipped to deal with any other kind.

In sum, hundreds of educational programs, as well as strong cultural traditions and legal activities, bolster conventional business. It is not easy for people to break tradition. As a result, people who have sought to develop fully self-managed businesses have regularly encountered discrimination against their form of enterprise. Lawyers have refused to help them; banks have refused to give them loans; government agencies have refused to provide technical assistance. State charters may even rule out their unique form of organization.[1]

Yet self-managed firms deserve public support for many reasons. Business is having its share of troubles. Productivity has declined in many industries, some are competing poorly against foreign firms, up to 80 percent of start-ups fail, and conventional businesses are typically strike-prone. Not least, government must continue to regulate the conventional system at all levels. The evidence is clear that self-managed firms can solve many of these problems, reduce the need for government regulations, and thereby save tax dollars.

In addition, self-managed firms show social and economic advantages over conventional businesses. In Chapter Three, we noted that firms taking steps toward worker participation and ownership save jobs and maintain local flows of capital; tend to be more productive and efficient; have less pilferage, absenteeism, labor turnover, and employee sicknesses; and give overall support to community development. Further, they provide a structure that enables employees to develop a sense of purpose and meaningfulness at work that can lessen the need for strikes and work stoppages. And finally, they can reduce the costs of middle management and bureaucracy. Although there are also problems in developing effective self-management, these firms are generally more efficient and humane than conventional firms.

Furthermore, empirical evidence suggests that the next potential stage of development for a fully self-managed firm—the worker cooperative (or employee-owned and -managed business)—will have even more advantages as a *business system*.[2] The most studied case of a cooperative business system is the Mondragon network in Spain, which began in 1956. This self-managed system, embracing both producer and retail cooperatives, is extraordinarily successful on every count: only 3 of 103 start-ups have been shut down; the firms' productivity outdistances conventional firms; they are highly profitable without need for layoffs (if workers are in surplus in one firm, they are transferred to a firm in short supply or sent for retraining); they use advanced technology; they do not have strikes; and they contribute significantly to community development. They are an important self-management alternative to conventional businesses that require government regulation.[3]

We also saw that businesses cultivating self-management practices in the United States—on their way to this more fully evolved form—not only exceed the economic performance of conventional business, but also offer personal rewards in human development. These findings suggest that the trends toward greater worker participation and ownership should be encouraged by public policies. Much is still to be learned about the most effective government support, but I would like to suggest here some policies and legislation that can encourage more effective levels of corporate self-management.

The Problems of Government-Mandated Self-Management

First, let me emphasize that I am *not* recommending legislation that *mandates* high levels of corporate self-management and ownership, even though such mandatory patterns have worked in some European countries. West German and Swedish statutes, for example, require co-determination in all major corporations in the private sector, which means that labor is represented on corporate boards and democratic councils that protect workers in such matters as hiring, firing, occupational health, and safety. Although some problems have arisen, most observers evaluate the long-range outcome of these changes positively; indeed, the West German co-determined companies have been among the world leaders in economic performance.

Over time, however, the cooperative arrangements of top leaders in organized labor, government, and business can lead to corporate and government bureaucracy and state corporatism, with many attendant problems. Such tripartite planning can lay the foundations for a centralized society oppressive to both small enterprises and workers at the bottom of the system. A government's tendency to impose solutions from a central capital without taking account of localities, a union's tendency to operate through its command system without taking account of all its workers, and similar manifestations of concentrated power are likely possibilities with such a system. Additionally, state corporatism has the potential to slow down economic growth over the long haul.

Some systemic problems are already visible within corporatist arrangements, including perhaps the recent slowdown in West Germany's economic growth. Analysts impute that slowdown to six things in particular:

1. The state-owned Bundespost has a near-monopoly on telecommunications services, stifling innovation and making it hard for foreign companies to sell equipment and services.

2. Strict government regulations make it difficult to enter service businesses, such as insurance or trucking.

3. The economy has an underdeveloped venture capital system, and one reason could be that it is dominated by a few big banks; indeed, this may be why Germany has had one of Europe's lowest rates of business start-ups.

4. Labor regulations impede laying off employees, even when companies are losing money.

5. Large subsidies to farmers and declining industries promote inefficiencies in the economy. In addition to the European Community's extensive subsidies for agriculture, Germany provides $5 billion a year to its 750,000 farms. This allows many inefficient farmers to scrape by even though their plots average just 42 acres.

6. Long-term subsidies support declining industries, such as coal and shipbuilding.[4]

But the strongest argument of all against strict legislative mandates for labor participation and ownership in the United States is that they would simply be counterproductive. The tradition in leadership and political life is far different from Europe's, and U.S. legislative mandates would almost certainly provoke strong resistance among both business executives and trade union leaders, which would obviously defeat the essential purpose of corporate self-management. The key policy question, then, is how government might encourage self-management on a *voluntary* basis.

Current Legislative Blocks to Self-Management

But new legislation cannot be easily conceived until laws inhibiting the development of corporate self-management are first eliminated. One example of an outmoded law is the once-useful Wagner Act, which now obstructs effective labor-management relations. If its assumption that there is a balance of power between labor and management was ever true in earlier years, it does not hold today.

Another example is the legislation on Employee Stock Ownership Plans (ESOPS). Joseph Blasi argues that the current law is inadequate and worse, blocks the development of self-management:

> Is employee ownership a revolution or a ripoff? It is a ripoff when it uses public tax expenditures to serve the interests of highly paid employees alone or to entrench existing management. It is a cheat when it denies employees voting rights on their stock and severely limits the rights and responsibilities to which owners are traditionally entitled. It is a disappointment when the meager amount of stock involved or the promise of stock only upon retirement undercuts a worker's sense of identification with the company. It is a poor incentive when it is not combined with short-term profit sharing that allows immediate participation in the success of the company. It becomes the pied piper of competitiveness when advocates claim that employees' owning "a piece of the action" automatically improves corporate economic performance.
>
> On the other hand, employee ownership could be considered revolutionary in terms of the commitment it can create among various work groups within an organization. It can elicit the American version of Japanese loyalty. It can go beyond wages and incentives to forge a joint sense of partnership by establishing a longer-term identification between the worker and the company.[5]

Blasi declares that four elements—employee ownership, profit sharing, labor-management cooperation, and work redesign—

could revive the corporation, but only if all four are applied in concert. Unfortunately, all labor legislation focuses on only the third. He would therefore redraw ESOP legislation to incorporate all four of these elements.

Blasi recommends a wide variety of measures to achieve his goals. For one thing, he believes a special commission made up of representatives of the Federal Reserve Board, the Department of the Treasury, the Department of Labor, academia, and the Senate and House Finance and Labor Committees should explore ways to redesign corporate finance mechanisms to favor a broadened ownership of wealth and restructuring of the ESOP. For another, he would like to see more equity given to employees with the least savings and access to credit; the limit on the amount of stock distributable to an employee substantially increased; and stock allocated on some more equitable basis than salary.

A host of other steps should be taken, in his view. The practice of excluding workers from stock equity because of age should be eliminated, and new legislation should set a limit on the number of part-time workers who can be excluded from ownership, since they represent a growing sector of the work force, yet currently constitute one of the most excluded groups. Also, labor law should be changed so that all aspects of the ESOP structure are open to collective bargaining by employees.

In addition, he believes that worker-owners should be able to protect their rights through their own (albeit minimum) involvement in the governance of the corporation, instead of depending on the complex rules and direct government regulation that encourage court cases. The current loophole allowing a company to set up a profit-sharing plan without giving employees voting rights should be eliminated where there is more than 15 percent employee ownership, and every 15 percent of employee equity in companies should entitle worker-owners to choose a member of the board of directors on a one-person, one-vote basis. Finally, there should be full pass-through voting rights on all stock in majority employee-owned companies, regardless of what form of employee-benefit plan holds the equity, although small businesses should be temporarily excused from this requirement where total ownership is slowly being transferred to employees over a limited number of years.

Possibilities at the State Level

It is heartening to note that several states are legislatively encouraging the development of self-management in promising ways. For example, the state of West Virginia helped underwrite a feasibility study when employees at Weirton Steel wanted to purchase the plant from National Steel; and Owned and Operated Supermarkets in Philadelphia received support from the state of Pennsylvania for a study of their worker buyout from A&P. The Connecticut General Assembly created an $8 million fund to reduce interest rates for worker-owned firms. California, under its Employee Ownership Act of 1983, authorized the state's Business Development Department and local development offices to give technical assistance to employee-owned firms. And Massachusetts provided a model for other states in establishing a sound legal basis for chartering worker cooperatives.[6]

The above examples of government support are the culmination of a long struggle by employees to be recognized as legitimate participants in, and owners of, corporations. Such support indicates a growing public awareness of the benefits that self-managed firms render the economy, but city, county, and state governments, and the federal government, too, could go much farther still removing barriers against them and more, encouraging their development.

I would like to describe one possible scenario at the state level that would require no special legislation and no significant cost. Let us assume that both the governor and the state legislature declare a policy of official support for worker participation and ownership. The governor then signs an executive order directing each affected state agency to report annually on what it has done to further the policy. The effect would be to cause agencies lending money to firms, supporting research on the economy, regulating stock ownership, and holding conferences and workshops for business and labor to focus some of their activities toward the goal of encouraging higher levels of self-management for business.

This would be no small matter in states that determine priorities for business. Massachusetts, for instance, has some number of agencies that grant business loans, including the Industrial Finance Agency, the Government Land Bank, the Community Development Finance Corporation, the Economic Stabilization Trust

Fund, the Technology Development Corporation, and the Product Development Corporation. Under this new policy, a company applying for funding would gain special attention by including a plan for making advances in employee ownership and self-management.

Each lending agency would emphasize the development of self-managed companies among their own particular constituencies. For example, the Community Development Finance Corporation in Massachusetts helps businesses to develop new systems of accountability to employees through ownership plans and management participation. Its communication of these priorities to over 60 CDCs, as well as to localities applying to create new CDCs, clearly has an influence on the development of self-managed businesses.

Following the gubernatorial executive order, let us say, a state agency was specifically charged with carrying out key responsibilities in connection with promoting self-managed companies, just as such agencies have been created in the past for conventional enterprises. Those responsibilities could include the following.

1. *Data collection and analysis for dissemination to interested firms, unions, and the public.* This could include gathering information on private agencies with expertise in consulting with self-managed companies; companies that have indicated an interest in self-management; colleges and universities offering programs and courses in corporate self-management; the activities of other states supportive of self-management; the legal problems of self-managed firms; potentially useful structural changes, such as model charters and bylaws; and strategies developing among business and unions to improve performance through self-management techniques.

2. *Consulting with business and unions on developing more effective self-management, and providing limited technical assistance on and promotion of the concept.*

3. *Supporting conferences on self-management and encouraging universities and private agencies to assume greater responsibilities in this area.*

4. *Formulating specific criteria defining a "relatively self-managed company,"* so that priorities can be clear for other state agencies. A special responsibility would be to investigate new methods for integrating the two separate trends of worker participation and worker ownership.

5. *Providing financial support and matching grants to universities for research on self-managed companies.* One key issue of research is how the trends of worker participation and ownership can be re-

inforced to become integral to the life of modern enterprise; another is the role of unions in the transition. By emphasizing support to private agencies to conduct conferences, perform research, and do consultation, the state signals the importance of development toward self-management without assuming primary responsibility for it.

6. *Studying privatization and self-management.* The agency could look into transferring the functions of certain state agencies to private self-managed companies as a method of reducing government costs, a buzzword in this era of conservative politics, which has seen proposals for privatizing everything from general hospitals to prisons and jails.[7] Although cities and states across the country have been saving money by transforming public agencies into private companies, they have always turned them into conventional businesses. But these functions could also be transferred to private entrepreneurs who are self-managing and accountable to their constituencies, a policy that would serve the double purpose of reducing government bureaucracy and strengthening what we have called the social sector.[8]

7. *Studying the feasibility of reduced interest rates on loans to relatively self-governed firms; tax advantages for owners interested in turning over their firms to employee ownership; and priority in state contracts to relatively self-governed firms.*

In conclusion, the scenario set out above is based on the assumption that if we are to proceed to a self-regulating system, the role of government should be confined to providing an environment in which self-managed enterprises can flourish. Government's task should not be to mandate changes, only to ascertain the kinds of private enterprise that best serve the public interest and then provide proper incentives for them to develop. Such public policies would also challenge conventional businesses to increase their own levels of employee participation and employee ownership, in their own interests as well as in the interests of their communities. (At the same time, state agencies promoting self-managed companies should not prejudice the letting of state contracts to conventional enterprises that have proved their merit.)

Most of these government incentive-mechanisms do not cost anything because they involve altering attitudes and policies in agencies already engaged in supporting business. But a special agency for promoting these firms *would* add costs. Therefore, that agency should itself eventually move into the private sector, and one of its tasks would be to determine how to encourage private research, consultation, and data gathering to replicate its own work so that it can eventually eliminate itself.

Self-managed companies help preserve jobs, improve the quality of work life, contribute to economic and community development, and maintain local stability. Fostering self-managed companies could work most effectively in concert with other programs aimed at reducing the costs to government of family instability, crime, delinquency, and drugs. Steps to reinforce trends toward self-management may enable the stabilization of communities that have been in decline, and new public policies could bring opportunity for autonomous economic life to develop once again.

Policies to Promote Social Investment

Chapter Four discussed how fiduciaries are increasingly using social criteria in deciding how to allocate capital. The government can also stimulate this trend at no added cost. The largest advance in that direction would be pension reform, since the U.S. pension system holds the greatest reserve of capital in the world today. Peter Drucker's seminal study *The Unseen Revolution* (1976), which predicted that pension funds would own half the corporate stock in the United States in the succeeding decade, made a number of recommendations in that regard, including publicly accountable boards of trustees representing the "new owners"—the employees—and adjustments in the "prudent-person" rule.

Although Drucker's proposed reforms are important, a still broader set of criteria is needed to guide pension fund investment. These would require government support for a professional field of investment that would at once promote capital allocation in the interest of beneficiaries and take the welfare of the overall economy into consideration. Government can reorient policies in this direction in much the same manner as discussed above for corporate self-management.

In addition, government can offer incentives for studies in finance with a social orientation. Investors could be taught in management schools to synthesize public and economic criteria in making their decisions. Legislation could foster private investment in the public interest by dealing with problems created in the stock market through computer programming for quick turnover; by taking into account the health of the economy as a whole; and by looking carefully at declining industries to see where firms can be supported to bring about good social and economic returns. Private investors could be encouraged to favor firms with good employee health and safety records, good environmental records, and good consumer safety records. Professional and legal guidelines would also be needed to channel allocations to where not only the economic returns but also the social standards are the highest. Investment history has shown that publicly oriented criteria can be effectively used even while high returns are primary.[9]

Problems in the U.S. economy are clearly connected to the national debt, which is intricately connected to world markets, and the resolution of the debt problem, in turn, is related to international organizations that monitor the circulation of global capital. New systems of governance are needed to handle the circulation of Eurodollars, watch over multinational corporations, and deal with trade problems in the global market. This means taking political steps to strengthen international law and establish a world court system, conducting joint studies on a revised monetary system, and supporting an international code of conduct for both capitalist corporations and socialist states so as to provide a common playing field in the world market. Issues in the global circulation of capital and the kind of public policies needed to treat them are discussed in more detail in the Appendix.

Policies to Promote Self-Regulation in Market Sectors

A basic premise of this book is that the lack of social norms and structures of accountability in the private market leads to a highly regulated market. While the development of employee self-managed firms can help to avert some government interventions, their systems of internal accountability would not sufficiently affect issues of competition between firms, and government regulations would still be needed for such problems as environmental pollution, product safety, and the conservation of natural resources. Thus there is a need for government to help advance self-regulation in this larger competitive market.

The Peril and Promise of Current Government Policies

Recent trends toward interfirm cooperation have been receiving some degree of government interest and support. For example, the "integrated system" is an arrangement in which cooperation to improve quality and reduce costs replaces competition for the lowest cost supplier. Fujitsu Fanuc and General Motors now have an integrated system in which Fanuc sells robots to GM and in the process learns factory technology to build better robots, while GM uses Fanuc's automation skills to compete in its market and simultaneously helps Fanuc attain worldwide sales based on high-volume customers wanting advanced robotics. Such systems can become so integrated that they develop products around each other.[10]

Cooperative systems like this one require study lest the long-term effect be to shut out competitors by exclusive purchasing arrangements. On the positive side, such systems could help firms overcome the problem of appropriability (technology spillover) through shared research, development, and manufacturing costs. Competition tends to lead firms to underinvest in new technology because innovators have limited capacity to extract "fees" from the imitators, who get a free ride on their competitors' investments. Cooperation thus could reduce the needless duplication of effort between competing companies while it stimulates investment.

Firms today are increasing their level of cooperation with one another because of the resulting economic advantages of lower costs, better product quality, and flexibility in the marketplace, and cooperation is becoming accepted and legally permissible because it is in the national interest, allowing firms to compete more effectively against foreign companies. Increasingly, there are new coalitions of rival firms cooperating for research and development; new partnerships of manufacturers, suppliers, and customers who seek lower costs, better products, and more efficient processes; and new consortia of capital and labor, along with new patterns of problem solving, planning, and coordinated action between business and government, aimed at achieving global competitiveness. For all these reasons, steps toward cooperation are supported by government, but without any attention paid to issues of self-regulation or social accountability. The future is thus full of both peril and promise.

As trends toward cooperation between firms begin to challenge the popular paradigm, they are also beginning to raise questions about its legality. To advance these cooperative practices, business leaders are now seeking to revise antitrust laws. Although such revisions in competitive practices in the value-added chain of business from suppliers to retailers could lead closer toward a self-regulated market, without a larger vision and social planning the immediate consequences could be monopolistic and highly detrimental to self-regulation.

Will new legislation favorable to cooperation lead toward mergers, centralization, and monopoly in the private sector, or can it lead toward greater decentralization of cooperating firms? Can competition be improved through legislation that encourages business cooperation to maintain the autonomy of firms? Let us now look at how legislation and other actions can encourage firms to deal with global competition through trade associations and business alliances designed for that purpose, encouraging business autonomy rather than monopoly.

The passage of the National Cooperative Research Act in 1984 marked a major shift in U.S. antitrust philosophy, since it allowed competitors to pool resources for joint research and development. The NCRA, which was designed partly to legalize changes already made in the marketplace, had been motivated by the effective formation of business alliances such as the Microelectronics and Computer Technology Corporation, a cooperative arrangement of 21 U.S. companies organized to rival Japan's Very Large Scale Integrated Circuit Technology Research Association (VLSI/TRA), a joint venture of the five largest Japanese mainframe computer manufacturers. These Japanese manufacturers were collaborating with the Nippon Telegraph and Telephone Company and were strongly supported by MITI, which provided half the VLSI/TRA program budget and helped to staff its laboratories. Faced with this kind of government-industry collaboration, U.S. companies had to find a new—and legal—way to cooperate in order to stay in the market.

Since the NCRA's purpose is to allow U.S. firms to compete more effectively in a global market, it does not interpret cooperation as being illegal in principle. The specific legality of any arrangement is judged by the standard of "reasonableness," taking into account all relevant factors affecting competition. However, it is not yet clear whether this act could backfire and promote noncompetitiveness in the domestic market.

The Japanese experience suggests that cooperation might lead to monopoly and a corporate state. To move into an era of integrated cooperation among competing firms, Japan both enacted legislation to provide for cooperation and promoted industry associations and antitrust immunity for interfirm cooperation in order to achieve its larger objectives in a global market.

For example, the entire Japanese computer industry of six firms coalesced to compete with IBM and its System 370. In 1980, the Japanese government supported the establishment of the Japan Robot Leasing Company, Ltd. (JAROL), a joint venture between 24 robot manufacturers and 10 insurance companies, to encourage the use of robots by small and medium-sized firms and to build a large domestic market. The Japan Development Bank provided JAROL with low-interest loans to allow easy leasing terms, and by 1982, Japan had 31,900 industrial robots in place, compared with 7,232 in the United States. Thus, success in the global market can come at the cost of the loss of free enterprise in the domestic market.[11]

Although other free market economies may do the same to compete, the trend also implies an increase in mergers and centralized government-industry collaboration, which is more like a step toward state corporatism than toward self-regulation. Such steps, unfortunately, do seem to be taking place in the United States. Recent Commerce Department studies, for example, recommend a wide range of remedies to avoid threats from outside competition, including "industry rationalization" through vertical and horizontal integration and mergers. In particular, mergers, cooperative partnerships, and industry cooperation are deemed necessary for joint research. These studies conclude that private industry will require greater collaboration among all of its organized divisions— labor, management, competitors, customers, and suppliers.

Such a conclusion would augur well in a carefully envisioned future based on structures for self-accountability, but points forebodingly to greater centralization under present circumstances.[12] The accounting world provides a recent example of how global competition pressures giants to merge. Arthur Andersen and Price Waterhouse sought hard to become the largest accounting firm in the world, with revenues of nearly $5 billion and a worldwide staff of 83,000 people, and only called off the deal at the last minute.[13]

It is essential to note that government policies view mergers as a form of cooperation, and therefore support them as being in the national interest. The problem for government policy, therefore, is to distinguish between mergers that lead to centralization and the threat of corporate statism and cooperation carried out among independent firms.

The Need for New Legal Foundations for Cooperation

Part of the promise of cooperation is seen in new definitions of the corporation's purpose offered by business scholars:

While the old premise of corporate purpose and governance is no longer valid, we are now undergoing the transition to the new premise where the corporation's purpose is to serve all of its constituents—customers, suppliers, shareholders, debt holders, and communities—in a balanced way. Management is now expected to give due regard to the "investments" of employees and affected communities along with that given to holders of equity and debt. If managers expect to receive the full commitment of employees toward improving productivity, for example, those employees must be assured a measure of employment security in return. In order to reach full potential, employees will expect and require participation in decisions that affect their work lives—in other words, a place in the governance process.[14]

But vital though all this is to a self-governing market, a definition of this sort is not complete. Without an awareness of the importance of intercorporate organization, including a plan for developing associational activity that produces norms and tribunals that function in the context of a balance of power, the proposed new corporate purpose "to serve all its constituents" will remain only a rhetorical ideal.

One promising line of development lies in what Thomas Jorde and David Teece call the "strategic alliance," which they define as "an alternative governance structure" that meets the problem of global competition. Their strategic alliances differ significantly from mergers and other types of coordinated activities in numerous ways. For one thing, they do not involve the acquisition of another firm's assets. They are less restrictive than mergers because they are temporary and are easily disassembled when circumstances warrant, and they are less comprehensive, since only a limited range of a firm's activities are drawn into such agreements. Strategic alliances are also different from exchange transactions, since exchange transactions, like licensing agreements with specified royalties, are unilateral. A strategic alliance is always bilateral; it can never have one side receiving cash alone, since it includes consortia and joint ventures that are required when an industry becomes fragmented.

Strategic alliances are especially important when an industry is endangered by foreign competition, and they are an alternative to government planning because they preserve the free market. Jorde and Teece note the irony that government policies treat such co-operative agreements less permissively than they do mergers.[15] In their view, Congress did not break any new ground with the National Cooperative Research Act because the cooperative arrangements it allows still fall under the traditional rule of "reasonableness." For example, the NCRA limits the antitrust recovery against joint research projects registered with the government to single damages, interest, and the costs of suit, thus eliminating the threat of treble damages that would be applied in the case of a collusive arrangement. But the NCRA provides a limited shelter *only* for research and development, and as a result, not many firms have taken advantage of this opportunity. A broader legal rationale for cooperation has yet to be established.

Arguing for a new legal foundation, Jorde and Teece note how antitrust laws discourage opportunities for beneficial cooperation, inhibiting joint efforts in large technological endeavors such as superconductors and high-definition television:

The limited nature of the NCRA will leave Sematech—after spending $1 billion over the next four years to develop what is expected to be the world's most advanced flexible computer-integrated semiconductor manufacturing facility—unable to operate it without substantial risk of an antitrust violation, for which it and its members would be exposed to treble damages. Even if antitrust enforcement agencies were not inclined to prosecute, private antitrust suits could be forthcoming. Until further legislation is passed, U.S. firms are likely to continue to muddle along with inadequate, uncoordinated, and unfocused, separate initiatives while foreign competitors take the lead.[16]

Smaller firms, too, could reap rewards from shared facilities such as flexible computer-integrated manufacturing, which are too expensive for individual second- and third-tier suppliers alone. Unfortunately, however, cooperative efforts by small firms to share costs in building such facilities are also clouded today because of antitrust uncertainties.

Under these circumstances, I propose the establishment of a federal commission charged with focusing on these issues. This commission could study how firms might cooperate more effectively against global competitors without participating in mergers. It could begin by identifying the needs of the business community, including the need for a "safe harbor" that exempts beneficial cooperative arrangements and strategic alliances from antitrust regulation, for an analysis of the pace and stage of technological change, coupled with the diverse technology and operational and strategic coordination needed to achieve success with a new product, and for new business strategies that can keep imitators at bay for a reasonable period of time.

At the same time, the commission must examine the larger picture of the future, beginning with a thorough review of the effectiveness of cooperation through decentralized forms of business as a means of coping with changes brought about by the global market. Such an examination should explore new roles for trade associations and business alliances, based on a decentralized system of authority, and should consider industrial structures that can lead to a social indexing of market norms, allowing the government to encourage firms to cooperate without monopoly for the benefit both of the larger industry and of the society as a whole.

The Role of Trade Associations

We have said that reducing the government's regulation of business requires (1) strengthening the authority of responsible trade and professional associations to democratically monitor the behavior of their member firms; (2) providing an opportunity for interindustry (peak) associations to deal with issues outside their internal lives; and (3) establishing conditions conducive to a balance of power among the corporations (and their associations) representing different stages in the vertical development of a product or service. We also discussed earlier why the conditions proposed here would avoid the legal problems raised by *Schechter* under the National Recovery Act.

Under these conditions, self-regulation should be permitted gradually, with firms first becoming structured to regulate themselves in the public interest through their own private associations, and then as parts of the chain from supply to consumption, regulating themselves in the public interest through vertical associations representing each level. One basis for the legality of this proposal rests in the development of indexes that would measure the structure of power in vertical stages of business within industries seeking to regulate themselves. Self-regulatory activity is already commonplace within certain market sectors, as we have seen, and this proposal would simply encourage that trend.

The key to effective self-regulation is the representation of all interested parties. A code of ethics may serve to govern an industry's own competing members, but even the most democratically organized association cannot monitor their collective behavior toward out-groups. Realtors can monitor their relationships with one another, but not those between individual realtors and home sellers and buyers, and physicians can monitor their behavior toward one another, but not the behavior of individual doctors toward patients, even though attempts to do so are laudable. For self-governance to work, the out-group must be represented in the private judicial system.

Although in-group monitoring is taking place in many market sectors in the form of interassociation monitoring between suppliers and producers, producers and distributors, and distributors and retailers, out-groups are only beginning to be represented. Government incentives are needed to further this basis for resolving conflicts. Indeed, the encouragement of the democratic construction of private judicial systems for competing associations stands at the core of planning for self-regulation in the U.S. economy.

New interassociation monitoring activities could be carried out experimentally by peak associations, including the U.S. Chamber of Commerce, the National Association of Manufacturers, and the AFL-CIO. More effective monitoring of health and safety in the workplace by trade associations working together with trade unions, for example, would reduce the need for OSHA to do so much of that job. Where unions do not exist, OSHA could encourage the development of worker councils, representing employees independent of management, to join with management on monitoring and enforcement procedures. Encouragement of interassociational self-regulation should thus be a top agenda item for any administration seeking to reduce the cost of government.

The Need for Social Indexing

As discussed earlier, social indexes that evaluate such issues as the voting structure, dues structure, and tribunal structure of trade associations are required before the Federal Trade Commission and the Antitrust Division of the Justice Department can begin authorizing them to increase their self-monitoring activities. As such social indexes are formally developed by government agencies and recognized as part of the legal determination of what constitutes a just basis for self-monitoring, more associations will be guided by them.

Another important step toward intercorporate self-regulation would be the establishment of a Council of Social Advisors that would operate concurrently with the present Council of Economic Advisors. The purpose of this new body would be to help government agencies to develop and operationalize social indicators to measure the changes taking place in such critical areas as health, safety, worker participation, corporate ownership, environmental protection, product safety, and pension plans.

There are precedents for the development of social indicators as a national policy. In 1968, the U.S. Commission on National Goals, concerned about the country's lag in the space race, took a new interest in social quantification, which culminated in this conclusion in its brief publication, *Towards a Social Report:* "For all of their virtues, the national income statistics don't tell us what we need to know about the conditions of American society. They leave out most of the things that make life worth living."[17] Five years later came the first published formulation of social indicators. *Social Indicators 1973*, and its supplement, *Social Indicators 1976*, showed a continued professional interest in the subject. The combined volume was 647 pages long, with 750 charts and tables covering such topics as population, housing, health and nutrition, public safety, work, income, leisure, social mobility, and participation. Although plenty of statistics were gathered, they appear with little commentary or theory.[18]

Meanwhile, the U.S. Bureau of the Census contemplated beefing up its social reporting by establishing three separate but interrelated "work centers": an information unit that would coordinate and integrate the bureau's social statistical research; a social indicator unit that would produce a triennial social indicators volume in cooperation with the United Nations; and a social accounts unit that would integrate various monthly and annual household surveys with other data sources, with the eventual aim of improved social monitoring.[19] Unfortunately, that plan never came to full fruition.

In the late 1970's, U.S. Senator Walter Mondale introduced the Full Opportunity and Social Accounting Act, which declared social accounting a national goal. It would have required the president to submit an annual social report to Congress, and emphasized the need to establish a permanent body to identify problem areas before they became so severe that they required government action. Although this act never reached the floor, such a program is clearly needed even more today. Such social monitoring could be conducted through the auspices of a Council of Social Advisors; and the data collected could serve as an operational foundation for government policies that would promote self-regulation in the economy.

The Need for Balance Between Vertical Stages of Product Development

As noted, one requirement of self-regulation is maintaining a balance of power between vertical stages of product development. This could be monitored by the Justice Department in the same sense that it normally monitors that balance within industries. One initiative taken by industry itself has been mentioned: the National Automobile Dealers Association, an arrangement between General Motors and retail auto dealers. Thanks to the tribunal organized privately by these opposing corporate groups at different vertical stages, dealers have a forum in which to vent any complaints of unfair treatment by the producer instead of routinely bringing their cases to the FTC or federal courts, as in earlier times. Although such a balance is essential to expand the power of self-regulation in the private sector, the law is not nearly so clear on the monitoring of vertical markets as it is in respect to horizontal markets.

A set of social indicators for each industry could tell the government and trade associations exactly where there is need for greater interorganizational balance for the purposes of self-regulation. To the degree that trade associations with opposing interests achieve that balance, they can begin to resolve the problems the federal government must otherwise solve for them. Needed legislation in this area would strengthen the legal basis for the Antitrust Division to act on monopolistic practices developing between vertical stages of product development within an industry.

Trade Associations as Economic Actors

Another major area affecting self-regulation concerns the ability of trade associations to operate for economic as well as nonprofit purposes. This is important because it would preserve the powers of self-governance at the level of small business while at the same time providing a decentralized alternative to the power that big business claims it needs to achieve certain tasks. The experience of Silicon Valley will demonstrate the problem.

Over the past two decades, Silicon Valley has been held up as an ideal example of business decentralization and social innovation, as inventive engineers quit jobs with big corporations to create their own small firms around a risky technology. But recently business scholars have observed drawbacks to this pattern of business development, arguing that the overabundance of small ventures has been taken to excess because the industries being broken up have lost their power to compete against corporate giants from overseas. The exodus of creative engineers from big U.S. companies saps these companies' strength and discourages them from making long-range investments; but the small companies do not have the capital to compete against foreign competition, and often have to sell their technological secrets for needed cash. Ironically, this provides a way for foreign companies to acquire the latest technology at bargain prices and win market dominance.

Clyde V. Prestowitz, a former chief trade negotiator with Japan, asks: "Can it be that the notion of individualism, so sacred to the United States, is also its fatal flaw—the basic strength that works against itself to reduce strength?" Charles Ferguson, a political scientist at the Massachusetts Institute of Technology, claims that "the time of entrepreneurship and instability, and the virtues of the one start-up engineer are virtually over in this industry."[20] The essence of these messages is that hundreds of small U.S. companies competing in the semiconductor market will simply lose out to Japan, which has fifteen giants. Furthermore, this problem is economy wide—semiconductors were only the beginning. The next industry that will lose in the same fashion is biotechnology. These are frontline industries that the United States cannot afford to lose.

I propose that such a process could be avoided through creative government policies that provide a legal foundation for trade associations to assume authority in declining industries. The idea of "intrapreneurship," which began within companies, should be extended to include relationships between companies. Intrapreneurship emerged when large companies that sought to develop new products allowed employees ("intrapreneurs") to start little internal "enterprises" outside the normal corporate bureaucracy. This process had mixed success, because even though they were free to innovate, many intrapreneurs believed they were not as financially well rewarded by the company as they would have been as independent innovators. (This was one reason for the exodus of creative engineers in Silicon Valley.)

The alternative proposed here is entirely different. Let the inno-

vative entrepreneur start his or her own company, but also allow it
to work within a federation of companies so as to stem the outflow
of inventions to foreign competitors. We can take a case that went
wrong in the computer industry to see how this proposed new social organization would work. Hard pressed for capital, LSI Logic, a
leader in semicustomized chips, had to cut a deal with Toshiba, in
which Toshiba got LSI's software technology and then became LSI's
sole supplier of the silicon wafers it needed. Under my proposed
new system, LSI could instead have received the capital it needed
as a loan from a new American trade association specifically created for the purpose of manufacturing silicon wafers. In turn, government would have provided this association with the capital
needed to establish a federated system of firms that would operate
in their joint interest to counter foreign competition. The board of
this model association would include representatives of LSI Logic
as well as other firms in the same industry. It would, in effect, be a
trade association with legal permission to go into production. Although the manufactured wafers would then be sold by LSI, some
of the profits would be shared by the members of the association.
In this way, arrangements with a foreign firm would be avoided, to
the benefit of the U.S. economy as well as the industry. Through
such an association, all U.S. firms in the industry could gain market power from the returns of the production process, as opposed
to the present arrangement, in which only a foreign competitor receives those returns.

Looked at in still another way, LSI would retain its autonomous
status as a company within its own federation, rather than operating under the command of a larger outside corporation. The association would assume responsibility for repaying the government
loan, and could also take on the distributing functions needed by
LSI Logic. The government might also confer added self-regulatory
powers on the association as long as it met the social standards devised for determining its capacity to maintain accountability to
member firms.

This is only one example of how trade associations operating as
economic units might excite a new stage of economic development.
Hundreds of unique scenarios could be written that would illustrate the advantages of a policy giving business more legal leeway
to cooperate for the purpose of advancing productivity in their
field. The legal foundations and preparations for such develop-

ments must be worked out through university research and new government policies. For example, studies are needed to model the types of associations that would avoid monopolistic practices while still keeping a competitive edge for member firms.

The Role of Peak Associations

A peak association can assume broader public responsibilities than can horizontal associations, particularly if it represents the interests of horizontal associations of competing firms at different stages of product development. No horizontal association by itself, for example, could monitor the norms of free entry and market concentration for which government agencies today have a responsibility, but competing firms within a value-added chain have an interest in monitoring tendencies toward monopoly, because they know that free entry keeps their prices down, and a peak association might do this in their interests within limits. Before any peak association was granted even limited power, to be sure, the FTC would have to ensure that it was democratically organized, and that its monitoring plan was accepted by its own members. An initial task of the association would be to keep the same statistics on concentration and entry now kept by the FTC or another federal agency. The figures are standard, and their public disclosure by the peak association would then become a minor force against large corporations taking steps to curb entry in their market area. The next steps toward "noncoercive" enforcement of the norms could be explored along the lines employed by the FTC. The FTC is known to have often been effective in getting consent decrees before court action after private consultations with companies about to engage in monopolistic buyouts.[21]

There are many other public responsibilities that peak associations could assume. For example, they could provide greater agency support to industries threatened by foreign competition, that is, increasing their competitive power by communicating crucial information on potential market invasions from overseas; consult on joint ventures in socialist countries; provide R&D ideas for breakthrough technology; and plan new markets with the aid of the U.S. Department of Commerce. They could also computerize industry-wide information on job openings, help standardize pension plans, and so forth. Each responsibility, however, would have to be evaluated to determine whether it meets the interests of member firms as well as the public interest. Although government can provide incentives for trade associations to move in this direction, it must be done on a voluntary basis where mutual interests are met.

Policies to Promote Associations' International Role

Although the Japanese model of integration is not suitable for the United States, it seems to me possible to keep the advantages of the Japanese system—strong leadership and vision at the top, planning between government and business leaders, and in particular the capacity of business and government to integrate their goals—without so complete a link between the state and the private sector and between national and individual interests. One step in this direction might be to establish a new federal agency whose mission would be to work with the existing order of trade and professional associations to advance the interests of U.S. business in a global market. Let us call this body the Agency for the International Development of Associations, or AIDA.

AIDA would be similar to MITI in certain respects. It would have an international focus, because all economically oriented national associations must now view their organization and their goals from a global perspective. To use Vogel's analogy, AIDA would function to some extent like the National Football League or the National Basketball Association. Its officials would set rules about the size of the team (in much the same way that the Antitrust Department already monitors "market shares") and would set rules of play that result in relatively equally matched teams of great competitive ability. At the same time, it would not interfere with internal corporate (team) activity or tell a firm's president how to manage, but would provide critical information that enabled that firm to cooperate with the others in "the league" (trade association) in improving their competitiveness as players in the world game.

AIDA would also propose legislation that in its judgment increased the capacity of firms to cooperate within decentralized trade associations under conditions of self-regulation and would provide model constitutions that enable trade associations to increase their ability to function as democratic entities.

But AIDA would have a different basic goal from MITI's. Its purpose would be to help associations become strong within themselves, to advance not only their business interests, but also their observance of the basic values of the public welfare, including affirmative action practices, freedom of exit and entry into trade areas, and social democracy. AIDA would have special powers to reward the member firms in these associations by going directly to bat for them as the need arose—helping them in the international market and in such matters as banking, tax breaks, land purchases, choice locations, and special permits and licenses. And it would work with top leaders to find ways to release proprietary information through peak associations that would enable them to make decisions regarding world markets without improperly or unfairly jeopardizing the competitive advantages of individual companies. In short, where MITI seeks to centralize corporate structures in global competition, AIDA would seek to decentralize ownership structures, while maximizing communications between companies and, where appropriate, sharing information and technology.

AIDA would study the local, regional, and national organization of trade associations to determine how balanced they are in terms of organizational power and would encourage a more equitable distribution. If adjustments could not be made on a voluntary basis, it would offer recommendations to the Antitrust Division on new enforcement policies and would help write legislation to encourage a more equitable distribution of corporate power, with a view to increasing the market's capacity for self-regulation.

AIDA would also help associations in their efforts to deal with the problems of declining industries. It would urge company presidents to specialize instead of conglomerize where it was in the national interest, and to update technology when they lagged behind other nations. It would teach trade associations how to help member companies reduce the impact of unemployment on communities by providing computerized information on job openings in neighboring companies, stimulating new local enterprises, and the like.

New enterprises might even be capitalized initially with AIDA's help, in order to keep a trade area developing in spite of occasional poor management or a declining market. In the process, AIDA would also help trade associations provide management training programs for their members and help firms open up new markets without jeopardizing the markets of their fellow members. The ultimate aim would be to provide the basis for trade associations to learn to do all this on their own, eliminating the necessity of supporting them in such projects in the future. Model projects sponsored by AIDA in the public interest might well lead other trade associations to replicate them in their own interest.

Some of these proposed activities already exist and simply need more support and development. For example, the peak National Association of Manufacturers, whose more than 13,000 member companies account for 85 percent of the manufactured products and manufacturing jobs in the United States, is most often thought of in connection with its self-interested lobbying efforts and its staunch antiunionism. But NAM also provides important support mechanisms for its members through national committees on employee relations, management training programs, environmental quality, and the like, all of which could become the organizational basis for AIDA's communications on issues in manufacturing. There are other trade associations related to manufacturing that help balance off NAM's power, such as the Chamber of Commerce, and they would have to be taken into equal consideration in formulating public policies in the manufacturing field that serve the broader public interest.

AIDA would also work with nonprofit organizations outside the business community, since its staff would understand how intricately related the market is to that entire sector. It would therefore be interested in the ways professional associations in accounting, chemistry, physics, engineering, economics, sociology, law, medicine, and hundreds of other fields connect with business in the public interest. For example, if AIDA decided that uniform accounting standards were needed to serve the public interest, it would communicate its concerns to professional accountants, leaving it to them to set national standards in corporate accounting; and it might arrange meetings between professional associations of accountants and major trade associations to deal with these matters. AIDA would work with professional associations of chemists and physicists to develop pollution standards, with medical associations to develop health standards, with engineering associations to develop construction standards, and so on.

Although such professional work has been going on for many years, it has never been integrated into the business system under a coherent policy encouraged by the government. For example, in 1972–73 the National Association of Accountants established an eight-member Committee on Accounting for Corporate Social Performance. This group wrestled with issues related to social responsibility, issuing reports with checklists under the headings of "community involvement," "human resources," "physical resources," "environmental contributions," and "product or service contribution," a taxonomy of social responsibility characterized by considerable detail and precision. Another example of an effort to delineate the content of social responsibility and to measure business performance is observed in the research of two accountant-scholars, Steven Dilley and Jerry Weygandt, who developed an annual report, tested with data from an electric power company, that provides a structured basis for social auditing for companies in the United States.[22]

AIDA could also work with investors to promote the public interest. If the Council of Institutional Investors, which manages billions of dollars in pension funds, continues to develop its concerns about hostile takeovers and "greenmail," and more of its members assert the importance of ethical criteria in their practices of investment, AIDA could serve as a counselor in talks between council leaders and business and trade association executives about social investment. In this way, the values of the society would be transmitted directly into the market through the power of a wider sector of nonprofit institutions, including such diverse groups as unions, states, religious institutions, and universities. Since they hold the capital that is invested in the profit sector, they are the owners of corporations, and their professional views on corporate conduct are entitled to be heard by trade associations, as well as at the annual meetings of the corporations themselves.

In facilitating communications between the vast nonprofit sector and business associations on such matters, AIDA would play a vital role in synthesizing social and economic factors. It would also help facilitate the changes needed by U.S. business to meet world competition, without destroying human values and the autonomy of the private sector. If an agency such as "AIDA" were established and operated as described here, it could set the private sector well on the way to becoming a social sector capable of functioning outside the government in the public interest.

Policies to Transform the Welfare State

Many of the principles and programs discussed in this book can be used to reduce the costs of the welfare state. While a plan for

overcoming all the costs of unemployment, public welfare, education and training programs, and the like is beyond our scope, the
basic idea is to transfer the capital that supports the welfare state
into a system that supports socially accountable business. Instead
of current practices such as tax credits, accelerated depreciation
rules, subsidized loans, loan guarantees, tariffs, quotas, marketing
agreements, welfare payments, and price supports, government
funds could be directed toward helping local, state, and regional
trade associations initiate businesses that open new markets and
thus do not compete with their members, and could reward those
firms that specialize in hiring disadvantaged and chronically unemployed people.

Unemployment

Under current public policies, it is profitable for companies to lay
off employees during economic downturns because they can transfer the responsibility for paying them to the state's welfare system
and reduce costs. When the economy improves, the companies re-
hire. This seems logical but it also promotes unemployment and
discourages firms from making long-term investments in training.

The alternatives are complex and must be tested. Some analysts
have suggested that in place of government job-training programs
that do not keep up with changes in job skills, the government
should provide unemployed workers with vouchers to cash in for
job training at companies that need workers. Half the training costs
would be financed by the government out of a payroll tax levied on
employees and employers. This plan would match training to specific market needs and ensure that companies finance part of the
training. But it does not transfer the welfare responsibility directly
to the private sector and keeps the govenment in the role of supplying financial support.

It is possible to go one step further and build capital reserves into
the private sector itself, or what I have called the social sector, to
handle job creation and job training. Job training could be transferred experimentally from the government to the nonprofit sector
through trade and professional associations. For example, trade
associations that set up training centers for workers in their own
industry and demonstrate that they are taking people off welfare
would become eligible for government funds to improve and expand their training operations. The government could ask that

endowments be established, that is, interest-bearing capital that could be accumulated just for the purpose of education and training. In this way, industrial associations would build up a reserve to handle their own job training and job transfers.

Many companies are too small to provide employees with adequate job training and retraining. But by joining forces through their trade associations, they can easily reach that scale. Indeed, job retraining could also be made available through industrial associations to workers who have been employed for some period of years at one job and wish to upgrade their skills. Robert Reich notes how the present tax code leads in the opposite direction. Companies that wish to desert their workers and communities by going overseas can deduct their costs of moving as a business expense, write off the plant and machinery left behind, and obtain tax credits and accelerated depreciation against new plant and machinery purchased at the new location. But the training costs that are incurred for preparing employees for new kinds of jobs cannot be deducted from current income. This policy generates social costs as workers and communities are left stranded within vast pockets of unemployment.[23]

Some analysts suggest a new tax code that permits individual companies to claim tax benefits for retraining their older workers for new jobs and also permits them to set aside an annual tax-deductible reserve fund for the development of human resources, based on the number of workers on the payroll. The accumulated funds would be used for retraining and upgrading the work force in single companies. But such a tax code should be designed at the same time to reward companies for turning to self-management and assuming the responsibility of retraining on their own.[24]

Reich believes that a significant part of the present welfare system will ultimately be replaced by government grants to businesses that agree to hire the chronically unemployed. These grants will pay a portion of the wages of these newly hired workers for a limited period of time, in an extension of the employment voucher concept. He believes that this system will be less expensive than welfare in the short run, and in the longer run will help get people off welfare by upgrading their skills. Firms that hire the chronically unemployed will have an incentive to give them on-the-job training in order to increase their contributions to overall productivity.

Reich has outlined the basic idea, but with the details yet to be carefully formulated.

Other social services—health care, Social Security, day care, disability benefits, unemployment benefits, relocation assistance—will become part of the process of structural adjustment. Public funds now spent directly on these services will instead be made available to businesses, according to the number of people they employ and the number of chronically unemployed they agree to hire. Government bureaucracies that now administer these programs to individuals will be supplanted, to a large extent, by companies that administer them to their employees. These social services will continue to be available to employees unless they attach themselves to another company. In this way, firms will become the agents of their employees, bargaining on behalf of their workers for different packages of government-supported social services and often purchasing them from private providers, who will be competing against one another to offer the best services at least cost.[25]

In this vision of things, the total package of benefits would be tied to a firm's specific production plans. For example, a decision to expand into new technology might require special emphasis on retraining, relocation, and day-care assistance, at least until the company's employees adjust to the new technology, schedules, and locations that the work requires.

In-Kind Benefits

To some extent, a trend of transferring welfare programs from government to business is evolving through the system of "in-kind benefits" that companies provide to employees and that is not part of employees' taxable income. This tax benefit is rewarding to companies and builds its own momentum. For example, an increase in employee wages is normally not as great as an increase in benefits such as health insurance and life insurance. The money that would have been paid to the government in taxes is now divided between the employees and the company.[26] In-kind company benefits that are exempt from income taxes are replacing direct government expenditures for social services, and thus reducing government bureaucracy.

At the very least, I believe such benefit programs should be managed jointly by representatives of both labor and management. Otherwise the firms cannot appropriately act as "agents of the employees," and the funds could be misused by top management. Such plans should also be linked to firms becoming accountable to their employees in a broader domain of management, through internal tribunals, councils, and board representatives; that is, they should demonstrate that they are becoming employee self-managed.

In effect, the federal government is now administering major social service programs such as health and life insurance and direct outlays in Medicare and Medicaid through American corporations. In addition, tax-deferred pension plans that are administered through firms have grown in size to compete with Social Security as the key means of saving for retirement. Other corporate tax-free benefits include subsidized cafeteria food, recreational facilities, home mortgage subsidies, relocation assistance, group legal services, and subsidies for children's private schooling. Increasingly, American corporations are sponsoring their own day-care programs and assisting employees to adopt children. Companies have developed programs to aid employees with problems of alcoholism and drug addiction, and have created counseling programs for emotional and family problems. Such benefits are growing more rapidly than direct social services from the government and becoming an increasing part of employee compensation.

But major inequities exist in these positive trends: benefit packages are likely to be supplied mainly for white-collar, salaried employees; the benefits are not spread uniformly throughout the enterprise system; smaller companies are not able to provide the level of benefits offered by larger companies; and the unemployed are receiving less help than ever before because of government cutbacks.

Employees in Japan do not face these problems because "justice" there decrees that everyone should share in a firm's benefits and workers should have lifetime guaranteed employment. Again, in Japan the risks of an economic downturn are shared by shareholders of companies and by government-linked banks rather than the employees. Workers are not laid off when sales decline because top managers take major cuts in pay before lower-level workers are laid off, and the government subsidizes small businesses as a safety net for the unemployed. Day care and job training are supplied by firms.

In the United States, one way to treat the problem of internal inequity of benefits among employees is to tie the governmental provision of benefits to the development of democratic self-management.

The development of self-management would lead toward the same end of employees sharing the cutbacks of an economic downturn.

Regional Inequities

Part of the problem of poverty, unemployment, and high welfare costs in the United States rises from the development of major dislocations of capital between regions. U.S. business is not organized on a regional foundation, as it is in Japan. Business moves nationally wherever it finds resources available. Thus major business investments will concentrate around key regions like Silicon Valley, while other regions like Appalachia remain capital-poor. Private investment, in turn, affects government welfare programs and the capacity of the local community to support roads, sewage treatment plants, and schools. One solution to this problem is to promote regional associations that can support capital allocation for development in their region.

In Japan, as we saw, trade associations are organized by regions, a policy that allows them to be represented relatively equitably. In the United States, one way to help redress the inequitable distribution of private capital would be a government program to establish new banks in poverty pockets. The banks would be financed with government-guaranteed bonds and shares of stock until they could become self-supporting. Some of the bonds and stocks could be made available to the state and union pension funds that have become such a significant source of capital in the country, thereby diverting the large amounts now invested in foreign securities to regional development.

The banks could be organized in a fashion similar to the famous Mondragon bank, which played so crucial—and successful—a role in the development of the Basque region of northern Spain. In making loans to new companies, the bank has had only three failures in the process of creating 110 industrial firms. Its success can be attributed in part to its maintaining close supervision over the development of the firms it finances, helping entrepreneurs to make careful business and marketing plans, and in part to its careful accounting procedures. The firms are designed to become fully worker-owned and -managed, with profits divided between an internal capital fund for (1) corporate R&D and expansion, (2) employee profit sharing, and (3) contributions to the local community. All firms capitalized by the bank elect representatives to its board of directors, on which the bank's own employees are represented as well. The bank also funds an institution for R&D that serves regional businesses. A system of consumer-owned retail establishments is capitalized with the help of these businesses, thus developing a mutually supportive producer-consumer link in the business organization of this creative regional system. Consumers and employees are represented on the retail firms' board of directors, offering an important model for regional development.

Conclusion

If the U.S. economy is to be socially governed, two concepts—self-governance and mutal governance—must guide public policies and scientific research in the future. Public policies can be directed toward increasing the economy's self-governing powers at all levels, keeping in mind the goal of productivity. In this process, they can also encourage new systems of mutual governance at all levels: workshops can be redesigned into autonomous groups, corporations can create opportunities for employee responsibility and become self-managed, industries can raise productivity through trade associations operating in the public interest, and nations can increase their economic strength by becoming an integral part of a system of mutually governed markets.

The principle behind all these proposals is that self-governance develops through higher systems of mutual governance at every level of the economy. At the bottom level, individual laborers can gain a greater degree of responsible power by working together through autonomous groups, while at the top, the U.S. government can gain a greater degree of power for the economy by working with other nations through a reorganized United Nations. New systems of mutual governance do not always work out effectively in practice, of course. Much depends on the social process—how the organizing is done—but I believe that a concept of social governance is the most promising path to the future.

Government is a symbol of authority as well as an expression of power. When the government adopts new policies that favor the social-economic development of business, that action by itself encourages private innovation. Furthermore, new government policies can help overcome existing regulations that stifle innovation. But the real source of change must come from voluntary action and experiments designed by participants in the private sector. There are thousands of ways for self-managed firms to develop successfully, depending on corporate size, geographic location, ethnicity, leadership styles, the maturity of employees, and so on. Government policy should not mandate only one form but should encourage the tryout of many different forms.

In sum, while government may be only one force for development, it can do a great deal to stimulate socially oriented investment and new types of associations that advance the economy beyond the framework of pure market competition. It can promote cooperative forms through which people monitor their competition, encourage industries to develop greater self-governing powers through joint research on new technology, generate an index system through a Council of Social Advisors (or other agency) to measure the larger human picture of business performance, authorize new codes of public conduct supplemented by private judicial systems, and help organize a consistent nationwide pension system under the aegis of the private sector, thus creating a new legal, healthy, and humane foundation for allocating capital. If such steps are taken, the economy could develop and thrive as never before. It could develop not only from the standpoint of economics, with its measures of higher productivity and material growth, but also from the standpoint of the social sciences, with its measures for higher degrees of self-governance and the cultivation of human resources.

The research world and the real world of the market are not far apart. When economists and sociologists work together in policy research, the conventional opposition between the social and the economic factors can diminish. Instead of an opposition, a synthesis can take place and begin to operate in the open market. Managers would learn to integrate high standards for a safe working life with high efficiency; employee representatives would learn to match their participation in higher management with greater productivity; investors would learn to optimize profits and human dignity concurrently in the world of finance.

If social and economic factors were to become consistently integrated, not only in research but also in policies that stimulate self-regulation in the market, we would be on our way to an entirely new economic order—and to a future not envisioned by policy makers today.

Conclusion

THE CHANGES and trends in the social organization of the market explored in this book foretell a major shift in the American economy. We have seen indications of this shift in an increasing amount of worker participation in higher management; a new pattern of worker ownership through employee pension funds and self-managed firms; a growing number of fiduciaries that allocate capital on the basis of social criteria; the growth of service and non-profit corporations that give a social character to business; and the development of trade associations that allow corporations both to compete and to regulate themselves in the public interest. We conclude our discussion by indicating one more signal that points to the growth of the social dimension in the business economy: a change in the definitions of key economic concepts.

A New Account of the Social Factor in Key Economic Concepts

Mainstream economists and business scholars are beginning to include noneconomic variables in the traditional economic concepts used for explaining market behavior. Six major concepts in particular appear to be changing:

1. *Wealth,* where the classical notion of wealth as material resources is broadened to include human resources

2. *Productivity,* where performance is now being judged by social criteria as well as economic criteria

3. *Marketing,* where the traditional notion of marketing as customer persuasion is being modified by the interpretation that it is in essence an exchange of values

4. *Corporation,* where the purpose is no longer defined solely as making a profit, and where selling is seen as a social engagement with customers

5. *Private sector*, where firms are now perceived to be socially accountable to various constituencies

6. *Technology*, where the definition now refers as much to advances in information shaped by interpersonal communications as to innovations in machinery.

Daniel Bell proposed that the meaning of a postindustrial economy could be interpreted through "theoretical formulations," the axial principle of the new age. Taken together, the redefinition of these theoretical categories by today's economists and business scholars indicates their growing recognition that the market economy has a social foundation. Let us examine each of these new interpretations in more detail.

Wealth

The field of economics has focused on the production of wealth since the days of Adam Smith, and so its redefinition is no small matter. In Smith's day, wealth was located in material resources. Smith himself wrote in *The Wealth of Nations*:

The labour of some of the respectable orders in society is like that of menial servants, unproductive of any value, and does not fix or realize itself in any permanent subject or vendible commodity which endures after the labour is past, and for which an equal quantity of labour could afterwards be procured. . . . In the same class we must rank . . . churchmen, lawyers, players, buffoons, musicians, Opera singers.[1]

Classical economists in the Smith tradition have always valued the physical objects of production and devalued services. Alfred Marshall broke new ground by pointing to the broader concept of "utilities," which included "trade," as the basis for study, but even in his work the original focus on material resources as the source of wealth never disappeared.

All economic entities must create wealth to maintain themselves, but how that wealth is created has changed through history. During the early extractive stage of society, wealth came from the earth's resources and was transformed into value by people's labor: metal became tools, animal skins became clothing, vegetation became food, and wood became fuel. During the manufacturing stage, people created value by using machines to transform material goods into more refined tools, clothing, food, and fuel. In the current services stage, wealth is found in human resources and the culture itself, and people create value by transforming the forms of social life through information and knowledge.

While the values of the extractive and manufacturing stages remain vital to a growing economy, they may now be understood as part of a broader term: culture. The deeper source of wealth today is found in the culture of a society, since natural resources and tools are of no value unless people are encultured to use them. The future of the postindustrial society therefore rests in transforming the culture. This means that the development of a more powerful economy requires changing the patterns of social organization in market life so that they reflect the fundamental values of society.

Distinguishing between the value of services and the value of utilities remains part of the dilemma in assessing the meaning of postindustrial society. Russell Lewis suggests that this problem continues today because an economics separated from the social sciences is incapable of treating the subject matter of services. Social and political relations in the economic order are either seen as an inferior form of wealth or praised beyond quantitative measure.

Those who deny to social or any other services full wealth status cannot allow them to be dealt with in the economist's language of utility. So here there is a division: commercial services are labelled "candyfloss," are described in fact in the language of nonutility and thus become candidates for persecution. Social services are, by contrast, promoted and extolled in the vocabulary of rights and privileges and political obligation.[2]

Lewis suggests that the problem also exists in socialist thought because Marx's theory of value was economically based: he was concerned with a loss in the human value of producing goods, not in the value to be found in services or in commerce itself. Socialist writers have since struggled with the distinction between social and economic categories, as the following excerpt from Alec Nove's *The Soviet Economy* suggests:

The present concept involves, among other things, the idea that a railway signalman is productive when he lets a freight train past his signal-box but unproductive when he performs an identical function on the approach of a passenger train. Similarly a typist at a factory is productive, but the girl in Gosplan, who may type the letter in reply, is unproductive because a line has to be drawn between "administration" and "productive enterprises," and the two typists find themselves on opposite sides of the line.[3]

Since productivity has always been associated with material wealth in the industrial society, many economists question the degree to which services actually generate wealth and are of value to a society. Admitting that the real problem is the difficulty of measuring services in terms of a price component and an output component, income statisticians have resorted to the use of employment as a proxy for output. But that is an unsatisfactory solution. As Jacques Nusbaumer notes:

The notion of intrinsic value, which is applicable to a good and which can be defined as the market value of which the good is the physical support, does not apply to a service which does not have an independent existence beyond the individual service act which alone determines its content. If it is true that one can establish a parallel between the value of a good and the value of a service on the basis of the notion of utility, there are also in this respect very great differences between a good and a service. The utility of a service only depends on the way it is being provided or supplied. Moreover, the qualities of a good are durable since they depend on the physical characteristics of the good, whereas the qualities of a service are as transient as the service itself. Consequently, it is difficult to compare the value of two services as can be done for two objects or goods serving the same purpose, and, in the absence of a precise definition of the quantity and objective value of services, it is not easy to evaluate their share of national output.[4]

Part of the problem lies in the fact that services are intricately related to industrial production (e.g., clerical work in a plant, consulting fees for technical design) and resistant to statistical separation. But the main problem stems from the logic of quantification itself. It is not possible *a priori* to calculate the unit cost of factors used in certain services, like banks, insurance companies, and shippers, in view of the nonmaterial character of their output. One can calculate salaries paid and depreciation of physical goods used, but the distinction between the cost and the objective value of services is not amenable to measurement because the unit of service is imprecise.[5]

Jonathan Gershuny speaks about "cost disease" in the service sector. He asserts that labor in the manufacturing sector demands higher wages when productivity increases but labor in the service sector has no equivalent rise in productivity, yet demands parity with labor in manufacturing. As a result, the price of final services (e.g., services supplied to households) "tends continuously to rise over time." But is it that there is no "equivalent rise in productivity," or simply the absence of an adequate measure of that productivity?[6]

Daniel Bell goes to the heart of the matter when he describes the postindustrial society in terms of a type of wealth found apart from the quantification of goods. "If an industrial society is defined by the quantity of goods that make a standard of living, the postindustrial society is defined by the quality of life as measured by the services and amenities—health, education, recreation, and the arts—which now are deemed desirable and possible for everyone."[7] The issue, finally, as more and more social scientists are coming to realize, is finding a way to measure social wealth.

Productivity

In postindustrial society, the basis for creating value lies in the transformation of society's cultural elements, particularly its key symbols. Since economic concepts such as wealth, marketing, corporation, private sector, productivity and all the other terms symbolizing the capitalist period are in fact the greatest symbols of modern society, a change in the meaning of these terms represents a basic transformation of the culture to that of the postindustrial market.

For example, the concepts of "efficiency" and "productivity" are part of this culture, intermediate values (means-values rather the end-values) important for judging the private sector. Broadly defined, efficiency is created by shortening the time period needed to achieve certain stated ends, while productivity is the capacity to realize more end-values in the shortest time. Although achieving these intermediate values of efficiency and productivity has been a key to the industrial period, their evaluation is now becoming more complex as we enter the postindustrial era.

William Torbert argues that we can expect the concepts of "effectiveness" and "legitimacy" to be added to the concept of efficiency and productivity in evaluating the future market system.[8] The concept of effectiveness is becoming used more frequently as a broader measure of the means-values toward higher ends that are now emerging as legitimate to pursue in the private—social—sector: public health, safety, environmental protection, income equity, and broader values such as freedom and social justice. As social indicators are developed to measure the effectiveness of the corporate system in realizing such broader values, productivity will be only one measure of the country's wealth.

Marketing

The nonprofit sector, in which it is legal to conduct business in the public interest without a profit motive, is steadily growing, and over the past decade, interest in nonprofit marketing has also been growing, through national conferences and new publications. This professional field of nonprofit marketing extends the marketing concepts of business to public and nonprofit organizations in ways that forecast basic changes in management theory. The theoretical disputes taking place in this area represent changes in basic outlooks on the purpose of marketing.

Philip Kotler, for one, argues that marketing can be looked at as more than just a managerial process aimed at persuading people to purchase a service or a product apart from meeting their needs; it can also be looked at as a social process that

seeks to bring about voluntary exchanges of values. Marketeers seek a response from another party, but it is not a response to be obtained by any means or at any price. Marketing is the alternative to force. The marketer seeks to offer benefits to the target of the market of sufficient attractiveness to produce a voluntary exchange. A museum seeking members, for example, tries to design a set of benefits that are appealing to potential members.[9]

Kotler and others explain that the marketing concept has undergone a gradual change through three stages: (1) restricted to business and competitive market transactions, (2) expanded to embrace all organizations that undertake customer or client transactions, and (3) extended to all organizations and to all "publics," such as unions, shareholders, and government, as well as traditional customers. Thus, museums, universities, libraries, and charities, as well as business firms, see a need to market their "cause"—in addition to their product—to gain political and financial support.

David Rados strongly disagrees with Kotler. As he sees it, the "correct theory" of marketing is based on influencing mass behavior—a direct carryover from the industrial period. Though Rados agrees that voluntary exchange is valuable for understanding many mercantile activities, he believes that the concept is stretched to meaningless limits. For example, the donors to an art museum may have good feelings in making their donations, but these are really self-generated and do not emanate from the museum. The government may persuade an adult to stop smoking, but what exactly is being exchanged? Hence, he argues, some marketing is exchange, but not all. Although Rados suggests that marketing is better conceived as a technique for obtaining a "behavioral response"—a technique for changing the behavior corporations use to get large numbers of people to do things—he admits that he is not fully satisfied with his own definition. His uncertainty is a perfect example of the transition now taking place between the profit and nonprofit sectors.[10]

In many business schools, marketing is still thought of as the "promotion of products in the interest of the firm," a vehicle for "securing the desired behavior" of a target audience in order to maximize profits, which generally means defining client groups that fall within a firm's sphere, finding out what customers want, determining how the product meets these wants, informing customers about the product and where it might be obtained, and deciding on a continuous basis what new products to add, subtract, modify, and upgrade to meet changing wants and circumstances. But Kotler's definition of marketing has been gaining ground because his definition is more inclusive. Business scholars in this tradition note that marketing includes the usual goals of persuasion in the corporate interest, but they add goals related to public needs and values. This altered definition leads them beyond the traditional market, a sign of the kind of cultural transition taking place in the postindustrial society.

The concept of "social marketing" has also begun to enter into business literature. This usually refers to marketing in the nonprofit sector, but it also includes a "concept sector" in which ideas are marketed by conventional firms. The theory here is that markets exist in the field of "concepts" and involve both persuasion and an exchange of ideas. The growth of consulting businesses ranging from engineering design to organizational development is one indication of this trend toward "idea marketing" in the economy. The theory of social marketing can go so far as to claim that all business is based in the idea market, since all enterprises and all marketing must start with an idea. It could theoretically extend even to the marketing of religious beliefs. The dissonance between the concept of marketing itself and the higher values of religion and cultural life—most of which cannot be marketed monetarily—becomes part of the problem to be resolved in the transition to a postindustrial society.[11]

The Corporation

For most business managers, the corporation's bottom line is making money, but this picture is changing. Theodore Levitt of the Harvard Business School goes so far as to observe that to say that the fundamental purpose of business is to make money is "as vacuous as to say that the purpose of life is to eat." He continues:

Eating is a requisite, not a purpose of life. Without eating, life stops. Profits are a requisite of business. Without profits, business stops. Like food for the body, profit for the business must be defined as the excess of what goes in over what comes out. In business, it's called positive cash flow. It has to be positive because the process of sustaining life is a process of destroying life. To sustain life, a business must produce goods and services that people will, in sufficient numbers, want to buy at adequate prices. . . . Besides all that, to say that profit is a purpose of business is, simply, morally shallow. Who with an audible heartbeat and moderate sensibilities will go to the mat for the right of somebody to earn a profit for its own sake? If no greater purpose can be discerned or justified, business cannot, morally, justify its existence. It's a repugnant idea, an idea whose time has gone.

Finally, it's an empty idea. Profits can be made in lots of devious and transient ways. For people of affairs, a statement of purpose should provide guidance to the management of their affairs. To say that they should attract and hold customers forces facing the necessity of figuring out what free people really want and value, and then catering to those wants and values. It provides specific guidance, and has moral merit.[12]

What has led business scholars like Levitt to include human values as part of the corporation's purpose? The reasons may be various. The growth of government regulatory agencies that monitor business behavior, professional associations that emphasize ethics, consumer advocates who use mass media to warn the public of corporate deceptions, the actions of competing corporations, and many other factors may be causing scholars and professional managers to think differently.

The rise of the nonprofit and service sector is certainly one factor. Although nonprofit managers sell social processes leading to nonmonetary values, they nevertheless often compete in the marketplace with regular businesses. The corporate university, for example, must sell its services to students on the basis of both their needs (not merely wants) and public needs, while selling its own performance. Its status as a service corporation changes the character of its marketing, since it must persuade students to buy not a product (e.g., a diploma) but a process, the process of learning, which is different from choosing a material good and then later consuming it. The rewards of the university are found in a process in which the producer (teacher) and the consumer (student) participate together in acquiring knowledge. The service contract is thus an exchange of values (à la Kotler) that is radically different from conventional business.

In this exchange, students must convince the university of their abilities to succeed in this endeavor, and the university must convince students of the quality of its faculty; this is symbiosis, a mutual relationship between producer and consumer. The university must persuade students not to purchase and value some thing, but rather to accept the desirability of the quality of the educational process and the value of the intellectual community in which they will participate. Although this includes such material things as housing and recreational facilities, the essence of what students are purchasing is found in a process and in their identification with an intellectual community to which they will now belong. Thus, students become a part of the "goods" they are buying through their life in the university community, and the valued product is actually themselves, discovered in the learning process. The consumption of knowledge therefore cannot be defined only as utility, as important as that may still be in a commercial society. It goes beyond the traditional market, that is, beyond the selling or purchasing of goods for money.

Likewise, the service economy—now the major portion of the market economy—is based on an activity, not on the production of goods: on a process, a performance, a deed, an effort, a mutual engagement. The old strategy of the profit corporation as an expression of the industrial economy can no longer be accepted either for nonprofits or for profit-based services in the new postindustrial economy.

In services, there is often a social value inherent in the activity itself that is more important than the economic value. Indeed, many service corporations are engaged in promoting noneconomic values. Hospitals must persuade patients of the primacy of health for themselves and their community, and then reconcile that health value with the economic factor. Their marketing must proclaim high standards in their medical practice and the quality of their professional staffs, including ethical standards of practice and human values. When service firms compete in a field like health, education, nutrition, environmental support, music, or drama, therefore, they are competing directly in the public interest.

The Private Sector

Many organizations involved in economic activities—a hospital, a community development corporation, a bank, a factory, or a retail store—can be incorporated as either profit or nonprofit, and people cannot tell the difference. It could therefore be said that the differences between the profit and nonprofit sectors are becoming obscured, that the two sectors are merging and their corporate goals are converging.

We have already seen how the nonprofit sector actually owns the profit sector through the billion-dollar investments of universities, religious institutions, and other nonprofit corporations, as well as labor's pension funds; how these nonprofit corporations also run conventional businesses; and how nonprofit trade associations and trade unions support and influence the direction of business policies. Thus, the two sectors are increasingly bound together and where they are different, there is a new tendency for each of them to learn from the activities of the other.

For example, until fairly recently nonprofits had very little consciousness of the importance of worker participation in management, but they are now showing growing interest in this process. And they have often had trouble raising income, particularly since profit is a dirty word to many nonprofit managers, yet they are now holding conferences on how to increase their incomes. Finally, many have had no notion of efficiency in the workplace; economizing—so vital to the competitive profit firm—has often been foreign to the thinking of nonprofit management. But they are learning all these things from the profit sector.

At the same time, the business corporation, typically known for maximizing profits, sometimes to the detriment of consumers and competing firms, is just beginning to gain that sense of social responsibility so taken for granted by most nonprofit corporations.

But it has not yet learned to decentralize authority effectively and productively, although many of its nonprofit counterparts that are making a good income are democratically decentralized through a confederation of branches.

What all this means is that a new synthesis is evolving in the private sector of the postindustrial economy, or as I have renamed it, the social sector. The private economy is becoming socialized through its own internal dynamic, with different norms and values emerging from those of the industrial period. This new culture is not yet fully visible, nor is its outcome fully predictable, because a complex diffusion is taking place between the two sectors today. This diffusion occurs as profits and nonprofits continue to learn from each other's failures and successes.

Equally important, major contradictions between the two sectors are beginning to be erased by corporations that manage to accommodate both interests. As a particularly refined expression of noneconomic values that must survive in a competitive market, community orchestras are a good example of the complex synthesis taking place between the subcultures of nonprofits and profits. Much as orchestra managers may want to distance themselves from the commercial sector, they have had to learn from business leaders how to turn a dollar. For example, the Boston Symphony Orchestra, hard pressed for paying customers, was linked, through an ingenious concept of organizing, to a profit-oriented corporation, the Boston Pops. The two are separate orchestras, but the Pops' profits help maintain the Symphony.

Business itself has entered more directly into the marketing of classical orchestras to make them self-supporting, and the transition in marketing illustrates the contradictions of the theories in the Kotler-Rados debate.

In Albany, New York, the Albany Symphony Orchestra had accumulated a deficit of $108,000 by the mid-1970s. At that point a local businessman, Peter Kermain, decided that the Albany Symphony Orchestra had to choose a niche that gave it a special advantage in attracting audiences. He decided to mix into the typical Mozart and Beethoven program at each concert little-known contemporary works by living American composers. At the same time, to keep audiences in their seats the orchestra always included some popular classical works performed by popular soloists. The Albany Symphony's programming innovation resulted in a 67 percent increase in ticket sales in seven years, the elimination of the orchestra's deficit, and an operating surplus in most years, a rarity among symphony orchestras.[13]

Observers say that the Albany Symphony Orchestra is not "lowering its classical standards" to make money but simply forging an opportunity to educate a larger public. A more widespread appreciation of classical music would mean a more dependable financial base for orchestras across the land. Has the Albany Orchestra now become a part of the profit economy, or has it altered its marketing strategies in order to survive in the competitive market by integrating profits into its cultural purposes? Whatever the answer, it is clearly part of a new class of organizations.

Another major example of the synthesis of the two sectors is the emergence of community development corporations. Organized as either profit or nonprofit entities, depending on the choice of their organizers, CDCs are a unique breed, at once democratic, nongovernmental, profit-seeking, and functioning in the interest of a whole town or neighborhood. Similarly, community development finance corporations are new kinds of banks, and community land trusts are new kinds of real estate agencies that alter the cultural landscape. Such social democratic corporations, operating as businesses but acting on behalf of the whole community, are resolving the conventional opposition between social and economic motives, providing new models for making profits while operating in the public interest.

Business competitors should soon be asking how much profit a CDC can make before it represents unfair competition, economists will be asking how far a CDC can expand its power in the locality without becoming a monopoly, and legal sociologists will be asking how a CDC can be organized to operate in the national as well as in the local interest. Basic changes in the professional definition of what constitutes business in the private sector are beginning to be introduced through these new community corporations.

This synthesizing trend, the mixing of profit and nonprofit sectors, cannot go much farther until many legal problems are solved. This requires new studies in public interest law. Many legal scholars still argue that the distinctions between the profit and nonprofit sectors exist for good reason, and a synthesis between them cannot be made. Lawyers are not ready for this transition, and law schools have not studied the cross-sector functions. Politicians are not ready for this transition either, and state legislatures have not drawn specifications on intermediate corporation types or settled on a tax policy for them. Schools of management must also introduce new curricula relevant to this synthesis.

To conclude, a new professional understanding of the private sector is developing. The issue is not whether the nonprofit sector will become as powerful as the profit sector, or whether the service economy can be more productive than the industrial economy. Rather, economists and business scholars are recognizing that the market operates on a social dynamic that continues to develop its own life and direction.

Technology

Thanks to the digitization of signals, information technology now makes services transportable and allows vast corporate networks to transfer, process, and retrieve information rapidly. Thus just as new technology sparked the Industrial Revolution, so new technology is sparking the service revolution. But this new technology could also lead to more unemployment, just as new technology in the industrial age often improved industrial productivity at the cost of a loss of jobs. But it might also be used to overcome this problem.

For one thing, information technology can allow us to identify where jobs are lost and where workers are needed in different industries, and to transmit that information across the country in ways that could never have been imagined before. Such information networks have not yet developed on a national scale in the United States, but they exist in other countries. Job placement is now fully computerized in Sweden, for example. Each employment office there has access to information about all job-seekers and all vacancies, and vacancies are filled quickly and efficiently, with substantial economic gains for the society. In the late 1960's, Sweden was one of the world's largest shipbuilders, with approximately 10 percent of the global market. When one of its last major shipyards was closed in 1986, more than 2,000 workers lost their jobs. Computerized information and teamwork on different levels transferred them to jobs in new businesses created in tandem with the shutdown; the entire shift was managed within a two-year period. Few other countries have had such a strong, unbroken industrial tradition, and few have moved so swiftly into the service economy without a severe loss of jobs.[14]

Moreover, the service sector is providing jobs for workers laid off from the industrial sector. One economist put it thus: "We can generate jobs by working less." Gershuny argues that advances in technology do not mean "job sharing," only the need for less work per week or year in the industrial sector and more jobs in the services. Societies have coped with the requirement for increasing levels of consumption of services, not by matching growth in labor productivity per hour with growth in the density of consumption per hour, but by providing more hours for consumption. As the length of work time in industry has declined since the mid-1950's, the consumption of services and employment in services have both grown. Major examples are leisure and tourist services, restaurants, clubs, and hotels. The task in the social market is to coordinate the decline in the need for work in industry with the rise in the need for work in the service economy. With the help of information technology, this transfer of jobs from one sector to another can be accomplished without the pain of mass unemployment and the cost of government welfare.[15]

The new role for technology does not stop there. The service sector is dependent on a special infrastructure centered on telecommunication systems, including cable television coupling with telephone networks for the selling of products and services. The situation is similar to that of the automobile industry at the beginning of the century, when automobiles were available before roads, gas stations, or garages; only after the Second World War, with the large-scale construction of roads, did the car and the truck begin to compete with the railroads. So it is with the services. Telecommunications now make it possible to transport the contents of a whole library to a living room or office, or to transport a banking service to a shopping center or to households and many other places connected to the bank's computer.

This development again challenges the traditional concepts of economics on what constitutes the wealth of a nation. Throughout the world, manufacturers are substituting information for material assets. Nearly every program to reduce inventories relies on the new information technology. A case in point is the Girard Bank. When it closed 18 of its full-service branches and increased the number of its automatic teller machines (ATMs) to nearly 200 at supermarkets and other stand-alone sites, it increased its deposit-taking locations by 50 percent, while the closings reportedly saved an amount equal to the $5.4 million in costs associated with the ATM program. The Girard Bank substituted information-wealth for asset-wealth.[16] Many observers believe such moves are only the beginning.

An Evolutionary Perspective on the Changing Market Economy

In sum, the modern economy can be defined conventionally as a market system in which people exchange things for money in their own private economic interest. The performance of this system has been evaluated by the field of economics largely in terms of wealth, productivity, efficiency, and the like, but a changing reality has led observers to increase the emphasis on the social factor and societal values, as shown by changes in the redefinition of those economic concepts. The indications are clear that if the economic order becomes increasingly defined by social scientists, the exchange system that had been latent should become more manifest, and then more consciously designed on a social foundation.

The market economy today is thoroughly identified with the "welfare state." There is not only growing government involvement in the operation of the market itself through interventions to cushion market failures and control business externalities, but also an enormous expansion in government services such as social insurance, welfare, public health, education, and housing. The welfare state would seem to be a permanent fixture, even though it is severely criticized by partisans on both the right and the left of the political spectrum.

Scholars on the Right argue that welfare activities have led to government bureaucracy and "overload," a failure of social programs to meet their goals, and the erosion of individual responsibility and independence. They claim that the welfare state is a result of the pressure of interest groups, notably trade unions and professionals, and is carried out by budget-maximizing bureaucracies within the state. This view of the state motivated the policies of the Thatcher and Reagan governments, which adopted monetarist and supply-side economic policies designed to reduce welfare expenditures and taxation.[17]

Scholars on the Left argue that the welfare state is a set of contradictions, in which big government supports big business with subsidies, and then legitimates the market system by supplying welfare for the poor and needy. They argue that there is a central contradiction in the welfare state's tendency to "commodify" and "decommodify" the economy at the same time. Commodification is needed to permit market mechanisms to operate for economic growth, but decommodification (government regulation) is needed to cope with the problems of an economic system that is out of control. This view of the state has led to governments seeking ever greater control over the market in the interest of democratization.[18]

This book has argued against the alternatives offered by either the Right or the Left in asserting that a new socially oriented economy is visible and emerging in the interstices of market life. If the latent aspect of the economy becomes more manifest, through the unfolding of the changes we have described, we may logicially anticipate an end to the welfare state and foresee its transformation into something significantly different, even though this change is not on the immediate horizon.

Although the social market has been advanced as a theoretical concept throughout much of this book, this concept also suggests a practical vision of how the economy might be organized in the future. It is a future in which noneconomic factors—societal values—will become a more deliberate part of the market, a future in which the society will operate the market through all its manifestations, including folkways, attitudes, associations, and social interactions. If associations are able to increasingly control the market in the public interest as we have suggested, there will be less need for state control. If nonstatist organizations become more pervasive in the public mind as self-regulating, people should more accurately perceive the social nature of exchange.

To try to imagine specific details of such a future is to get into the utopian, but a vision of the changing process is important, for that vision itself can become a determinant of the future. But that future also rests crucially on what happens in the global economy. As things stand, the competition for world markets simply tends to increase the power of national governments, because corporations require ever more subsidies and government support to stay afloat. Under these circumstances, nation-states promise to become more and more like global corporations competing against one another for economic advantage in a world that has not yet developed a "society." Without new levels of social alternatives that promote cooperation in global markets, the result of these competitive trends should be an expansion of state capitalism at world levels. Without new social inventions to modify the existing state of affairs, the logic of the immediate future is a world of competing corporate states.

To curb the growth of governments caused by competitive global markets thus becomes a vital issue today. During this century, half the world's population has lived under statist economies, a startling repudiation of the market system. Even though socialist states to-day appear to be moving radically toward a moderate position on government controls and free markets, the outcome could be an East-West synthesis characterized by neocorporatism. The intro-duction of market incentives does not in itself imply an immediate diminution of the power of the corporate state under socialism.[19]

But if there is reason for pessimism in the years ahead, there is also reason for hope. Under pressure from their own populations against a stagnant and monopolistic state far removed from the power of people to manage it properly, these nations are under-going a major revolution in political thought and economic plan-ning. Socialist leaders are also looking for inventions in the market that may offer the possibilities that we have been examining in this book. For example, if the Ministries of Light and Heavy Industry in socialist states become part of the private sector, they might very well become decentralized and democratically constituted in a manner that we have been discussing for industrial associations in the market economy. At the same time, there are also many signs of interest among socialist states in developing worker self-management in the nonstatist sector. In addition, Third World leaders have been resisting the pattern of state controls by creating other patterns of social development standing between traditional capitalism and state socialism.[20]

At the end of this century, perhaps the socialist and capitalist states may stand together, still in a struggle, taking steps toward the fulfillment of that dream of the nineteenth-century philoso-phers, a dream to be realized in its own time.

The vision of a new societal order characterized by self-regulating economies shaped by social norms and values and operating in the public interest with minimum state involvement is important to cultivate for the simple reason that it would help to promote that development. Without any social vision or planning, the modern market could easily continue its self-destructive path toward statism. The history of government intervention in the private, economistic, and unsocialized market testifies to its lack of economic stability and responsibility. That market has led constantly to not only government controls and regulations but violent revolutions and state command systems. Without such a vision, and the necessary public policies to make it a reality, the next decades could produce not only an economic recession but even a political regression to something like the fascist regimes of an earlier day. The future, therefore, depends on how people deal with social problems in the years to come.

Through a vision of both the immediate and intermediate future—combined with social, not merely state, planning—the humanizing aspects that exist in the market system today may grow in prominence. Indeed, the vision we have been examining here is not utopian in the sense of approaching a noneconomic ideal, since it builds on the virtues of capitalism. The economic factor, represented by productivity and profitability, is not reduced or eliminated in this vision, but on the contrary, enhanced. All the evidence suggests that a future economy based on self-regulation should be even more productive and profitable than the economy today. But it should also be richer in the cultural values such as justice and freedom.

Finally, a social vision is not an absolute requirement for a more promising future, even though it should increase the probability of a desirable outcome. Indeed, without a vision, it is conceivable that the normal conflict between conservatives and liberals in America today could by itself push the economy in the direction of greater self-regulation. The interest of conservatives in reducing government controls, combined with the interest of liberals in creating social responsibility in the market, could provide the necessary dynamic for creating new social policy.

Interestingly, both liberals and conservatives have expressed views approaching our vision of a socially based economy. For example, the liberal economist Robert Kuttner writes:

Let us first concede the obvious: no radical democrat should be too comfortable with a behemoth state as the sole instrument of social justice. None other than Karl Marx, in one of his more infelicitous phrases, called for the eventual "withering away of the state." Indeed, the early socialists were roused to indignation by the appalling effects of early capitalism on the traditional security of the individual. They hoped to restore community by means of voluntary, cooperative association, not to enlarge the state. The reality of the twentieth-century communism mocks that vision. For an American radical democrat, the association of social justice with statism has to be troubling. Measures that promote social justice without expanding the domain of the state are always preferable to measures that enlarge it.[21]

From the more conservative side we can cite George Cabot Lodge and Richard Walton, who write:

> If the purpose of the corporation is merely the satisfaction of shareholders, its focus will necessarily be short term, the cost of capital will be high, and insufficient funds will be invested in the innovation required for competitiveness. For the focus to be long term, the purpose of the corporation must include the welfare of the community and the employees. The welfare of the community must be defined reliably at different levels so that the government policies can assist—not thwart—the achievement of corporate purpose. The welfare of the employees must be similarly well-defined, keeping in mind the good of the corporation as a whole.[22]

The shared interests of both liberals and conservatives, despite the ongoing conflict between them, suggests one basis for anticipating the development of a social market. But I would still argue that this development becomes more likely when public policy is guided by social planning and a vision of the market that encourages its own self-development.

Appendix

The Global Market

The only security for Americans today, or for any
people, is in the creation of a system of world order
that enables nations to retain sovereignty over their
own culture and institutions but that creates a workable authority for regulating the behavior of nations
in their relationships with one another.

> Norman Cousins,
> World Federalist Association

MORE THAN 20 percent of U.S. industrial production is now exported, accounting for about one out of every six manufacturing
jobs. Two of every five acres of agricultural land are used for exports; about one-third of all corporate profits are derived either
from foreign investments or from exports; and about 1,500 banks
are linked to international banking and Third World loans, which
means that large amounts of consumer savings are at risk in the
international market.[1] There is no question that the United States
has become part of a world market that powerfully affects the entire domestic economy.

The growth of the global market is due partly to the new export-
able capital that has developed in a number of nations and partly to
the rapid growth in communications, transportation, and computer technology. The globe has become a village marketplace,
with millions of capital transactions taking place every day. Nothing of its size and complexity has ever existed before, nor, paradoxically, has there ever been so great an equity in power side by side
with so great an interdependence among so many nations with so
many goods to exchange.

The New Global Organization of Markets

From 1815 to the First World War, Great Britain dominated the international economy; from the end of the Second World War to the 1970's, the United States was the undisputed world leader. But today no single nation is paramount, and as a result, new power relationships continue to emerge. In some regions, nations set rules that other nations then break. Certain nations dominate particular products, but their markets are also interdependent with other markets controlled by other nations, and all markets are shaped by various national policies.

Although big nations were long accustomed to setting the terms of trade, smaller nations are now collectivizing to assert their own needs. OPEC, the first major instance of such banding together, forced "the seven sisters," a cartel of multinational oil companies, to take a back seat. The European Economic Community has already heightened the standing of less powerful nations and could possibly join with Eastern European countries and the Soviet Union to form an entirely new European market. Although the Andean Pact may not be as familiar a collectivity, it has had significant influence in controlling the entry of multinationals into the member states; and Third World debtor nations have talked of ways to organize against the creditor nations. Regional coalitions of nations operating in their collective self-interest are a reality, and other coalitions are no doubt in the offing.

Although these new coalitions are restoring the balance of power, they are not the total answer, since the global market is still largely unregulated and highly unpredictable. Many economists foresee that if some aspects of the global market do not come under some kind of international control, the outcome could be unsettling for everyone. For example, the money market is shaped by constant "wholesale transactions" that occur in the blink of an eye, in a manner that at times approaches lawlessness. Multinationals, which operate without any common codes of conduct, are a constant menace to the political stability of the Third World nations they have moved into, as well as a source of their development. And the recently evolved global stock market has created uncertainties in capital flow and a volatility that could spell future disaster in world finance.

Although the absence of control by one nation is a positive step, the lack of any central control in the global market could eventuate

in economic anarchy. Lawless markets have led to serious dis-
equilibrium in the past, and astute observers see in the global market a constant tendency toward collapse, with nations rising and
falling together in extreme ups and downs. The issue, then, is
*whether the global market should operate under new systems of mutual
governance, that is, whether it can be managed by democratic institutions
that maximize the principle of free enterprise.*

Most international observers of the global market would agree
that a solution requires more than just new trade agreements and
new regional alliances among private corporate actors. The developing relationships are so complex that they cannot be separated
from politics. Regulating the international stock market, monitoring exchange rates, revising international trade policies, establishing codes for multinational corporations, and many other related
global problems cannot be resolved without the involvement of all
the nation states.[2] Before we explore some of these solutions, let us
look in more detail at how the global market affects the U.S. economic system.

Trade and Total Debt

In 1985, the United States became a net debtor for the first time
since before the First World War, and in 1986 it surpassed Brazil as
the world's largest debtor nation. In fact, for several years now, the
economy has been staggering under the drag of government debt,
corporate debt, farm debt, consumer debt, and the trade deficit.
Total debt rose from $1.6 trillion in 1970 to $4.6 trillion in 1980 and
to $7 trillion in 1986.[3] Much of this debt load is tied to the world
market.

Consumer debt alone doubled from $371 billion in 1980 to $740
billion in 1986, and this is apart from home mortgages, which grew
by $760 billion in the same period, as finance firms and banks
pushed credit cards and adjustable mortgages to their limits. Imports have been stimulated by high consumer demand, helping to
cause a major trade deficit. Furthermore, consumers borrow to buy
foreign products and thereby add both to the trade deficit and the
interest debt. The Federal Reserve then tightens credit (interest
rates go up), and the dollar rises in the world market, but when the
dollar rises, U.S. products are not easily sold abroad to balance the
trade deficit. However, when the dollar is falling, there are other
reasons to raise interest rates, which can fuel a recession. The con-

sumer market thus requires constant surveillance for its connection to the global market and its impact on various other aspects of economic activity and policy.

The rise in U.S. government debt has been caused by many things, including the tax cuts and military buildup of the Reagan years, interest payments, and social expenditures. From 1979 to 1986, the government's interest burden grew from $42 billion to $136 billion, and by then debt service accounted for 13.7 percent of the federal budget, as opposed to 8.8 percent in 1980. Thus, debt interest is a cause of more indebtedness. A substantial share of this money goes to foreign bondholders who reinvest it in the stock market and contribute to its fluctuations.

U.S. corporate debt rose to $500 billion between 1984 and 1986. Corporate debt was 95 percent of net worth in 1980 and 115 percent in 1985. One cause was "paper entrepreneurialism," the result of corporate raiding, corporate defenses such as a company's buying back its own stock in order to shrink supply and raise prices, and the like. Not only do corporate funds flow into the stock market, intensifying its ups and downs as firms buy one another out, but the buyout process has crossed national borders. In recent years, more than 600 large U.S. companies have acquired non-American owners.

The trade deficit amounts to $150 billion or so annually, with imports surging and exports stagnating. Many have noted the irony of the role postwar U.S. aid has played in making the nation's former enemies, Japan and Germany, economic forces to reckon with. Beyond this, free trade and the U.S. consumer have contributed mightily to Japan's phenomenal growth, and to the EEC's 50 percent growth in 1984 and 25 percent in 1985.

Third World products also satisfy U.S. consumer demand. The International Monetary Fund's deflationary pressure on the Third World reduces domestic buying and increases exports; indeed, Third World exports of manufactured products to the United States doubled between 1980 and 1984, while those of Europe declined slightly. By 1985, the United States was buying two-thirds of Third World manufacturing exports. Much of this was due, of course, to the intracompany transactions of multinational corporations. Although encouraging imports to the United States has made Second and Third World countries dependent on the United States as their biggest customer, it has also made the United States dependent on them as its providers.

Third World nations owe a large debt to the United States, but a significant aspect of this "interdependence" is turning into U.S. "dependency" because Third World nations have recognized their collective power to renege on their obligations. Since wholesale, absolute refusal would have a major impact on the U.S. banking system and could create a serious recession in the economy, the IMF has tried to help Third World nations to increase their savings and investment, partly by urging them to reduce welfare and government expenditures, and has encouraged them to emphasize production and sales to the United States. Although this has enabled some debt repayment, it also has serious drawbacks. Cutting back on welfare programs to invest more in production for sales abroad increases the level of poverty and aggravates social problems, which can bring on political rebellion. This sequence can then direct U.S. capital into foreign aid and military assistance, a reinvestment with no return on the dollar. The United States is thus intricately and politically bound into overseas markets. To protect itself, it has supported strong military regimes and backed dictatorships in the Third World, adding to both military outlays and its own government debt crisis.

World Market Position

From 1950 to 1965, U.S. business productivity grew at 3 percent a year; from 1965 to 1973, the figure fell to 2 percent, and since 1973, it has barely moved, with an average growth of about 1 percent a year. Manufacturing productivity is in a worse position. Although it grew at 2.5 percent a year from 1950 to 1985, this rate contrasts with Japan's 8.4 percent yearly growth, Germany's and Italy's 5.5 percent, France's 5.3 percent, Canada's 3.5 percent, and Britain's 3.1 percent. The U.S. per capita GNP, a major indicator of a nation's economic standing, slipped below Japan's in 1986 and also trails the per capita GNP of West Germany, Switzerland, Sweden, and Denmark. The average wage for white males aged 25–30 (a bellwether indicator of progress) declined from 1973 to 1983 by 26 percent in constant dollars, and the national savings rate has continued to go down.[4]

Some statistics seem to show that things are improving. Although the trade deficit remains high and imports have invaded many U.S. industries, the U.S. Department of Commerce has asserted that total U.S. output has been maintained, the implication being that nothing fundamental has happened to the economy except for the growing deficit. The 1988 Economic Report of the President declared that the "shares of real manufacturing output and final goods output have been remarkably stable for 25 years." But other evidence suggests that such optimism is unwarranted. For example, at the request of eight congressional committees, the Office of Technology Assessment recalculated the Commerce Department findings and concluded that manufacturing's share of GNP is declining.[5]

Economists estimate that as many as 30 million people have been dislocated by corporate restructuring during the past decade. The Fortune 500 companies alone have eliminated 2.8 million jobs since 1980. Much of this change is in reaction to foreign competition. Furthermore, many key industries have desperately sought trade protection, and textiles, steel, autos, and machine tools have obtained it. Even Silicon Valley's top businesses have looked for shelter, and today the service sector (now 75 percent of the domestic market) is headed in the same direction.[6]

U.S. producers long dominated the domestic market, but over the period 1962–88 their share of the steel and auto markets fell from 95 percent to 74 percent. Electronics slipped even more steeply, from 90 percent (in 1966) to 40 percent. Many other industries are experiencing similar declines.[7]

U.S. corporations themselves are a basic part of the problem, specifically the multinationals, whose purpose has become, in the words of Business Week, "to maximize worldwide profits, without regard to source of product or national boundaries."[8] Overseas operations drained off more than $200 billion in investments between 1980 and 1984 alone. Simultaneously, many companies began shutting down all their operations in the United States, leading to extensive layoffs, the destruction of whole communities, and overburdened welfare programs.[9] Furthermore, these companies often now sell their products back to the United States under various nations' protectionist policies. Because of all these developments, businesses are becoming more and more intricately involved in foreign policy.

In recent years, the growth of international banks has created even greater problems in the domestic market than the flight of manufacturing overseas, accelerating the need to establish new systems of governance over the global market. Instantaneous electronic communication enables vast sums of money to be moved anywhere in the world in a matter of seconds. In a market economy in which speculation plays a powerful role in the transfer of money, such capability leads to instability and raises the likelihood of market collapse, as rumors race through international trading rooms, with no time to verify them. In 1984, rumors floated in the international banking community about the inability of Continental Illinois National Bank, the eighth largest bank in the United States, to collect on defaulted loans; in a matter of hours billions of dollars were withdrawn. Continental was reportedly overextended in risky foreign loans; about 40 percent of its deposits were in Eurodollar accounts, and as a result it was near bankruptcy until the federal government assembled a $7.5 billion rescue package.

Continental is hardly an isolated case. In 1986, 138 banks failed, the largest number in one year since the Great Depression; the pace accelerated in 1987. (In contrast, only ten banks toppled in 1981.) U.S. money has become international money, pointing up the serious need for joint governance of the worldwide circulation of capital.

Military Expenditures

The biggest reason for the U.S. government deficit is the defense budget: between fiscal year 1979 and FY 1988, defense outlays rose by $175 billion, and the overall deficit by $143 billion. Government borrowing to finance those enormous deficits forced interest rates higher, causing the value of the dollar to skyrocket, and the prices of U.S. goods overseas to go up. Between 1981 and 1987, the nation's trade position thus deteriorated rapidly. By 1987, the deficit was six times greater than at the beginning of the 1980's, and foreign debt was close to $300 billion and rising.[10] In only five years, escalating military costs, paid for wholly on credit, had turned the United States into the world's largest debtor. To a major degree these expenditures were responsible for the abrupt growth of the trade deficit in the 1980's and the subsequent economic decline. A few examples follow:

1. U.S. government-supported research priorities, in their emphasis on weapons rather than commercial products, have been the exact opposite of policies pursued by America's major trading partners. Only 25 percent of the U.S. government research budget relates to products for the civilian market, compared with 70 per-

cent in Europe. And while the United States under the Strategic Computing Initiative spends $600 million for such specialized military applications of supercomputers as battle-management programs, Japan spends $700 million on the supercomputer's commercial applications. In cutting-edge technologies (e.g., lasers and artificial intelligence), defense projects account for 70–80 percent of U.S. R&D expenditures.

2. The highly specialized weapons technology that the U.S. taxpayer has supported plays a relatively small role in international trade. Though weapons research accounts for 75 percent of government-funded research, weapons account for no more than 4 percent of U.S. exports.

3. When U.S. defense does result in technologies with potential commercial spin-offs, other countries often jump ahead in marketing them. For example, Japan now has the lead in small machine tools and in ceramics applications, technologies originally developed through U.S. military research.

4. In the competition for public finances, U.S. education has taken second place to military programs, starving the resources needed to train and maintain a high-quality, skilled work force. Currently, U.S. expenditures on education are barely three-fourths of military expenditures. West Germany, by contrast, spends 40 percent more on public education than on military defense, Japan 500 percent more.

The miraculous changes taking place in Europe since the end of 1989 offer hope that we may soon begin to have massive arms reductions, but even with these changes, the global structure remains unstable, and the cause for insecurity among nations overall has not disappeared. Thus, the arms race will still be with us for a long time, with vastly destructive results. The arms race has not only been devastating to the U.S. economy; it is also destroying Third World attempts to repay debts and develop productive trade with the United States and other nations. Some developing nations continue to purchase huge amounts of military equipment and build up their armies, while the continuing need of industrialized nations to export weaponry has distorted trade profiles, inhibited the import of capital goods, created financial problems, and in general been highly unproductive for the Third World.[11]

All UN reports on military spending have emphasized its negative economic consequences. The Palme report, for example, stressed that in industrialized countries it constrained the number of civilian jobs, was inflationary, carried serious opportunity costs, short-changed health and education, and caused foreign exchange short-ages.[12] It is widely agreed that the arms race and economic develop-ment are closely tied to each other and must be solved together.[13]

Political scientists argue that the key to solving the problems that have developed in the global economy lies in establishing world-wide security, and that the way to do that is a system of inter-national governance. Improved relations between the Eastern and Western blocs are a necessary but not sufficient step. The issues of security are global. This means beginning with a fundamental re-form of the United Nations and strengthening its agencies dealing with the world economy.[14]

Toward Global Alternatives

I believe that new systems of international governance are essen-tial to release capital for economic development and to assure its equitable use. Steps to accomplish this would include reinvigorat-ing the UN and its affiliated agencies, reforming the world mone-tary system and broadening the base of the World Bank and the International Monetary Fund, dealing with environmental prob-lems caused by regional and economic inequities, creating new codes of conduct for multinational corporations, and strengthen-ing local communities connected to the global circulation of capital.

Strengthening the United Nations

UN reform has been studied in many academic and political circles, and this is not the place to review all the work that needs to be done. But a few reforms that need support immediately can be listed here.[15]

1. *Develop a more effective world trade and monetary system.* For ex-ample, create an international fund to moderate commodity price fluctuations and help single-crop countries diversify their econo-mies; implement UNCTAD (UN Conference on Trade and Develop-ment) proposals to make the world trading system more respon-sive to Third World nations; develop regional monetary networks and a centralized international credit reserve system.

2. *Devise a stronger code for multinational corporations.* For example, formulate rules that would lessen the tendency of firms to over-

exploit and monopolize the resources of host-nations and their workers.

3. *Increase the use of and support for the International Court of Justice.* For example, repeal the Connally reservation, which allows the United States to refuse judgments of the court in its own self-interest.

4. *Improve the UN's peacekeeping capability.* For example, authorize the recruitment and training of a permanent peacekeeping force.

5. *Establish a more stable UN income arrangement.* For example, use deep-seabed revenues, multinational licensing fees, a one-cent levy on international mail, satellite communication fees, ocean and atmospheric pollution penalties.

6. *Modify veto power in the Security Council.* For example, bar a permanent member from voting on the admission of a new member when it is one of the parties in a dispute.

7. *Provide a more equitable General Assembly voting structure.* For example, adopt the "binding triad" formula discussed periodically, requiring concurrent majorities based on nationhood, population, and UN financial contributions.

8. *Organize an international ocean authority.* For example, press for a broad ocean authority to manage ocean resources and protect the ocean environment.

9. *Create an international disarmament organization* that would monitor the arms race and initiate disarmament treaties, verify arms limitations agreements, oversee step-by-step phased disarmament, and establish procedures for enforcing treaties.

10. *Support UN economic programs and agencies.* For example, create a single UN development authority and reorganize the Economic and Social Council to ensure coherent planning.

11. *Improve the dispute-resolution process.* For example, provide specific procedures for third-party involvement in disputes through mediation services and panels of arbitrators.

12. *Establish a global resources program to monitor the depletion of nonrenewable resources and to suggest guidelines for the preservation of the "world commons."* For example, monitor the military use of nonrenewable resources and create a global system for the storage and distribution of food reserves.[16]

Such proposals require careful study, for they must be in the interest of the United States as well as that of other nations. If undertaken, they would help cut U.S. defense expenditures, would reduce government debt significantly, and would release funds for programs that stimulate the private economy.[17]

Building a New Monetary System

The role of the U.S. dollar in the global market is central to the gradual decline of the U.S. economy; hence, we take some time to discuss this problem, whose solution requires a system of mutually governed finance. The story begins with the Bretton Woods Conference of July 1944, which created the International Monetary Fund (IMF) and the World Bank. Although parts of the system arrived at have lasted for nearly half a century, it is beset by major problems.[18]

The keystone of the Bretton Woods agreement was the establishment of a world monetary system.[19] The central bank of each nation was to stabilize the value of its currency in the world market within 1 percent of the official value established by the IMF. If the value of its currency fell below that 1 percent, the central bank was to take some of its dollars in reserve to buy its own currency, increasing the demand for its currency. If the central bank could not stabilize its currency within the 1 percent range, it had to consult with the IMF about measures to be taken. First, the nation in question might borrow dollars from the IMF to replenish its reserves to maintain the equation. If this did not work, the IMF would look more carefully at the nation's structural problems as a condition for making additional loans. If nothing succeeded, it meant currency devaluation.

Between 1946 and 1950, several methods were devised to move dollars from the United States to Europe and maintain international liquidity for commerce. Though the World Bank now focuses largely on developing nations, its original purpose was to finance reconstruction in war-devastated countries. Point Four and the Marshall Plan, inaugurated by President Harry S. Truman, were also designed to keep the flow of dollars going abroad to help Western Europe, Greece, and Turkey get back on their feet. Later, as U.S. military installations were added overseas, dollars began moving from the U.S. Treasury through the military in support of international trade.

As foreign countries recovered and accumulated dollars, the system began to run into real difficulties. Thanks in part to speculative runs on Fort Knox, U.S. gold reserves fell by $4 billion between

1955 and 1960, to about $18 billion. Efforts to restore stability by the Kennedy and Johnson administrations did not correct the situation. Finally, in late 1968, a two-tier agreement provided for a dual market for gold: in the official market, it would still sell at $35 an ounce, the rate agreed to at Bretton Woods; in the free market, the price would be permitted to fluctuate. This set the stage for the collapse of the gold-dollar link. That officially occurred in 1971, when President Richard Nixon suspended the convertibility of dollars into gold and imposed a 10 percent surcharge on all imports to restore some balance to the U.S. international monetary flows. Since then, other governments have been obliged to float dollars on the open market.[20]

A second approach to the growing instability of the world monetary system saw the creation of a reserve unit called the Special Drawing Right (SDR). In 1967–68, the United States dropped its objections to SDRs and helped the move toward them as credits that could be drawn on by member nations through the IMF. Once dollars could be converted into SDRs instead of gold, the United States persuaded European and Japanese bank managers to use this alternative. Backed initially by the dollar and since 1974 by a basket of currencies and gold, SDRs are becoming something of a world currency in their own right.

In the past few decades, U.S. dollars overseas (Eurodollars) have become the primary basis of world finance. The Eurodollar system works in the same manner as private banking in the United States except that it deals in huge amounts of money. It is called "wholesale banking." In 1976, the House Committee on Banking, Currency, and Housing conducted a comprehensive study of the banking system and declared that the volume of international banking was extraordinary and asked how it could continue without any regulatory authority. At the same time, the Joint Economic Committee of Congress warned that the financial operations are largely hidden from view and understood only by the bankers.[21]

Some economists assert that the largest share of the holdings in U.S. banks and savings and loans are in Eurodollars beyond the reach of any regulatory safeguards. The FDIC and the FSLIC, for example, do not insure these foreign deposits. By one estimate, 1 trillion (or more) Eurodollars were supporting the international trade and banking reserve systems in 1984, but no one knows how close to the mark that is because Eurodollars escape being counted by any monetary census takers. It is clear enough, though, that the growth of what *Business Week* describes as "stateless money," circling the globe in a matter of seconds in a stateless banking system,[22] has been phenomenal, and that international commerce has become totally dependent on this new supranational system.

U.S. banks, moreover, are as heavily involved in overseas operations as U.S. industry, though less visibly so. For example, the First National City Bank of New York (Citibank) has 1,490 offices in 94 countries. It generated 67 percent of its deposits and 60 percent ($448 million) of its net income from abroad. It operates around the clock. Out-of-service deposits are lent overnight by Citibank, and all other banks, to financial centers in such places as Hong Kong and Singapore, where it is daytime. Such overseas operations affect not only local and national market policies but government policies as well.[23]

Howard Wachtel, author of *The Money Mandarins*, argues that the excessive supply of unregulated Eurodollars, Third World debt, and exchange instabilities are closely related, the result of international monetary deregulation after Bretton Woods. He points out that the wild swings in exchange rates are influenced largely by money flows that have nothing to do with international trade. In 1984, for example, world trade was worth about $2 trillion, as against financial flows worth anywhere between $20 trillion and $50 trillion. In his view, global financial stability therefore requires a re-regulation of the international monetary system.

It seems clear at this stage that the billions of dollars the developing countries and the Eastern European nations owe to private supranational banks cannot be repaid under the present system. Wachtel believes that the solution lies in establishing a public-debt authority under the joint management of the World Bank and the IMF to act as an intermediary. Initially subscribed through public allocations that would otherwise go toward short-term private-bank bailouts, the authority could leverage this capital for additional borrowing from the Eurodollar system. Once sufficiently funded, it would offer to buy existing debt obligations from the supranational banks and deal directly with the debtor nations. An important stabilizing effect of this proposal is the reduction of the Eurodollar overhang: placing some of the Eurodollars under public control would reduce the amount of footloose supranational money.

As the quid pro quo for this onetime bailout, the supranational banks would come under more regulatory authority. Wachtel proposes, for example, that a reserve requirement imposed against Eurodollar accounts would slow the rate of growth of supranational money, make the Eurodollar system less profitable for supranational banks, and restore public influence over global capital. The policy could be implemented by the Federal Reserve. He would also have the banks provide more timely and accurate reporting about their activities, reportage as extensive as that required of U.S. domestic banks.[24]

The foregoing are modest proposals for international monetary reform. The Brandt Commission recommended completely reorganizing the World Bank to bring it more closely in line with the administrative decentralization called for in the bank's original Articles of Agreement. Regional offices, it proposed, would respond better to problems in the field and should be fitted into a structure that would "encourage autonomy and genuine decentralization." Further, the organizational structure should include more Third World representation and be made more democratic.[25]

Both sets of proposals have many ramifications and require wide-ranging analysis. Most important, they demonstrate that economic efficiency is a function of social organization, a truism that applies from local to global markets. The basic problem of organization cannot be seen when the financial market is interpreted as a spontaneously emerging natural system. The market is not simply biological or, alternatively, statist; it is social, that is, humanly created. Careful study should precede determining how it should be socially governed at every level.

Resolving Environmental Problems

Many writers have predicted a world environmental crisis ahead. Scientists differ in their judgment about the critical nature of the crisis, but some certainly agree with the dramatic predictions of Jeremy Rifkin:

> The year is 2035. . . . Phoenix is in its third week of temperatures over 130 degrees, and the project to cover the city with air-conditioned domes is still unfinished.
> Holland is under water. Bangladesh has ceased to exist. Torrential rains and rising seas there have killed several million people and forced the re-

maining population into makeshift refugee camps on higher ground in Pakistan and India.

In central Europe and the American Midwest, decades of drought have turned once fertile agricultural lands into parched deserts. Tens of millions of people continue to trek northward—the greatest mass migration in recorded history. Canada's population swells from 20 million to 200 million in less than four decades. Forest fires rage out of control over millions of acres in the Pacific Northwest, while the Mississippi River, closed to commercial traffic earlier in the century, becomes a vast earthen plain, allowing people to cross over by foot for the first time in human memory.

Welcome to the Greenhouse World of the 21st century. It is not science fiction; it is based on current projections by climatologists and environmental scientists.[26]

In the 1980's, which saw the five warmest years since record keeping began, global warming emerged as a central concern of international policy makers. Top NASA scientists are now fairly certain that gases released by human activities are trapping the sun's radiant heat much like a glass roof. Carbon dioxide released from fossil fuel combustion alone accounts for about 40 percent of the greenhouse effect. Slowing the warming will require a fundamental redirection of energy policies to limit the use of fossil fuels. Most writers agree that this cannot be done except through international organization.

Over the centuries, people have cut away the earth's rich mantle of forests to make room for crops and grazing, and to obtain wood for fuel and lumber. The planet's forested area has shrunk so far since the Industrial Revolution that the future climate of the earth is critically dependent on saving what is left. But to do so depends in part on curbing world competition in business, and again most writers agree that the problem cannot be solved by the policies of any single business corporation or nation-state.

The most recent UN demographic projections show world population doubling in size before leveling off around 10 billion sometime late in the next century. Most of the 5 billion will be added in the Indian subcontinent, the Middle East, Africa, and Latin America—regions where life-support systems are already collapsing. The population growth in these areas is related to environmental problems in ways that vitally affect wealthy nations. Moreover, the disparities in living standards around the world are extreme. The world has 2 million millionaires but over 100 million homeless people; Americans spend $5 billion each year on special low-calorie diets, while the world's poorest 400 million people are so undernourished they are likely to suffer stunted growth, mental retardation, or death. Though the connection between the poor and the rich nations in managing human survival is not yet fully understood, it is clearly a vital one.

The problem is all the stickier because the poor themselves are now a major ecological threat. Moving into marginal lands under population pressure, they raze the rain forests, plow steep slopes, and overgraze fragile rangeland. Economic deprivation and environmental degradation have therefore come to reinforce each other to create an environmental crisis that threatens to engulf the globe. The chain of events that is contributing to the serious environmental crisis in the world today thus leads from the very rich to the very poor.[27]

Many observers conclude that a strong United Nations is required to deal with these issues. Methods must be found to help reduce the world population growth by half before the year 2000, to negotiate an agreement to cut global carbon emissions by 20 percent, and to allow Third World countries to retire their debts in exchange for adopting sustainable development practices. All these steps and others—such as developing a world grain reserve equivalent to 80 days of consumption, reforesting 320 million acres of land in Third World countries, raising the average fuel economy of cars to 50 miles per gallon, and emphasizing research on photovoltaic cells and electric cars—must be the responsibility of a global association of nations showing concern for human survival.

Creating Codes of Conduct for Multinational Corporations

As a result of mounting social and corporate costs for corporations operating in the global market, codes of conduct are gradually being developed. Sometimes this is at the initiative of individual firms, but the practice is not as effective as regional and global efforts along those lines. General Electric, for example, now monitors its global operations, with 117 auditors who roam the world looking for anything amiss, but this is plainly done in its own self-interest.[28] Whole industries, however, have put codes in place with more promise for the future, as has the International Chamber of Commerce.[29] Regional governments have also written codes for multinationals. The Andean Code is only one of many, including the OECD guidelines.

Global codes are also being devised under the auspices of the UN's Centre for the Study of Transnational Corporations, and three others are already in place: the International Labor Organization's Tripartite Declaration on Principles Concerning Multinational Corporations; the UN's Mutually Agreed Equitable Principles and Rules for the Control of Restrictive Business Practices; and the UN Commission on Trade and Development's Transfer of Technology Code. Even so, rules governing corporations in world markets are still far from complete.[30]

Corporate codes are not developed simply out of a concern for ethics, as important as that may be. A major reason is also to avert litigation and marketing conflict—that is, for economic efficiency. There were enormous costs attendant on the legal battle over the sale of infant formulas by the world's largest food corporation, Nestle. The Infant Formula Action Coalition, the principal litigant, spent $3.5 million, and Nestle spent $10 million. Such costs could be prevented by establishing rules of the game ahead of time.[31]

There has also been some discussion of developing a global charter for multinational corporations that would prohibit such actions in host-nations as acquiring stock in or participating in interlocking controls over their firms, and would require various types of disclosure and international obligations to host-nations. Global rules can "even the playing field" for all corporations, lessen the likelihood of their being nationalized by rebel regimes and, according to international lawyers, lay the foundation for changes in international law ensuring fair competition, something that should ultimately be in the interest of everyone.[32]

Community Building: From the Local to the Global Level

One solution to making peace in the new world will come about through making new connections between opposing regional trade communities such as the EEC and Comecon (as the defense alliances of NATO and the Warsaw Pact also realign themselves). But equally critical issues today involve establishing worldwide financial institutions that include the excluded nations—small nations like Honduras and Burma, as well as big nations like China and India. There is a need for world development institutions that include the poorer nations as a part of the construction of a world community.

Finally, worldwide planning must take account of local domestic markets, because they are interdependent with nations in all global decisions. It is essential to take account of local communities in a global organization that regulates the circulation of world capital.

In some ways, the world community may be seen as the local community, writ large. A community is found not so much in government as in the common life of people who work, play and make decisions together; less in the established institutions of a locality than in the network of associations; less in the judicial order than in the common recognition that people are fallible; less in the business contract than in people's common desire to find creative solutions to their problems; less in the maintenance of territorial boundaries than in recognizing the inspiring beauty of the diversity of people and the land on which they live; less in perpetuating traditions than in having a shared vision of the future. That search for wholeness in the opposing mix of associations, together with the capacity of people to respond quickly to human need, is what a community—local or global—is all about.

Even if defense expenditures could be reduced by new worldwide security arrangements, releasing funds to stimulate the U.S. economy to compete effectively with other nations, and even if international agreements on finance, corporate conduct, and many other aspects of world commerce allowed fair and efficient trade, one issue would remain. International capital must be decentralized and come under the power of people in local communities around the world. A way must be found for international capital to reduce the power of government over people and promote real community life.

The global circulation of capital under the present organization of markets increases the centralization of corporate states. We see that competing corporations must centralize their administrations as armies do in battle, and nations themselves are in competition with one another today without world law, tending collectively to centralize their administrations through their diplomatic combat. This structure of international competition has devastating effects on local communities.

Global capital disenfranchises local communities because powerful corporations buy and sell local property, both land and firms, in competition for the greatest return on invested capital. Local people lose control over their property, and the result is a series of social and economic problems in the villages, towns, and cities across the world.

The unregulated circulation of capital on the world scene has always been a bane to Third World countries, whose local communities have been destroyed with the advent of foreign capital. The growth of metropolitan centers in the Third World, encircled by slums built by peasants attracted by new jobs in the city, had seemed a natural part of capitalist growth. But now the inner cities of the First World, the United States in particular, are also beset by crime and drugs as neighborhoods have crumbled and been lost to local control.[33] The movement of local capital to metropolitan centers over the last 50 years seemed to most observers an integral part of the ecology of capitalist competition.[34] But as capital has begun to move from the nation out to world centers, the problem is coming home to roost. The United States is becoming a colony of foreign investors. A third of downtown Houston and Minneapolis and almost half of downtown Los Angeles are already foreign-owned. Local real estate markets are dependent on decisions made by distant investors. The result is an exacerbation of community problems, gang violence, and drug addiction, and skyrocketing government costs.[35]

I believe that international agreements should concentrate on directing capital effectively back to local markets while maximizing its world circulation at its most efficient levels. To do this requires a special kind of decentralized market organization: local ownership arrangements that allow capital to keep circulating at global levels while simultaneously keeping it under reasonable control by people in local neighborhoods, villages, towns, and cities. Cooperation at the world level "evens the playing field" between nations, but it requires special policies to increase local resources. It requires creating international policies that advance the common welfare of local residents as a principled basis for global development.[36]

Toward a Mutually Governed Global System

Solutions to the problems created by U.S. dependency on the global market do not readily emerge from standard economic textbooks, because they require an integrated outlook on the politics and the sociology of international organization. At the global level, the political issue, for the United States, as for all nations, is common security. At the national level, the task is to find a new way for corporations to set public norms and mediate conflict through the oppositional dynamics of professional and trade associations, and for firms to confederate in order to compete more effectively against foreign competition. At the local level, the solution lies in developing enterprise federations and community corporations that can influence global capital and distribute its benefits equitably among local citizens.

Can governments allow nonstatist and democratic associations at the global level to set rules for a free market? Can such associations help transform a volatile monetary system into a self-regulating world economy? The answer may be found in new systems of mutual governance. Although the vast changes occurring in Europe today look promising, without broader links to other regions and larger global networks, they will also create new instabilities. These rapid and still unpredictable changes in the organization of Europe reemphasize the need for establishing a transregional, broader base for a socioeconomic organization. There is a vital need to create world institutions to monitor changes in the larger global economy for the common good.

But the ultimate problem is a faulty paradigm that must be repaired. Constructed from neoclassical economics, this paradigm shapes modern thought and policy without an integral view of the connections between social and economic factors. Solving our economic problems will remain elusive until social factors are seen to be as important as economic factors in determining market behavior, at the global as well as the national and local levels.

Notes

Notes

Chapter 1

1. It is important to keep in mind that one cannot use these categories as a means of easily characterizing any single writer. For example, Marx criticized the prevailing view that the market had solely economic foundations by arguing that it had a social foundation, suggesting that he belongs in economic sociology; yet in certain parts of his own work, he took a Ricardian view of the market in the manner of a classicist. His work also drew from economic anthropology, where he could be located with good reason; yet many social economists count him as one of their own, and many historians would see him as one of the founders of social history. Similarly, the writings of other major analysts to be mentioned fall complexly between these trends of thought. Therefore, these categories should be seen largely as "constructed types"; many writers would fall in more than one if the whole body of their work were examined.

2. J. E. King indicates a prior use in Mazerne-Turquet (1611). Because the relationship between the state and the economy it signified was so appropriate to the times, King suggests that even earlier usages might be found. J. E. King, "The Origin of the Term 'Political Economy,'" *Journal of Modern History*, 20 (1948): 230–31.

3. Ben B. Seligman, *Main Currents in Modern Economics* (New York: Free Press, 1962), p. 269. Seligman notes that Jevons refers to the change of name in his Preface to the Second Edition, in which he stresses his concern with formal relations.

4. Daniel Bell, "Models and Reality in Economic Discourse," in Daniel Bell and Irving Kristol, eds., *The Crisis in Economic Theory* (New York: Basic Books, 1981).

5. Thorstein Veblen, "The Preconceptions of Economic Science III," *Quarterly Journal of Economics*, 14 (1900): 240–69.

6. This advance is generally traced back to J. R. Hicks and G. J. Stigler, since they defined the core of marginalist theory as based on methodological individualism and marginal productivity theory deriving from the subjective theory of value. See J. R. Hicks, "Marginal Productivity and the

Principle of Variation," *Economica*, 12:79–88; and G. J. Stigler, *Production and Distribution Theories* (New York: Macmillan, 1941).

7. Paul Samuelson, *Economics: An Introductory Analysis*, 3d ed. (New York: McGraw-Hill, 1955).

8. The problem with this view from a sociological perspective is not simply that the U.S. economy is so much different from other cultures than could be indicated by these rudimentary ideas (most economists know this), but that such phrases get repeated routinely in textbooks as though they were universally true. Furthermore, even these phrases do not apply accurately to the U.S. economy. A brief example: "The core of a private enterprise economy, then, consists of an interchange between individuals and businesses." Lloyd Reynolds, *The American Economy* (New York: McGraw-Hill, 1987), p. 2. This does not define the core of the economy that, as I see it, is essential to an understanding of its future, since it ignores the role of associations, institutions, customs and a larger culture that determines market behavior, even more than individuals.

9. Frank H. Knight, "On the Most Important Economic Problem," *Problems of United States Economic Development* (New York: Committee for Economic Development, 1958) 1:273.

10. Peter O. Steiner, "Markets and Industries," in David Sills, ed., *International Encyclopedia of the Social Sciences* (New York: Macmillan, 1968), 9:575–76.

11. Lester Thurow, *Dangerous Currents: The State of Economics* (New York: Random House, 1983), p. 220.

12. *Ibid.*, pp. 222–23.

13. John Commons finds von Wieser's first book, *Natürliches Wert* (1889), highly individualistic, and his second, *Gesetz der Macht*, highly collectivistic. In *Grundriss der Sozialökonomik (Social Economics)* von Wieser contrasts the "simple economy" of a supposed isolated being with the "social," "state," and "world" economy. Commons traces institutional economics back to his thought. See John Commons, *Institutional Economics: Its Place in Political Economy* (Madison: University of Wisconsin Press, 1961), 2:667–68. Von Wieser rejected the classical notion of competition as the ideal state of the economy and had an interest in the development of trade unions as a basis for balancing the unequal power structure in a bourgeois society. The state's objective, he believed, should be the protection and development of social production rather than the satisfaction of wants. For a broader interpretation of von Wieser's work, see Seligman, *Main Currents*, pp. 283 ff.

14. Some of the work of institutional economists appears in the *Journal of Economic Issues*, published by the Association for Evolutionary Economics.

15. Pareto's principle of optimality posits that the well-being of some

people can be increased without detriment to others. Pareto made a distinction between the maximum utility *of* a community, which might lead to wealth with unequal incomes, and the maximum utility *for* a community, which might lead to equal incomes but less wealth; thus the concept *for* a community stressed the impact on the group as a whole, whereas that *of* a community emphasized the interest of the individual. Critics argue that a concept decreeing an optimality where the rich get richer and the poor get no poorer has serious shortcomings. At the same time, the language describing the nature of welfare and its measurement became quite cumbersome and difficult, so that interest in the idea has waned.

16. See David Novick, "Cost-Benefit Analysis and Social Responsibility," *Business Horizons*, Oct. 1973, pp. 63–72. The reader can pursue the tradition of welfare economics in more detail by reading Allen Feldman, "Welfare Economics," in John Eatwell, Murray Milgate, and Peter Newmann, eds., *The New Palgrave: A Dictionary of Economics* (London: Macmillan, 1987), 4:981 ff. For example, welfare economists have described how the marginal costs to a factory emitting smoke that is damaging to the local community can be calculated and may over the long run bring the factory to change its business policy in the larger interest of itself and the community. One example given by Feldman on the case of factory smoke emphasizes the reciprocal nature of externalities. Cost-benefit studies suggest remedies based on common law doctrines. Thus, according to the economist R. H. Coase, if two neighboring factories are involved, the polluter damages the pollutee only because of their proximity, e.g., the smoking factory harms the other only if it happens to be located close downwind. Coase rejects the notion that the state must step in and tax the polluter. The common law of nuisance can be used instead. If the law provides for the upwind factory's clear right to emit smoke, the downwind factory can contract with the upwind factory to reduce its output, and if there are no impediments to bargaining, the two firms acting together will negotiate an optimal outcome. See R. H. Coase, "The Problem of Social Cost," *Journal of Law and Economics*, 3 (1960):1–44.

17. One leading figure in this new association is the sociologist Amitai Etzioni, whose book *The Moral Dimension: Toward a New Economics* (New York: Free Press, 1988) provides a stimulus for the new group's orientation. "Socio-economics," Etzioni says (p. 16), "seeks to construct a cross-disciplinary bridge between exchange and structure, bridging together the market, polity and society; in the study of choice, it combines the study of reason with values and emotions. . . . Socio-economics brings positive (logical-empirical) and normative (prescriptive) considerations closer together, without losing the distinction between factual and value-judgements."

18. Mark Granovetter, "Economic Action and Social Structure: The Prob-

lem of Embeddedness," *American Journal of Sociology*, 91 (1985):481–510. Some economists have suggested that fundamental changes in conception are imminent however. Albert O. Hirschman contends that noneconomic factors may play a crucial role in the whole analysis of economic institutions. Hirschman, *Rival Views of Market Society* (New York: Viking, 1986). See also Amartya Sen, "Rational Fools: A Critique of the Behavioral Foundations of Economic Theory," *Philosophy and Public Affairs*, 6 (1977):317–44. For a review of the general disinclination of economists to take serious account of the social factor in markets, see Bernard Barber, "The Absolutization of the Market," in G. Dworkin, G. Bermant, and P. Brown, eds., *Markets and Morals* (Washington, D.C.: Hemisphere, 1977). For a review of studies on the borderline between disciplines, see Louis Levy-Garboua, *Sociological Economics* (London: Sage, 1979).

19. The reason for the current lack of conceptual integration between the fields of sociology and economics is first, the popular belief that the market is rooted in an economic base while social factors play only a secondary role in the conduct of the market economy; and second, but equally important, the fact that the contemporary market is legally structured to rest on economic foundations. The second point requires much research attention; indeed, it was only in the 1930's that corporations were permitted by the courts to give a percentage of their profits to charities, as opposed to maximizing returns to their stockholders. But today the very concept of stockholder is changing in professional studies to the concept of "stakeholder," reflecting a broader concept of social responsibility for business in the legal system. Thus, the significance of social economics as a field of research remains vital, because it serves as a monitor of social change taking place in the marketplace and also because the research itself acts as a force to bring social issues to public awareness and into public policy.

20. I include under my review of economic sociology many ideas shared with economic anthropology, and I do this for simplicity. My apology to anthropology, but I assume for our immediate purposes that the two fields are in sufficient accord on basic ideas that stand apart from traditional economics to make my point. There is much to be said at another time about the differences between sociology, with its subject of society and accent on modern times, and anthropology, with its subject of culture and accent on early societies. The term economic anthropology became popular after the publication of Melville Herskovits's *Economic Anthropology* (1952), a republication of his earlier *The Economic Life of Primitive Peoples* (1940), which he revised in light of a critical review by the neoclassical economist Frank Knight in 1941. This dialogue sparked off a debate that persists today between the "formalists" (i.e., neoclassical economists) and the "substantivists," described in the discussion of Karl Polanyi. For more on this de-

bate, see J. S. Kahn and J. R. Llobera, *The Anthropology of Pre-Capitalist Societies* (London: Macmillan, 1981).

21. Neil J. Smelser, *The Sociology of Economic Life* (Englewood Cliffs, N.J.: Prentice-Hall, 1963), p. 32. Here we see reliance on the economic model (e.g., the need for scarcity and the omission of the associational life in exchange systems).

22. Max Weber, *Economy and Society*, ed. Guenther Roth and Claus Wittich (New York: Bedminster Press, 1968), pp. 4, 63, 82. In the Weberian tradition, the "market situation [*Marktlage*] for any object of exchange" means "all the opportunities of exchanging it for money which are known to the participants in exchange relationships and aid their orientation in the competitive price struggle." From this perspective, the market is a system in which participants choose to exchange objects for money according to the opportunities they see available to them in a competitive relationship. Studies of the social market in this tradition lead the researcher to enter into the "market situation" in which people find themselves in a position of *choice*, able to determine the extent and type of opportunities that are available, the degree to which money exists as a basis for their exchange, and the degree and type of competition that are present in the situation. Further, following Weber, "'Marketability' [*Marktgängigkeit*] is the degree of regularity with which an object tends to be an object of exchange on the market." And "'market freedom' is the degree of autonomy enjoyed by the parties to market relationships in the price struggle and competition." Finally, "regulation of the market" is the condition in which there is a substantive restriction on marketability or market freedom through (1) tradition, (2) convention (patterns of social disapproval), and (3) law.

23. But there are still important distinctions. Critical for our purposes is Weber's conception of market regulation as socially determined from within the economy as well as by law.

24. It is noteworthy that in Marx's thought the social factor explains not only the dynamics of the economy, but also consciousness: "It is not the consciousness of men that determines their social being but on the contrary, their social being that determines their consciousness." Karl Marx, *Selected Writings in Sociology and Social Philosophy*, tr. Thomas Bottomore (London: McGraw-Hill, 1964), pp. 64–65.

25. Polanyi's work has been detailed in many articles. For a relatively recent set of articles, see "Special Section on Karl Polanyi," *Telos*, Fall 1987. The fundamental schism between the fields of social economics and economic sociology is most evident in a critique of Polanyi's work by the sociologist Bernard Barber, who argues that Polanyi's idea of a "disembedded" system of market exchange takes attention away from examining just how intricately interdependent the market is with other parts of the societal

system. Barber, "Absolutization of the Market," p. 27. The economist Albert Hirschman takes a similar position, arguing that social scientists must start "embracing complexity" in their studies of the market. Hirschman, "Rival Interpretations of Market Society," *Journal of Economic Literature*, 20 (1982):1483.

26. Karl Polanyi, *The Livelihood of Man*, ed. Harry Pearson (New York: Academic Press, 1977), pp. 20 ff.

27. The central feature of reciprocal, or nonmarket, economies is that goods are allocated on the basis of social norms held by various groupings: families, neighborhoods, networks of friends, voluntary associations, etc. Land use, inheritance, the movement of things from person to person, and the like are determined by the culture's social expectations; and practices relating to how goods are transferred, who makes the transfers, the means of transfer, and so on are determined by the group's norms. A reciprocal economy may readily be observed in some aspects of what is currently referred to as the "informal economy." See Jonathan Gershuny, "The Informal Economy," *Futures*, 11.1 (1979):3–15. The central feature of redistributive economies is the physical movement of goods to a central place for distribution. The development of such systems is closely associated with the development of a political order. Redistributive economies are exemplified by the vast bureaucratic empires of ancient Mesopotamia and Egypt. A modern example is the tax system of market economies, where income is drawn to the government from one sector of the population and allocated to another for special purposes, such as (in American society) for corporate subsidies and welfare programs. For the application of Polanyi's theories to early societies, see George Dalton, ed., *Tribal and Peasant Economies* (New York: Natural History Press, 1967).

28. For a Marxist critique of *Economy and Society* see Alvin Gouldner, *The Coming Crisis of Western Sociology* (New York: Avon Books, 1971), pp. 304–13.

29. Kenneth Boulding, "Economics as a Moral Science," in Boulding, *Economics as a Science* (New York: McGraw-Hill, 1970).

30. Gary Becker, *The Economic Approach to Human Behavior* (Chicago: University of Chicago Press, 1976). See also Becker, *A Treatise on the Family* (Cambridge, Mass.: Harvard University Press, 1981). For example, Becker explains the economic virtues of people faking altruism, because they can then benefit from the altruism of others without contributing their share. This simulation is said to be limited mainly by the "transaction costs" of faking and the difficulty of being a completely successful faker. This mode of economics thus becomes comprehensive to the study of all human behavior but to my mind, it distorts social reality.

31. Richard Swedberg, "Economic Sociology: Past and Present," *Current Sociology*, 35.1 (Spring 1987).

32. Pirenne argued: "I shall not ask what one can call such a navigator as Romano Mairano (1152–1201) if, in spite of the hundreds of thousands of francs he employed in business, the fifty per cent profits he realized on his operations in coasting trade, and his final failure, one persists in refusing to him the name of capitalist." Henri Pirenne, "The Stages in the Social History of Capitalism," *American Historical Review*, 19 (1914):496.

33. Sombart defined capitalism by three elements: a basic spirit (a set of values and attitudes), an economic organization, and a "technique" or mode of technology. Writing in the Hegelian tradition, he found the first element essential to the development of the second and third. As he saw it, "early capitalism" began in the 13th century and lasted to the middle of the 18th. In the second period, "full capitalism," the spirit of the enterprise became rationalistic, calculating, and competitive, with a Faustian spirit of "unlimited acquisition." "Late capitalism" appeared after the First World War, at which time the "spirit of enterprise" passed into a new phase because of increasing government regulation. It was more oriented to the public interest, and employment began to look like civil service. Werner Sombart, "Capitalism," *Encyclopedia of the Social Sciences* (New York: Macmillan, 1930), vol. 3. See also the discussion of Sombart's *Der Moderne Kapitalismus* (untranslated) in Frederich Nussbaum, *A History of the Economic Institutions of Modern Europe* (New York: Crofts, 1935).

34. Dobbs argued: "If we are speaking of Capitalism as a specific mode of production, then it follows that we cannot date the dawn of this system from the first signs of the appearance of large-scale trading and of a merchant class, and we cannot speak of a special period of 'Merchant Capitalism,' as many have done. We must look for the opening of the capitalist period only when changes in the mode of production occur, in the sense of a direct subordination of the producer to a capitalist. This is not a point of terminology, but of substance; since it means that if we are right, the appearance of a purely trading class will itself have no revolutionary significance." Maurice Dobbs, *Studies in the Development of Capitalism* (New York: International Publishers, 1947), p. 17. Commons set the date for the transition from merchant capitalism to employer capitalism in the United States as the two decades from 1850 to 1870. "During these twenty years the number of patents leaped from less than 1,000 per year to more than 12,000 per year. This is the period when the railways created a national market and the patent office a factory system. The third stage, Banker Capitalism, had its forerunner in the commercial banking of the decades of merchant capitalism with their short-time credits needed for the marketing of commodities. But the banking syndicates, or the investment bankers of the twentieth century, affiliated with commercial banks, rise to a dominant position in the consolidation of industries, the sale of securities, and control of boards of directors whose corporate securities they have sold and

for which they have become supposedly responsible." John R. Commons, *Institutional Economics: Its Place in Political Economy* (New York: Macmillan, 1934), pp. 121–22.

35. Political capitalism took five forms: *pariah capitalism* (e.g., the Parsis of India, Occidental Jewry); *imperialist capitalism* (e.g., the Roman and British empires, where profit interests dominated); *colonial capitalism* (e.g., imperial expansion dominated by economic interests, such as guaranteed trading monopolies, shipping privileges, compulsory labor); *adventure capitalism* (e.g., charismatically led raids on foreign countries for treasure, from tombs to mines); and *fiscal capitalism* (e.g., farming out tax collection to private enterprises, as in ancient Rome and France, or the Catholic Church's leasing the sale of indulgences to Italian merchants as compensation for their loans to the Vatican). Max Weber, *General Economic History* (New York: Collier Books, 1961), pp. 207–9.

36. *Ibid.*, pp. 275 ff. Weber showed a close affinity to the late Marx when it came to defining the commercial instruments emerging in the market and to the early Marx with his definition of "free labor" in the market. For example, Weber said of labor: "It is in contradiction to the essence of capitalism, and the development of capitalism is impossible, if such a property-less stratum is absent, a class compelled to sell its labor services to live; and it is likewise impossible if only unfree labor is at hand. Rationalistic capitalistic calculation is possible only on the basis of free labor; only where in consequence of the existence of workers who in the formal sense, voluntarily, but actually under the compulsion of the whip of hunger, offer themselves, the costs of products may be unambiguously determined by agreement in advance." At the same time, Weber's thesis that a religious ethic (Calvinism) served as the trigger for the development of capitalism placed him closer to the Hegelian tradition. *Ibid.*, p. 269.

37. Robert Wilson, "Exchange," in John Eatwell, Murray Milgate, and Peter Newmann, eds., *The New Palgrave: A Dictionary of Economics* (London: Macmillan, 1987), 1:202–3. One promising connection between economic and sociological perspectives on exchange theory may be developing in the work of Harrison White. White formulated his model of markets, the so-called W(y) model, in technical papers written between 1976 and 1979, and he is still at work elaborating it. He has proposed to provide a basis for "embedding economists' neoclassical theory of the firm within a sociological view of markets, . . . almost the inverse of longstanding preconceptions of how sociology relates to economics." White, "Production Markets As Induced Role Structures," in Samuel Leinhardt, ed., *Sociological Methodology* (San Francisco: Jossey-Bass, 1981), p. 44. See also White, "Markets and Hierarchies Revisited," unpublished paper, Harvard University, Department of Sociology, 1978; and his "On Markets," Harvard University, RIAS Program Working Paper no. 16, 1979.

38. Marcel Mauss, *The Gift*, tr. I. Cunnison (New York: Free Press, 1954).

39. Claude Lévi-Strauss, *The Elementary Structures of Kinship* (Boston: Beacon Press, 1969).

40. George Homans, *The Human Group* (New York: Harcourt Brace Jovanovich, 1950).

41. Peter Blau, *Exchange and Power in Social Life* (New York: Wiley, 1964). See also Peter Ekeh, *Social Exchange Theory: The Two Traditions* (Cambridge, Mass.: Harvard University Press, 1974). Let us apply these abstract notions of social exchange theorists to an actual case. The American Association of Security Dealers was created by dealers who experienced many personal costs as well as rewards. It gradually enlarged and members established guidelines on trading behavior. Indeed, it has become a powerful collectivity in itself, acting on individual members, and requires balance through another corporation, the government, which regulates it through the Securities and Exchange Commission. Following Blau, the action of the "smallest unit of interaction" by a stockholder is determined by the norms of these two major associations, but there is still a dynamic interaction of small units within the whole system that in turn acts to shape the behavior of the associations. It is a social system especially important to observe as the stock market undergoes more instabilities in the future. Exchange theory has been systematized over the years and now includes many testable propositions detailing people's relationships in their social exchanges. For elaborations, see Richard Emerson, "Exchange Theory, Part I: A Psychological Basis for Social Exchange" and "Exchange Theory, Part II: Exchange Relations and Network Structures," in J. Berger, M. Zelditch, and B. Anderson, eds., *Sociological Theories in Progress* (Boston: Houghton Mifflin, 1972), pp. 38–87. For a descriptive review and interpretation of the work on exchange theory, see Jonathan Turner, *The Structure of Sociological Theory* (Homewood, Ill.: Dorsey Press, 1982).

42. Robert Ayers, *Banking on the Poor* (Cambridge: MIT Press, 1983), pp. 1–35.

43. See Patricia A. Adler and Peter Adler, eds., *The Social Dynamics of Financial Markets* (Greenwich, Conn.: JAI Press, 1984), vol. 2.

44. The disdain for state ownership of property in the days of Marx and Engels is made clear in many of their comments. Explaining why he believed the state tends to take over industries for economic reasons and why that does not represent socialism, Engels wrote: "But of late, since Bismarck went in for state ownership of industrial establishments, a kind of spurious socialism has arisen, degenerating, now and again, into something of flunkeyism, that without more ado declares all state ownership, even of the Bismarckian sort, to be socialistic. Certainly, if the taking over by the state of the tobacco industry is socialistic, then Napoleon and Metternich must be numbered among the founders of socialism. Otherwise,

the Royal Maritime Company, the Royal porcelain manufacturer, and even the regimental tailor shops of the Army would also be socialistic institutions, or even, as was seriously proposed by a sly dog in Frederick William III's reign, the taking over by the state of the brothels." Engels went on to discuss the necessity of a proletarian takeover and the concept that the state is not "abolished" but simply "dies out." The real authority rests in "society." Frederick Engels, "Socialism, Utopian and Scientific," in *Selected Works of Karl Marx and Frederick Engels* (New York: International Publishers, 1970), pp. 427 ff.

45. The idea of a "social contract" as the basis of a citizen's rights and duties can be traced back, although in imprecise form, to Plato and Epicurus and to Cicero and the *lex regia* of the Roman law. As a systematic and coherent notion, the social contract is related more to the Reformation and the Counter-Reformation, becoming the weapon of religious and political doctrines. See H. J. Laski, "Social Contract," in *Encyclopedia of the Social Sciences* (New York: Macmillan, 1934), vol. 14.

46. The major contractarians of the 17th and 18th centuries, Thomas Hobbes, John Locke, and Jean-Jacques Rousseau, represented the beginning of the social contract movement. Each writer's definitive work dealing with the "contract" (Hobbes, *Leviathan*; Locke, *The Second Treatise of Civil Government*; and Rousseau, *The Social Contract*) focuses on two basic areas: (1) individual rights and (2) the problem of consent. My own view is that this concept applies to the development of a social market. For a reference to its application to intracorporate relations, see Litsa Nicolaou-Smokovitis and Severyn T. Bruyn, *A Theoretical Framework for Studying Worker Participation: The Psychosocial Contract* (Athens, Greece: National Centre of Social Research, 1978). The concept can explain the basis for separating major divisions of state socialist industries into the private sector by giving them social constitutions. This protean concept suggests that we view the American private sector as a social republic. See Severyn T. Bruyn, *The Social Economy* (New York: Wiley, 1977), chaps. 4–7.

47. Adam Smith, *The Wealth of Nations* (New York: Modern Library, 1937), p. 423.

48. This interpretation and the quotation from Marx's *Essay* are drawn from Lloyd D. Easton and Kurt H. Guddat, trs. and eds., *Writings of the Young Marx on Philosophy and Society* (New York: Anchor Books, 1967), pp. 14–15.

49. Karl Marx and Frederick Engels, *The German Ideology* (New York: International Publishers, 1965), pp. 53–54.

50. *Ibid.*, p. 50.

51. Emile Durkheim, *Socialism and Saint-Simon*, ed. Alvin Gouldner, tr. Charlotte Sattler (Yellow Springs, Ohio: Antioch Press, 1958), pp. 21–22.

52. I resist naming the new economic order because any given name

soon becomes the basis for impassioned pursuit, often through the agency of the state. The names "socialism" and "communism" represent only one consequence of this passion to create a new order based on a fixed picture of a changing reality. Indeed, the use of "ism" in our language has come to represent a fixed order of things that actually defies reality. Such terms as Protestantism, Catholicism, Quakerism, Methodism, and Judaism, and even descriptive terms like patriotism and nationalism, represent fixed views of the world. But it is impossible to fix the identity of such changing worlds as the Catholic or the Protestant without causing distortions of reality and misinterpreting the complexities in the dynamic, real world. When people identify with a fixed picture of the world and try passionately to create it in their own image, it loses a central quality of itself—its vitality and capacity to evolve. My interest here is less in a fixed picture of the future than in the revelation of a changing reality that can be perceived through a new interpretation of the meaning of sociality in the everyday life of the market. Hence the future is seen through an interpretation of the evolving present: the social market.

Chapter 2

1. We can even give an example of this phenomenon in Yugoslavia today, where workers own and manage their own firms, yet government controls remain strong, not only because the system devolved from state socialism in the Soviet Union and not only because it operates in a context of ethnic and provincial conflict that requires strong government controls, but also because it shows the need to regulate a competitive market of labor-managed firms. Yugoslavia is partial testimony to the failure of a labor-managed system by itself to evolve toward what Marx described as a "withering away of the state," or what this book refers to as a "self-regulated system."

2. Daniel Bell, *The Coming of Post-Industrial Society: A Venture in Social Forecasting* (New York: Basic Books, 1973), p. 378.

3. This sociological concept is parallel in some respects to the Freudian concept of the conscious and unconscious, but we are dealing in this case with a public mind and a social structure. Merton added the concept of latent and manifest dysfunctions as consequences that detract from the adaptation of the system. I am not treating the question of adaptations and maladaptations at the abstract level in this Mertonian tradition, but they do become relevant in middle-range analysis. At this abstract level, we are working simply with the idea of consciousness and intent. Thus, there are differences at this level from Merton's more sophisticated terms, but these terms still lead easily to middle-range analysis of adaptations, as indicated later. The emergence of the "latent economy" cannot be generalized as adaptive because unforeseeable changes will occur at middle-range levels

of organization. As profit corporations increasingly come to look like non-profits, and nonprofits to look like profits, for example, the resulting changes can have consequences that may not all be legal, intentional, or adaptive in the evolving system. Merton's middle-range analysis therefore becomes important for studying the adaptiveness only of middle-level changes. Here is where functional analysis is important. See Robert Merton, *Social Theory and Social Structure* (Glencoe, Ill.: Free Press, 1949).

4. I note throughout the book how mainstream economists focus on the profit sector, even though the academic field takes a broader view. The focus on the profit sector is visible in most economic textbooks, but the tendency also appears in references to "economic" in dictionaries written by economists. "Economic indicators," for instance, measure the conditions of "business." Nevertheless, even though the broader scope of economics, defined as the allocation of goods and services based on "scarcity," is a concept applicable across both profit and nonprofit sectors, it is still a much narrower scope of inquiry than is needed to understand the deep changes taking place in the economy today. See *The McGraw-Hill Dictionary of Modern Economics* (New York, 1983), p. 150.

5. Things are changing, with economic principles becoming manifest and more important in marriages today, although money making is not yet deemed the main purpose of marriage. Though the problems of the family are not our main concern here, they illustrate how the relationship between the manifest and the latent economy is changing. The social and economic factors can be very subtle and complexly related at any place where earning an income makes a difference in society. A social concept of the economy reaches far into the life of the family and requires study by social economists and economic sociologists.

6. Mirra Komarovsky, *Blue-Collar Marriage* (New York: Random House, 1967), p. 237.

7. Carol Stack, *All Our Kin: Strategies for Survival in a Black Community* (New York: Harper & Row, 1974).

8. Lowenthal himself calls this economic system "the social economy," since its transactions are embedded in a network of social relationships people maintain over time. Martin Lowenthal, "The Social-Economy in Working Class Communities," in Gary Gappert and Harold M. Rose, eds., *The Social Economy of Cities* (Beverly Hills, Calif.: Sage, 1975).

9. The shift in emphasis first became apparent when Herbert Simon suggested that the concept of profit maximization be dropped in favor of "multiple goals." The corporation was acting under a number of constraints, and therefore its overall aim was "satisficing." See Herbert Simon, "On the Concept of Organizational Goal," *Administrative Science Quarterly*, 1964:1–22. For a more recent view on this matter and corporate stakeholders, see R. Edward Freeman and David L. Reed, "Perspective on

Corporate Governance," *California Management Review* 25.3 (Spring 1983): 88–106.

10. We shall look at specific cases in Chap. 5. Here I am simply indicating the complex interaction of the two sets of oppositional categories at a middle-range level. I have defined the manifest economy broadly as the profit sector in terms of public consciousness, but at the middle-range level of analysis there are degrees of consciousness of intent and consequence that operate in the nonprofit university to bring about dysfunctions. The social factor is manifest in its noneconomic goals (the advancement of learning), but in this example the system is operating dysfunctionally within the laws of the nonprofit sector. On the other hand, the economic factor is manifest in the goals of the business corporation, but the system is operating dysfunctionally within its legal order. Further, the corporate gift is dysfunctional in the system not only because it is illegal, but also because it causes a lot of trouble and "lost time," thereby hindering the realization of corporate goals of efficiency and productivity.

11. To illustrate this point, a number of the changes in SEC rules that have taken place through the social investment movement have broadened the opportunity for stockholder protest. One case involves the Sisters of Loretto, a teaching order of the Catholic Church, who became concerned that the Blue Diamond Coal Company was not treating miners fairly. The conflict between social and economic purposes was vividly illustrated when the Sisters won the right to purchase stock in the company in order to influence the company to implement social goals along with its economic goals. See Robert Schwartz, "The Blue Diamond Coal Company Case," *The Social Report* (Boston College) 3 (June 1982):5. For many concrete examples of organizational conflict in the field of social investment, see Ami Domini, with Peter Kinder, *Ethical Investing* (Reading, Mass.: Addison-Wesley, 1984).

12. In both cases, the social drive to dominate kept people from seeing the economic consequences. Perhaps the leaders of the over-evangelizing church were so driven by their desire to "save souls" that they paid no attention to the debts being accumulated in carrying out the church's mission. And perhaps the corporation's owner was so ego-involved in dominating other companies that he failed to notice that his firm was seriously losing money as a result of his unfriendly takeovers. Both the collective drive of the soul-saving church and the ego-drive of the corporate owner and his lawyers represent the social factor gone out of balance, resulting in economic damage.

13. These cases are based on my talks with leaders and people-on-the-streets interviews during a visit to Cuba in 1977.

14. The idea of making money is still frowned on by many leaders in socialist countries because of its past association with capitalism, just as

many corporate managers still frown on the social factor. The general director of the Moscow International Business School, Valeri Kazikaev, expressed such caution as late as 1989 in recruiting lecturers from the Harvard Business School. See Jan Fitz Simon, "Perestroika, to a Degree," *The Boston Globe*, Oct. 10, 1989:1. The shift taking place in socialist countries toward recognizing the economic factor parallels the shift in the United States toward recognizing the social factor in the market, but I believe both factors require study together to maximize their constructive role in the market.

15. Albion Small, *Adam Smith and Modern Sociology* (Chicago: University of Chicago Press, 1907); Charles Horton Cooley, *Social Process* (Carbondale: Southern Illinois University Press, 1966); Robert Park, *Human Communities* (New York: Free Press, 1952), p. 507. Small treated Smith's more popular *The Wealth of Nations* as a sociological study that emphasized the economic process. *Adam Smith*, p. 1.

16. The result was the worst of ironies. During the socialist struggle to overcome the divided class structure, the state in fact became the basis for the fulfillment of the self through socialist idealism. Everything that Marx abhorred—state bureaucracy and idealism—came to fruition because of what he believed was realism (i.e., the need for violent revolution).

17. George Herbert Mead, *Mind, Self, and Society*, ed. Charles W. Morris (Chicago: University of Chicago Press, 1934); Mead, *The Philosophy of the Act*, ed. Charles W. Morris (Chicago: University of Chicago Press, 1938). I discuss this idea in relation to "economic governance" in Severyn Bruyn, *The Social Economy* (New York: Wiley, 1977), pp. 225–29.

18. Riesman spoke of the transition in social character from being "tradition-directed" under feudalism, to being "inner-directed" under 19th-century capitalism, to being "other-directed" in the market of his day (the 1950's). He was not pleased with the tendencies of "other-directed" people to base their conduct on the opinions of other people and on external authorities. The "other-directed" personality, a consequence of industrial society and the rise of the middle class, was preoccupied with consumption and the "human factor" in productive spheres. Similarly, Fromm wrote about the development of the "exploitive orientation" of 19th-century capitalists (who could easily say "the public be damned") and the emergence of the "marketing orientation" in the "public relations" of their successors. Fromm saw people selling themselves in the market to get ahead and thereby losing their integrity. Both writers saw how the market structure had badly shaped social character and looked hopefully toward a change in the economy of the future. Neither had a clear picture of what kind of new market structure would foster the wished-for moral character, but both knew that the structure of character was related to the market structure. Riesman spoke hopefully of the "autonomous" person

who could take account of tradition and his or her own inner drives and listen to the opinions of others without becoming solely directed by those opinions. Fromm spoke of the development of a "productive orientation," in which the individual could become free to make creative decisions within a "sane society" whose market was socially organized. See David Riesman, in collaboration with Reuel Denney and Nathan Glazer, *The Lonely Crowd* (New Haven, Conn: Yale University Press, 1950); and Erich Fromm, *Man for Himself* (New York: Rinehart, 1947).

I should mention two other writers who are separate in their work but uniquely related in their theories. One is the psychologist Fritz Kunkel, whose categories of self-development are similar to Fromm's, but who saw the problem of a limited "ego identity" being solved through an expansion of the "I" to the "We." The other is the sociologist Amitai Etzioni, who sees the market economy as needing a structural resolution between the "I" and the "We." See Fritz Kunkel and Ruth Gardner, *What Do You Advise?* (New York: Ives Washburn, 1946); and Fritz Kunkel, *Creation Continues* (New York: Scribner's, 1947). See also Amitai Etzioni, *The Moral Dimension: Toward a New Economics* (New York: Free Press, 1988).

19. For example, we will see in a later chapter how the social factor is becoming manifest in profit corporations through social research, how the informal (associational) life of the corporation shapes policy, how ethical (social) criteria are being used not only by nonprofit churches and universities, but also quietly, in less visible ways, by profit-oriented banks and fiduciaries, etc. How quickly a social orientation becomes fully manifest in the profit sector depends on how quickly certain changes take place (e.g., social investment by banks, employee ownership in big business), and whether Congress advances or restricts legislation regarding such practices.

20. I shall discuss this trend in the private sector later. Note that it has already invaded the public sector to a significant extent. Governments at all levels—city to federal—have been giving workers greater opportunity to participate in management and alter the workplace. In Milwaukee, for example, city and county governments have provided tuition subsidies for workers to keep abreast of their fields, and have offered job-sharing, four-day weeks, unpaid parental leave for fathers as well as mothers, and much more. The executive director of the local chapter of the American Federation of State, County and Municipal Employees, says, "We've had a long-running, formal relationship with the city so we've been able to get at these issues early." As the county Executive views it, the city has only responded to a trend that is evident everywhere. "There has been a sea-change. Employers value their employees more. We're fitting the job to the employee and not the employee to the job." Peter T. Kilborn, *New York Times*, Oct. 12, 1989:1, D25.

21. Bell, *Coming of Post-Industrial Society*, p. x.

22. Other students of the market economy have described how the economy has become much more resilient, with more emphasis on public relations, a greater concern for employees, and a special regard for the public interest. While recognizing that the rude forms of capitalism still exist in raw competition, profiteering, and rigid command systems, they claim that the old traits are being modified. Writing in 1930, Werner Sombart described such developments as part of "late capitalism," and showed how the system had become more institutionalized and employee-oriented, less risky in some respects, and more publicly oriented. Sombart, "Capitalism," in *Encyclopedia of the Social Sciences* (New York: Macmillan, 1930), vol. 3.

23. Léon Walras, *Elements of Pure Economics* [1874] (New York: Kelley, 1954), p. 84.

24. E. Mansfield, *Microeconomics: Theory and Applications*, 2d ed. (New York: Norton, 1976), chap. 7. This image of the marketplace is similar to what Emile Durkheim defined as a "social fact" and Gustav LeBon described as the "collective mind." In other words, participants in the market functioned as a collective entity, in which all individuals acted together under one theme of action, and the market was in essence conceived as a superior personality, never having to answer for its actions and further, seemingly never making a mistake.

25. Perhaps in the United States a few markets—like agriculture and the stock market—approximated perfect competition for a short time. Farmers may have believed that as producers they were independent and free, but the belief gradually faded with increasing government involvement and eventually regulation by the Department of Agriculture. The stock market also experienced uncontrollable fluctuations, with the result that it too was circumscribed by government legislation and oversight by the SEC. Many other markets became regulated as the government came to speak for both the less powerful "minority" actors, such as labor and the consumer, and for the larger society. Through such regulation, government was addressing the imbalance of power in the social organization of the economy.

26. Peter Kropotkin, *Mutual Aid: A Factor of Evolution* [1902] (Boston: Extending Horizons Books, n.d.); Kropotkin, *Fields, Factories, and Workshops Tomorrow* [1898] (London: Allen & Unwin, 1977).

27. Lewis Coser, *The Functions of Social Conflict* (New York: Free Press, 1956).

28. Francis Sutton, Seymour Harris, Carl Kaysen, and James Tobin, *The American Business Creed* (New York: Schocken Books, 1962), p. 40. In this book, top scholars in economics examined the ideology of American business by studying the institutional advertisements of large corporations and the literature of such business associations as the U.S. Chamber of

Commerce, the Committee for Economic Development, and the National Association of Manufacturers.

29. For many years, food manufacturers calendar-dated their products for inventory control but disguised the information by codes. By 1975, 12 states had developed some form of dating regulation. Car manufacturers and dealers in the past regularly falsified odometers to dupe customers into believing that vehicles were newer than they actually were. Public outrage led 37 states to prohibit odometer tampering, and Congress passed the Motor Vehicle Information and Cost Savings Act, which requires a written, true-mileage disclosure statement at the time of sale for all self-propelled vehicles, except those over 24 years old or those exceeding 16,000 pounds. At the same time, the Federal Energy Act of 1975 required labels on all cars, beginning with 1977 models, disclosing the estimated mileage per gallon and annual fuel costs of 15,000 miles.

30. In Britain, unemployed people who start new businesses can continue to receive their unemployment benefits for a period. The aim is to stimulate business start-ups and help them succeed, thereby providing employment not only for would-be entrepreneurs, but also for their labor forces. For more on these systems, see S. M. Miller, "Social Programs Are Now Economic Programs," *Social Policy*, Winter 1988:44–45.

31. John Commons, *Institutional Economics: Its Place in Political Economy* (Madison: University of Wisconsin Press, 1961), 2:709.

32. Some of these latent dimensions in the retail business have been revealed in a study by Barry Bluestone, *The Retail Revolution: Investment and Labor in the Modern Department Store* (Boston: Auburn House, 1981).

33. These interim changes are depicted by Rosabeth Kanter, *The Change Masters* (New York: Simon & Schuster, 1983).

34. R. W. Boyden, "The Breakdown of Corporations," in Andrew Hacker, ed., *The Corporation Take-Over* (New York: Doubleday, 1965).

35. Charles Hecksher, *The New Unionism* (New York: Basic Books, 1988), pp. 10–11.

36. Robert MacIver, *Society* (New York: Holt, Rinehart & Winston, 1962), pp. 233–34.

37. The terms vary among business scholars. Some writers substitute "influencers" or "claimants" for stakeholders, but the term refers to those who maintain a stake in the organization the way a shareholder maintains shares. See Henry Mintzberg, *Power In and Around Organizations* (Englewood Cliffs, N.J.: Prentice-Hall, 1983), p. 23.

38. Barnaby Feder, "A Nonprofit Institution That Counts on Profits," *New York Times*, May 27, 1988:D1, D5.

39. Gregory Gray gives illustrations of borderline activities: "The nonprofit Children's Television Workshop netted $8 million in 1983 by marketing miniature versions of Kermit the Frog, Big Bird, and other Sesame Street characters and products. . . . Chicago's Lincoln Park Zoo earns

up to $10 thousand per week on stuffed animals, jewelry, and souvenirs. . . . Many YMCAS are operating membership-only health clubs which are subsidized at least in part by funds donated through the United Way and local community chests." Gray, "Nonprofits in Competition with Private Enterprise: Where Is It Leading?," *Nonprofit World,* 3 (January–March): 1–9.

Chapter 3

1. There is of course much scholarly dispute about the role of Marx's early thought in the 1844 *Manuscripts,* as opposed to his later work in *Das Kapital,* but that dispute is not germane to our discussion. The distinction between the humanist orientation of Marx, with which scholars like Leszek Kolakowski might identify, and Marx's later scientific orientation, with which scholars like Louis Althusser might identify, is cogently discussed by Michael Harrington, *The Twilight of Capitalism* (New York: Simon & Schuster, 1976), pp. 166ff.

2. Marx was mindful to distinguish the workers' role in the capitalist system from the slaves'. Workers owned their own labor and could therefore market themselves, whereas slaves were a commodity marketed by others. More recent writers have pointed to an extension of this problem among employees such as salespeople, models, and corporate careerists, who sell their personalities, smiles, and appearances to advance the profits of a firm over which they have no control. See Erich Fromm, *Man for Himself* (New York, Rinehart, 1947).

3. "The product of labor is that which has been embodied in an object, which has become material: it is the objectification of labor. Labor's realization is its objectification. In the sphere of political economy this realization of labor appears as loss of realization for the workers; objectification as loss of the object and bondage to it; appropriation as estrangement, as alienation." Karl Marx, *Economic and Philosophic Manuscripts of 1844,* ed. Dirk Struik (New York: International Publishers, 1964), p. 108.

4. Developed by Lukacs in the early 1920's to amplify Marx's work, the term "reification" was later employed by Marxist humanists. Georgy Lukacs, *History and Class Consciousness,* tr. Rodney Livingstone (Cambridge, Mass.: MIT Press, 1971).

5. These arguments in social theory are highly technical and not part of my main argument. Marx owed a great debt to Hegel's brilliant work in this area. Furthermore, scholars recognize that Marx's externalizing of the Hegelian spirit (*Geist*) into a critique of political economy was both an advance in social thought and an inadequate restatement of the fundamental problem Hegel posed—an advance because it allowed students of the subject to see how the problem of alienation must be interpreted as a function of the economic order, as well as of the mind; inadequate because it failed

to explain the more fundamental problem of cultural development as part of a profounder dialectic. Some scholars contend that neither Hegel nor Marx ever came to terms with alienation's full meaning and significance, but to discuss this issue would carry us beyond the point. Briefly, Ralf Dahrendorf argues that the concept of alienation "has no place in empirical social science, since no amount of empirical research can either confirm or refute it." Dahrendorf, *Essays in the Theory of Society* (London: Routledge & Kegan Paul, 1968), p. 13.

6. Leland Stanford is an interesting example of a capitalist who bridged such class differences and acted with a larger human interest in the later years of his life. During his last decade this railroad magnate and notorious "Robber Baron" had a social vision of an economy based on the principle of cooperation. He advocated an end to capitalism, not through a revolutionary takeover but through the gradual replacement of the conventional corporation by cooperative systems such as worker-owned businesses. As a U.S. Senator, Stanford introduced a number of bills to give worker cooperatives the proper legal structure and sources of credit to flourish in the United States. When he founded Stanford University as a memorial to his late son, he made the cooperative vision "a leading feature lying at the foundation of the University." Although his bills never made it out of committee and his vision for Stanford University was left unrealized, he stands with notable U.S. labor leaders and with millions of unnoticed Americans who fought hard with a vision for social development. See Lee Altenberg, "An End to Capitalism: Leland Stanford's Forgotten Vision," *Sandstone and Tile* 14.1 (Stanford Historical Society, Winter 1990): 8–20.

7. Harry Braverman, *Labor and Monopoly Capital: The Degradation of Work in the Twentieth Century* (New York: Monthly Review Press, 1974).

8. Michael Buroway, *Manufacturing Consent: Changes in the Labor Process Under Monopoly Capitalism* (Chicago: University of Chicago Press, 1979).

9. Richard Edwards, *Contested Terrain: The Transformation of the Workplace in the Twentieth Century* (New York: Basic Books, 1979).

10. Richard Edwards, Michael Reich, and David Gordon, eds., *Labor Market Segmentation* (Lexington, Mass.: Heath, 1975).

11. Maurice Dobbs, *Studies in the Development of Capitalism* (New York: International Publishers, 1963), pp. 265–66. Few people in the United States today recognize the historic significance of labor's struggle as its strength and vision rose, fell, and rose again. The full story of labor is not taught in conventional history books, and many people see the labor movement today as having lost its power, seemingly in decline. But the importance of this movement cannot so easily be dismissed from history or the public mind.

12. Michael Reich, "The Evolution of the United States Labor Force," in Richard Edwards, Michael Reich, and Thomas Weisskopf, eds., *The Capi-*

talist System (Englewood Cliffs, N.J.: Prentice-Hall, 1972), pp. 175, 181. In the 1930's, industrial unionism arose as a mass movement. Some four million workers, many semiskilled and unskilled, were organized into the Congress of Industrial Organizations (CIO). The movement reached its peak in the massive sit-down strikes of 1936–37, when tens of thousands of workers successfully occupied factories to force their recognition as legitimate bargaining agents. By 1947, union membership had reached 14.8 million, or about 24 percent of the labor force. In 1960, about half of all blue-collar workers were union members, four-fifths of them in the mining, manufacturing, and construction industries.

13. Charles C. Hecksher, *The New Unionism: Employee Involvement in the Changing Corporation* (New York: Basic Books, 1988), p. 16.

14. Ibid.

15. Ibid., p. 160.

16. Quoted and discussed in ibid., p. 161.

17. The most complete program treating the problem of rule-based approaches may be the Work Environment Act of 1977 in Norway, which holds that rules cannot be developed for all relevant hazards, such as human stress or ergonomics. Bjorn Gustavsen and Gerry Hunnius, *New Patterns of Work Reform: The Case of Norway* (Oslo: Universiteforlaget, 1981).

18. A theory of self-development is implied in social management, based on the premise that the self is an entity constructed in a social context. This idea, which as we noted began with Hegel in the 19th century and was developed by George Herbert Mead and others in the 20th, holds that for selfhood to develop, each person must participate with others in wider and wider sets of groups. American management has been finding that when workers participate with others in higher levels of authority, they often increase not only their own personal resources but also the effectiveness of the firm through their understanding of the larger organizational system of which they are a part.

19. For an elaboration on corporatism, see Phillipe C. Schmitter, "Democratic Theory and Neocorporatist Practice," *Social Research* 50.4 (Winter 1983): 885–928.

20. Carmen Sirianni, ed., *Worker Participation and the Politics of Reform* (Philadelphia: Temple University Press, 1987), p. 23. Worker participation programs developed in the 1970's by General Motors, Ford, and Chrysler, in cooperation with the United Auto Workers, were found to add significantly to productivity and profitability, and expanded rapidly to other corporations in the 1980's. These programs, which came to be called quality of work life (QWL), quality circles, labor management participation teams, and employee involvement plans, have now become the rule in big companies like the Fortune 500.

21. For a detailed discussion of the data suggesting the continuation of

both trends, see Corey Rosen, Katherine Kline, and Karen Young, *Employee Ownership in America* (Lexington, Mass.: Heath, 1986). I discuss the way these U.S. corporations have developed worker participation and ownership through the assistance of the government, unions, and communities in Severyn T. Bruyn and Litsa Nicolaou-Smokovitis, *The International Social Economy* (New York: Praeger, 1989), chap. 3.

22. Michael Quarry, Joseph Blasi, and Corey Rosen, *Taking Stock* (Cambridge, Mass.: Ballinger, 1986), pp. viii, 1.

23. *People and Productivity: A Challenge to Corporate America* (New York: Office of Economic Research, New York Stock Exchange, 1982), p. 44. The report concluded that one in seven companies with more than 100 employees had some kind of human resource program, involving 13 million workers overall. There are also several thousand labor-management committees operating today. See Vernon G. Talbott, "A Brief History of Labor-Management Committees," *Workplace Democracy* 56 (Spring 1987):7.

24. The fully self-managed company is owned by its workers, who vote on a per-person rather than a per-share basis and are represented at significant levels of management, including the board of directors. Probably only about 1,000 such firms exist in the United States, but many thousands appear to be heading in that direction. Christopher Gunn discusses ten requisites defining a fully self-managed company in *Workers' Self-Management in the United States* (Ithaca, N.Y.: Cornell University Press, 1984), p. 35.

25. William Foote Whyte, "New Approaches to Industrial Development and Community Development," in Warner Woodworth, Christopher Meek, and William Foote Whyte, eds., *Industrial Democracy: Strategies for Community Revitalization* (London: Sage, 1985), pp. 20 ff.

26. Cited in Barry Bluestone and Bennett Harrison, *The Deindustrialization of America* (New York: Basic Books, 1982).

27. Christopher Meek and Warner Woodworth, "Worker-Community Collaboration and Ownership," in Woodworth et al., eds., *Industrial Democracy*.

28. Don Stillman, "The Devastating Impact of Plant Relocations," in Mark Green, ed., *The Big Business Reader* (New York: Pilgrim Press, 1983), p. 140.

29. Floyd Agostinelli, *Community Development Credit Unions* (Washington, D.C., 1977). See also Graham Rice, "Difficulties in Keeping Financial Capital in the Community," in Richard Schramm, ed., *Financing Community Economic Development* (Ithaca, N.Y.: Program in Urban and Regional Studies, Cornell University, 1981).

30. The matter of local communities maintaining a balance of inside-outside control is discussed in Severyn T. Bruyn and James Meehan, *Beyond the Market and the State: Innovations in Community Development* (Philadelphia: Temple University Press, 1987).

31. Many of these experiments are described and summarized by John Simmons and William Mares, *Working Together* (New York: Knopf, 1983).

32. Samuel Bowles, David Gordon, and Thomas Weiskopf, *Beyond the Wasteland* (New York: Anchor Press, 1984).

33. Robert Reich, "The Next American Frontier," *Atlantic Monthly*, March 1983:43. Robert Cole estimates that one out of eight workers in Japan is participating in quality circles and finds that this makes a difference in productivity. Robert Cole, *Work Mobility and Participation* (Berkeley: University of California Press, 1979). Ezra Vogel points out how feather-bedding and labor's inflexible insistence on work rules contrast with Japanese styles of participatory management. He says that low productivity in the United States is due partly to workers' fear of losing their jobs, in contrast to Japanese workers, who eagerly seek technological change because they have a guarantee of permanent employment and a high level of participation in corporate governance. Ezra Vogel, *Japan as Number One* (New York: Harper & Row, 1979), p. 151.

34. Michael Conte and Arnold Tannenbaum, *Employee Ownership* (Ann Arbor: University of Michigan Survey Research Center, 1980), p. 3.

35. Thomas Marsh and Dale McAllister, "ESOPs Tables," *Journal of Corporation Law*, 6 (Spring 1981):612–16.

36. Many of these studies are reported in Rosen, Klein, and Young, *Employee Ownership*, p. 48.

37. Simmons and Mares, *Working Together*, p. 65.

38. Studies of Japanese firms have demonstrated the advantages of developing a more cohesive and participatory work force. An early argument was made by William Ouchi, *Theory Z: How American Business Can Meet the Japanese Challenge* (Reading, Mass.: Addison-Wesley, 1981).

39. Mike Parker, *Inside the Circle* (Boston: South End Press, 1986). On workers' views of such attempts as an insidious management ploy to gain stronger control over labor, see Richard Edwards, *Contested Terrain* (New York: Basic Books, 1979); and Harry Braverman, *Labor and Monopoly Capital* (New York: Monthly Review Press, 1974).

40. Raymond Russell, *Sharing Ownership in the Workplace* (Albany: State University of New York Press, 1985), chap. 4.

41. Ibid.; Melinda Schlesinger and Pauline Bart, "Collective Work and Self-Identity," in Frank Lindenfeld and Joyce Rothschild-Whitt, eds., *Workplace Democracy and Social Change* (Boston: Porter Sargent, 1982), p. 153.

42. Corey Rosen, personal communications, 1985–89.

43. Personal interviews with members of the personnel department and employees at John Lewis Partnership.

44. Carole Pateman, *Participation and Democratic Theory* (Cambridge: Cambridge University Press, 1970), p. 105.

45. Edward S. Greenberg, "Producer Cooperatives and Democratic

Theory: The Case of the Plywood Firms," in Robert Jackall and Henry Levin, eds., *Worker Cooperatives in America* (Berkeley: University of California Press, 1984).

46. In the United States, an average of 1,247 working days per 1,000 employees lost to strikes in the period 1964–73; the British and French figures were 633 and 277. In countries where labor shared authority at the top, the time lost was negligible—an average of just 43 hours in Sweden and West Germany. See, for example, L. Foresebäck, *Industrial Relations and Employment in Sweden* (Stockholm: Swedish Institute, 1976), p. 67.

47. For comparative studies on the effects of labor participation in higher management, see Charles King and Mark van de Vall, *Models of Industrial Democracy* (New York: Mouton, 1978); and David Jenkins, *Industrial Democracy in Europe* (Geneva: Business International, 1974). As self-managed companies develop, unions continue to play an important role in defending the rights of workers by assisting them in obtaining proper pension funds and low-interest loans, by consulting with members on personnel problems, and so on. The assumption of these studies is that the overall economic costs of the adversarial system are thereby significantly reduced.

48. Josip Obradovic and William Dunn describe the political nature of the first strike in Yugoslavia, by miners in 1958, over the issue of low personal income, a problem caused not by management but by their position in the system of distribution. The relatively high costs of production and the relatively low prices of coal were at fault, and the miners protested to the government, which set the prices. Because they received no response from any of the political bodies—the League of Communists, the trade union, the state organs at the commune and district levels, the republic of Slovenia, or the federation—a strike became the only effective means for realizing their demands. Their protests were complicated by the fact that the media announced nothing about the strike because such reports were discouraged at the time. The character of strikes in socialist states can thus have a larger political significance than strikes in capitalist nations based on labor-management disputes. Obradovic and Dunn, *Workers' Self-Management and Organizational Power in Yugoslavia* (Pittsburgh: University of Pittsburgh Press, 1978).

49. These observations on the causes of recent strikes in Yugoslavia are based on papers presented at a conference on worker self-management ("Social Stratification: Comparative Perspectives"), Interuniversity Center, Dubrovnik, April 1986.

50. William Foote Whyte and Kathleen King Whyte, *Making Mondragon* (Ithaca, N.Y.: ILR Press, 1988).

51. Severyn T. Bruyn, *The Field of Social Investment* (Cambridge: Cambridge University Press, 1989), pp. 51 ff.

52. Russell, *Sharing Ownership;* Bowles et al., *Beyond the Wasteland.*

53. Gunn, *Workers' Self-Management,* p. 111.

54. Edward S. Greenberg, "Industrial Self-Management and Political Attitudes," *American Political Science Review,* 75 (March 1981).

55. Simmons and Mares, *Working Together,* p. 232.

56. Lyman D. Ketchum, "A Case Study of Diffusion," in Albert Cherns et al., eds., *The Quality of Working Life* (New York: Free Press, 1975), vol. 2.

57. Greenberg, "Producer Cooperatives," p. 184. See also Katrina Berman, *Worker-Owner Plywood Companies: An Economic Analysis* (Pullman: Washington State University Press, 1967); Paul Bernstein, *Workplace Democratization* (Kent, Ohio: Kent State University Press, 1976).

58. Joyce Rothschild-Whitt, "The Collectivist Organization: An Alternative to Bureaucratic Models," *American Sociological Review* 44 (Aug. 1979): 509–27.

59. Will Conrad, Kathleen Wilson, and Dale Wilson, *The Milwaukee Journal* (Madison: University of Wisconsin Press, 1964). See also "Partners in Ownership," updated periodically by the Journal Company.

60. My visit to West Germany provided an opportunity to observe large-scale businesses in which labor has 50 percent board representation and worker councils at the level of middle management, as well as inter-plant councils, government-labor-management tribunals, and ombudsmen. I also witnessed this same organization in U.S. subsidiaries in that country, such as Xerox and G.M.'s Opel plant. There were problems in these structures, but the visit suggested to me that U.S. firms can adjust to major changes in administration and still remain highly productive, as is the case for the West German affiliates. Employees in smaller self-managed companies, such as Scott-Bader in Wallaston, England, told me of the tendency for the work force to number around 500. But the expansion of a firm is not ruled out under a decentralized system of management. See David Mead-Fox, "Worker Self-Management in Ireland," Ph.D. dissertation, Department of Sociology, Boston College, 1990.

61. Lindenfeld and Rothschild-Whitt, *Workplace Democracy.* See also Jane Mansbridge, "Town Meeting Democracy," *Working Papers for a New Society,* 1 (May 15, 1973).

62. "Employee Ownership," *Business Week,* May 15, 1989:116. See also "The Payoff from Teamwork," ibid., July 10, 1989:56.

63. Louis Putterman, "Some Behavioral Perspectives on the Dominance of Hierarchical Over Democratic Forms of Enterprise," *Journal of Economic Behavior and Organization,* 1982.3:140. See also "On Some Recent Explanations of Why Capital Hires Labor," *Economic Inquiry,* 22 (1984):171–87. Such definitions seem to me overfocused on the firm itself, in isolation from the rest of the system, as though firm members alone could have "ultimate discretion over all matters," like "what products to produce in

which quantities." Such an approach fails to recognize the power of the larger external market to influence these decisions. I deal with this faulty perception in Part III.

64. The technical arguments on these issues can be found in Daniel Egan, "Organizational Degeneration in Self-Managed Firms: A Theoretical Survey," Working Paper, Program in Social Economy and Social Justice, Department of Sociology, Boston College, May 1989.

65. Avner Ben-Ner, "On the Stability of the Cooperative Type of Organization," *Journal of Comparative Economics*, 8:247–60; Hajime Miyazaki, "On Success and Dissolution of the Labor-Managed Firm in the Capitalist Economy," *Journal of Political Economy*, 92.5:909–31. Both references are cited by Daniel Egan, who finds these economic models inadequate because they (1) fail to take account of noneconomic factors, (2) fail to be supported by empirical tests, and (3) do not reflect the literature on labor-managed firms that reject taking on hired labor. Egan, "Organizational Degenerations," p. 15. See also the analysis by Raymond Russell, "The Role of Culture and Ethnicity in the Degeneration of Democratic Firms," *Economic and Industrial Democracy*, 5:73–96.

66. For studies of the Mondragon model, see Robert Oakeshott, *The Case for Workers' Coops* (Boston: Routledge & Kegan Paul, 1978); Thomas Henk and Chris Logan, *Mondragon: An Economic Analysis* (Boston: Allen & Unwin, 1982); and Chris Clamp, "The Mondragon Experiment," Ph.D. dissertation, Program in Social Economy and Social Justice, Boston College, 1985.

67. Erik Furubotn and Svetozar Pejovich, "Property Rights and the Behavior of the Firm in a Socialist State: The Example of Yugoslavia," in Furubotn and Pejovich, eds., *The Economics of Property Rights* (Cambridge, Eng.: Ballinger, 1974).

68. Jaroslav Vanek, "The Basic Theory of Financing of Participatory Firms," in Vanek, ed., *Self-Management* (Baltimore: Penguin Books, 1975). The structure for combining basic and user owners in the same firm was devised and implemented by a number of consulting agencies, including the Industrial Cooperative Association (Somerville, Mass.) For a technical discussion of this structure, see David Ellerman, "Horizon Problems and Property Rights in Labor Managed Firms," *Journal of Comparative Economics*, 10:62–78. Note that state laws in Connecticut, Maine, Massachusetts, New York, and Vermont have been altered to create a better legal structure for producer cooperatives.

69. Oliver E. Williamson, "The Organization of Work: A Comparative Institutional Assessment," *Journal of Economic Behavior and Organization*, 1980.1:5–38.

70. The empirical research on the issues of income equity, internal structure, middle-management resistance, union resistance, organiza-

tional development, and community relations in self-managed firms is discussed in Bruyn, *Field of Social Investment*, pp. 82 ff. See also Robert Jackall and Henry M. Levin, eds., *Worker Cooperatives in America* (Berkeley: University of California Press, 1984).

Chapter 4

1. For Marx, when people buy something, like labor or machines, that "thing" becomes their capital, that is, a "commodification" of labor. When business has products waiting for market, that inventory is its capital; when it sells its products, its profit is its capital. These phases from production to distribution represent the "metamorphosis" of capital, that is, stages in the development of capital. But capital itself is none of these things. Capital is a social process that Marx described in three formulas: This process begins in early societies where commodities (C) are bartered against one another, which he describes as $C-C$. In a more advanced stage of society, money (M) begins to facilitate a much greater number of transactions in the market. The formula then becomes $C-M-C$. Now money has become the medium of exchange. People make commodities and exchange them for money, which in turn permits them to purchase another commodity. The commodities still have some use value in the exchange system. Finally, through the growth of the capitalist society, there is a new equation, $M-C-M$. At this point, capitalism has emerged as a system, because the exchange for money is the focus; it is at the beginning and the end of the equation. People with money and a desire for profit invest in the production of a given commodity because it will give them the highest yield. The "use value" of a commodity is no longer the primary interest of producers, because commodities are looked on primarily for their exchange value in the market. The focus is on the money (profit, rent, interest), without much thought of the product's social use or its impact on people. Money begets money. Monetary value generates additional monetary value.

2. The neoclassical economist assumes that people in all stations of life will economize: one more unit of capital will be invested only if the profit it will help to produce is going to be greater than the cost; one more acre of land will be cultivated only if its yield is going to be more than its rent; new laborers will be hired only if the value of their output will exceed their wages; consumers will buy one more unit of a good if it adds one more unit of utility (satisfaction) for them. The market will thus accurately fix the costs that have to be paid to meet the patterns of demand set by the consumer market. According to this theory, the distribution of income is determined by these predictable market operations: interest (or profit) represents the reward to be paid to the marginal efficiency of capital; wages represent the marginal efficiency of labor; and rent represents the marginal

efficiency of land. The whole theory is based on the assumption that people are motivated by money, forgetting that there are other motives in the marketplace.

3. Joan Robinson, "Capital Theory Up to Date," in E. K. Hunt and Jesse Schwartz, eds., *A Critique of Economic Theory* (New York: Penguin Books, 1972), p. 233.

4. Alfred Marshall was prescient on this matter when he said that "capital consists in a great part of knowledge and organization." Marshall, *Principles of Economics* (New York: Macmillan, 1961), p. 138.

5. Capital is often identified with physical property, but it is also defined as the means for producing wealth, which is seen as the higher resources of a society. In a broad sense, *capital is anything that can be used effectively to achieve wealth as an end.* Wealth, the end value for which capital is used, though often identified with capital, is changing its meaning today. A nation's wealth is coming to mean not only property, but the whole way of life of society—its culture, which is to say, its wealth—lies in both the society's material and its human resources. Thus, while Marx saw capital as money used destructively to maintain the dominance of an elite class and the exploitation of labor—that is, money used by the rich for the pursuit of more money to maintain the class system—capital is far more complex than that, owing to its potential for accomplishing higher purposes.

6. In one dictionary definition, "capital" refers to a "stock of accumulated wealth," such as the amount of property owned by an individual or corporation at a specified time (as distinct from the income received during a given period) or an aggregation of economic goods used to promote the production of other goods (instead of being valuable solely for immediate enjoyment). Although wealth includes both property with money value and all objects of economic utility, it is also seen as those "energies, faculties, and habits, directly contributing to make people industrially efficient" and "an abundance of things desired." *Webster's Collegiate Dictionary,* 5th ed. (Springfield, Mass.: Merriam, 1937).

7. Mark Clayton, "How Quarterly Treadmill Keeps Mills of America Muddling," *Christian Science Monitor,* Aug. 17, 1987: 16.

8. Robert Reich, *The Next American Frontier* (New York: Times Books, 1983), p. 147.

9. Linda Sandler, "Mania to Buy Back Stock Is Going Too Far," *Wall Street Journal,* Sept. 18, 1987.

10. S. M. Miller and Donald Tomaskovic-Devey, *Recapitalizing America* (Boston: Routledge & Kegan Paul, 1983).

11. Edward Prescott and Michael Visscher, "Organizational Capital," *Journal of Political Economy,* 88 (June 1980): 446–61. The authors describe "organizational capital" as (1) information on employees' suitability for particular tasks and information on employees' ability to work as teams, and (2) firm-specific human capital vested in individual employees.

12. John Tomer, "Organizational Change, Organization Capital and Economic Growth," *Eastern Economic Journal*, 7 (Jan. 1981). See also John Tomer, "Management Consulting for Private Enterprise," Ph.D. dissertation, Rutgers University, 1973.

13. Alfred Chandler, *Strategy and Structure* (New York: Doubleday, 1966).

14. Peter Drucker, *Management* (New York: Harper & Row, 1973), p. 574.

15. Subsequent sections discuss whether a very large but decentralized (federalized) corporation may be more bureaucratic or less bureaucratic and thus more self-managing. This aspect of the decentralizing trend is another mode of change that may or may not become more effective, depending on the way it is done; that is, the effectiveness of particular steps toward de-bureaucratization depends on the social process. See also the analysis in Severyn T. Bruyn, *The Field of Social Investment* (New York: Cambridge University Press, 1977), pp. 170–71.

16. Scott Buchanan, *The Corporation and the Republic* (Santa Barbara, Calif.: Center for the Study of Democratic Institutions, 1958).

17. These figures were reported in *New Options*, 48 (May 30, 1988): 7–8. See also Corey Rosen, Katherine Klein, and Karen Young, *Employee Ownership in America* (Lexington, Mass.: Heath, 1986).

18. Ralph Landau, "U.S. Economic Growth," *Scientific American*, June 1988. Landau draws part of his argument from Robert Solow, the Nobel Prize–winning economist, who describes economic growth as the sum of the inputs of capital and labor, each weighted by a coefficient reflecting its average contribution to the value of products. It is also measured by a third variable representing increases in "factor productivity," that is, the combined productivity of capital and labor. Most economists recognize that the third variable includes such elements as more efficient resource allocation and economies of scale, as well as many social, educational, and organizational factors that serve to improve the quality of labor and management. Solow and others estimate that as much as 85 percent of U.S. economic growth per capita is attributable to increases in productivity or technological change.

19. Landau argues that the rate of U.S. savings has been dismal compared with that of other nations, which is part of the reason for our lack of capital sources for investment in technology. According to the 1987 Economic Report of the President, at least 50 percent of net investment in the United States came from abroad, mostly because U.S. companies have not been able to count on domestic savings for investment capital. Indeed, the situation is so bad that economists today recognize that the cost of servicing foreign debt is becoming a heavy drag on economic growth. As long as the U.S. savings rate remains unable to cover productive investment in the country, the pool of available investment capital will have to be supple-

mented from abroad. In sum, the United States has been consuming too much and producing too little. Government policies that stimulate domestic savings, therefore, go hand in hand with investment in new technology. Some alternatives to this problem are discussed in Chap. 11.

20. Walter Adams and James Brock, *The Bigness Complex: Industry, Labor and Government in the American Economy* (New York: Pantheon Books, 1986), p. 52.

21. Horizontal collaborations in R&D among business rivals are different from research cooperatives in such regulated industries as the Electric Power Research Institute, the Gas Research Institute, and Bell Communications Research Corporation, which pool industry resources to conduct research.

22. William Ouchi and Michele Bolton, "The Logic of Joint Research and Development," *California Management Review*, 30 (Spring 1988).

23. Richard Clarke, "Collusion and the Incentives for Information Sharing," *Bell Journal of Economics*, 1984:383–94.

24. Russell Johnston and Paul Lawrence, "Beyond Vertical Integration—The Rise of the Value-Adding Partnership," *Harvard Business Review*, July–Aug. 1988:94–101.

25. Ibid., p. 95.

26. Michael Piore and Charles Sabel, *The Second Industrial Divide* (New York: Basic Books, 1984).

27. Johnston and Lawrence, "Beyond Vertical Integration," p. 100.

28. I trace the dilemmas in this paradox in Bruyn, *The Social Economy* (New York: Wiley, 1966), pp. 226–29.

29. Simon Kuznets advances a broad concept of capital that runs close to my argument of corporate development. He says that organizational behavior in the large-scale, limited-liability firm is very different from the older personal type of firm. It requires *a capacity to cooperate* that would not have been expected of people accustomed to an entirely different form of economic relations. Simon Kuznets, *Economic Growth and Structure: Selected Essays* (New York: Norton, 1965), p. 100.

30. Louis Lowenstein, *What's Wrong with Wall Street* (Reading, Mass: Addison-Wesley, 1988).

31. *Business Week*, April 18, 1988:58, citing the findings of Data Resources, Inc., University of Michigan, based on a Federal Reserve Board Survey for 1983.

32. Another solution to this situation is for employees to own the corporations in which they work. Aware of the destructive effects of their actions, they would be less likely to do anything to harm corporate performance.

33. *Labor and Investments* (Industrial Union Department, AFL-CIO:1981), vol. 1.

34. "Council Heading for the Crossroads," *Pensions and Investment Age*, July 8, 1985.

35. Peter Drucker, *The Unseen Revolution: How Pension Fund Socialism Came to America* (New York: Harper & Row, 1976), p. 91.

36. I note in Part III that firms may become increasingly linked to broad policies of trade associations that express societal standards. If this happened to a sufficient extent, self-managed firms would then need *less outside guidance* from social investors who press these public issues on corporate management today. In this development, there is a broader role for trade associations in setting standards on behalf of the larger society, through balanced systems of competitive power in value-added chains. As these associations assume new roles in helping member firms train and structure management (the alleged function of outside takeovers today), they could also lead to firms' greater productivity.

37. *The Social Investment Forum* (Boston, Mass.), Oct. 1, 1989:1. Italics in original.

38. Amy Domini and Peter Kinder, *Ethical Investing* (Reading, Mass.: Addison-Wesley, 1984), pp. xii–xxiii.

39. Joseph M. Queenan, "Rewards of Virtue: Do-Good Portfolios Do Better," *Barron's*, Nov. 30, 1987:68.

40. Some observers criticize the practice of social investment on the grounds that adding social principles as a criterion for buying stock narrows the range of choice and therefore lessens the opportunity for economic returns. Other observers suggest that the reason social investors do as well as they do is because the range of corporate stock available for selection in the United States is so broad that successful investment is possible regardless of which stocks are chosen.

41. Michael Leibig, "Social Investments and the Law," *Studies in Pension Fund Investments* (Conference on Alternative State and Local Policies), Aug. 3, 1980.

Chapter 5

1. But the concept of a social sector can have more than an analytical reference. It can also have a normative reference in the sense that it posits guidelines through which the private sector can become more accountable both to corporate constituencies and to the public at large. This normative dimension is treated in Severyn T. Bruyn and Litsa Nicolau-Smokovitis, *The International Issues in Social Economy* (New York: Praeger, 1989).

2. Daniel Bell, whose book *The Coming of Post-Industrial Society* (New York: Basic Books, 1973) generated an entire literature, asserted that "if an industrial society is defined as a goods-producing society—if manufacture is central in shaping the character of its labor force—then the United States is no longer an industrial society." He described the transition of economic sectors from primary to secondary to tertiary; of technologies from raw materials to energy to information; of methodology from common sense to

empiricism to abstract theory; of axial principles from traditionalism to economic growth to the centrality of knowledge.

3. David Rados, *Marketing for Non-Profit Organizations* (Dover, Mass.: Auburn House, 1981), pp. 3–4. Rados points to the bewildering variety of nonprofits, including the Council on Abandoned Military Posts, the American Concrete Institute, the National Association of Music Executives in State Universities, the Association of Gay Psychologists, the I Have Lived Before Club, the Antique Outboard Motor Club, the National Association of Membership Directors of Chambers of Commerce, the Ancient Mystic Order of Bagmen of Bagdad Imperial Guild, and the American Medical Association. Some nonprofit corporations are part of what we normally think of as the profit sector: the New York Stock Exchange and the Metropolitan Life Insurance Company. Associated Press is nonprofit, as are some 23,000 U.S. credit unions, 6,000 museums, 700 opera companies, and 1,400 symphony orchestras. In 1970, there were 6,000 nonprofit hospitals, as opposed to 900 profit ones.

4. Howard Oleck, "Nature of American Non-Profit Organizations," *New York Law Forum*, 17 (Spring 1972): 1066, quoted in Rados, *Marketing for Non-Profit Organizations*, p. 5.

5. Eli Ginzberg, Dale Hiestand, and Beatrice Reubens, *The Pluralistic Economy* (1965), quoted in Bell, *Coming of Post-Industrial Society*, p. 147.

6. Virginia Hodgkinson and Murray S. Weitzman, *Dimensions of the Independent Sector* (Washington, D.C.: Independent Sector, 1984), p. 1. Other figures of note: government, an independent part of the nonprofit sector, employed 18.2 percent of the labor force and accounted for 15.2 percent of the national income in 1974, and 17.6 percent of the labor force and 14.0 percent of the national income, in 1980.

7. There are substantial advantages to organizing a corporation. First, ownership can be transferred freely among parties. Second, individual owners are not responsible for the corporation's debts and liabilities, and the corporation is not responsible for claims against its owners. Third, the corporation can enter into contracts, sue and be sued, and buy, hold, and sell property. Fourth, the corporation has a perpetual existence, continuing beyond the withdrawal of its owners. Because of these advantages, the corporate form remains the dominant choice for people wanting to organize for social objectives.

8. Severyn T. Bruyn, *The Field of Social Investment* (Cambridge: Cambridge University Press, 1987).

9. *Wall Street Journal*, Aug. 25, 1976:1, reported in Rados, *Marketing for Non-Profit Organizations*, pp. 8–9.

10. *New York Times*, Jan. 18, 1969:1, quoted in ibid., p. 9.

11. C. Cacace, *Employment and Occupations in Europe in the 1980s* (Strasbourg: Council for Cultural Co-operation, quoted in J. I. Gershuny and I. D. Miles, *The New Service Economy* (New York: Praeger, 1983), p. 15.

12. G. B. Thomas, "Manpower Problems in the Service Sector," *Manpower Problems in the Service Sector* (Paris: OECD International Seminars, 1966).

13. Victor R. Fuchs, *The Service Economy* (New York: National Bureau of Economic Research, 1968).

14. T. P. Hill, "On Goods and Services," *Review of Income and Wealth*, 23 (1977): 315–38. See also A. Gartner and F. Reisman, *The Service Society and the Consumer Vanguard* (New York: Harper & Row, 1974).

15. Gershuny and Miles, *New Service Economy*, p. 24. There are, of course, inbetween services, such as television repair, that do not involve an end activity directly with the consumer or provide a service directly for the producer.

16. G. J. Stigler, *Trends in Employment in the Service Industries* (Baltimore, Md.: Johns Hopkins University Press, 1956), p. 138.

17. H. I. Greenfield, *Manpower and the Growth of Producer Services* (New York: Columbia University Press, 1966), p. 10.

18. Ernest Mandel, *Late Capitalism* (London: New Left Books, 1975); Gershuny and Miles, *New Service Economy*. See also James O'Connor, "Productive and Unproductive Labor," *Politics and Society*, 5.3:297–356.

19. C. Browning and J. Singelmann, *The Emergence of a Service Society* (Springfield, Va.: National Technical Information Service, 1975).

20. J. Singelmann, *From Agriculture to Services* (Beverly Hills, Calif.: Sage, 1978). See also P. T. Bauer and B. S. Yamey, "Economic Progress and Occupational Distribution," *Economic Journal*, 61 (Dec. 1951).

21. For Riddle, "services are neither of lesser size or importance than the other sectors, nor do they have a parasitical dependence on manufacturing activity. Rather, services are industries that play a vital and dynamic role in any functioning economy, and that stimulate growth in other sectors." Dorothy Riddle, *Service-Led Growth* (New York: Praeger, 1986), p. 7.

22. Ibid., p. 2.

23. E. Sasser, "Match Supply and Demand in Service Industries," *Harvard Business Review*, 56.2:133–48.

24. J. Galbraith, *Designing Complex Organizations* (Reading, Mass.: Addison-Wesley, 1973).

25. Peter Mills, *Managing Service Industries* (Cambridge, Mass.: Ballinger, 1986), pp. 8–9.

26. Nevertheless, many writers argue that the tendency toward decentralization is generally true for service companies. For example, Christian Gronroos argues that the internal structure of service firms is necessarily different from that of industrial firms. "Organizational structures which have been successfully applied in the industrial sector seem to be a potential danger to growing service firms. Various activities are more interrelated in a service firm than in a company producing consumer goods." And a "customer"-oriented company requires more interdependent organizational innovations. Moreover, Gronroos sees special strengths in the

smallness of service companies: "decisions are made near the market [and] made quickly [with] better knowledge of the desires of the customers, . . . good interactive marketing performance is easier to achieve, . . . internal marketing is easier, [and] quality control . . . is easier to handle." Gronroos, "Innovative Marketing Strategies and Organizational Structures for Service Firms," in L. Berry, G. Shostack, and G. Upah, *Emerging Perspectives on Services Marketing* (Chicago, Ill.: American Marketing Association, 1983), pp. 19–20.

27. James L. Heskett, *Managing in the Service Economy* (Boston: Harvard Business School Press, 1986), pp. 147–52.

28. Put concretely, the church has a manifest social orientation when it receives sacrificial gifts from its members as a measure of religious commitment, but its latent side exists in the fact that most members receive their salaries from the profit sector, and the church, in turn, invests heavily in corporate stock in the profit sector. While the church cultivates values that transcend the economic ones of the market, it is rooted in the same market system.

29. Although the market may be seen as existing in every exchange in which people see that the value of traded objects can be translated into money, analysts have always observed social factors present in every transaction as well. It is simply not observed by the controlling public image. At the same time, most people would probably recognize that not all human values can be translated into economics. The highest act of love or expression of human courage transcends the capability of monetary exchange.

Chapter 6

1. Although the root concept of "social" embraces the political realm, including the concept of power as a key dimension of the economy, it is broader than that. This point is important to note because some economists who dissent from the mainstream substitute a purely political analysis for an economic analysis, assuming that power and politics are the only reality, and miss the larger sociological character of the economy. Since such a political analysis focuses on the interplay between the government and the economy, these writers recommend giving the greater power to government because it is democratic and representative of the people. For a clearly written dissent from mainstream economics illustrating this approach, see Robert Kuttner, *The Economic Illusion: False Choices Between Prosperity and Social Justice* (Boston: Houghton Mifflin, 1984).

2. Although trade associations may display more of the individualistic ethic than the medieval guilds did they also represent a larger sense of the "we" needed in the development of economic life and discussed as a concept by Amitai Etzioni, *The Moral Dimension: Toward a New Economics* (New York: Free Press, 1988), pp. 6–9. This "we-ness," or sense of community,

so essential to the success of a trade association is discussed in the next chapter, but it can be seen as a problem throughout our case studies, a problem of balancing the values of the individual and the community.

3. Katherine Gruber, ed., *Encyclopedia of Associations* (Gale Research Corp.: Detroit, 1990). There were 3,806 associations in 1988, 3,861 in 1987. The slight drop in number appears to be due to mergers between associations.

4. This section draws on Peter Farago, "Regulating Milk Markets: Corporatist Arrangements in the Swiss Dairy Industry," in Wolfgang Streeck and Philippe C. Schmitter, eds., *Private Interest Government* (Beverly Hills: Sage, 1985), pp. 168–81.

5. This section draws on Frans van Waarden, "Varieties of Collective Self-Regulation of Business: The Example of the Dutch Dairy Industry," in ibid., pp. 197–220.

6. This study is reported in T. Lynn Smith, *The Sociology of Rural Life* (New York: Harper, 1947), pp. 491–92.

7. Harold Lough, *The Cheese Industry*, U.S. Department of Agriculture, Agricultural Economic Report no. 294 (Washington, D.C., July 1975).

8. Ibid., p. 19. Also noteworthy are the changes in the concept of property ownership with the introduction of technology. Local milk routes were once the transferable property of individual haulers, but the transition to bulk pickup has seen a movement toward the manufacturing firm's ownership of routes.

9. Alden Manchester, *The Public Role in the Dairy Economy* (Boulder, Colo.: Westview, 1983), p. 85. If one looks closely at the buyer-seller relationships, it becomes clear that the *organization of the parties* involved makes a difference in terms of market behavior. Manchester notes how each dairy farmer has a sole customer, who must take his total output, loaded out at a prearranged time of day, at a mutually agreeable price. The processor, on the other hand, has many customers, who make a variety of products that sell at different prices, with each item fabricated daily from the uncertain volume of raw milk purchased from a fixed set of dairy farmers, who are paid monthly an average price based on the mix of final products sold. These are basic organizational differences that affect power and market price.

10. Rowland Bartlett, "Bring Federal Order Class I Pricing Up to Date and in Line with Antitrust Regulations," *Illinois Agricultural Economics*, 14 (Jan. 1974): 2.

11. Ronald Knutson, "Cooperative Bargaining Developments in the Dairy Industry, 1960–70," *Farmer Cooperative Research Report*, 19 (Washington, D.C.: Government Printing Office, 1971).

12. Tanya Roberts, *Review of Recent Studies* (Washington, D.C.: Public Interest Economic Center, 1975), pp. 25–32; David Front, "Farmer Size and Regional Distribution of the Benefit Under Federal Milk Market Regu-

lation," Bureau of Economics Staff Report to the Federal Trade Commission, 21 (May 1978), reported in Michael McMenamin and Walter McNamara, *Milking the Public* (Chicago: Nelson Hall, 1980), p. 33.

13. This section draws on Bert de Vroon, "Quality Regulation in the Dutch Pharmaceutical Industry: Conditions for Private Regulation by Business Association," in Streeck and Schmitter, *Private Interest Government*, pp. 128–67.

14. PHC was registered with the Dutch government and the European Economic Council in Brussels and operated until 1977.

15. G. Beudeker, "Het Beshuit Verpakte Geneesmiddelen," *Pharmaceutisch Weekblad*, 98:814, quoted in de Vroom, "Quality Regulation," p. 134.

16. This section draws on Jane A. Sargent, "The Politics of the Pharmaceutical Price Regulation Scheme," in Streeck and Schmitter, *Private Interest Government*, pp. 105–27.

17. In 1958, ABPI published its Code of Advertising Practice and made compliance with it a condition of membership. The code was not regarded as a restrictive practice; the industry was ready to accept self-regulation in the interest of the safety of medicines, but not in regard to membership prices and profitability. Nevertheless, during negotiations, ABPI conducted a review of its constitution and rules, and agreed to changes that became effective in April 1961.

18. Pharmaceutical Manufacturers Association, *Annual Survey Report: 1975–1976* (Washington, D.C.: PMA, 1976), p. 10.

19. U.S. Senate Judiciary Committee, *Administered Prices: Drugs* (Washington, D.C.: Government Printing Office, 1961).

20. Jerome Schnee and Erol Caglarcan, "Economic Structure and Performance of the Ethical Pharmaceutical Industry," in Cotton M. Lindsay, ed., *The Pharmaceutical Industry* (New York: Wiley, 1978), p. 33.

21. Raymond Bauer and Mark Field, "Ironic Contrast: U.S. and U.S.S.R. Drug Industries," *Harvard Business Review*, Sept.–Oct. 1962: 94.

22. "Physician Ownership of Pharmacies," *Journal of the American Pharmaceutical Association*, n.s. 5 (May 1965): 276.

23. There are other trade associations important to the industry that are not so relevant to the issues we are discussing. For example, the Pharmaceutical Manufacturers Association is a nonprofit scientific, professional, and trade organization whose stated policy is to focus on scientific and professional improvement and avoid distributive conflicts.

Chapter 7

1. Daniel Bell, *The Coming of Post-Industrial Society* (New York: Basic Books, 1973), p. 481.

2. The market share of an acquired firm at this writing (1989) cannot ex-

ceed 5 percent. U.S. Department of Justice, *Merger Guidelines*, III (A), *Fed. Reg.* 28,493,28,497 (1982), reprinted in *California Law Review*, 71 (1983): 649, 655–57.

3. Douglas Greer, *Industrial Organization and Public Policy* (New York: Macmillan, 1980), pp. 18–19.

4. The economic success of Japan is a special case in certain respects, notably in the demilitarization that allowed it to pour its resources into economic development, while other nations poured theirs into national defense; and Japan's decision to exploit the large, money-rich U.S. consumer base. But Japan's economic expansion is increasingly criticized and feared by other nations. Although the expansion's destructive tendencies are softened by the focus on business markets, Japan's economic imperialism is nevertheless the natural outcome of any nation-state seeking to expand without international institutions to constrain its movement and govern the global market. Therefore, any concern about Japan's expansion should be a concern extended to *all* nation-states. This problem can be resolved by strengthening the United Nations and other international institutions, as discussed in the Appendix.

5. Ezra Vogel, *Japan as Number One* (New York: Harper & Row, 1979).

6. Vogel notes that Japanese business leaders are surprised at the narrow interests of American businessmen, who focus only on their own companies and are badly prepared to consider the economy from a broader perspective. On the other hand, senior U.S. business executives have been impressed with the statesmanlike leadership of their Japanese counterparts. Many Japanese executives not only have had a broad training in European history and literature, Chinese classics, Marxism, and modern economics, but also have a bold philosophic vision for the future. Ibid., p. 117.

7. Ibid., p. 110.

8. In popular belief, prices are regulated "spontaneously" by firms competing horizontally along similar product lines as each firm independently seeks to match or beat competitors. This mode of autonomous pricing is not observable in our cases, but that is not because it does not exist; I simply did not focus on this aspect of the competitive process.

9. Empirical studies of all aspects of these cases are not available to us, so we cannot evaluate the degree of influence (or dominance) that might exist in this aspect of the milk producer–cheese association relationship. I am simply selectively noting the logic of market self-governance exhibited in these cases.

10. See, for example, H. Assad, "The Political Role of Trade Associations," in William Evan, *Interorganizational Relations* (Philadelphia: University of Pennsylvania Press, 1978).

11. Recall, in this connection, the contention of the sociologist Robert Merton that a deep contradiction existed in 20th-century American society between its cultural goals and the structural or institutional means avail-

able to achieve them. Like Durkheim before him, Merton believed that the attempts of people to adapt to this contradiction led to a state of tension, frustration, and anomie, which also resulted in various forms of rebellion. Merton, *Social Theory and Social Structure* (Glencoe, Ill.: Free Press, 1949). Although Merton's focus was on the incapacity of individuals to adapt to the contradictions between our society's cultural values—expressed through their desires, hopes, and dreams—and the institutional means available to achieve them, a case could be made that there is also a disjuncture between the societal values most people hold and the ability of the market system as currently organized to express these values. We have seen how trade associations are beginning to introduce societal values into the operations of the market through their own cooperative activities.

12. Later, I indicate how that decentralized and independent pattern of development can be fostered. Chapter 11 proposes a government agency called the Agency for International Development of Associations (AIDA), that would work with firms and trade associations in a fashion parallel to that of MITI, but whose function would be to encourage and enable trade associations to become self-regulating. It would reward those associations that democratize their structures, develop systems of social accountability with their constituencies, create self-management training programs, and supply welfare and training programs for their unemployed workers. Although AIDA would seek a close working relationship with such trade associations, it would also respect the full autonomy of associations to take their own directions in a process of self-development. AIDA would also cultivate interassociation committees that offered private conflict mediation procedures, and would work with various professional associations such as chemists and physicists to help set societal standards with industry on the environment, and with biologists to provide guidance in standards regarding biotechnology, and with social scientists to enable business to create organizational studies on the effectiveness and profitability of decentralized operations.

13. Berle articulated this view in lectures at Robert Hutchins's Center for the Study of Democratic Institutions in Santa Barbara, Calif., but suggestions can be found in various of his books. See, for example, Adolf Berle, *Power Without Property* (New York: Harcourt Brace, 1959). The guild socialist movement began with Arthur Penty's book *The Restoration of the Guild System* (1906) and was advanced by A. R. Orage and S. G. Hobson. It was central to the work of G. D. H. Cole. See his *Guild Socialism Re-Stated* (London: Parsons, 1920). See also N. Carpenter, *Guild Socialism: An Historical and Critical Analysis* (New York: Appleton, 1922).

Chapter 8

1. For example, courts prohibit trade associations from regulating members' holding practices. The leading case involves the National Society of

Professional Engineers; the Supreme Court held that its code's blanket prohibition of competitive bidding by members violated Section 1 of the Sherman Antitrust Act.

2. Advisory Opinion File 6737038 (May 30, 1967), quoted in George Webster, *The Law of Associations* (Mathews-Bender, New York; a loose-leaf binder service, updated regularly for libraries), p. 9-4.

3. Public Law 91-366, signed July 31, 1970: "Any duly organized and existing jewelry trade association shall be entitled to injunctive relief restraining any person in violation of this Act from further violation of this Act and may sue therefore as the real party in interest in any district court of the United States in the district in which the defendant resides or has an agent, without respect to the amount in controversy."

4. *American Brands, Inc.* v *National Association of Broadcasters*, 308 F. Supp. 1166 (D.D.C. 1969).

5. Webster, *Law of Associations*, p. 9-18.1.

6. There is a great deal of developing case law on trade associations, but the trade association polity is based on more than that. Association executives argue that a set of customs, folkways, and administrative policies supporting their existence is yielding a new measure of maturity, and that even though some associations have engaged in malpractices, most are an important, morally developed part of the free enterprise system.

7. Howard Oleck, *Non-Profit Corporations and Associations* (Englewood Cliffs, N.J.: Prentice-Hall, 1956), pp. 259–60.

8. N.Y. Stock Corporation, L para. 46, quoted in ibid., p. 258.

9. Webster, *Law of Associations*, p. 2-37.

10. *Goldfarb* v *Virginia State Bar*, 421, U.S. 773; *Oglesby and Barclift, Inc.* v *Metro MLS, Inc.* (E.D. Va. 1976), 1976-2 C.C.H. Trade Cases 61064.

11. Webster, *Law of Associations*, pp. 2-55, 2-64.2.

12. Amitai Etzioni argues that Durkheim's theory of social solidarity was an example of oversocialization in an attempt to counter the utilitarian view that moral values were the product of individual adults. Etzioni, *The Moral Dimension: Toward a New Economics* (New York: Free Press, 1988). The proposed indexes are designed to seek a balance between over- and undersocialization. See also Dennis Wrong, "Oversocialized Concept of Man in Sociology," *American Sociological Review*, 26.2 (1961): 183–93.

13. *McCreery Angus Farms* v *American Angus Association*, 379 F. Supp. 1008 (S.D. Ill. 1974), affd 506 F. 2d 1404 (7th Cir. 1974), cited in Webster, *Law of Associations*, p. 9-5. We will return to the Angus case.

14. Ibid., p. 9-14. Additional precautionary steps for an association include avoiding discussion of a case with any concerned party prior to its final determination. In this manner, judicial members of the association avoid prejudicial error.

15. McQuire, *Business and Society* 286 (1963), quoted in Webster, *Law of Associations*, p. 9-1.

16. *American Column and Lumber Co. et al.* v *United States*, 257 U.S. 377 (1921).

17. C. Wilcox, *Public Policies Toward Business*, 3d ed. (Homewood, Ill.: Richard Irwin, 1966), p. 129.

18. Alden Manchester, *The Public Role in the Dairy Economy* (Boulder, Colo.: Westview, 1983), p. 247.

19. Alfred Chandler, *Strategy and Structure* (Cambridge, Mass.: MIT Press, 1966), p. 287.

20. Ibid., pp. 382–83.

21. The literature on the disadvantages of corporate hierarchy and command bureaucracy is vast. The problems of a command bureaucracy are summed up in such phrases as "information impactedness," "sunk costs," "red tape," "communications distortions," "impersonality," and "narrow calculative commitment." Steps to overcome these problems are suggested by the work of Chandler—for example, moving from the decentralized firm to a corporate federation. The role of power in studies of business organization is discussed by J. Pfeffer, *Organizational Design* (Arlington Heights, Md.: AHM Publishing, 1978).

22. Kathryn Harrigan, *Strategies for Vertical Integration* (Lexington, Mass.: Heath, 1983), p. 2.

23. Severyn T. Bruyn, *The Field of Social Investment* (New York: Cambridge University Press, 1987), pp. 118 ff.

24. National Industrial Recovery Act, para. 3(a), 48 Stat. 196 (1933).

25. *A.L.A. Schechter Poultry Corp.* v *United States*, 295 U.S. 495 (1935).

26. Federal Trade Commission Secretary Joseph W. Shea to Earl W. Kintner, May 22, 1967, cited in Ivan Hill, ed., *The Ethical Basis of Economic Freedom* (Chapel Hill, N.C.: American Viewpoint, 1976), p. 495.

Chapter 9

1. Tocqueville argued that at every moment American citizens were reminded that it was their duty as well as in their own interest to be useful to their fellows. "At first it is of necessity that men attend to the public interest. . . . By dint of working for the good of his fellow citizens, he in the end acquires the habit and taste for serving them." Alexis de Tocqueville, *Democracy in America*, tr. George Lawrence (Garden City, N.Y.: Doubleday, 1969), pp. 512–13, 692–93.

2. See, for example, William M. Sullivan, *Reconstructing Public Philosophy* (Berkeley: University of California Press, 1986).

3. Report of the Council for Public Interest Law, Mitchell Rogovin and William D. Ruckelshaus, co-chairmen, "Balancing the Scales of Justice."

4. For more on the social welfare function, see Jerome Rothenberg, "The Measurement of Social Welfare," in Carl J. Friedrich, ed., *Nomos V: The Public Interest* (New York: Atherton Press, 1962), pp. 107–14.

5. Burton Weisbrod, ed., *Public Interest Law: An Economic and Institutional Analysis* (Berkeley: University of California Press, 1978), p. 5.

6. The conflict between equity and efficiency is described in Arthur Okun, *Equality and Efficiency: The Big Tradeoff* (Washington, D.C.: Brookings Institution, 1975). Possibilities for integrating the two concepts are proposed in Robert Kuttner, *The Economic Illusion* (Boston: Houghton Mifflin, 1984).

7. It is not critical to our purposes to discuss the meaning of "public interest" in any detail. An opposing argument, however, should be distinguished. Richard Musgrave equates the public interest with efficiency alone and not with equity, in "The Public Interest: Efficiency in the Creation and Maintenance of Material Welfare," in Friedrich, *Nomos* V, pp. 107–14.

8. Russell Settle and Burton Weisbrod, "Occupational Safety and Health and the Public Interest," in Burton Weisbrod, ed., *Public Interest Law* (Berkeley: University of California Press, 1978), pp. 285 ff.

9. Steve Kelman, *Regulating America, Regulating Sweden: A Comparative Study of Occupational Safety and Health Policy* (Cambridge, Mass.: MIT Press, 1981).

10. Arthur Snow and Burton Weisbrod, "Consumerism, Consumers, and Public Interest Law," in Weisbrod, *Public Interest Law*, pp. 404 ff. This issue continues in other papers; see Kenneth Arrow, "Gifts and Exchanges," discussion Paper no. 240, Institute of Economic Research, Harvard University (May 1972).

11. Discussed in Snow and Weisbrod, "Consumerism," p. 426.

12. Ibid., pp. 426 ff.

13. In labor-management disputes in the Netherlands, each party appoints a judge and agrees on a third party to chair the tribunal. The experience has been that the judges act professionally and do not simply vote on behalf of the parties that appointed them—much like the justices of the U.S. Supreme Court, who whether appointed by a Republican or a Democratic president cannot be counted on to follow a party line.

14. Oliver Williamson, *The Economic Institutions of Capitalism* (New York: Free Press, 1985), p. 119. The quotation about Ford is from H. C. Livesay, *American Made* (Boston: Little, Brown, 1979), p. 175. The question of whether labor was dominated or consumers exploited in the process does not enter into Williamson's judgment about such moves. He argues that these vertical attempts were unsuccessful simply because they cost too much in the long run.

15. From Williamson's standpoint, Whitman's Candies was wise to use a number of different methods to merchandise its product, because costs were predominant in the decisions. He notes that wholesalers were bypassed in the sale of high-grade, packaged candies. Control of the wholesaling function was arguably more important for quality-control purposes. Small, inexpensive bar and packaged candies were sold through the usual

jobber and wholesale-grocer network, while high-grade packaged candies were sold directly to retailers so that the company could regulate the flow of the perishable items and avoid alienating customers. In other words, the process was a wholly rational one calculated on transaction costs and economic incentives.

16. Examples of how ethical codes and practices result in collective goods can be found in Gene Laczniak and Patrick Murphy, *Marketing Ethics* (Lexington, Mass.: Heath, 1985); and Richard Farmer and W. Dickerson Hogue, *Corporate Social Responsibility* (Lexington, Mass.: Heath, 1985).

Chapter 10

1. Durkheim asserted that the capitalist system had led to the disintegration of community life; the market, competitive and anomic (normless), was a major cause for urban social problems such as crime and suicide, and it was so ruthless in its destruction of communal life that it indirectly destroyed personal well-being. The medieval craft and merchant guilds that had maintained normative communities had been virtually eliminated, and the accent now was on egoism; Durkheim therefore recommended creating new occupational communities and a new social solidarity within the market economy. Emile Durkheim, *Suicide*, ed. John Spaulding and George Simpson (Glencoe, Ill.: Free Press, 1951).

In the spirit of Durkheim's concern, social scientists began to look more critically on the corporation as an institution and to search for ways to improve the conditions of employment and the work community, the two phenomena that defined so much of a person's life in terms of status, power, and the fulfillment of human values. This interest in cultivating a sense of community and mutual support in the corporation led to a human-relations movement in industry, with many studies of organizational development carried out by the best talents in social theory. But Durkheim was really referring more to the normlessness *between* corporations. Since the market system created a competitive process that was as destructive of the individual as it was of the larger community, he was concerned with how the ruthless market could become socialized so that solidarity could develop between competitive enterprises and intercorporate communal values could be cultivated along with the values of the individual.

These questions were similar to those of Marx, who also concluded that the modern emphasis on competition and individuality was destructive to community life, although he interpreted this problem in the context of a self-destructive class structure. Since for Marx the class structure constituted the moving dynamic of history, crucial questions from his perspective included whether a future based on the values of community could be formulated without a revolution, whether a community could be created beyond the confines of the state without a classless society, and whether some sort of economic organization could introduce both community and freedom simultaneously into the chaotic marketplace. The questions raised by Durkheim and Marx, although clearly philosophical, serve as a theoretical background generating ideas for research and it is now time to formulate models of the economy sensitive to them, since the relationship of the individual to the community is not only a sociological question of long standing, but critical to studies of the social market.

2. Alfred Chandler, *The Visible Hand* (Cambridge, Mass.: Harvard University Press, 1977), p. 1.

3. Ibid., Introduction.

4. In this tradition, Oliver Williamson takes corporate analysis into the field of exchange and makes transaction cost rather than Chandler's "administrative coordination" the basic unit of analysis. Williamson, *The Economics of Discretionary Behavior* (Englewood Cliffs, N.J.: Prentice-Hall, 1964); Williamson, "A Dynamic Theory of Interfirm Behavior," *Quarterly Journal of Economics*, Nov. 1965.

5. Andrew Martin, unpublished paper, "Is Democratic Control of Capitalist Economies Possible?" My reference to this essay is drawn from an interpretation by Robert Kuttner, *The Economic Illusion* (Boston: Houghton Mifflin, 1984), p. 268.

6. Gabriel Kolko, *The Triumph of Conservatism* (New York: Free Press, 1963), pp. 4–5.

7. Many of these issues are argued in terms of business ethics. See S. Prakash Sethi and Cecilia Falbe, eds., *Business and Society* (Lexington, Mass.: Heath, 1987).

8. Robert Reich, *The Next American Frontier* (New York: Penguin Books, 1983), pp. 230–31.

9. For contrasting reviews of this history, see Meyer et al., *Environments and Organizations*; Frank Fischer and Carmen Sirianni, eds., *Critical Studies in Organization and Bureaucracy* (Philadelphia: Temple University Press, 1984); and Henry Mintzberg, *Power In and Around Organizations* (Englewood Cliffs, N.J.: Prentice-Hall, 1983). See also Oliver Williamson, *The Economic Institutions of Capitalism* (New York: Free Press, 1985).

10. Oliver Williamson, *Antitrust Economics* (New York: Basil Blackwell, 1987), p. 74.

11. Alvin Gouldner, "Organizational Analysis," in Robert Merton, Leonard Broom, and L. S. Cottrel, Jr., eds., *Sociology Today* (New York: Basic Books, 1959), pp. 404–5.

12. J. Rogers Hollingsworth and Leon N. Lindberg, "The Governance of the American Economy: The Role of Markets, Clans, Hierarchies, and Associative Behavior," in Wolfgang Streeck and Philippe C. Schmitter, eds., *Private Interest Government* (Beverly Hills, Calif.: Sage, 1985), p. 221. See also Paul Lawrence and David Dyer, *Renewing American Industry* (New York: Free Press, 1983).

13. The issues in synthesizing social and economic goals are being debated in a field called "social marketing." See Philip Kotler, *Marketing for Nonprofit Corporations* (Englewood Cliffs, N.J.: Prentice-Hall, 1975), chap. 5.

14. G. Teubner, "Substantive and Reflective Elements in Modern Law," *Law and Society Review*, 17 (1983): 239–85.

15. Claus Offe, "Competitive Party Democracy and the Keynesian Welfare State: Some Reflections on Their Historical Limits," in S. Clegg, G. Dow, and P. Boreham, eds., *The State, Class and the Recession* (London: Croom-Helm, 1983).

16. Robert Reich, "Why the U.S. Needs an Industrial Policy," *Harvard Business Review*, Jan.–Feb. 1982:76.

17. Thorstein Veblen, *The Portable Veblen* (New York: Viking, 1948), p. 543.

18. K. W. Kapp, *Social Costs of Business Enterprise* (Nottingham, Eng.: Spokesman-B. Russell Foundation, 1978).

19. For studies on this problem in health, pollution, occupational disability, unemployment, drugs, and other areas of social concern, see John Ullamn, ed., *Social Costs in Modern Society: A Qualitative and Quantitative Assessment* (London: Quorum Books, 1983).

20. Two books representing different generations can represent this vast literature: Edgar Heermance, *Codes of Ethics* (Burlington, Vt.: Free Press, 1924); and Paul Bernstein, *Workplace Democratization* (Kent, Ohio: Kent State University Press, 1976).

21. The traditional literature in organizational studies presents a case for the hazards of norm making and enforcement within corporations, much of which applies to organizations seeking to become democratic. For example, A. M. Pettigrew's description of a decision made by a British company to purchase a specific computer indicates the power of information control. The department head was able to influence the board of directors by systematically filtering out information from both the computer manufacturers and his own personnel. He was a gatekeeper for information that never became visible to the board as a whole. Pettigrew, *The Politics of Organizational Decision-Making* (London: Tavistock, 1973). For a series of studies on the problems associated with private organizations assuming greater social responsibilities, see Meyer et al., *Environments and Organization*.

22. Alvin Gouldner, *Patterns of Industrial Bureaucracy* (Glencoe, Ill.: Free Press, 1954).

23. Christopher Stone, *Where the Law Ends* (New York: Harper Torchbooks, 1975).

24. Murray Weidenbaum, *The Future of Business Regulation* (New York: Amacon, 1979).

25. Ian Maitland, "The Structure of Business and Corporate Social Re-

sponsibility," in S. Prakash Sethi and Cecilia M. Falbe, eds., *Business and Society* (Lexington, Mass.: Heath, 1987).

26. Harry Braverman, *Labor and Monopoly Capital* (New York: Monthly Review Press, 1974), pp. 298–304.

27. David Kinzer, *Health Controls Out of Control: Warning to the Nation from Massachusetts* (Chicago: Teach 'em, 1977); John D. Steinbruner, *The Cybernetic Theory of Decision* (Princeton, N.J.: Princeton University Press, 1974).

28. Roland Warren, *The Community in America* (Chicago: Rand McNally, 1972).

29. See Howard Aldrich, "Centralization Versus Decentralization in the Design of Human Service Delivery Systems," in Rosemary Sarri and Yeheskel Hasenfeld, eds., *The Management of Human Services* (New York: Columbia University Press, 1978); and Jeffrey Pfeffer and Gerald Salancik, *The External Control of Organizations* (New York: Harper & Row, 1978).

30. On the educational sector, see Jerome Murphy, "The Paradox of State Government Reform," *Public Interest*, 64 (Summer 1981): 124–39. On the health sector, see Anne Somers, *Hospital Regulation: The Dilemma of Public Policy* (Princeton, N.J.: Industrial Relations Section, Princeton University, 1969).

31. W. Richard Scott and John W. Meyer, "The Organization Societal Sectors," in Scott and Meyer, eds., *Organizational Environments* (Beverly Hills, Calif.: Sage, 1983), p. 137.

32. John Meyer and Brian Rowan, "Institutionalized Organization: Formal Structure as Myth and Ceremony," *American Journal of Sociology*, 83 (Sept. 1977): 440–63.

33. The following are examples of supportable hypotheses. (1) Technical sectors will attempt to control and coordinate their production, buffering them from environmental influences. (2) Technical sectors will succeed to the extent that they develop efficient production and effective coordination. (3) Institutional sectors will not attempt to control or coordinate their production closely but will seek to buffer or decouple these activities from organizational structures. (4) Institutional sectors will succeed to the extent that they are able to acquire types of personnel and to develop structural arrangements and production processes that conform to the specifications of that sector. See Meyer and Scott, *Organizational Environments*, p. 141.

Chapter 11

1. The difficulties are discussed in more detail in Severyn T. Bruyn, "The Community Self-Study: Worker Self-Management Versus the New Class," *Review of Social Economy*, Fall 1984: 388–412.

2. The literature on our prototype of the worker cooperative indicates that its economic performance in the United States rates favorably with the

performance of conventional firms, despite the unfavorable social and educational climate in which it must compete. Derek Jones, "U.S. Producer Cooperatives: The Record to Date," *Industrial Relations*, 18 (Fall 1979): 342–57.

3. William Foote Whyte and Kathleen King Whyte, *Making Mondragon: The Growth and Dynamics of the Worker Cooperative Complex* (Ithaca, N.Y.: ILR Press, 1988), p. 3.

4. Steven Greenhouse, "Why Germany's Growth Is Slow," *New York Times*, Dec. 31, 1987: D1, D4.

5. Joseph Blasi, *Employee Ownership: Revolution or Ripoff?* (Cambridge, Mass.: Ballinger, 1988). For policy recommendations, see pp. 239 ff.

6. In 1986, Bruce Scott and George Cabot Lodge of the Harvard Business School filed for legislation with the state of Massachusetts. They proposed that the Commonwealth reward firms that (1) established an incentive-compensation plan tied to overall firm performance, (2) made a commitment to train and retrain all employees, (3) agreed to collaborate with state and federal programs to improve work-force productivity, and (4) created a fund to promote job creation and long-term opportunity, to be administered by a board representing all employees. Workers' compensation pay was to be exempt from state income taxes, and firms could deduct their contributions to the job-creation fund from corporate income taxes. This legislative bill failed, but the co-op charter bill succeeded.

7. E. S. Savas, *Privatizing the Public Sector: How to Shrink Government* (Chatham, N.J.: Chatham House, 1982).

8. This process can be done well only by a careful targeting of the services in the interest of the community. For some of the ramifications of the process, see Ted Kolderie, "What Do We Mean by 'Privatization'?" *Society*, Sept.–Oct. 1987: 46–51.

9. The details of such guidelines are discussed in Severyn T. Bruyn, *The Field of Social Investment* (Cambridge: Cambridge University Press, 1987).

10. George Lodge and Richard Walton state that integrated systems are taking off in all markets, including the financial. Merrill Lynch sponsored a $1.5 billion leveraged buyout of Jack Eckerd Corporation and interpreted it as managing "an integrated capital-raising process." It meant bringing together 29 banks, 7 private institutional investors, and hundreds of buyers of publicly offered debt. Lodge and Walton, "The American Corporation and Its New Relationships," *California Management Review*, 31.3 (Spring 1989): 14–16.

11. Ibid., pp. 17–18.

12. In addition to "industry rationalization" through mergers and acquisitions, the Commerce studies recommend greater government financial assistance to defense research to maximize commercial competitiveness on the grounds that the lack of competitiveness is a national security problem. Critics argue that the dangers of such protectionism lie in the de-

velopment of global command systems that eventually produce foreign political resistance and higher military costs. See ibid., pp. 17–19.

13. Spokesmen in the U.S. accounting field argue that the only way to keep up with global competition and compete with multinationals is "to become a large multinational ourselves." Anthony Flint, "Accounting's 'Big Eight' Shrinking," *The Boston Globe*, July 7, 1989:69–70.

14. Lodge and Walton, "The American Corporation," pp. 20–21.

15. Thomas Jorde and David Teece, "Competition and Cooperation: Striking the Right Balance," *California Management Review*, Spring 1989: 25–37.

16. Ibid., pp. 33–34.

17. Mancur Olson, "The Plan and Purpose of a Social Report," *Public Interest*, 15 (Spring 1969): 86.

18. For discussions by sociologists on the need for social indicators, see Arthur B. Shostack, "How Long Before We Get a Volume of Social Indicators?," *Contemporary Sociology*, 7 (1978): 719–22; and A. L. Stinchcombe and J. C. Wendt, "Theoretical Domains and Measurement in Social Indicator Analysis," in K. C. Land and S. Spilerman, eds., *Social Indicator Models* (New York: Russell Sage Foundation, 1975).

19. M. S. Weitzman, "The Developing Program on Social Indicators at the U.S. Bureau of Census," *Social Indicators Research*, 6.19 (1979): 239–50.

20. Andrew Pollack, "A Look at Entrepreneurs: Doubts on the American Ideal," *New York Times*, June 14, 1988:1, D6.

21. Joe S. Bain, *Barriers to New Competition* (Cambridge, Mass.: Harvard University Press, 1962). The condition of entry for new firms is a structural factor that carries direct implications for market behavior. If entry is easy, the degree of "pricing discretion" for existing firms may be limited even though the firms occupy what appear to be dominant positions in the market. For this reason, it can be misleading to look at market concentration without also considering entry barriers. A common entry barrier is the reputation of established products. A new firm may calculate that its initial sales will be limited because of consumer loyalty to established brands, and that to break into the market, it will have to cut prices. Another barrier is the "absolute cost advantage" of established firms, which occurs because these firms possess superior factors of production, have agreements with suppliers that assure them of more favorable terms than any new entrant can obtain, or simply have superior knowledge of production and marketing because of their long experience in the field.

22. These reports address occupational health and safety records, minority and female recruitment and promotion patterns, the environmental and pollution consequences of production activities, and community relations efforts such as charitable contributions and facility beautification. Steven Dilley and Jerry Weygandt, "Measuring Social Responsibility: An Empirical Test," *Journal of Accountancy*, Sept. 1973.

23. Robert Reich, *The Next American Frontier* (Penguin Books, 1983), p. 240.

24. This practice is typical of the advanced worker cooperatives organized today and exemplified in the Mondragon model. Another scheme that encourages self-reliance would be to make payroll contributions to the unemployment insurance system depend on the extent to which former employees have been forced to use the system in the past. A company that tends to lay off many employees at every downturn would have a higher unemployment insurance premium than an identical company that keeps its workers employed. But I think a still better alternative is to provide strong incentives for employee self-management. We have frequently noted the many advantages of the fully self-managed company, not the least of which are keeping a continuous flow of capital circulating locally, and helping to maintain stability in local institutions. Over the long haul, it is important to study the degree to which peak associations could begin to handle unemployment compensation programs when they have achieved the degree of accountability we have discussed in earlier chapters.

25. Reich, *Next American Frontier*, p. 248.

26. Reich notes that a wage increase of about $1,000 enriches the employee by only $666, assuming the employee is in a 33 percent tax bracket, whereas an increase in the value of employee benefits (health insurance, life insurance, etc.) by, say, $833, makes the employee $167 richer than the salary increase would and also saves the company $167 ($1,000 less $833). Since the $334 that is now divided between the employee and the company is money that would have otherwise been paid in taxes, the result is the same as if the government had offered the employee and company a grant of $334 to split between them. In-kind benefits therefore go directly to firms rather than through the government bureaucracy. Ibid., pp. 249–50.

Conclusion

1. Adam Smith, *An Inquiry into the Nature and Causes of the Wealth of Nations* [1776], ed. E. Cannan (New York: Modern Library, 1904), 1.2:314. See also John Stuart Mill, *Principles of Political Economy* [1848] (London: Routledge and Kegan, 1968), where he asserts that the economic process is aimed exclusively at producing utilities embodied in outward objects.

2. Russell Lewis, *The New Service Economy* (London: Longman, 1973), p. 100.

3. Quoted in ibid., p. 26.

4. Jacques Nusbaumer, *The Services Economy: Lever to Growth* (Boston: Kluwer Academic Publishers, 1987), p. 12.

5. Ibid., pp. 12–13.

6. Jonathan Gershuny, "The Future of Service Employment," in Orio Giarini, ed., *The Emerging Service Economy* (New York: Pergamon Press, 1987), p. 108.

7. Daniel Bell, *The Coming of Post-Industrial Society: A Venture in Social Forecasting* (New York: Basic Books, 1973), p. 483.

8. William Torbert, *Managing the Corporate Dream* (Homewood, Ill.: Dow Jones–Irwin, 1987).

9. Philip Kotler, *Marketing for Nonprofit Organizations* (Englewood Cliffs, N.J.: Prentice-Hall, 1982). See also Kotler, "A Generic Concept of Marketing," *Journal of Marketing*, 40 (July).

10. David Rados, *Marketing for Non-profit Organizations* (Dover, Mass.: Auburn House, 1981), pp. 14–18.

11. See, for example, Seymour Fine, *The Marketing of Ideas and Social Issues* (New York: Praeger, 1981).

12. Theodore Levitt, "Marketing and Corporate Purpose." Paper delivered as part of the Key Issues Lecture Series, New York University, March 2, 1977.

13. Philip Kotler and Alan Andreasen, *Strategic Marketing for Nonprofit Organizations* (Englewood Cliffs, N.J.: Prentice-Hall, 1987), p. 1.

14. See *Sweden Works* and *Fact Sheets on Sweden* (Stockholm: Swedish Institute, 1987). A unique feature of the Swedish labor-market policy is the role accorded to management organizations and labor unions. Representatives of both sides sit on boards of directors at all levels of the Labor Market Administration.

15. Gershuny, "Future of Service Employment."

16. "Electronic Banking," *Business Week*, Jan. 18, 1982:76.

17. See R. Mishra, *The Welfare State in Crisis* (Brighton: Wheatsheaf Books, 1984). I would argue that deregulation does not solve the problems that caused government regulation in the first place. If the economy is not organized to solve the root problems in society, the government will simply create new agencies and regulations to deal with these problems again in the future.

18. See J. O'Conner, *The Fiscal Crisis of the State* (New York: St. Martin's Press, 1973); C. Offe, *The Contradictions of the Welfare State*, ed. J. Keane (London: Macmillan, 1979). I would argue that decommodification cannot be achieved successfully through the state, but must be accomplished through the introduction of self-accountability systems in the private sector, based on social management, social investment, and the cooperation of firms in the public interest, which together would reduce the necessity for government controls.

19. For the powerful statement that stimulated this movement, see Mikhail Gorbachev, *Perestroika: New Thinking for Our Country and the World* (New York: Harper & Row, 1987).

20. On the matter of Third World dissatisfaction, see James Wunsch and Dele Oiowu, *The Failure of the Centralized State* (New York: Sage, 1988).

21. Robert Kuttner, *The Economic Illusion* (Boston: Houghton Mifflin, 1984), p. 22.

22. George Lodge and Richard Walton, "The American Corporation and Its New Relationships," *California Management Review*, 31.3 (Spring, 1989): 22. Lodge is a Republican who envisions a communitarian society evolving from the business system. For some of his further thoughts, see his *The New American Ideology* (New York: Knopf, 1975).

Appendix

1. C. Fred Bergsten, "The United States and the World Economy," *Annals of the American Academy of Political and Social Science*, 460 (March 1982): 12.

2. *Symposium on Global Security for the Twenty-First Century: Proceedings* (New York: United Nations, 1987).

3. These figures and those that follow on this debt are drawn from an analysis in Michael Moffitt, "Reaganomics and the Decline of U.S. Hegemony," *World Policy Journal*, 4 (Fall 1987): 553 ff.

4. Tom Peters, "Facing Up to the Need for a Management Revolution," *California Management Review*, 30 (Winter 1988): 8.

5. Robert Kuttner, "U.S. Industry Is Wasting Away—But Official Figures Don't Show It," *Business Week*, May 16, 1988:26.

6. James Brian Quinn and Christopher Gagnon, "Will Service Follow Manufacturing into Decline?," *Harvard Business Review*, Nov.–Dec. 1986: 103.

7. Gary Willard and Arun Savara, "Patterns of Entry: Pathways to New Markets," *California Management Review*, 30 (Winter 1988): 58.

8. "'Made in U.S.A.' Means Little to the Multinationals," *Business Week*, April 10, 1978:60.

9. Ralph Kozlow, "Capital Expenditures by Majority-Owned Foreign Affiliates of U.S. Companies, 1985," *Survey of Current Business*, 65 (March 1985): 24; Barry Bluestone and Bennett Harrison, *The Deindustrialization of America* (New York: Basic Books, 1982).

10. Ruth Leger Sivard, *World Military and Social Expenditures, 1987–88* (Washington, D.C.: World Priorities, 1987), p. 39. Except as noted, the following data are drawn from this source.

11. Signe Landgen-Backstrom, "The Transfer of Military Technology to Third World Countries," *Bulletin of Peace Proposals*, 1977, no. 2.

12. *Common Security: A Programme for Disarmament*, report of the Independent Commission on Disarmament and Security Issues under the chairmanship of Olof Palme (London, Pan Books, 1982).

13. *The Relationship Between Disarmament and Development*, UN publication Sales no. E82.IX.1. See also Augusto Varas, "Military Spending and the Development Process," *Disarmament: A Periodic Review by the United Nations*, 9 (Autumn 1986).

14. Richard Falk, *The Promise of World Order* (Philadelphia: Temple Uni-

versity Press, 1987); Saul Mendlovitz, ed., *Legal and Political Problems of World Order* (New York: Fund for Education Concerning World Peace Through World Law, 1962).

15. On the need for reforms, see Lester Brown et al., *State of the World* (New York: Norton, 1988).

16. For an elaboration of these points, see *The Campaign for U.N. Reform: Study and Action* (Wayne, N.J.: Campaign for U.N. Reform, 1988).

17. Gorbachev's speeches to the United Nations in the late 1980's and much of the planning reported from sources in the Soviet Union suggest that the steps I have outlined here have become real options for the United States. Various U.S. congressional leaders had been seeking to implement them even during the earlier resistant Soviet policies. For example, on October 8, 1985, Representative Jim Leach of Iowa introduced a joint resolution to establish a U.S. commission on improving the effectiveness of the United Nations. (It was referred to the Committee on Foreign Relations.) The proposed commission's aims were to identify the UN's strengths and weaknesses in order to recommend to the president and Congress ways to improve its effectiveness. Special attention was to be given to such matters as the role of the Security Council; the use of the International Court of Justice; the creation of standing peacekeeping forces; the role of UN institutions in helping to enforce arms control agreements; formal and informal decision-making procedures; the advisability of weighted voting; the administrative efficiency of agencies; and alternative nongovernmental sources of revenue. The next logical steps for UN reform are outlined in Grenville Clark and Louis Sohn, *Introduction to World Peace Through World Law* (Chicago: World Without War Publications, 1973). See also Richard Falk, Friedrich Kratochwil, and Saul Mendlovitz, *International Law* (Boulder, Colo.: Westview, 1985).

18. The discussion that follows is indebted to Howard Wachtel, *The Money Mandarins* (New York: Pantheon Books, 1986).

19. The system was constructed on certain premises, notably that U.S. currency would be universally accepted in international transactions, and that other currencies would be pinned to a fixed rate of $35 per ounce of gold. To maintain confidence in the dollar's stability, the United States was pledged to redeem any unwanted dollars in gold.

20. The dollar had to go down because it had been overvalued, but the downgrading also made U.S. exports cheaper. The fall of the dollar could have been rapid and disastrous over the next few years except for the unanticipated action of the OPEC countries, which increased oil prices while accepting only dollars for payment. The dollar was given a lucky support system until other measures of stability could be found.

21. Richard F. Janssen, "Rapid Growth of Eurodollar Market Prompts Debate Over Wisdom of Imposing Control," *Wall Street Journal*, Aug. 3, 1979:34; U.S. Congress, Joint Economic Committee, *Some Questions and*

Brief Answers about the Eurodollar Market (Washington, D.C.: Government Printing Office, 1977), p. 1.

22. "Stateless Money, a New Force on World Economies," *Business Week*, Aug. 21, 1978:76–77.

23. "Citibank's Pervasive Influence on Internal Lending," *Business Week*, May 16, 1983:124.

24. Wachtel, *Money Mandarins*, pp. 207–10. In the succeeding discussion, Wachtel expands much further on how to develop exchange rate stability. This is important because rate instabilities are a major cause of high interest rates.

25. Willy Brandt, *North-South: A Program for Survival* (Cambridge, Mass.: MIT Press, 1980), pp. 248–49.

26. Jeremy Rifkin, "The Greenhouse Doomsday Scenario," *The Washington Post*, July 31, 1988:5.

27. For a fuller account of this argument, see Alan B. Durning, "Poverty and the Environment: Reversing the Downward Spiral," *Worldwatch Paper* 92, Nov. 1989.

28. William Hartley, "More Firms Now Stress In-House Auditing," *Wall Street Journal*, Aug. 22, 1977.

29. *International Chamber Rules of Conciliation and Arbitration* (Paris: ICC Publishing, Nov. 1987).

30. Kathryn Sikkink, "Codes of Conduct for Transnational Corporations: The Case of the WHO/UNICEF Code," *International Organization*, 40 (Autumn 1986).

31. Archibald Alexander and Robert Swinth, "A Value Framework for Assessing the Social Impacts of Multinational Corporations," *Essays in International Business* (University of South Carolina Center for International Business Studies), 7 (Nov. 1987).

32. An analysis of how multinational corporations have decentralized their operations over the decades and a discussion of a world charter for them can be found in Severyn T. Bruyn, *The Social Economy: People Transforming Modern Business* (New York: Wiley, 1977), pp. 241–97. See also *The United Nations Code of Conduct on Transnational Corporations* (New York: United Nations, 1986).

33. This problem is discussed in more detail in Severyn T. Bruyn, *The Field of Social Investment* (Cambridge: Cambridge University Press, 1987), chap. 7.

34. The pattern of neighborhood deterioration in city life with the shift from locally controlled capital to nationally controlled capital began to be studied by a "Chicago school" of sociologists, led by Ernest Burgess and Robert Park in the 1930's; it was a sociological tradition that continued for the next three decades as the standard ecological theory of city growth. See Stuart Queen and Lewis Thomas, *The City: A Study of Urbanism in the United States* (New York: McGraw-Hill, 1939). The deleterious consequences

on national and local community life because of the international control of capital has been a focus of sociological studies in "world system theory" promoted by analysts such as Immanuel Wallerstein, *The Capitalist World-Economy* (Cambridge: Cambridge University Press, 1979). For a critique of Wallerstein's view (which leaves out the regional capital powers of socialist states), see Peter Worsley, "One World or Three?," in David Held et al., eds., *States and Societies* (New York: New York University Press, 1983).

35. An awareness of these interconnections is developing among Third World groups and community workers in the United States. See David Morris, "Local Self Reliance," *Building Economic Alternatives* (Washington, D.C., Coop America), 12–13 (Winter 1987–Spring 1988): 3; *Women and Global Corporations* 9.1 (1988); Boston Women's Health Book Collective, *Women in Development* (Philadelphia: New Society Publishers, 1984).

36. The alternatives are just beginning to be understood, many of which I believe hold the potential for future development. They include the decentralizing of corporations into confederations where autonomy is more local, in contrast to conglomerates that leave communities quickly and go overseas; increased control of firms by their employees, who treasure their home base and keep capital circulating locally; and the practice of social investors, who seek to strengthen capital formation in poor communities. In addition, three new types of community-oriented corporations—community development corporations (CDCs), community development finance corporations (CDFCs), and community land trusts (CLTs)—are being created in the United States. Support for these new organizations, which allow local citizens to gain direct control over the use of capital in their neighborhoods, could be part of the new socioeconomic criteria of an international finance that seeks to rebuild community life instead of destroying it. For a detailed discussion of how CDCs, CDFCs and CLTs operate in the United States, see Severyn T. Bruyn and James Meehan, eds., *Beyond the Market and the State* (Philadelphia: Temple University Press, 1987).

Indexes

Author Index

Subject Index

Library of Congress Cataloging-in-Publication Data

Bruyn, Severyn Ten Haut, 1927–
  A future for the American economy: the social market / Severyn T.
Bruyn.
    p.   cm.
  Includes bibliographical references and index.
  ISBN 0-8047-1872-5 (cloth : alk. paper):
    1. United States—Economic policy—1981– 2. United States—Social
policy—1980– 3. Financial institutions—Social aspects—United
States. I. Title.
HC106.8.B78   1991
338.973'001'12—dc20
                                                              90-20724
⊗ This book is printed on acid-free paper   CIP